BARRY ST. CLAIR

MAKING
JESUS LORD

John's
Book

VICTOR BOOKS®
A DIVISION OF SCRIPTURE PRESS PUBLICATIONS INC.
USA CANADA ENGLAND

Moving Toward Maturity Series

Following Jesus (Book 1)
Spending Time Alone with God (Book 2)
Making Jesus Lord (Book 3)
Giving Away Your Faith (Book 4)
Influencing Your World (Book 5)

Produced in cooperation with   REACH OUT MINISTRIES
3961 Holcomb Bridge Road
Suite 201
Norcross, GA 30092

All Bible quotations, unless otherwise indicated, are from the *Holy Bible, New International Version,* © 1973, 1978, 1984, International Bible Society. Used by permission of Zondervan Bible Publishers. Verses marked TLB are taken from *The Living Bible,* © 1971, Tyndale House Publishers, Wheaton, IL 60189. Used by permission. Other quotations are from the *King James Version* (KJV).

Chapter opening and "Making It Personal" illustrations by Joe Van Severen.

Library of Congress Catalog Card Number: 83-51369
ISBN: 0-89693-293-1

4   5   6   7   8   9   10   Printing/Year   95   94

CONTENTS

SPECIAL THANKS

To Rod Minor, Debbie Hayes, and the Reach Out Ministries office staff for working on this project with me.

To Randy Drake and Rob Lassiter for their creative artwork and design.

To Jane Vogel and the Victor Books team for their unceasing participation and unending patience.

To the youth ministers from across the country who have tested this material and given valuable suggestions.

To my wife Carol and my children Scott, Katie, Jonathan, and Ginny, who have loved me and encouraged me in my ministry.

To the Lord Jesus Christ for teaching me the things in this book.

A WORD FROM
THE AUTHOR

Jesus Christ has made positive changes in my life. He can change your life too. And He can use you to change others!

Just make yourself AVAILABLE, and Jesus can:

> Help you know Him better.
> Work in your life to make you a more mature Christian.
> Motivate you to share Christ with others.
> Use you to help other Christians grow toward maturity.
> Make you a spiritual leader.

My goal for you is: "Just as you received Christ Jesus as Lord, continue to live in Him, rooted and built up in Him, strengthened in the faith as you were taught, and overflowing with thankfulness" (Colossians 2:6-7).

When that is happening in your life, then just as $2 \times 2 = 4$, and $4 \times 4 = 16$, and on to infinity, so Jesus can use you to multiply His life in others to make an impact on the world. How? One Christian (like you) leads another person to Christ and helps him grow to the point of maturity. Then the new Christian can lead another person to Christ and help him grow to maturity. And so the process continues. God gives you the tremendous privilege of knowing Him and making Him known to others. That is what your life and the Moving Toward Maturity series are all about.

The Moving Toward Maturity series includes five discipleship study books designed to help you grow in Christ and become a significant part of the multiplication process. *Making Jesus Lord* is the third book in the series. The other books are:

God's desire and my prayer for you is that the things you discover on the following pages will become not just a part of your notes, but a part of your life. May all that's accomplished in your life be to His honor and glory.

PURPOSE

This book will help you discover why it is important to have Jesus as Lord. It will teach you to make decisions about making Jesus Lord in various areas of your life.

A disciple is a learner and a follower. As you learn to make Jesus Lord, you will learn about Jesus Christ and how to become more like Him. When that happens, you will be able to say with the Apostle Paul:

> We Christians have no veil over our faces; we can be mirrors that brightly reflect the glory of the Lord. And as the Spirit of the Lord works within us, we become more and more like Him (2 Corinthians 3:18, TLB).

Before you begin doing the Bible studies in this book, make the commitment to let Jesus Christ bring to completion all He wants to do in your life. Remember: God cares more about what is being developed in your life than about what you write in this book.

USES FOR
THIS BOOK

1. **GROUP STUDY**   You can use this book as a member of an organized study group (Discipleship Family) led by an adult leader.* Each member of this group signs the commitment sheet on page 11, and agrees to use the book week by week for personal study and growth.

2. **INDIVIDUAL STUDY**   You can go through this book on your own, doing one lesson each week for your own personal growth.

3. **BUDDY STUDY**   You can ask a friend who also wants to grow to join you in a weekly time of studying, sharing, and growing together.

4. **ONE-ON-ONE DISCIPLESHIP**   After you have mastered and applied each Bible study in this book to your own life, you can help another person work through his own copy of the book.

---

*The Leader's Guide for the *Moving Toward Maturity* series can be purchased at your local Christian bookstore or from the publisher.

PRACTICAL HINTS

(How to get the most out of this book)

If you want to grow as a Christian, you must get specific with God and apply the Bible to your life. Sometimes that's hard, but this book can help you if you will:

1. **Begin each Bible study with prayer**
   Ask God to speak to you.

2. **Use a study Bible**
   Try the *New International Version* or the *New American Standard Bible*.

3. **Work through the Bible study**
   - Look up the Bible verses.
   - Think through the answers.
   - Write the answers.
   - Jot down any questions you have.
   - Memorize the assigned verse(s). (Use the Bible memory cards in the back of the book. Groups should select a single translation to memorize, in order to recite the verse[s] together.)

4. **Apply each Bible study to your life**
   - Ask God to show you how to act on what you're learning from His Word.
   - Obey Him in your relationships, attitudes, and actions.
   - Talk over the results with other Christians who can encourage and advise you.

IF YOU'RE IN A DISCIPLESHIP FAMILY

▶ *Before* each group meeting, set aside two separate times each week to work on the assigned Bible study. If possible, complete the whole Bible study during the first time. Then during the second time (the day of or the day before your next group meeting), review what you've studied. This time should not be part of your time alone with God each morning. Do not use your time alone with God to work on your lesson.

▶ *After* you have discussed each Bible study with your Discipleship Family, complete the *Assignment* section of the study during the following week.

▶ Take your Bible, this book, and a pen or pencil to every group meeting.

PERSONAL COMMITMENT

I, _____ , hereby dedicate myself to the following commitments:

1. To submit myself daily to God and to all that He wants to teach me about growing as a Christian.

2. To attend all weekly group meetings, unless a serious illness or circumstance makes it impossible. If I miss more than one meeting, I will withdraw willingly from the group if it is determined necessary after meeting with the group leader.

3. To complete the assignments without fail as they are due each week.

4. To be involved in my local church.

I understand that these commitments are not only to the Lord but to the group and to myself as well. I will do my very best, with God's help, to completely fulfill each one.

Signed _____

GET READY... GET SET!

Discovering Jesus' credentials

This was the first day of practice. At first I felt scared and kind of awkward. But Coach gave us a talk about being a team. You know, after we practiced for a while, it felt pretty good. But I've got a long way to go!

Can you recall the first day you started something new (a class, a sport, a musical instrument, etc.)? How did you feel?

different

Name one talent you have that you're really proud of.

running long distance

How long have you been doing it? How did you get to be good at it? Write a short paragraph that describes your learning process from the point you started until now.

I've been doing it for a long time.

Did you learn on your own, or did someone teach you?

Who contributed to your learning process?

COACHING CREDENTIALS

Having Jesus as Lord of your life is kind of like having a teacher or coach to help you be the best person you can be. What did Nicodemus say that Jesus was? (John 3:2)

_____

Jesus Christ wants to teach you everything you need to know about being a Christian. But is He really qualified to do that? Let's look at His teaching credentials for being Lord of your life.

1 **He Created You**
Read John 1:1-18, substituting "Jesus Christ" for "the Word" (Jesus is the Living Word of God). Compare that passage to Colossians 1:15-16 and describe how Jesus Christ was in on the creation of the world and, more specifically, *your* creation.

_____

_____

_____

Read Psalm 139:13-16. Since Jesus created you, He knows how you work best. What does Jesus Christ know about you?

_____

_____

Jesus Christ made you, and He knows all about you.

2 He Identifies with You

Picture in your mind a story where the two main characters are a wicked leader (Evil Ruler) and a brave lad (Fearless Young Man). The people in the country where this story takes place have been starved, cheated, and oppressed by Evil Ruler. Fearless Young Man has grown up under Evil Ruler's reign and decides to save his people by overcoming Evil Ruler. If you want to know the end of the story, read John 1:14.

Jesus Christ came to earth as one of us. Through His death, He crushed Satan's rule on this earth forever. And because He lived here for 33 years, He knows what we go through every day. "We do not have a high priest [Jesus Christ] who is unable to sympathize with our weaknesses, but we have one who has been tempted in every way, just as we are" (Hebrews 4:15).

Read Luke 4:1-13 and find out how Jesus faced the same temptations you have.

_____

_____

_____

_____

_____

Jesus had struggles just like you have.

3 He Redeemed You

Redeemed means to "rescue." How did Jesus rescue you? (1 Corinthians 6:20; Romans 14:9)

_____

_____

_____

Another definition for *redeem* is "to recover ownership by paying a specified sum," or "to ransom." If a gang kidnapped your best friend, how much would you pay as a ransom to get him back?

_____

What ransom did Jesus pay for you?

_____

Jesus has paid to regain ownership of your life, so He has the right to be the Lord of your life. Jesus redeemed you at an expensive price.

JESUS' RESPONSIBILITIES AS LORD

"OK," you say, "I can see that Jesus is qualified to teach me and be Lord of my life, but what is a *lord* supposed to do anyway?" Three Greek words in the New Testament describe Jesus' role as Lord. Let's look at what each one means.

Despotes (master) — The meaning here is "unlimited power." Jesus can overcome anything when His unlimited power is in operation.

Basileus (monarch) — This word is more commonly used in the Orient to mean "all power and authority." A monarch's word is law. And because Jesus is God, He is always the truthful authority — the Boss.

Kurios (lord) — A lord, in this sense of the word, is the "owner." Wisdom and love are suggested in this word. Jesus as Lord is wise and loving.

Now it's time for you to put it all together. Keep the meanings of these three words for *lord* in mind, and write your own definition of what it means for Jesus Christ to be Lord.

_____

_____

_____

_____

_____

_____

_____

_____

_____

What does that definition mean to you personally?

_____

_____

_____

_____

_____

_____

_____

_____

_____

Jesus wants His lordship to become a reality in your life. How does that take place? As you go through this study of *Making Jesus Lord,* you will examine some very specific areas of your life: dating and sex, parents, attitudes, habits, thoughts, friendships, temptation, and material possessions. You will learn how the lordship of Jesus Christ affects each of those areas. You can do two things to get ready to acknowledge Jesus as Lord of your life.

1 Desire
The psalmist says, "O God, You are my God, earnestly I seek You; my soul thirsts for You, my body longs for You, in a dry and weary land where there is no water" (Psalm 63:1). This kind of desire comes when we get

desperate! When we get tired of running our own lives, God will give us a desire to do it His way. Are you to the point where you are willing to let go and let God take over?

_____

The more we see who Jesus really is, the more the desire develops in us to please and worship Him. You will begin to see Jesus more clearly throughout the rest of *Making Jesus Lord.* But right now, evaluate where you stand as far as wanting Jesus to be the Lord of your life:

Are you tired of running your own life? _____ Why?

_____

_____

What things do you know about Jesus that cause you to want to give yourself to Him as Lord?

_____

_____

_____

What doubts do you have about making Jesus the Lord of your life?

_____

_____

_____

Whatever your desires are at this moment, stop right now and pray that God would give you the desire to make Jesus the Lord of your life. Write your prayer here:

_____

_____

_____

_____

2 Decide

When Paul realized on the road to Damascus who Jesus was, he said: "What shall I do, Lord?" Jesus told him: "Get up and go into Damascus. There you will be told all that you have been assigned to do" (Acts 22:10).

What did Paul do? He nailed down his commitment to make Jesus Lord right then and there. Look at his response: "I was not disobedient to the vision from heaven. First to those in Damascus, then to those in Jerusalem and all Judea, and to the Gentiles also, I preached that they should repent and turn to God and prove their repentance by their deeds" (Acts 26:19-20). You need to nail down your own commitment to making Jesus Lord of your life *right now*. Do it by faith, realizing that He will increase your desire for His lordship as time goes by. Silently, in your own words, let Jesus know that you have decided to make Him the Lord of your life. After you have committed to make Jesus your Lord, fill out the statement below.

Today, _____, I asked Jesus to be
              Date
Lord of my life.
      Signed: _____

Complete this Bible study by memorizing Psalm 63:1.

ASSIGNMENT

1 One of your assignments for this week (and throughout this book) is to spend time alone with God every day. Each day you should read and study a short passage from the Gospel of Mark. This week, during your daily time alone with God, use the following Bible readings. Record your observations in a notebook or journal.

- ✔ Day 1: Mark 1:1-11
- ✔ Day 2: Mark 1:12-13
- ✔ Day 3: Mark 1:14-15
- ✔ Day 4: Mark 1:16-20
- ✔ Day 5: Mark 1:21-34
- ✔ Day 6: Mark 1:35-38
- ✔ Day 7: Mark 1:39-45

2 Complete *Bible Study 2*.

2

NO PAIN, NO GAIN

Looking at the costs and benefits

Today the coach told me that I have
the potential to be really good if
I practice and get more rest
(which means I'll have to get to
bed earlier). I was really excited
to hear that until I realized that
I might have to give up hanging
out with my friends after school
and staying out late on school nights.

When you make Jesus Lord, you face some of these same choices. You have to lose something in order to gain something else. In this Bible study, you will take an honest look at the price you are willing to pay. On the other hand, you will also discover many benefits to having Jesus as Lord.

PAYING THE PRICE

Look up Matthew 16:24-26. Paraphrase these verses in your own words.

> If you follow me you must forget yourself & live for me. For how good is it if you have the whole world and give up your soul

Those are pretty strong words, aren't they? Let's take a closer look at what Jesus is really asking us to do.

1 Deny Yourself

What does it mean to deny yourself? It means that you get rid of your "I, me, mine" approach to life — by making a sold-out commitment to Jesus Christ. The world teaches, "Look out for number one." But Jesus says to forget yourself because:

➤ He has taken over the responsibility of looking out for you.

➤ You don't have to worry about yourself.

➤ He wants to motivate you to be your very best for Him.

➤ You don't have to get hung up on yourself.

26

Name one specific way that you are still looking out for number one.

_____

_____

_____

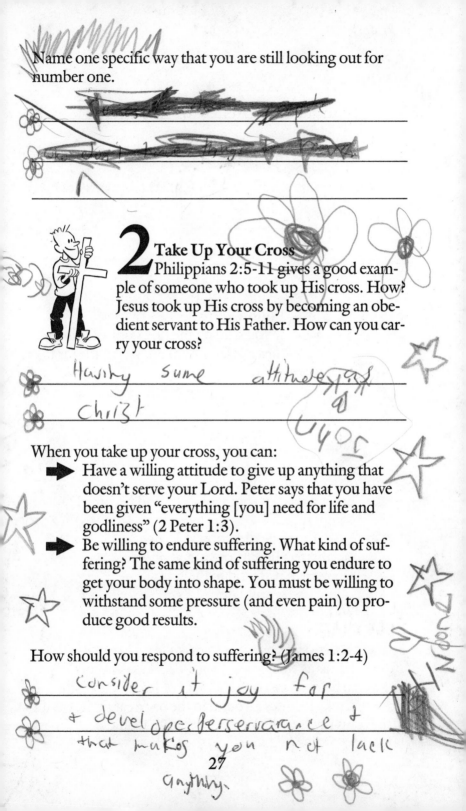

2 Take Up Your Cross

Philippians 2:5-11 gives a good example of someone who took up His cross. How? Jesus took up His cross by becoming an obedient servant to His Father. How can you carry your cross?

Having sume attitudes as christ

When you take up your cross, you can:

➤ Have a willing attitude to give up anything that doesn't serve your Lord. Peter says that you have been given "everything [you] need for life and godliness" (2 Peter 1:3).

➤ Be willing to endure suffering. What kind of suffering? The same kind of suffering you endure to get your body into shape. You must be willing to withstand some pressure (and even pain) to produce good results.

How should you respond to suffering? (James 1:2-4)

consider it joy for + develope perserverance + that makes you not lack anything.

What does God promise to do when you suffer? (1 Peter 5:10)

_He will restore you &
make you strong & whole_

What is the result of suffering for Christ? (Romans 8:17)

We share in his glory

3 Follow Jesus

If you studied the first book of this series, *Following Jesus*, sum up what it means to follow Jesus.

_You submit your
life to him_

When you follow Jesus you:

▶ Enter a relationship with Him and become His companion.
▶ Go in the same direction as Jesus.
▶ Submit to His authority in your life.
▶ Obey Him now and in the future.

GOOD DEALS

So there are costs if you want to make Jesus Lord. But there are good deals as well. Many times we ask: "What do I have to give up before I can be a follower of Jesus? Can I still smoke, drink, and mess around in the backseat of the car if I make Jesus my Lord?" A better question would be, "What activities do I have the privilege of giving up in order to follow Christ and get in on all of the good deals He has for me?"

Just as a sleek, fast car can really move with the right person behind the wheel, you can move down the road of life in the right direction with megahorsepower when Jesus is in your driver's seat. Having Him there allows you to live life at its very best.

Here are some of the good deals Jesus has to offer:

1 You Will Make Good Decisions

Another way of saying "Jesus is Lord of my life" is to say "I am in the center of God's will for me." When you have decisions to make, God will give you specific guidance.

Look up Proverbs 3:5-6. As you think of one big decision you are facing right now, how do these verses apply to your decision?

Just trust in him I
do what he wants

2 You Will Have Satisfaction

How do your mouth and body feel when you are really thirsty?

Dry

Jesus is your spiritual thirst quencher.

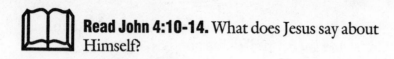 **Read John 4:10-14.** What does Jesus say about Himself?

_____

_____

In what way do you need satisfaction right now? Be specific.

_____

_____

Jesus is "a river of life" flowing out of you. He satisfies your thirst for meaning in life.

 **3 You Will Lead a Victorious Life**
Examine what Paul says in 1 Corinthians 15:57: "But thanks be to God! He gives us the victory through our Lord Jesus Christ." Think of a time when you were victorious. How did it feel?

_____

_____

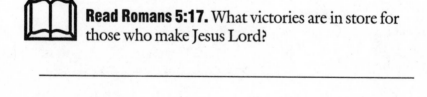 **Read Romans 5:17.** What victories are in store for those who make Jesus Lord?

_____

_____

_____

4 Your Future Has Hope

Lots of things make life tough these days: broken homes, low grades, and people who hate you, to name a few. Name one thing that is discouraging you.

_____

What does 2 Timothy 2:11-12 say will happen if you hang in there?

_____

No matter how bad things look right now, you have a bright future.

5 Your Character Will Change

Read Romans 8:28-29. Being "called according to His purpose" is another way of saying "He is Lord of my life." What will happen as a result of Jesus being your Lord in every area of your life?

_____

_____

"Conformed to the likeness of His Son" means you will begin to have His character qualities. What are some of Jesus' qualities that you would like to develop?

_____

_____

_____

_____

_____

_____

📖 **Reread Matthew 16:24-26.** "Whoever wants to save his life will lose it, but whoever loses his life for Me will save it" (v. 25). By making Jesus Lord, you "lose your life" (so to speak) because you turn everything over to Him. But in doing so you gain real life and all of the positive benefits that go along with it. Only then can you find the life that God wants you to enjoy.

Among the things you will have to lose in order to gain are your material possessions. What do you think of when you hear the word "materialism"? After checking a dictionary, write your definition here.

_____

_____

From now on, every Bible study session will conclude with a short Life Change sheet to help you apply God's truths to your own life. The following page contains a Life Change sheet dealing with the issue of materialism. Your part in making this lesson personal is to work through that sheet, thoroughly studying the Scripture passage and answering the questions that follow.

Complete this Bible study by memorizing Matthew 16:24.

ASSIGNMENT
1 Have a time alone with God every day this week, using the following Bible readings.
- ✔ Day 1: Mark 2:1-12
- ✔ Day 2: Mark 2:13-17
- ✔ Day 3: Mark 2:18-28
- ✔ Day 4: Mark 3:1-12
- ✔ Day 5: Mark 3:13-19
- ✔ Day 6: Mark 3:20-30
- ✔ Day 7: Mark 3:31-35

2 Complete *Bible Study 3*.

LIFE CHANGE

ISSUE: Material Possessions
BIBLE STUDY: Matthew 6:19-34
(See "How to Study a Passage of Scripture" on page 139. Use the space below to record your comments.)

_____

_____

_____

My weaknesses in the area of material possessions are:

_____ Clothes _____

_____

My strengths in the area of material possessions are:

_____

_____

ACTION POINT
Based on my study of Matthew 6:19-34, I need to make Jesus Lord of my material possessions by:

_____

_____

I will take the following specific step of action to begin to overcome the grip of material possessions on my life:

_____

_____

_____ will pray with me about this.

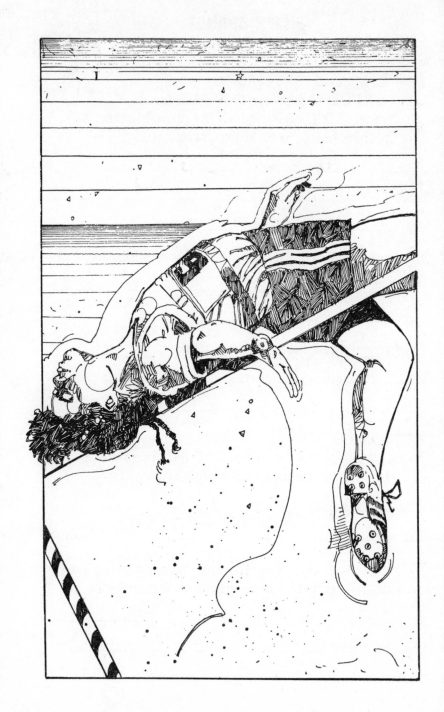

WHAT'S THE DIFFERENCE?

Experiencing Jesus' greatness

Today the coach said, " 80 percent of the people in the world don't know what's happening, 15 percent watch what's happening, and 5 percent make things happen." I really want to be part of that 5 percent, but I'm not sure where to start.

Have you ever thought about the difference between someone who is successful and someone who is not? Think of someone you know who is really successful and write his or her name here.

_____Tom Hanks_____

How do you think that person became successful?

_____Perserverence, hard work_____
_____talent_____

The people who succeed in life make a decision somewhere along the way to become somebody special. Making Jesus Lord means that you have chosen to become someone special because Jesus is special. Why is He so special? For starters, He is God.

When the Bible refers to God, He might be called the Father, the Son (Jesus), or the Holy Spirit. God is three persons in one, and one person in three. That's kind of mind-boggling, isn't it?

The word to describe all three persons of God is the Trinity, or Godhead. Let's look at some illustrations to get a rough understanding of the Trinity.

Each side of this triangle is equal, but distinct from the other two sides. Like a person can be a father, son, and husband at the same time, so too God has three identities in one.

Or imagine you are taking your SAT and see the following question. What would your answer be?

Which of the following has the chemical compound H_2O?
(A) Water
(B) Steam
(C) Ice
(D) All of the above

You science majors would select (D) without a blink. You know that H_2O is a chemical compound with three different forms. This is a beautiful mystery. Ice is no more and no less H_2O than water or steam, yet the three compounds look quite different. In a similar manner, God reveals Himself in different ways, yet the Father, the Son, and the Holy Spirit are equal parts of the one God.

WHAT IS GOD LIKE?

If you really want to know what a person is like, you don't just look at his outward appearance. You look deeper inside to see what kind of *character* he has. Is he dependable? Honest? Loving? If he is a loving son, he will be a loving husband and a loving father.

God is like that. His character as the Father, Son, and Holy Spirit is the same — just expressed differently. Let's look at some of His qualities in order to begin to grasp what He is like.

1 **God Is Great**
Take a map of the world and spend several minutes pinpointing and listing some of the countries you have never seen. Then find your state. How big is it compared to some of the countries you have never even seen?

Big

God created the universe. Our galaxy is only one of many, many galaxies contained in the universe that God made. Our solar system is one of many in our galaxy. Planet Earth is one of the planets in our solar system. So your state is a small part of a country on a continent that is a small part of a planet in a galaxy that is only a small part of the universe that God created. Get the picture? Here's how Psalm 145:3 says it: "Great is the Lord and most worthy of praise; His greatness no one can fathom."

Look at Isaiah 40 and list some of the ways God is great.

verse 12 _____

verses 15-17 _____

verses 21-22 _____

verse 23 _____

verses 25-26 _____

2 **God Is Consistent**
He never changes. You could pull out some of your grammar school pictures to see how you have changed. But your changes haven't all been physical. Sure, you're a lot taller and stronger than you used to be. But you're probably a lot more mature as well. List a few ways you are more mature now than when you were in grade school.

_____

But God never changes. He can't mature the way we do because He is already perfect. He told Moses, "I am who I am" (Exodus 3:14) which means, "I am the self-existent One who never changes." Take a closer look at some of God's consistencies.

His truth is consistent. Think of a time when you said something you wanted to take back. Then read Psalm 119:89; Isaiah 40:8; 45:23; and John 14:6. What do those verses tell you about God's truth?

_____

_____

His purpose is consistent. Read Numbers 23:19 and Hebrews 7:21. Why is it that God never needs to reverse His plans?

_____

_____

3 God Is Holy

A.W. Tozer said, "Holy is the way God is. To be holy He does not conform to a standard. He is that standard. He is absolutely holy with an infinite, incomprehensible fullness of purity that is incapable of being other than it is" (*The Knowledge of the Holy,* Harper and Row). That is quite a statement. Rephrase it in your own words.

_____

_____

_____

Read and study Isaiah 6:1-8. Based on that passage, what do you think holiness is?

_____

_____

How did Isaiah respond to God's holiness?

_____

_____

What does God want us to be?

_____

Why?

_____

To be "holy" means to be "set apart." You are set apart because you belong to God. Romans 6:11 and Ephesians 2:1-6 tell you who you are set apart *for* and what you have been set apart *from*.

I am set apart *for* _____

I am set apart *from* _____

How did God set you apart from sin?

_____

_____

_____

BEING SET APART

Ephesians 4 describes some practical ways in which you can be holy. Paul begins the chapter with the word "Therefore," so it's important to know what he was saying *before*. The passage you just read (Ephesians 2:1-6) sums up what Paul's "therefore" refers to. Paul is saying that because you have died to sin and are alive to God, you *can* become holy by putting off your old (sinful) nature and putting on the new (godly) one.

Study the following chart and Ephesians 4:25 — 5:8 to see where you need to put off your old personality and put on your new personality in Christ.

MAKING THE CHANGE

From	To	Because
Falsehood	Truthfulness	We're all members of one body
Wrong anger	Controlled anger	You should not give the devil a foothold
Stealing	Useful labor	You can share with those in need

From	To	Because
Unwholesome talk	Words that build others up	You can benefit those who listen
Bitterness and rage	Kindness and compassion	You should not grieve the Holy Spirit
Brawling and slander	Forgiveness	Jesus forgave you
Sexual immorality, impurity, and greed	Love	You are holy
Obscenity, foolish talk and coarse joking	Thanksgiving	You are the light of God

Perhaps you see several areas listed above that you feel you need to improve in your life. That's OK. But a common problem that young people face is the next to the last category: "Sexual immorality, impurity, and greed." Specifically, how is your dating life? At the end of this session is another Life Change sheet—like the one you did last week on materialism. Right now, complete the questions for this week's Life Change issue: sex and dating.

Complete this Bible study by memorizing 1 Peter 1:15-16.

ASSIGNMENT

1 Have a time alone with God every day, using the following Bible readings:

✔ Day 1: Mark 4:1-12
✔ Day 2: Mark 4:13-20
✔ Day 3: Mark 4:21-34
✔ Day 4: Mark 4:35-41
✔ Day 5: Mark 5:1-20
✔ Day 6: Mark 5:21-43
✔ Day 7: Mark 6:1-6

2 Complete *Bible Study 4.*

ISSUE: Sex and Dating
BIBLE STUDY: 2 Corinthians 6:14−7:1
              1 Thessalonians 4:3-8
Use the space below to record your comments.

_____
_____
_____
_____

My weaknesses in the area of sex and dating are:

_____
_____

My strengths in the area of sex and dating are:

_____
_____

ACTION POINT
Based on my study of 2 Corinthians 6:14−7:1 and
1 Thessalonians 4:3-8, I need to make Jesus Lord in my sex
and dating life by:

_____
_____

I will take the following specific step of action to insure that
I keep my dating and sex life within God's standards:

_____
_____
_____ will pray with me about this.

TOTAL CONFIDENCE

Growing in faith

The coach said today that if I can develop more confidence, I can probably make the first team. But how can I become more confident? I want to be the best I can be!

What does it take to reach your full potential in a sport?

_____

What does it take to reach your full potential as a Christian?

_____

_____

The two questions above might have a lot of the same answers (practice, obedience, etc.). But another big prerequisite for living to your full potential is faith—believing that you can. Jesus Christ has great plans for you.

Look at Jeremiah 29:11 and write down what He tells you about those plans.

_____

_____

Read Matthew 10:29-31. How important does God think you are?

_____

_____

GOD'S FAITHFULNESS

You recognize the value of your life when you begin to exercise your faith and understand Jesus' plans for you. But how can you develop that kind of faith? The first step is to try to understand God better, because God is the source of faith.

**Praise the Lord,
all you nations; extol Him,
all you peoples.
For great is His love
toward us,
and the faithfulness
of the Lord
endures forever.
Praise the Lord.
(Psalm 117)**

God's faithfulness causes His love and mercy to continue toward you. What does Lamentations 3:22-23 reveal about God's faithfulness toward you?

_____

_____

_____

The two words "never fail" describe God's faithfulness.

Study the following verses and list some things that God is faithful to do in your life.

1 Corinthians 1:9 _____

1 Corinthians 10:13 _____

2 Thessalonians 3:3 _____

1 John 1:9 _____

God's faithfulness *to* us should inspire faith *in* us. Let's say you really need some help in algebra, and a fellow student

51

offers to meet you after school and help you. If he didn't show up, how would you feel?

_____

If he missed two or three appointments, would you keep trying to meet with him?

But if he made it to every meeting and helped you, wouldn't you begin to think, *Hey, here's someone I can count on*? Faith in God develops in the same way. God proves to you that He can be trusted, and you begin to have faith in Him.

How has God proven Himself trustworthy to you? Give a specific example.

_____

_____

How can you give Him additional opportunities to prove Himself faithful?

_____

_____

When God says He will do something, He *always* does it. And because God is faithful, you can develop faith in Him.

OUR FAITH
What is the biblical definition of faith? (Hebrews 11:1)

_____

52

_____

_____

_____

Faith is confidence in your mind, your feelings, and your actions that God will come through.

An example of what faith is not – A man walks across Niagara Falls on a tightrope. People applaud. He walks across it again with a wheelbarrow. People get really excited. Do those people have faith that the tightrope walker knows what he is doing? You might think so. But suppose the guy asks for a volunteer to go across the Falls in his wheelbarrow. That is the test of how much the people believe in him. Genuine faith isn't sitting back and watching others. It is developed only when risk is involved.

An example of what faith is – When you sit down in a chair, do you worry about whether or not it will hold you up? Of course not. Why? Based on the evidence and your experience, a chair's purpose is to hold you up when you sit on it. As long as you're standing up, you are not expressing any faith. Faith comes when you sit down, relax, and put all your weight on the chair. Sitting down is one of many simple acts of faith we take every day. Everyone has faith in something. But what is really important is the *object* of your faith.

Jesus is the only object of your faith who will *never* let you down.

Let's take a closer look at what faith is.

Faith Is Confidence
Reread Hebrews 11:1. What do you think the following phrases refer to?

● "What we hope for" _____

_____

● "What we do not see" _____

_____

How can you "be sure" of such things?

_____

_____

Faith Is Believing in Your Mind
Read Hebrews 11:6. What are the two things you must believe intellectually in order to have faith?

_____

_____

What is God's response when you meet those requirements?

_____

_____

Abraham was known for his faith. Read Romans 4:18-21. What does it mean to be "fully persuaded"?

_____

_____

Are you fully persuaded that God can do what He promises? Why or why not?

_____

_____

Faith Is Action
Read Mark 11:24. According to that verse, how does faith become an action?

_____

_____

**You put into practice
what you believe every day.
All the rest is just
religious talk.
(Peter Lord)**

Without action, faith does not exist. Faith is a *total* trust in God. He wants us to *act* on what we believe.

Through learning how to totally trust God, you can reach your maximum potential as a person and at the same time glorify Him.

Look again at Romans 4:20-21. How can your potential and God's glory fit together according to these verses?

_____

_____

Now jot down one thought from each of the following verses on how you can reach your maximum potential and give glory to God through your life.

Romans 10:17 _____

Hebrews 11:8 _____

Hebrews 13:7 _____

1 Peter 1:6-7 _____

2 Peter 1:5-9 _____

One of the most important characteristics of a friendship is faithfulness—being able to be counted on. In order for a friendship to succeed, you need to trust the other person and have faith in him. To make this lesson on faith and faithfulness personal to your own life, work through the Life Change sheet on the issue of "Friendships." Think about how God's faithfulness and your faith can make you a better friend.

Complete this Bible study by memorizing Hebrews 11:1.

ASSIGNMENT

1 Have a time alone with God every day this week, using the following Bible readings.

✔ Day 1: Mark 6:7-13
✔ Day 2: Mark 6:14-29
✔ Day 3: Mark 6:30-44
✔ Day 4: Mark 6:45-52
✔ Day 5: Mark 6:53-56
✔ Day 6: Mark 7:1-23
✔ Day 7: Mark 7:24-30

2 Complete *Bible Study 5.*

LIFE CHANGE

ISSUE: Friendships
BIBLE STUDY: 1 Samuel 18:1-5
Use the space below to record your comments.

_____

_____

_____

_____

My weaknesses in the area of friendships are:

_____

_____

My strengths in this area of friendships are:

_____

_____

ACTION POINT
Based on my study of 1 Samuel 18:1-5, now I need to make Jesus Lord of my friendships by:

_____

_____

I will take the following specific step of action to strengthen my existing friendships and/or develop new ones.

_____

_____

_____ will pray with me about this.

FOR REAL

Knowing the truth

I heard a rumor at school today that the coach didn't really play for the pros like he said he did. I really believed him when he talked about the "old days," but after today, I'm not sure who to believe.

People talk about Jesus Christ in a lot of ways. You probably hear a lot of negative rumors about Him at school. Most of them probably aren't true, but they can stir up some doubts about His faithfulness. Let's look at some of the rumors about Jesus and then examine the proof so we can know for sure that Jesus was who He said He was.

PROOF POSITIVE

Rumor #1
Jesus Christ was merely a good teacher.

Proof #1
Jesus is more than just a good teacher. Only one person has ever fulfilled the Old Testament prophecies referring to the "Messiah" — Jesus Christ. Look up the prophecies listed on page 63 and see how they were fulfilled.

These are only a few examples. Jesus Christ fulfilled over 300 prophecies from the Old Testament. So He is obviously much more than a good teacher. In C.S. Lewis' classic book, *Mere Christianity* (Macmillan), he says:

A man who was merely a man and said the sort of things Jesus said wouldn't be a great moral teacher, he would either be a lunatic on the level with a man who says he is a poached egg, or else he would be the devil of Hell; you must make your choice.

Either this was and is the Son of God, or else a madman or something worse. You can shut Him up for a demon, or you can fall at His feet and call Him Lord and God. But don't come up with any patronizing nonsense about His being a great moral teacher. He hasn't left that alternative open to us.

Prophecy	Fulfillment	What Happened?
Psalm 16:9-11	Acts 2:25-32	
Psalm 22:1	Matthew 27:46	
Psalm 34:20; 22:16-18	Matthew 27:35; Luke 23:33; John 19:33-37	
Psalm 110:1	Acts 2:34-36; Hebrews 1:3	
Isaiah 53:7	Luke 23:8-9	
Isaiah 53:9	Luke 23:33, 50-53	

Rumor #2
The prophecies that Jesus fulfilled were written during or after the time of Jesus.

Proof #2
In *Evidence That Demands a Verdict* (Here's Life), Josh McDowell points out that the Greek translation of the Hebrew Scriptures (known as the Septuagint) was completed by the year 250 B.C. So there had to be *at least* a 250 year gap between the written prophecies of Christ and their fulfillment.

Read 2 Peter 1:20-21. What further proof does that passage provide regarding prophecies?

_____

_____

Evidence clearly indicates that Jesus was born many years after the prophecies about Him were written.

Rumor #3
Jesus wasn't really God. He was just a great religious figure.

Proof #3
Like C.S. Lewis said, no great religious figure would ever have made the claims Jesus made. What were some of Jesus' claims, and what evidence did He provide to prove He was telling the truth? Look up the following passages, and then decide if Jesus supported His claims to be God.

Claim	Evidence	Your Observations
John 6:35	John 6:1-14	
John 7:37	John 2:1-11	
John 8:12	John 9:1-25	
John 11:25-26	John 11:38-44	

📖 **Read Matthew 3:16-17.** Someone else believed Jesus' claims to be God — His Father. What indications did God the Father provide to support Jesus' claims?

_____

_____

📖 **Read Matthew 14:25-32.** Other people believed Jesus was God. What did those people say about Jesus?

_____

_____

Rumor #4
Jesus is equal to Muhammad, Confucius, Buddha, and other great religious leaders.

Proof #4
If you go to the graves of Muhammad, Confucius, or Buddha, you will find their bodies enshrined there. But that's not true of Jesus Christ. His grave is empty. Why? Because Jesus Christ was raised from the dead and ascended to heaven to be with the Father. Examine the following proof.

📖 **Jesus prophesied His resurrection.** Rephrase Luke 18:31-34 in your own words.

_____

_____

Jesus' tomb was empty. Read Matthew 27:57 – 28:7. What proof of Christ's resurrection do those verses provide?

_____

_____

Jesus appeared to people after His death. Read the following passages and make a list of those who saw Jesus alive after His death.

Matthew 28:1, 8-10 _____

Matthew 28:16-20 _____

Luke 24:13-16, 28-31 _____

Luke 24:34 _____

Luke 24:36-43 _____

John 20:14 _____

John 20:26-28 _____

John 21:1-14 _____

1 Corinthians 15:3-8 _____

Because of the proof of His resurrection, there can be *no* comparison of Jesus to other religious leaders.

Rumor #5
Jesus was a Jew who died 2,000 years ago. He doesn't have anything to do with my life today.

Proof #5

This proof is up to you. From your personal experience, how can you prove that Jesus is who He said He was and that He is still active today?

_____

_____

_____

_____

_____

TRUST AND OBEY

We can learn from the example that Christ has set for us. The one factor that allowed Jesus to be who He was and do what He did was His perfect obedience to His Father. Look at these examples.

➤ Jesus was obedient in baptism (Matthew 3:13-17).
➤ Jesus was obedient in every detail of His life (John 6:38).
➤ Jesus was obedient even in death (Matthew 26:36-46).

Determine from the above passages what motivated Jesus to obey His Father.

_____

_____

Define obedience as you see it expressed through Jesus' life.

_____

_____

The greatest factor that will allow you to discover power and purpose in life is your obedience to God. When you make Jesus Lord, you become obedient to Jesus Christ and do what you know He wants you to do. And you experience some positive results of your obedience.

You Will Be Wise

Read Matthew 7:24-27 and rewrite this parable to apply to your own life.

_____

_____

_____

You Will Experience God's Love and Fellowship

Look at John 14:23. What does that verse mean to you?

_____

_____

You Will Know Jesus Better and Better

Read John 14:21 to see how that happens.

_____

You Will Be an Overcomer

What promise does 1 John 5:3-4 hold for those who keep God's commandments?

_____

_____

Name one area of your life where it is really tough for you to be obedient to Jesus Christ.

_____

_____

Perhaps my toughest test of obedience happened while I was in college, playing basketball on a scholarship. One day while I was reading the Bible I came across Matthew 6:33: "Seek first His kingdom and His righteousness, and all these things [food, clothes, etc.] will be given to you as well." When I read that verse, I realized that playing basketball was more important to me than Jesus Christ. I struggled with the thought of *not* playing. I had played basketball since I was in first grade. The summer before my senior year in high school, I practiced eight hours a day — basketball was my life.

I didn't want to quit, but I kept thinking, *What comes first, basketball or Jesus Christ?* Finally one day my parents and I talked, cried, and prayed about my decision, and I knew that I needed to quit basketball.

After making that decision, I discovered how Jesus really takes care of us when we obey Him. I thought that quitting basketball would leave a big void in my life. As soon as I quit, God put me in touch with a person who got me involved in working with students. Then a year and a half later, God gave me the opportunity to play for a basketball team that traveled all over the country playing major colleges and universities. But in addition to playing basketball, we shared our faith in Jesus Christ with the crowds of people who came to the games. I gave up basketball to seek Jesus first, and He gave basketball back to me.

You probably know of several tough areas where you need to start being obedient to Jesus Christ. Let's take just one — your parents — and make it really personal to your life right now. Work through the Bible study on your Life Change sheet and then answer each question. Focus your thoughts on how your obedience to your parents will help you obey Jesus.

Complete this Bible study by memorizing John 14:21.

ASSIGNMENT

1️⃣ Have a time alone with God every day this week, using the following Bible readings:

   ✔ Day 1: Mark 7:31-37

✔ Day 2: Mark 8:1-13
✔ Day 3: Mark 8:14-21
✔ Day 4: Mark 8:22-26
✔ Day 5: Mark 8:27-30
✔ Day 6: Mark 8:31–9:1
✔ Day 7: Mark 9:2-13

2 Complete *Bible Study 6.*

LIFE CHANGE

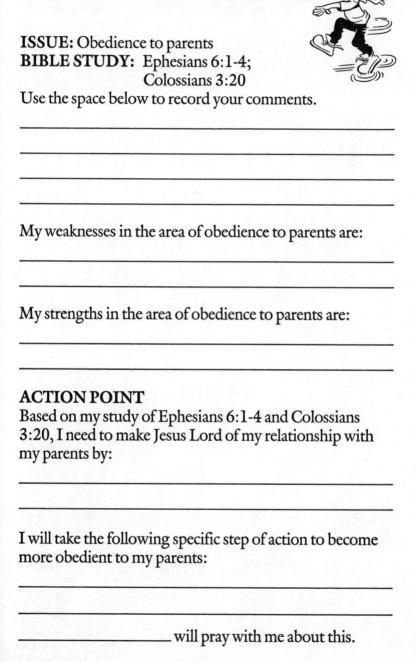

ISSUE: Obedience to parents
BIBLE STUDY: Ephesians 6:1-4;
Colossians 3:20
Use the space below to record your comments.

_____

_____

_____

_____

My weaknesses in the area of obedience to parents are:

_____

_____

My strengths in the area of obedience to parents are:

_____

_____

ACTION POINT
Based on my study of Ephesians 6:1-4 and Colossians
3:20, I need to make Jesus Lord of my relationship with
my parents by:

_____

_____

I will take the following specific step of action to become
more obedient to my parents:

_____

_____

_____ will pray with me about this.

Go For It!

Changing your attitudes

Today during practice, one of the guys cussed me out because he got ticked off at me. I wanted to punch his lights out. It's hard to have the right attitude about people like him.

What would you do in a similar situation?

Ignore the person and stay away from them.

Why?

So that way the wan't get any more mad at you.

Your attitudes determine your actions just like your genes determine what you look like. I heard a story once that demonstrates the relationship between attitudes and actions. A guy named Steve Trass ran away from home and got a job in a lumber camp. He had lived a sheltered life and was kind of a sissy. One day he wrote home: "I hate this place. It's the worst place I've ever seen. The men are crude and nasty. I feel out of place."

But one night everyone in the camp went to town to get drunk—except for Steve. After the men had left, some guys from another lumber camp came to raid Steve's camp. Steve was scared and he didn't know what else to do, so he grabbed a nearby axe handle and turned out the light. As soon as the strangers came through the door, he started swinging. _Thud! Thud! Thud!_

Pretty soon the men from the other camp retreated. When Steve turned on the light, he saw seven bodies lying on the floor. That night he wrote home again: "I love this place. This is a place for men who are brave and strong. I am going to stay and make my fortune." This time he signed his letter "Your son, Axe Handle Trass." What a change of attitude!

ATTITUDE CHECK

Do you recognize any of the following attitudes?

"I hate school."

"Gotta make my move on that girl!"

"My teacher came over on the *Mayflower!*"

"This stuff tastes like dog food."

"My parents have no right to tell me what to do."

If you are guilty of these thoughts (or worse), *you need a change of attitude.*

But don't exchange one bad attitude for another. You need to know what the right attitudes are. Jesus is a perfect example of someone with proper attitudes. Let's take a look at some of those attitudes and try to imitate them (as Paul challenges us to do in Philippians 2:5).

1 Jesus Didn't Strive for Ambition and Success

He gave up His own desires and goals for His Father's desires and goals. Read Philippians 2:3. What two negative attitudes are named there?

Seltishness and conciet

How do you struggle with those attitudes?

I struggle a lot with them.

What positive attitude should replace those negative ones?

Kind

 Philippians 2:6 describes how Jesus displayed that positive quality. Write what He did here.

Jesus "made Himself nothing." That means He poured out His own desires just like a glass of water. We need to pour out our attitudes of pride, selfishness, conceit, stubbornness, and defensiveness. Which of these attitudes do you need to get rid of?

selfishness and defens

Emptying yourself may cost you your hopes, dreams, and desires.

 **2** Jesus Gave Up His "Rights" to Serve Others

What does Philippians 2:7 say about Jesus' "rights"?

 Read Mark 10:45. What else can you learn about Jesus' attitude?

he didn't come to be served but to serve and give his life a ransom for man

78

Many servants in Old Testament times were *hired*. They were paid wages and had certain rights. But the New Testament introduces the concept of a *bond* servant — someone who had no rights and was only the property of a master. Jesus was a *bond servant*. He voluntarily gave up His rights in order to glorify God and to serve men.

Look up Philippians 1:1 and 2 Corinthians 4:5 (in the *New American Standard Bible*), and you will discover that the Apostle Paul called himself a bond servant. Who was his master?

Christ Jesus

People in our society think they have rights. Do you? Defend your answer.

Yes, because people should be able to do things.

How do you develop Jesus' servant attitude? By giving up your "rights." Since your last Life Change sheet was about parents, here are some practical ways to apply a servant attitude to your parents.

1 *Look at life from your parents' perspective.* How does your father feel about his job right now? His friends? His age? His relationship with your mom?

He likes his job and his friends. He's 46 and has a good relationship with my mom

79

What about your mom? How does she feel about her life? Her feelings of self-worth? Your dad? Does she ever feel lonely?

She likes her life and her husband. She sometimes feels lonely.

2 *Ask your parents' advice for problems you are facing.* What do you need their advice about right now?

nothing

Name a recent bad decision you might not have made if you had consulted your parents first.

I went downtown after school and they didn't know where I was

3 *Show appreciation for your parents.* Here are some suggestions to get you started.

➡ Take them out to dinner and *you* pay.
➡ Pick up your clothes.
➡ Clean up your room.
➡ Remember their birthdays and anniversary.
➡ Take out the trash.
➡ Vacuum the house.

What will you do this week to show appreciation for your parents?

Clean up my room

4 *Pray for your parents.* Make sure you remember your parents during your prayer times in your daily time alone with God. Use a "Record of Intercession" (see page 139 in *Spending Time Alone with God*) and record your prayer requests for your parents.

5 *Ask forgiveness from your parents when you do something wrong.* Does tension exist between you and your parents? Have you caused *any* of it? If so, you need to go to them and tell them you're sorry. Practice saying this out loud: "I was wrong. (Explain how.) Will you forgive me?" After you rehearse your apology several times, ask for your parents' forgiveness and record what happens.

6 *Tell your parents you love them.* People are different. Your parents might respond positively, negatively, or indifferently when you say "I love you." But either way, it's important that they know you love them. (And don't just *say* it. *Show* it.) Their response can help you determine more specifically what to pray for them. Record their response here.

You can tell if you have a servant's attitude by the way you react when someone treats you like a servant.

3 Jesus Gave Up His Life for Death on the Cross

Read Philippians 2:8. Jesus struggled to be "obedient to death" in the Garden of Gethsemane (Matthew 26:38). The Bible pictures Jesus with "sweat . . . like drops of blood" as He was struggling to obey His Father.

Read Matthew 26:39. Did Jesus want to die?

yes he did

Why did He decide to willingly give up His life?

Because he didn it to save all people.

You will never learn to live until you learn to die.

4 Jesus Knew He Would Be Victorious

Read Philippians 2:9-11. What two things did God do as a result of Jesus' attitudes?

He lifted him high and gave him a name that surpasses everyone

What two things should we do as a result of Jesus' attitudes?

Read 1 Peter 5:5-6. What should we do to imitate Jesus' attitudes?

put on the apron of humility on toward each other.

You must go through the Cross to get to the Resurrection.

Everything you do costs something (time, money, energy, etc.). The real question is whether or not you want to pay the price. If a football team wants to get to the state championship in December, they must practice in the sweltering heat of August. If a student wants to make the grades to get in one of the best colleges, he has to give up certain activities and study every night. If you want to set your sights on developing attitudes that will make you more like Christ, you must humble yourself before Jesus as Lord. Then His exciting promise is that He will exalt you, lift you up, and make you a winner in life.

Are your attitudes like those that Jesus displayed? Or do you need "a change of attitude"? Your attitudes will determine your actions. To make this lesson personal, complete this session's Life Change sheet on "Attitudes," doing a Bible study of the passage of Scripture and then answering each question.

Complete this Bible study by memorizing Philippians 2:5.

ASSIGNMENT

1 Have a time alone with God every day this week using the following Bible readings.

✔ Day 1: Mark 9:14-29
✔ Day 2: Mark 9:30-32

✔ Day 3: Mark 9:33-37
✔ Day 4: Mark 9:38-41
✔ Day 5: Mark 9:42-50
✔ Day 6: Mark 10:1-12
✔ Day 7: Mark 10:13-16

2 Complete *Bible Study 7.*

LIFE CHANGE

ISSUE: Attitudes
BIBLE STUDY: Matthew 5:1-12
Use the space below to record your comments.

_____

_____

_____

_____

My weaknesses in the area of attitudes are:

_____

_____

My strengths in the area of attitudes are:

_____

_____

ACTION POINT
Based on my study of Matthew 5:1-12, I need to make
Jesus Lord of my attitudes by:

_____

_____

I will take the following specific step of action to make sure
my attitudes reflect the lordship of Christ in my life:

_____

_____

_____ will pray with me about this.

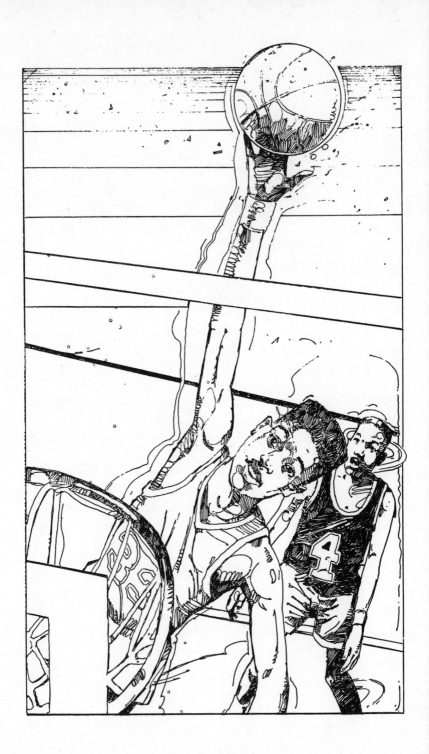

TURN HIM LOOSE

Living in the power of the Holy Spirit

This week has been the roughest yet. I have taken a beating in practice every day. I wish I had more strength and power.

I had a roommate in college who could be more than a little intimidating on the basketball court. I was a skinny six-foot guard, but he was a 6′4″, 210-pound All-American. We used to play one-on-one. I would come back to the dorm room exhausted and humbled after spending much of our playing time with the ball stuffed down my throat.

My roommate would beat me time after time, and his victories began to take their toll as I began to lose my confidence. One afternoon, I was sitting in my room thinking about possible ways to defeat him. I fell asleep and the next thing I knew, I was dreaming that Michael Jordan (probably the best basketball player who ever lived) was stuffed inside my body. I still looked like me on the outside, but inside I had become the best basketball player around.

The next day my roommate and I went to the gym to play our usual one-on-one. I decided to play it cool, so I dribbled the ball off my knee one time so he wouldn't suspect anything. But then I thought, *OK, Michael baby, get loose!* I turned around and shot a perfect skyhook. It stripped the net. The next time I got the ball, I dribbled downcourt, put the move on my roommate, and slam dunked it right over his head. When he got the ball, I made him eat it . . . and I didn't even ask if he wanted salt and pepper on it. He never knew what hit him, because I obviously wasn't playing my normal game.

Have you ever wished you could be stronger than your normal self? When?

_____

_____

Jesus has given Christians an edge in the game of life. He has stuffed the person of the Holy Spirit right down inside them. What good does that do? Jesus said that "when He, the Spirit of truth, comes, He will guide you into all truth. He will not speak on His own; He will speak only what He hears, and He will tell you what is yet to come. He will bring glory to Me by taking from what is Mine and making it known to you" (John 16:13-14).

Having the Holy Spirit is like having "extra ability" as you face the test of living for Christ each day. Check out His promise to you in Ephesians 3:20-21: "Now to Him [Jesus] who is able to do immeasurably more than all we ask or imagine, according to His power [the Holy Spirit] that is at work within us, to Him be glory in the church and in Christ Jesus throughout all generations, for ever and ever!" The Holy Spirit gives you power to live the Christian life.

POWER FACTS

What do you really know about the Holy Spirit? Let's look at some of the "power facts" about Him.

1 **The Holy Spirit Is God**
He is the third person in the Trinity. Remember the diagram from *Bible Study 3*?

Look up the following verses and record the evidence they give to show that the Holy Spirit is God.

Matthew 28:19-20 _____

John 14:26 _____

1 Corinthians 12:13 _____

2 The Holy Spirit Has Been Working Since the Beginning of Time

How do the following verses confirm the Holy Spirit's early ministry?

Genesis 1:2 _____

Haggai 2:5 _____

3 The Holy Spirit's Work Was Evident in the Life of Jesus

How do the following verses of Scripture verify the Holy Spirit's work?

Luke 1:35 _____

Luke 4:1 _____

Luke 4:14-21 _____

John 1:32 _____

Romans 8:11 _____

Hebrews 9:14 _____

4 The Holy Spirit Inspired the Bible

Read and summarize what the following Scripture verses say about the Holy Spirit's role in the writing of the Bible.

John 16:13 _____

Acts 1:16 _____

2 Peter 1:21 _____

Does the fact that the Holy Spirit was the source of knowledge for all of the Bible writers give you more confidence in God's Word? Why?

_____

_____

5 The Holy Spirit Helps Us to Believe in Christ

Read John 14:15-17. How does the Holy Spirit bring us to Christ?

_____

_____

_____

_____

Can unbelievers possess the Holy Spirit?

_____

_____

How can a non-Christian grieve the Holy Spirit? (Matthew 12:31-32)

_____

_____

6 The Holy Spirit Comes to Live Inside of You

What do the following verses reveal about a Christian's relationship with the Holy Spirit?

John 7:37-39 _____

1 Corinthians 12:13 _____

2 Corinthians 3:6 _____

Galatians 4:6 _____

Ephesians 1:13-14 _____

7 The Holy Spirit Changes Your Life

The following verses will help you see how the Holy Spirit living in you will make you more like Christ.

Ezekiel 36:26-27 _____

John 14:26 _____

Acts 1:8 _____

Romans 8:13-16 _____

1 Corinthians 12:4-11 _____

Galatians 5:22-23 _____

Philippians 3:3 _____

Write a statement describing the work of the Holy Spirit in
your life by paraphrasing 2 Corinthians 3:18.

_____

_____

THE POWER PACT

After you received Christ, your body became the temple of
the Holy Spirit (1 Corinthians 3:16). You need to be willing to allow the Holy Spirit to operate within His temple.

Study and outline Romans 8:1-11, giving an expla-
nation of what happens when the Holy Spirit fills
you. Use this basic diagram to help you.

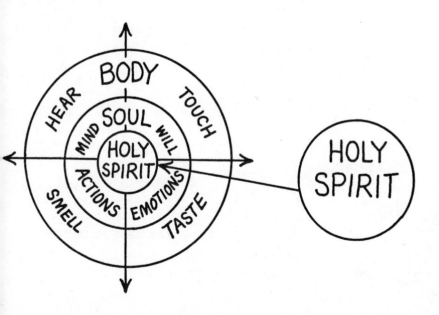

Why do you need to be filled with the Holy Spirit? Be specific.

_____

_____

Is anything in your life preventing you from being filled with the Holy Spirit?

_____

_____

The following steps will help you learn to be filled with the Holy Spirit *daily* so you will remain under His control. Pray through each step as you ask God to fill you with His Holy Spirit.

1 Recognize
That the Holy Spirit lives within you permanently because you have asked Christ into your life. Read 1 Corinthians 6:19-20. What do you need to do? Why?

_____

_____

2 Realize
That God wants you to be completely controlled by His Spirit. (This is the heart of allowing Jesus to be your Lord.) What command does God give you in Ephesians 4:17-18?

3 Repent

Of any sin in your life. Do certain things in your life displease God? Jesus provided forgiveness and deliverance from sin on the cross. His forgiveness becomes real when you confess your sin to Him (agree with God about it). His promise to you in 1 John 1:9 will then become special to you. What sin(s) do you need to confess right now?

_____

_____

4 Renounce

Abandon *your* desires in order to follow *God's* desires. What does Galatians 2:20 teach about dealing with your desires?

_____

_____

What desires do you now control that you need to turn over to the Holy Spirit?

_____

_____

_____

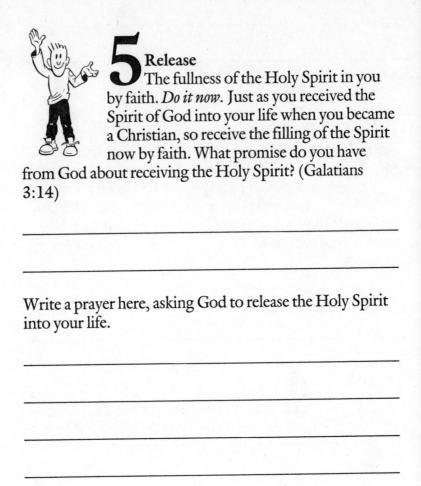

5 Release

The fullness of the Holy Spirit in you by faith. *Do it now*. Just as you received the Spirit of God into your life when you became a Christian, so receive the filling of the Spirit now by faith. What promise do you have from God about receiving the Holy Spirit? (Galatians 3:14)

_____

_____

Write a prayer here, asking God to release the Holy Spirit into your life.

_____

_____

_____

_____

N ow that you understand how the Holy Spirit can change your life and give you more strength and power, let Him do that. Again, the Life Change sheet will examine just one area that most people need to change. As you think through your "habits," complete the study from Ephesians and answer all the questions.

Complete this Bible study by memorizing Ephesians 5:18.

ASSIGNMENT

1 Have a time alone with God every day this week, using the following Bible readings.
- ✔ Day 1: Mark 10:17-31
- ✔ Day 2: Mark 10:32-34

✔ Day 3: Mark 10:35-45
✔ Day 4: Mark 10:46-52
✔ Day 5: Mark 11:1-14
✔ Day 6: Mark 11:15-19
✔ Day 7: Mark 11:20-26

2 Complete *Bible Study 8.*

ISSUE: Habits
BIBLE STUDY: Ephesians 5:1-18
Use the space below to record your comments.

_____

_____

_____

_____

My weaknesses in the area of habits are:

_____

_____

My strengths in the area of habits are:

_____

_____

ACTION POINT
From my study of Ephesians 5:1-18, I need to make Jesus
Lord of my habits by:

_____

_____

I will take the following specific step of action to get rid of
my bad habits and replace them with habits that honor
God.

_____

_____

_____ will pray with me about this.

8

GET IN SHAPE!

Throwing off the hindrances

Last night we played our biggest rival, and I ran out of steam during the third quarter. I really feel like I let the team and the coach down. Monday I'm going to ask Coach how I can build up my endurance so I can finish stronger than I started.

Paul once challenged the Galatian church: "You were running a good race. Who cut in on you and kept you from obeying the truth?" (Galatians 5:7) The writer of Hebrews tells us to "throw off everything that hinders and the sin that so easily entangles, and let us run with perseverance the race marked out before us" (Hebrews 12:1).

What hinders us from running the race with endurance? Let's look at some common hindrances and then see how we can "throw them off."

HINDRANCES TO SERIOUS "RUNNERS"

A list of those hindrances is found in Galatians 5:19-21. Let's take one group at a time and see how they hinder Jesus' control of your life.

1 Sexual Immorality, Impurity, and Debauchery
These days it is pretty acceptable to participate in casual sexual relationships. If you are a virgin, you might even be an outcast (in the eyes of the people at school, that is). But what does God think about sexual purity?

Read 1 Thessalonians 4:3-6. What should you avoid?

_____

_____

What do you need to do instead? Why?

_____

_____

104

Why is sex outside of marriage such a problem? When you don't wait for the proper person, time, and place (marriage), your focus is more on, "I need to gratify my sexual desires" than, "This is an expression of my love for you." You end up using the other person to fulfill your own selfish motives. By learning to control your sex life, you will be more able to respond with love and concern to the other person. A lack of control in this area indicates that sex is more important to you than Jesus is.

2 Idolatry and Witchcraft

Idolatry is giving ultimate worth to someone or something other than God. Some of our idols seem innocent enough. Others are obviously wrong. Below are three common idols you might be tempted by. (Of course, there are many, many more.)

➤ Popularity. In school, recognition is the name of the game. The emphasis always seems to be on grades, elections, or dating. What does Paul say about popularity? (Galatians 1:10)

_____

_____

Why is it wrong to put too much emphasis on trying to please others?

_____

_____

➤ Pride. Egotistical pride makes you think you are more important than you really are. What does Peter encourage us to replace pride with? (1 Peter 5:5) Why?

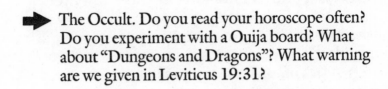 The Occult. Do you read your horoscope often?
Do you experiment with a Ouija board? What
about "Dungeons and Dragons"? What warning
are we given in Leviticus 19:31?

3 Hatred, Discord, Jealousy, Fits of Rage, Selfish Ambition, Dissentions, Factions, and Envy

These are all negative emotions that keep you from living
in harmony with other people. Here are a couple of specific
examples.

Bitterness. With all of the hurt that goes with broken homes and unfulfilled expectations, it's easy to
see why students experience so much bitterness today. But bitterness eats away at you.

Read Hebrews 12:15. What happens when we remain bitter over a period of time?

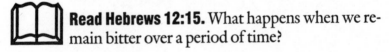 Envy and jealousy. Do you resent the accomplish-
ments and prosperity of other people?

You can find some good advice in Proverbs 14:30.
Summarize that advice. (Use *The Living Bible* if
possible.)

4 Drunkenness, Orgies, and the Like

This set of hindrances refers to the "party spirit." You are probably familiar with the following symptoms.

➡ Escapism. Drugs, alcohol, television, and even video games have become popular ways of escape, today more than ever. But people have tried to escape reality for centuries.

Read Proverbs 23:29-35 to discover one popular way people tried to escape during Bible times. What method did they use?

_____

_____

What are the results of trying to escape reality in that manner?

_____

_____

_____

➡ Pleasure. The overwhelming desire for pleasure expresses itself in a lot of different ways: the acquisition of clothes, cars, stereos, trips, and so forth. A person who overemphasizes pleasure always has to manipulate his outward circumstances in order to be happy.

Read Proverbs 21:17. What happens if you love pleasure too much?

_____

_____

Selfishness is the bottom line for someone who puts pleasure above all else.

THROWING OFF YOUR HINDRANCES
What are the three biggest hindrances that interfere with your relationship with Jesus Christ?

_____

_____

Read Galatians 5:16. What is the key to throwing off those hindrances that bog down your spiritual growth?

_____

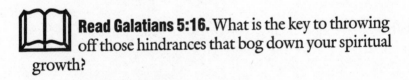

Before you can *run* a good race, you have to learn to *walk* by the Spirit.

In the last chapter, you learned how to be filled with the Spirit. But how do you "walk by the Spirit" every day?

1
Be Filled Continually with the Holy Spirit (Ephesians 5:18)
This happens when you allow Him to control or influ-

ence you totally. At first the Holy Spirit might bring to light an area of your life that needs to be changed. *Walking* in the Spirit takes place when you yield that area to the Lord day by day. You continue to allow the Holy Spirit to shed light on and change you in that area. Eventually, you ask Him to control your behavior *all the time*.

2 Do Not Quench the Holy Spirit (1 Thessalonians 5:19)

What does it mean to "quench" the Holy Spirit? It's when you choose not to do what He directs you to do. For example, when you feel prompted by the Spirit to call a friend, but don't, you've quenched the Spirit. You can say no or ignore Him, but His prompting is always for your own good, or the good of others.

3 Do Not Grieve the Holy Spirit (Ephesians 4:30)

The Holy Spirit is grieved whenever you deliberately choose to sin. For example, when you know it's not right to date a non-Christian, but choose to do it anyway, you grieve the Spirit. By doing so, you say yes to sin and no to God.

GETTING BACK ON TRACK

What do you do when you know you're no longer walking with the Spirit because you've quenched or grieved Him? You stay on track by learning to breathe spiritually. Physical breathing comes naturally for you.

You've been breathing all the time you have been working on this chapter, but you haven't even noticed it. You exhale, ridding your lungs of all their carbon dioxide impurities. Then you inhale to take in the life-giving oxygen your body needs.

In a similar way, spiritual breathing keeps your spiritual life healthy. And after you practice it for a while, it will become like your physical breathing — a natural process.

You *exhale* by confessing. Confession means you get specific and identify the source(s) of whatever has caused the problem. Then you confess (agree with God) that you have quenched or grieved the Spirit.

You *inhale* by claiming two things: God's cleansing (1 John 1:9) and God's filling of the Holy Spirit (Ephesians 5:18). The great thing about breathing is that you can do it as often as you want or need to. If you are undergoing a particularly difficult ordeal, you will probably breathe a little harder than normal. Spiritual breathing works the same way, so don't hesitate to do it as often as you need to. God wants you to walk by the Spirit, so begin to practice your spiritual breathing exercises right away.

Beginning to walk by the Spirit is the first step you can take toward getting in shape. Are you walking in the Spirit? To make this session really personal in your life, work through the Life Change sheet on "Temptation." Review Galatians 5:19-21 and specifically name some of the temptations that hinder you from walking with the Spirit.

Complete this Bible study by memorizing Galatians 5:16.

ASSIGNMENT

1 Have a time alone with God every day this week, using the following Bible readings:
  ✔ Day 1: Mark 11:27-33

✔ Day 2: Mark 12:1-12
✔ Day 3: Mark 12:13-27
✔ Day 4: Mark 12:28-34
✔ Day 5: Mark 12:35-40
✔ Day 6: Mark 12:41-44
✔ Day 7: Mark 13

2️⃣ Complete *Bible Study 9.*

ISSUE: Temptation
BIBLE STUDY: James 1:2-4, 12-22
Use the space below to record your comments.

_____

_____

_____

_____

My weaknesses in the area of temptation are:

_____

_____

My strengths in the area of temptation are:

_____

_____

ACTION POINT
From my study of James 1:2-4, 12-22, I need to make
Jesus Lord over my temptations by:

_____

_____

I will take the following specific step of action to prepare
myself to overcome any temptation I face:

_____

_____

_____ will pray with me about this.

CHANGED AND REARRANGED

Improving your thoughts

Now that we are moving toward the end of the season and the playoffs, I can look back and see how I've improved. I feel great, even though I also see a need to keep getting better. But what's next? When will I know I've "arrived"?

In making Jesus Lord, hopefully you have experienced similar feelings of "What's next?" or "When do I get this thing licked?" You have seen Jesus change many areas of your life, but you wonder, "How much more is He going to change?"

CHANGED STATUS
More changes occurred when you became a Christian than you may be aware of. You weren't just changed — you were totally rearranged! A picture of how you were changed and rearranged is given in Romans 6:3-11.

Christ died (6:3).	Christ was buried (6:4).	Christ was raised from the dead (6:4).
When you received Christ, you died.	When you received Christ, you were buried.	When you received Christ, you were raised from the dead.

Repeat the following phrases twice to help them sink in:
- Christ died, so I died.
- Christ was buried, so I was buried.
- Christ was raised from the dead, so I was raised from the dead.

According to Romans 6:4, you were raised to live a

_____ life.

You may say, "I don't *feel* dead," or "I don't *feel* new!" On the first sunny day of summer you may not *feel* the sun

116

burning your skin. But the next day you can both see and feel the change that has taken place.

Some things have to be recognized and accepted by faith. So here's how to act on your faith:

➡ Know what God says about you (Romans 6:6, 9).
➡ Count yourself as dead to sin and alive to God (Romans 6:11).
➡ Yield yourself to God (Romans 6:13).

As you grow and then look back, the reality of your new life is something that you can be sure of.

CHANGED THINKING

How much will you change? After you become a new person on the inside, you will begin to notice outer changes as well. The following chart lists some of those changes.

Before you became a Christian	After you became a Christian
You were dead in your transgressions and sins (Ephesians 2:1).	You became alive to God (Ephesians 2:5).
You were controlled by what *you* thought was right or wrong (Ephesians 2:3).	You are controlled by what *God* says is right and wrong (Ephesians 2:10).
You were a slave to sin (Romans 6:6).	You are a son of God (Galatians 4:7).

How does the new you on the inside become the new you on the outside too? As your old self (the one before you became a Christian), you learned how to think and act a certain way. But that old self died. Since you have become a Christian and received a new self, you can now begin to think and act differently. How? Study the following chart, and then fill in the missing words from Colossians 3:1-4.

Christ was raised (3:1).	Christ is seated above (3:1-2).	Christ will appear (3:4).
You were _____ _____ _____.	Set your_____ on things_____ _____.	You will _____ with Him in__ _____.

Now read Ephesians 4:22-24. In your own words, how will you be changed?

_____

_____

_____

Many of your outward changes depend on your inner *mind-set* — learning to think a new way. This quote breaks down the process for you.

Sow a thought, reap an action.
 Sow an action, reap a habit.
  Sow a habit, reap a lifestyle.
Sow a lifestyle, reap a destiny!

In other words, your thoughts determine your destiny.

A.W. Tozer said, "The most important thing about you is what you think about Jesus, because what you think about Jesus will determine who you are and how you behave."

How can you sow thoughts that will eventually reap a destiny of being "conformed to the likeness of His Son"? (Romans 8:29) Two ways: *putting off* and *putting on*.

Putting Off
When you exercise, you sweat. When you sweat, your clothes begin to stink. If you're a slob, you might continue to wear your sweaty clothes for several days until they get really rank. But if you are a self-respecting person, you will take those clothes off, take a shower, and then put on some clean clothes.

You need to "put off" unclean thoughts just like you would put off rank, smelly, stinking clothes.

Read Colossians 3:5-9. What are some of those thoughts that need to be put off?

_____

_____

_____

_____

_____

List some of *your* thoughts that fall into the above categories. Be honest.

_____

_____

_____

_____

What happens if you decide *not* to put off those types of thoughts? Imagine you are a fish and you see an absolutely gorgeous worm dangling down in the water. You swim up to look at the worm. *Hmmmm*, you think, *it looks pretty good, but I'd better stay away. I've been told that there is usually a hook tied to a string which is tied to a pole at the end of that worm.*

You swim away, but you can't get that big, fat, juicy worm out of your mind. You keep imagining how good that worm would taste, so you swim back and look at it again. You think, *No, looks good but I'd better pass.* Yet you continue to swim around it and around it again — kind of checking out the situation.

The more you swim, the better that worm looks. You think, *I can just feel it going down my throat and how good it will taste.* Finally, *chomp* — you take the bait, you're hooked, and you're dead.

James 1:13-15 describes a similar process:
> ➤ Source of evil thoughts (Satan's hook) — James 1:13
> ➤ Lure (the worm) — James 1:14
> ➤ Initiator (you, the fish) — James 1:14
> ➤ Enticement (thinking about your temptation) — James 1:14
> ➤ Birth of Sin (acting on your thoughts) — James 1:15

➤ Growth of Sin (getting hooked on a bad habit)
  — James 1:15
➤ Death (you are caught in your sin) — James 1:15

Once you reach the "Growth of Sin" stage, you are caught in a cycle like this one:

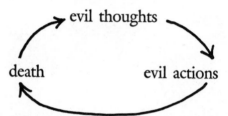

evil thoughts

death   evil actions

You can't control the source (Satan). Sometimes you can't even control the lure (bait) he tosses at you. But you *can* control your thoughts about it. "Set your minds on the things above, not on earthly things" (Colossians 3:2).

Putting On
Read Colossians 3:12-17. As your mind is renewed, positive changes will take place in your life. Make a list of the qualities with which you should clothe yourself.

_____

_____

_____

_____

These changes will occur as you "think on these things." What things?

121

Read Philippians 4:8 and list what you are to think about.

_____

_____

_____

_____

How can you learn to think on these things? Here are some practical suggestions.

1 *Develop a habit of consciously thinking about your life in Christ.* Repeat these statements each day:
➤ "I am dead to myself" (Colossians 3:3).
➤ "I am alive to Christ" (Romans 6:4).
➤ "My life is hidden with Christ in God" (Colossians 3:3).
➤ "Christ is *in* me" (Colossians 1:27).

2 *Memorize Scripture.* The practice of committing God's Word to memory will renew your mind. Write down some of the verses you have memorized word for word that help you keep your mind on "things above."

3 *Resist temptation.* Because you are a new creature in Christ, it should be very difficult for temptation to get to you.

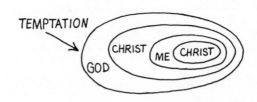

Remember: Your life is hidden with Christ in God (Colossians 3:4). Think of yourself as protected from temptation without and within. If you are tempted, you have Jesus Christ living inside you. You are *dead* to sin (and dead men don't respond to temptation). You are *alive* to Christ, so let Jesus deal with any temptation you face.

So when you get up in the morning,
when some ungodly thought comes to mind,
when you are afraid, lonely, or pressured, or
when you have idle time . . .
THINK ON THESE THINGS.

To make this session specific for you, select one area of your thought life (refer back to your list from Colossians 3:5-9) and work through the Life Change sheet.

Complete this Bible study by memorizing Colossians 3:1.

ASSIGNMENT
☐ Have a time alone with God every day this week, using the following Bible readings.
- ✔ Day 1: Mark 14:1-2
- ✔ Day 2: Mark 14:3-9
- ✔ Day 3: Mark 14:10-11
- ✔ Day 4: Mark 14:12-16

✔ Day 5: Mark 14:17-21
✔ Day 6: Mark 14:22-26
✔ Day 7: Mark 14:27-31

2 Complete *Bible Study 10*.

ISSUE: Thought Life
BIBLE STUDY: Philippians 4:8
Use the space below to record your comments.

_____

_____

_____

_____

My weaknesses in the area of my thought life are:

_____

_____

My strengths in the area of my thought life are:

_____

_____

ACTION POINT
From my study of Philippians 4:8, I need to make Jesus
Lord of my thought life by:

_____

_____

I will take the following specific step of action to rid my
mind of unclean thoughts and "set my mind on things
above":

_____

_____

_____ will pray with me about this.

10

WHO OWNS YOU?

Making your choice

Today was the final game of the year. As I look back, it's encouraging to see how much I've improved. All of the hard work has really paid off. After the game, one of the college coaches offered me a scholarship to play next season. I'm really honored and excited, but I'm sure the demands will be even tougher.

Making Jesus Lord does not insure that your life will become easier. In fact, the challenges usually seem to get harder. But we have a promise as we move ahead: "My God will meet all your needs according to His glorious riches in Christ Jesus" (Philippians 4:19).

Matthew 13:44-46 tells two parables to describe making Jesus Lord. What parallels do you see between these parables and the opening illustration about accepting the scholarship?

_____

_____

_____

In order to get a clearer picture, think of making Jesus Lord this way: Jesus hands you a blank check in exchange for a blank sheet of paper. Let's examine that concept more closely.

A LIVING SACRIFICE
The blank check Jesus gives you represents everything you need to live life at its very best. Check out these verses to discover some of the promises included in Jesus' "blank check."

Romans 8:32 _____

Ephesians 1:3 _____

2 Peter 1:3 _____

In return for Christ's provisions, you need to give Him your life as a blank sheet of paper — with no restrictions. He can write on it whatever He desires for you.

Romans 12:1-2 explains how the process works. Paul's first word is "Therefore," so he is referring back to what he had been saying in the earlier chapters of Romans. Basically he is saying that in light of this fantastic relationship that you have with God, and because of everything Jesus has done for you, you need to "offer your bodies as living sacrifices." What do you think that means?

_____

_____

When Paul says "offer your bodies," he means to put all of your mind, feelings, desires, and physical abilities at Jesus' disposal. He means you should offer yourself to God, just as sacrifices were put on the altar in the Old Testament.

How can you present your body on the altar? You have to make a willing choice to lay down your life and let God remove anything that competes with Jesus' desires for you. But Paul says you are to be a *living* sacrifice. What kind of living sacrifice are you to be? (Romans 12:1)

_____

_____

From your studies so far in *Making Jesus Lord,* what do you think it means to be a *living* sacrifice?

_____

_____

_____

Romans 12:9-21 gives several suggestions on how you can present your body to Christ. What are some of them?

_____

_____

_____

_____

_____

A CHANGED LIFE

When you make that big decision to "offer your body as a living sacrifice," then you can live every day "on the altar." As you learn to think of yourself as a sacrifice, you can know that Jesus is changing your life daily.

How? Look at Romans 12:2. "Do not conform any longer to the pattern of this world" means you shouldn't try to be someone on the outside that you aren't on the inside.

Have you ever caught yourself doing something you shouldn't or not doing something you should because of pressure from other people? How did you feel?

_____

_____

_____

"Be transformed by the renewing of your mind" means

that you should begin to act on the outside like you already are on the inside. Your new life in Jesus Christ gives you the power to control all you do and say. What is one way that Jesus Christ is transforming your actions? Be specific.

_____

_____

Renewing your mind is the key to a changed life. If your thinking doesn't change, your actions won't either. Look back at the example you gave where you were doing or not doing something because of pressure from others. If you had concentrated on having Jesus Christ inside you, how might that situation have had different results?

_____

_____

Romans 12:2 ends by saying that "you will be able to test and approve what God's will is — His good, pleasing, and perfect will." After you have received the blank check of promises from Jesus and given Him your life as a blank sheet, the quality of your life in Christ will develop from "good" to "pleasing" to "perfect." It just gets better and better!

How is the Christian life getting better for you?

_____

_____

Why? _____

_____

GOD'S TROPHY

To bring everything together, look back to Romans 8:28-29. God promises to use *every* circumstance in your life for good when you are called according to His purpose (which you are). His purpose for you is "to be conformed to the likeness of His Son." In other words, you become like Him in everything you do.

The issues you have been working on throughout this book have helped you focus on some specific areas in your life that need to change. But those changes are already present *inside* you, because the Holy Spirit lives in you.

 Read 2 Corinthians 3:18. Who are you compared to?

_____

_____

The positive qualities that result from those inward changes will begin to be reflected in your behavior more and more as Jesus is Lord of your life.

Have you ever known anyone who was awarded a trophy? A trophy is special to its owner because it represents something the owner is proud of. When you make Jesus Lord of your life, you become God's trophy. Your life should reflect God to others. When they see you, they should also see something about Him.

A trophy belongs to the person who has his name on it, and that person can do whatever he wants with his trophy. Remember: you are God's trophy, and He owns you.

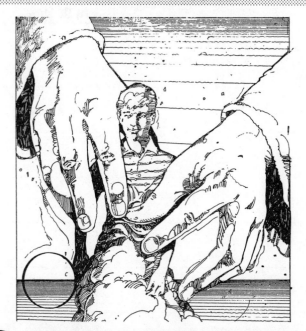

R ight now is a good time for you to be sure what Jesus is doing in your life. Sometimes the things He is working to change in us are different than what we want to change about ourselves. So take a few minutes and look back over the past 10 weeks to see where *He* has been working.

As you evaluate the Life Change sheets from the past eight weeks, take time to pray. Review each sheet and ask yourself: *What has God already done in this area?* Focus on the *Action Point* sections and determine any further action God might want you to take in each area. After you have finished reviewing all eight sheets, spend time in prayer and select the area that is most important for God to work on in your life *right now*.

Topic	What God Has Already Done	What God Is Leading Me to Do Now
Material Possessions		
Dating and Sex		
Friendships		
Parents		
Attitudes		
Habits		
Temptation		
Thought Life		

What specific area do you think is most in need of corrective action right now?

_____

What does God want you to do next?

_____

_____

Complete this Bible study by memorizing Romans 12:1-2.

To close this study of *Making Jesus Lord*, spend a few minutes flipping back through each of the chapters to review what you studied. Then write in your own words what you feel you have learned about Jesus' lordship in your life. How has your commitment to Him changed since you began this study?

_____

_____

_____

ASSIGNMENT

Have a time alone with God every day this week, using the following Bible readings.

- ✔ Day 1: Mark 14:32-42
- ✔ Day 2: Mark 14:43-65
- ✔ Day 3: Mark 14:66-72
- ✔ Day 4: Mark 15:1-15
- ✔ Day 5: Mark 15:16-47
- ✔ Day 6: Mark 16:1-14
- ✔ Day 7: Mark 16:15-20

The next book in the Moving Toward Maturity series, *Giving Away Your Faith*, will help you learn how to share the life you have in Jesus Christ with others.

HOW TO STUDY A PASSAGE OF SCRIPTURE

OBSERVATION (Use with *Title* and *Key Verse* sections of your Bible Response Sheet.)

Pray first for the Holy Spirit's guidance, and then read the passage carefully. Read with an open mind, ready to receive and obey what God has to teach you.

INTERPRETATION (Use with the *Summary* section of your Bible Response Sheet.)

Step One — Read the verses preceding and following the passage in order to understand the proper setting and context.

Step Two — Ask yourself these questions about the passage: *Who? What? When? Where? Why?* and *How?* Write down your insights and any unanswered questions you may have.

Step Three — Look up unfamiliar terms in a standard dictionary or a Bible dictionary.

APPLICATION (Use with the *Personal Application* section of your Bible Response Sheet.)

Step One — Look for:

Promises to claim	*Commands* to obey
Attitudes to change	*Actions* to take
Challenges to accept	*Examples* to follow
Sins to confess	*Skills* to learn

Step Two — Describe how the passage applies to your life by asking yourself these questions: "How can I make this passage personal?" "How can I make it practical?" "How can I make it measurable?" Be specific.

MEMORIZATION
Find a verse or passage of Scripture that speaks to you personally, and memorize it. During the Moving Toward Maturity series, concentrate on memorizing the verses as they are assigned. You will find specific steps to Scripture memorization on page 130 of *Spending Time Alone with God.*

BIBLE MEMORY CARDS

Each memory verse on these cards is printed in the *New International Version* (NIV) and in the *King James Version* (KJV). The verses correspond with the Bible studies in this book. Cut out the cards and packet along the solid black lines. Make the packet, insert the cards, and follow the instructions on the packet. ENJOY THE BENEFITS OF SCRIPTURE MEMORIZATION!

2. COST OF DISCIPLESHIP
Matthew 16:24 (NIV)
Then Jesus said to His disciples, "If anyone would come after Me, he must deny himself and take up his cross and follow Me."

1. SEEKING GOD Psalm 63:1 (NIV)
O God, You are my God, earnestly I seek You; my soul thirsts for You, my body longs for You, in a dry and weary land where there is no water.

3. HOLINESS 1 Peter 1:15-16 (NIV)
But just as He who called you is holy, so be holy in all you do; for as it is written: "Be holy, because I am holy."

4. FAITH DEFINED Heb. 11:1 (NIV)
Now faith is being sure of what we hope for and certain of what we do not see.

5. OBEDIENCE John 14:21 (NIV)
Whoever has My commandments and obeys them, he is the one who loves Me. He who loves Me will be loved by My Father, and I too will love him and show Myself to him.

6. ATTITUDES Phil. 2:5 (NIV)
Your attitude should be the same as that of Christ Jesus.

2. COST OF DISCIPLESHIP

Matthew 16:24 (KJV)
Then said Jesus unto His disciples, "If any man will come after Me, let him deny himself, and take up his cross, and follow Me."

1. SEEKING GOD *Psalm 63:1 (KJV)*
O God, Thou art my God; early will I seek Thee: my soul thirsteth for Thee, my flesh longeth for Thee in a dry and thirsty land, where no water is.

3. HOLINESS *1 Peter 1:15-16 (KJV)*
But as He which hath called you is holy, so be ye holy in all manner of conversation; because it is written, "Be ye holy; for I am holy."

4. FAITH DEFINED *Heb. 11:1 (KJV)*
Now faith is the substance of things hoped for, the evidence of things not seen.

5. OBEDIENCE *John 14:21 (KJV)*
He that hath My commandments, and keepeth them, he it is that loveth Me: and he that loveth Me shall be loved of My Father, and I will love him, and will manifest Myself to him.

6. ATTITUDES *Phil. 2:5 (KJV)*
Let this mind be in you, which was also in Christ Jesus.

7. HOLY SPIRIT   Eph. 5:18 (NIV)
Do not get drunk on wine, which leads to debauchery. Instead, be filled with the Spirit.

8. LIVE BY SPIRIT   Gal. 5:16 (NIV)
So I say, live by the Spirit, and you will not gratify the desires of the sinful nature.

9. THINGS ABOVE   Col. 3:1 (NIV)
Since then, you have been raised with Christ, set your hearts on things above, where Christ is seated at the right hand of God.

10. LIVING SACRIFICE
Romans 12:1-2 (NIV)
I urge you, brothers, in view of God's mercy, to offer your bodies as living sacrifices, holy and pleasing to God — which is your spiritual worship. Do not conform any longer to the pattern of this world, but be transformed by the renewing of your mind. Then you will be able to test and approve what God's will is — His good, pleasing, and perfect will.

PACKET
FOR
CARDS

Cut out.
Fold *in* on dotted lines.
Tape short flap to back on outside edges.

INSTRUCTIONS:
Always carry this packet with you.
Memorize a verse a week.
Daily review each verse you've learned.
Have someone check your progress each week.
Apply each verse to your daily life.

7. HOLY SPIRIT Ephesians 5:18 (KJV)

And be not drunk with wine, wherein is excess; but be filled with the Spirit.

8. LIVE BY SPIRIT Gal. 5:16 (KJV)

This I say then, walk in the Spirit, and ye shall not fulfil the lust of the flesh.

9. THINGS ABOVE Col. 3:1 (KJV)

If ye then be risen with Christ, seek those things which are above, where Christ sitteth on the right hand of God.

10. LIVING SACRIFICE

Romans 12:1-2 (KJV)

I beseech you therefore, brethren, by the mercies of God, that ye present your bodies a living sacrifice, holy, acceptable unto God, which is your reasonable service. And be not conformed to this world: but be ye transformed by the renewing of your mind, that ye may prove what is that good, and acceptable, and perfect, will of God.

MAKING
JESUS LORD
Bible Memory Packet

Adventures
in
the
Mainstream

Coming of Age with Down Syndrome

Greg Palmer

Woodbine House ✦ 2005

All rights reserved. Published in the United States of America by Woodbine House, Inc., 6510 Bells Mill Rd., Bethesda, MD 20817. 800-843-7323. www.woodbinehouse.com

Library of Congress Cataloging-in-Publication Data

Palmer, Greg.
  Adventures in the mainstream : coming of age with Down syndrome / by Greg Palmer.— 1st ed.
    p. cm.
  ISBN 1-890627-30-5
1. Palmer, Ned. 2. Palmer, Greg—Diaries. 3. Down syndrome—Patients—United States—Biography. 4. Down syndrome—Patients—Education—United States. 5. Down syndrome—Patients—United States—Family relationships. 6. Parents of children with disabilities—United States—Diaries. I. Title.
  RJ506.D68P347 2005
  618.92'858842'0092—dc22

Manufactured in the United States of America

First Edition

10   9   8   7   6   5   4   3   2   1

Table of Contents

Virere facillimum non est.

—*Kermit the Frog*

I grew up on Mercer Island, across Lake Washington from Seattle. It was a much more rural place then than it is now. Some mornings we'd eat breakfast watching deer grazing on our front lawn. It was the kind of suburb-to-be where every kid had a collection of Indian arrowheads he found, and Cub Scouts enjoyed almost real "wilderness experiences" in their own back yards.

Nine months of every year, from 1952 to 1965, I usually rode a big yellow bus to and from school. The different schools I attended were spread around the island, but the bus always seemed to take the same route to get to them. I got very familiar with the particulars of that drive, and not just who got on and where, but the scenic attractions as well. Like the Sanborns' dog. She could run faster than the bus and proved it

Introduction

every morning for a decade. Or the still functional earthen dam that I could see for just a moment while passing by a deep, green ravine near my house.

Every day the bus went through one of the island's first housing developments, a place called Mercerwood, where fifty new homes had been laid out on a once-forested hillside. They were very nice houses for the 1950s, occupied mostly by Boeing engineers and East Coast transplants who didn't mind what then seemed like an extremely long commute into Seattle—twenty minutes on a bad day. One of the bus ride's regular attractions was in Mercerwood, on the front lawn of a house that was a little bigger than the others.

I have never known his name or where he came from. He was just there one day, and then every day, watching us go by. I saw him first when we were both about eight years old. I assumed the bus was going to stop for him, that he was another new kid. We were getting a lot of new kids back then, whose parents were forerunners of a Mercer Island invasion that would triple the population within a few decades and drive the deer away forever. But the bus didn't stop. Gordon, the driver, slowed to a crawl, peered through his door at this little kid standing alone, and then pulled away. We drove by, for the first time of a thousand times, and left him. That afternoon he was there again, watching us come home. If it didn't seem so crazy, you might have thought he'd been there exactly like that, all day long, waiting for us.

He was the first person with Down syndrome I had ever seen. I didn't know the term then, and it wasn't used anyway, at least by kids. Somebody told me he was a "Mongoloid Idiot," a re-tard, and that's why he wasn't on the bus with us, why he didn't have to go to school.

We grew up together, he and I, in the same place but in completely different worlds. It was a rare day when he wasn't there to watch the bus go past. I came to depend on seeing him, just like I depended on seeing the Sanborns' dog. He never smiled, but just stared at the bus with what writer Paul Goodman called "the open look." Goodman was talking about cats and the way they stare at you. But the description certainly fit this kid.

I waved at him a few times that first year. He didn't respond, except to look more directly at me. Eventually I stopped waving because I didn't want him to think I was making fun of him. From then on he always looked in my window, and I always sat on the right side of the bus to see him. I don't really know why. I remember he was always carefully dressed for the weather, with a thick coat in the winter and his plaid Pendleton shirt buttoned up to the neck. Somebody inside that house cared about this boy and made sure he was presentable.

Only once during all those years was I around him off the bus. One warm summer day when I was fifteen, some friends and I were walking through Mercerwood. I spotted him a block away, on the other side of the street near his home, just standing there. One of my friends lived nearby. I asked him about the kid, what he knew about him. The answer, to my surprise, was that he knew almost nothing, even though they had been neighbors for years.

"I'll tell you one thing I know," my friend said. "He's the best rock thrower I ever saw. He can hit a mailbox fifty yards away. I've seen him do it. So you don't want to piss him off, because he can get you from a long ways off. His pockets are full of rocks." We all stopped and looked at the kid, thinking he might throw a rock for us. He didn't look back.

My friend laughed. "He could be a hell of a pitcher, if he was only smart enough to learn the game." Then we took off up the hill. It never occurred to any of us to ask him to come along.

My second son, Ned, was born in September of 1981. It was a relatively easy birth, producing this very red little eight-and-a-half pounder. A few moments after he arrived, as I was counting his fingers and toes, he stuck his tongue out at me, and left it there. At the time I thought it was cute. I was to learn later that it was an "indication."

That afternoon our pediatrician stopped by to see the new Palmer. Dr. Dassel looked at Ned in his maternity ward crib and then came by Cathy's hospital room. He asked us if he could run some tests on our infant son. "I think there's a 30 percent chance he's Down syndrome," Dr. Dassel said matter-of-factly. "And the test results could take two weeks, so we should get started as soon as we can." We agreed to the tests, of course, and Steve Dassel left us sitting alone in that room, stunned and silent, at the beginning of the longest two weeks of our lives.

That day, and many times since then, I've thought about the kid by the side of the road. In twelve years I never heard him speak, or saw him talking to anyone else. I never saw him laugh or even smile. He seemed to have no present, no past, and certainly no future.

Cathy and I had an advisor at the time Ned was born, an aging psychiatrist who was an old friend of my father's. He told us to forget our new son existed. We should never see him again, he said, never even think about him. "Have another child if you want to and get on with your lives. This one will be all right. I can pull some strings and get him into Fircrest."

Fircrest was and still is an institution for the developmentally disabled, north of Seattle. At one time, the place took care of a thousand people, although that number has dropped a lot. My father's friend said that immediate institutionalization was what people did in these cases, if they could afford it.

And he was right; it's what many parents did do, although he was thirty years out of date.

Thirty years. Or just about how much older than Ned the Mercerwood kid would be. Whoever his parents were in that big house, they obviously could have afforded to dump their son in an institution and forget him, just as we were being advised to do. But they didn't. They chose to raise him in their home, and that is certainly to their credit. So it's probably unfair to them to say that it's the only thing to their credit. He deserved a better life than just watching everyone else's life. We all do. And it was their responsibility to help him find it.

Cathy and I didn't consider institutionalizing Ned for a moment, even though there were people who told us we would ruin our lives trying to raise him. He was and is our son, and we have loved him from the beginning with all our hearts. After all these years I still find it appalling that anyone ever thought we could possibly drop him on an institution's doorstep and walk off. And I think of all those infants who actually were tossed away, infants now in their fifties and sixties, waiting to die in the only home they have ever known.

We vowed to keep Ned with us, but we also vowed to make his life as complete and satisfying as we could, given our resources and his abilities. In that, we have been very lucky. Our resources are pretty good, and Ned's abilities are in many ways phenomenal. That certainly doesn't mean it's always been easy, and I hope it doesn't mean that parents in different circumstances, with kids who have different abilities, won't find something worthwhile, maybe even enjoyable, in what follows. This is most emphatically not a how-to book or an instructional manual. It's a relatively straightforward, true chronicle of the most important time in Ned's life so far, with a bit too much musing on various things by his father. I'm no expert in anything, just somebody who's been at it a while, somebody who agrees with the late Frank Zappa that we're all bozos on this bus, trying in every way we can to help our kids find good lives.

I was in high school the last time I saw the boy by the side of the road. I was mostly driving then, and didn't have to go through Mercerwood. I'd almost forgotten about him. But one day I took the bus, and there he was, older and taller, but standing in the same spot, with the same open look.

I've been in Mercerwood only once since leaving the island to go to college. That was ten years ago, when Ned was thirteen. It was Saturday, and he and I had driven across the floating bridge from our home in Seattle so I could show him his dad's old boyhood haunts. We started up Mercerwood hill, and I found myself automatically looking at that house. It was a different color, and the front yard had changed a lot. But it was the same place, even if it didn't look so big and impressive any more.

I slowed down, but I didn't stop. I wanted to tell my son about a boy I knew. I wanted to explain to Ned that one of the reasons he has a lot going on in his life is because years ago his father knew a kid who stood in front of that house. But I didn't think Ned would understand, maybe because I don't really understand it myself. I just know that the specter of that boy has both haunted me, and motivated me, since the day Dr. Dassel made his visit. Some day I may be able to explain it to Ned, but that particular afternoon, we just went on up the hill to the high school.

By now that boy by the side of the road would be in his late fifties, almost a decade past the life expectancy of people with Down syndrome who were born in the 1940s. I'll never know what happened to him, whether by some miracle he found a life worth living. I can only hope. But I did finally figure out what he did all day while we were in school, what he must have been doing.

He threw rocks.

Greg Palmer
Seattle, December, 2004

There is a lie at the heart of what follows, or at least a false representation, and that is the relative absence in this journal of Ned's mother, Cathy. Although it is true that I have spent more time with Ned than she has in the last decade and a half, the reasons for that are entirely logistical. Until recently she has been working at a time-intensive job for somebody else. Being self-employed for the past fourteen years, I've had more freedom to adjust my life and my schedule to Ned's needs, especially on weekdays. And also, this is my journal, not hers, so understandably I'm in it more than she is.

An Admission of Sorts

But make no mistake. From the day of his birth, Cathy has been every bit as involved as I have in raising Ned, and making him feel part of a family that loves and respects him. Conjecture about the impact that individual parents have on their children is usually pointless, but I think Ned is the functional, artistic, and social young man that he is more because of her influence than mine. Ned would probably agree if he thought about things that way. Fortunately, he doesn't. He knows he is ours, and we are his, and that's all he needs or cares to know. The three of us have always been in this together.

This book is for Cathy, with love. As a fine young poet once wrote:

...If there weren't any girls, it's girls I'd miss.

You said it, Ned.

1. Very religious in my own way
2. Kind of musical, especially fond of the guitar
3. A sense of humor
4. A tendency to look at things in a historical perspective
5. Well educated from many ways, including school, videos, personal reading of books and magazines
6. I think I'm neat and tidy
7. Explorer of places

List of Personal Characteristics

8. Explorer of people
9. Hard worker
10. A story teller, and a fan of story telling
11. Singer
12. Actor
13. Playwright
14. Collector of many things, especially action figures, videos, recorded music, song books, and information about the Titanic, volcanoes, natural disasters, and rock and roll
15. A great host at parties
16. A good brother

Ned Palmer
May, 2001

The Expedition

Monday, June 17, 2002, Midnight

Aboard the M.S. *Endeavour*, in the English Channel, off Bournemouth

My original plan was to begin this journal on September 3, 2001. That was Ned's twentieth birthday, and the week he started his last year in public school—the oldest, smallest senior at Nathan Hale High School in Seattle. On that birthday, Ned wasn't a teenager any more. He was officially a young man, just twelve months from the time when we are able to fend for ourselves, drink alcoholic beverages nationwide, find the love of our dreams, and begin repaying the state for its past support and future protection. Or so society and the law tell us. It should have been a perfect occasion to begin a journal about his transition from child to adult, to start finding answers to the question I've been asking myself for a long time: Can a very verbal, very social young man with Down syndrome find safety and happiness in a world where his parents will ultimately desert him, in a most inconsiderate way, by dying?

Starting this work on his twentieth birthday made a lot of sense. It would have looked exactly right on the outline, if I had ever done an outline. Except there was nothing special about that day, no matter how important it might have been symbolically. In my experience you don't spend much time thinking about symbolism when you're raising a child with developmental disabilities. You're too wrapped up in the details of daily living. Ned's twentieth birthday was no exception.

His birthday gifts nine months ago reflected the world between boyhood and manhood that he occupies now. There were toys, of course, but his main gift was what he wanted most, a video camera he planned to use to "record history." And he got some CDs—old rock, the *Best of the Limelighters*, the soundtrack from *Amadeus*—and additions to his songbook collection. At his birthday nine months ago we went out for a burger lunch with his classmates—Lily, Santosh, and Matt. Besides the cuisine, it was ostensibly a very adult affair, a quiet lunch with a few friends, not worth writing about. At least that's what I told myself at the time.

In retrospect, I realize that I couldn't start writing about him then as an adult, or on the verge of becoming an adult, because that seemed so far from happening. When I looked at Ned on that September third, he was still a little boy, with his little boy friends and his little boy lunch. A twenty-year-old little boy. That scared the hell out of me. I've heard parents bemoaning the fact that their children have grown up and gone off to their own lives. They long for those days when Junior automatically took their hand to cross the street, found delight in an ice cream cone, and slept with stuffed animals and action figures. Ned still does all these things, and he is twenty. A child growing up and going away is sad; a child not able to grow up, and with no place to go, is something far worse. In modern society, without the large families we used to have to shelter and nurture our very old, very young, and very threatened, it means that no matter what his mother and I do, some day Ned will have to depend on the kindness of strangers.

If Ned is to thrive in his world to come, he must be able to function with adults who don't particularly care whether he thrives or dies. That's why we're on this cruise around the British Isles. In a very real sense, it's a shakedown cruise for his adult life. For the next eleven days, we will be part of an adult, normally functioning community of strangers. We'll eat every meal with people we didn't know twenty-four hours ago, and have adventures with them as well. We'll sit in the lounge in the evenings and have adult conversations. We'll begin friendships, form alliances, and probably create a few enemies as well—in any group of people there's almost always somebody who dislikes you as much as you dislike him. And if it goes as I hope, Ned will assume a positive and contributing role in this short-lived but intense community.

I'm calling it a cruise, but more accurately, we are on an expedition. "Cruise" implies aged white folks sitting around eating huge meals many times a day, wandering into the shipboard casino every evening to yank at slot machines and toss the bones, and being entertained in King Neptune's Showroom by people who know Wayne Newton personally. On such cruises, the outside world drifts by more or less unnoticed.

Ned and Dad. (Photo by Fred Milkie.)

I've been on one like that with my mother, hated it, and vowed never to do it again.

Last year, after my mother died, I asked my father if there was anything he wanted to do and had never done. The rest of the sentence—"before you die too, or get so feeble you can't do it"—was implied, and we both knew it. "I've always wanted to see castles on the Rhine," my father said, to my surprise. Historically, my father has not been a happy traveler.

The ships that take tourists up the Rhine are mostly flat, fat, ugly tubs with casinos, Herman Göering Shipboard Showrooms and accommodations for three hundred and fifty insurance sales people. They are the kinds of boats I knew my father would loathe. He's spent his life on or near the sea, and boats are important to him. Boats that look like a Las Vegas Holiday Inn lying on its side would not be boats he would enjoy. But a travel agent told me that there was this small company, Lindblad Expeditions, that journeyed up the Danube from Vienna to Frankfurt, in less massive boats on more educationally-based trips. Lindblad eschewed casinos and showrooms, and had a ship's staff that featured historians and writers, not Elvis impersonators and blackjack dealers.

"How about the Danube instead of the Rhine?" I asked my father.

"As long as there are castles," he said. We spent seven splendid days on the river, and walking through places like Bamburg and Nuremberg. And because we took the trip less than a month after the 9-11 attacks on New York and Washington, more than half the booked passengers didn't show up, so we had lots of room. We saw many castles, and my father had a very good time.

When our older son, Ira, graduated from high school, his grandfather gave him a car as a graduation present. Ned didn't need a car. Ned will never need a car, though I'm not sure he realizes that. When Ira turned sixteen and got his driver's license, Ned talked a lot about how he could hardly wait until he could get his driver's license too. But as the three subsequent years went by, he mentioned it less and less. By the time Ned was sixteen, the possibility that he might get a driver's license and a car and cruise the boulevard himself simply didn't come up in conversation with me, although Cathy says he mentioned it a few times to her. When told he would have to take both a written test and a driving test, he let the matter drop. To our relief, we never had to tell him that he wasn't ever going to be a driver.

It's one of the mysteries of Ned. He has never made the slightest reference to the fact that he's different from other kids, even though he's spent most of his school days surrounded by other Special Ed students who are obviously atypical of the general school population. Didn't he notice that some of his colleagues in Room 104—the Special Ed headquarters at his high school—couldn't talk, or would suddenly start screaming for no apparent reason? Was he unaware that some of them wore football helmets all the time and others were in wheelchairs? During high school he took many regular classes, including U.S. History, Washington State History, Horticulture, Photography, and four years of choir. He must have noticed the difference between the students he saw in those classes and the Room 104ians, whose medical conditions he can describe in detail. Yet he apparently doesn't see any connection, physically or intellectually, between them and himself. For Ned, his situation simply isn't an issue, and on those occasions when his disability might have to be part of a discussion with us, I guess he does whatever it takes to avoid that discussion. He doesn't ask why he isn't getting a driver's license.

Ned wasn't going to get what his brother did for graduation, but it was important to me that Ned get something from his grandfather. Not so much important for Ned. He has a lot of things and gets a lot of gifts. But important for my father and our family.

For some of the people around us, Ned's formal graduation from high school was seen as a kind of self-esteem gimmick, a conspiracy between his parents and teachers to make him think he's just as good as everybody else. You would never say to the parents of a typical kid, "He's graduating from high school! Isn't that cute!" But I heard something close to that from a lot of people a few months ago. They weren't trying to be condescending, necessarily. They just didn't understand that even if Ned's educational goals weren't the same as those of the others in the class of 2002, they were still goals he had to strive to achieve. They were goals he *did* achieve. And to their credit, his classmates throughout the school understood that a lot better than most adults did.

At the graduation ceremony last week, the Nathan Hale High School Class of 2002 was seated on folding chairs on the football field, with us parents staring down at them from the stands. After the speeches about the future lying ahead as it does, and a song or two, the graduates were called up one by one to receive their diplomas. When the class president announced "Nathaniel Palmer!" there were cheers, and for the first and only time that day, a lot of those kids spontaneously stood and applauded. It is a moment that I will remember, and cherish, for the rest of my life.

He deserved the various graduation events and ceremonies, he deserved the post-graduation all-night party, and he deserved a gift from his grandfather. As a former traveler with Lindblad, I'm on their mailing list. Each month, letters arrive describing some new and wonderful expedition. Last March the trip being promoted was called "The Wild Isles," an almost complete circumnavigation of Britain and Ireland that started in London and went clockwise around to Inverness, Scotland. I went to Grandpa and suggested what might be nice to give Ned was a trip, and he agreed.

So here we are at the end of the first day of the expedition, sliding by Bournemouth in the middle of a clear, warm night aboard the M.S. *Endeavour,* flagship of the Lindblad line. One of my particular fascinations is a British comedian named Tony Hancock. He grew up in Bournemouth, where his parents operated a hotel. In the mid-1950s, still a relatively young man, he was one of the most famous and beloved people in England, star of a television comedy series called *Hancock's Half Hour*. But Hancock, like too many comedians, was beset by devils, most of them of his own devising. He couldn't figure out why he wasn't happy, even though he had ten times more of everything than he ever dreamed of achieving. After years of wealth, fame, and adulation, he drank himself into failure. In 1968, trying to make yet another comeback in Australia, he killed himself. His suicide note said, "Things seemed to go wrong too many times."

It's 2:00 a.m. now. Ned is sleeping (I hope) two decks below, with his video camera for recording history charged, loaded, and ready. I'm sitting in an empty ship's lounge, with the English Channel bubbling by outside, thinking of Ned and Bournemouth, Tony Hancock, and lives that go wrong too many times. And how you can possibly keep that from happening, especially for those you love, those you have both a duty and a desire to protect, even from beyond the grave.

Tuesday, June 18, 2002, 10 p.m.

Aboard the M.S. *Endeavour,* Dartmouth Harbor

We spent the day at sea, getting to Dartmouth across the swells of the Channel, too far out to see either the English or French coast most of the time. Without even knowing it, Ned passed Southhampton, from which his beloved *Titanic* sailed to her doom. Later on he contented himself with the knowledge that we probably sailed right over the spot where bandleader Glenn Miller went into the drink during the war, never to play "Little Brown Jug" again.

Ned's interest in Glenn Miller and the *Titanic* has much to do with the fact that in both cases people died in tragic and unanticipated ways. We've never really known how or why this fascination with unexpected death began. The first work I did for PBS was a four-part documentary series titled *Death: The Trip of a Lifetime.* Between celebrating the Day of the Dead in Tzintzuntzan, Mexico, in 1991, and visiting a drive-thru funeral parlor in Pensacola, Florida, in 1993, I went around the world, talking to people of different cultures and seeing the ways they ritualize death, dying, and grief. I even staged my own funeral, and wrote the worst eulogy for myself I could think of. ("I didn't know Greg personally, but many people seemed to like him..." being my favorite line in it, delivered with unctuous disinterest by George Ray, the same guy who does the pledge pitches on our local PBS station.) But Ned's obsession with what Dryden called "The Grand Perhaps" preceded the series. In fact, my coworkers on the death documentary, were very surprised at how knowledgeable I was about our local graveyards and cemeteries when we began production. (The difference, incidentally, is that a graveyard is usually next to and operated by a church, and a cemetery is usually private or municipal. Always a good trivia question for when the party gets dull.) By then I'd already visited them all with Ned many times, especially a place called Lakeview on Capitol Hill in central Seattle, which, like thousands of municipal cemeteries, was apparently named so people would confuse it with a housing development.

Many of our region's famous historical persons are buried in Lakeview, including Arthur Denny and most of his family. Denny was the Illinois farmer who led a party of settlers to Seattle on the schooner *Exact,* arriving from Portland, Oregon, in 1851. He saw what he thought could become a good deepwater port and decided to stay, even though the cold, nasty rain made the women in his party burst into tears the minute they hit the shore. Much of their distress centered on Arthur's hapless brother, David, who had gone on ahead of the main party with instructions to build a cabin for the new arrivals. By the time the *Exact* dropped anchor, David had the walls up but hadn't yet gotten around to installing a roof. On the wet side of the Cascades, this was a mistake. It made for a cold, damp night.

Arthur, David, and a handful of others were the first white settlers in a place they initially named New York Alki, and then Duwamps, and finally called Seattle. That was as close as their Illinois tongues could get to the name of a local Indian chief. He was a fine old chief, who helped the new arrivals take whatever they wanted and didn't kill them for their rapacity, as he probably should have. Arthur Denny staked out his own farm in an area we Seattleites now refer to as "downtown." Ever the visionary was Arthur Denny. Eventually he became a rich but reportedly compassion-free visionary. He let his poor brother go bankrupt in various ill-conceived ventures, like public transportation and a water system, that the future city desperately needed but David had no idea how to manage. David's not in Lakeview with the rest of his family, but way out north in a cemetery called Washelli, built on the site of his last farm. Ned and I like to think he'd rather be there, next to his beloved wife, Rebecca, than lying for eternity under a plinth in honor of his brother.

By most accounts Arthur Denny was a tight-fisted man who wouldn't have given Ned the time of day. Ned lionizes him anyway, and has since he learned we are distantly related, on my mother's side. Ned developed his fascination with Seattle history because of this extremely tenuous, last-inch-of-the-shirttail family connection. He's even given guest lectures to elementary school classes about the Denny Party and Northwest history. A year ago, on the 150th anniversary of the Dennys' arrival in Seattle, a new plaque was unveiled at their landing site on Alki Point to commemorate the event. Ned attended, of course, and before the actual ceremony told the woman running the event of his familial connection to the Denny family, and his devotion to Arthur. When the time came to unveil the plaque, without any prior consultation with us, she called Ned—"Arthur Denny's descendant"—out of the crowd to pull the velvet cord. He was extremely pleased, although those present whose last name actually was Denny clearly were wondering, "Who the hell is this kid?"

Not far from where Arthur Denny lies buried is Lakeview's most famous deceased duo, film star Bruce Lee and his son Brandon. Whenever we're at the cemetery, we are approached by heavily muscled young men of various ethnicities, all wearing black tee shirts and driving SUVs with California plates. They're trying to find the Lee graves, and Ned walks them over like he's the cemetery concierge. "While you're here," he will say, strolling along, "You might want to go up the hill there to visit Arthur Denny, the founder of Seattle and my great-great-grand-uncle." If the buff young men don't excuse themselves very quickly, they get a history of Seattle that can last an hour or more.

The suggestion may seem facetious, but the best possible work for Ned in adulthood could be in the funeral industry; probably not dealing with bodies, however, which he would most certainly find yucky. He's more interested in the administrivia of death, things like names, dates, gravesites. He should be an obituary writer. Some years ago, we discovered a website called Find-A-Grave, which has pictures of the graves of thousands of the famous and near famous, along with brief biographies. Ned has spent hundreds of hours happily cruising around this website, both at home and during computer class at school. He's especially indignant when someone he considers important, like the late composers Joe Raposo of *Sesame Street* and Malvina "Little Boxes" Reynolds, isn't there.

(Last year a teacher's aide at school thought Ned's fascination with Find-A-Grave was morbid and unhealthy. Without talking to us or Ned's main teacher, he told Ned he was forbidden to cruise Find-A-Grave during school computer time. Ned finally told me about it, and I headed for school that afternoon. I informed this guy that he was denying an historian one of his principal sources of information. "Oh, really?" he said, with a sneer. So I asked him some questions: "Do you know George Washington's date of birth? What day he died? How about Lincoln, know when he was born? Do you know where Buddy Holly is buried, and what's carved on his tombstone?" He couldn't answer any of these questions, but Ned could and did, including the bit about the great-looking Fender Stratocaster carved into Buddy's stone in Lubbock. And that was that. It's rare when one can deal so easily and effectively with the petty bureaucratic mind.)

I think it's possible Ned's fascination with the realm of the dead allows him to view life's most frightening aspect—its end—not as a personal experience that *will* happen, but only as something that *has* happened to others. There was evidence today of his desire to separate himself from real, possible death and instead fictionalize it, ritualize it, make it an historical rather than an actual and eventual certainty.

At 9:30 this morning, the ship's loudspeaker told us to go to our cabins to prepare for lifeboat drill, the "Mandatory Lifeboat Muster" now required on all passenger ships. The young man who can recite by heart the lifeboat scenes in the recent *Titanic* film was extremely reluctant to do any of this. I thought he'd come bouncing up the stairs wearing his lifejacket and humming "Nearer My God to Thee," but no. I had to fight with him to put on the lifejacket, and then physically force him to accompany me to our Assembly Station in the lounge. When we finally got there, a ship's officer told us what would happen "in the unlikely event of a real emergency." Ned stared at his shoes and pretended he was somewhere else, doing something else. Then we had to go to our assigned lifeboat out on deck and stand there for a while until the Captain declared "all clear." Ned was having none of it. I thought he would enjoy reliving part of the *Titanic* story in the exact same waters the *Titanic* passed through, but it became the biggest hassle of the trip so far.

The reason for his reluctance is conjecture, but I'd be willing to guess it's because Ned is so familiar with what happens next. The other lifeboats don't come back to get you, you slip into the frigid water, the life drains out of you in twelve minutes, you're dead at the bottom of the sea, and they roll the credits. He's seen it, but he has never felt it before. And he never wants to again.

I saw much the same thing last year on September 11. Ned came down for breakfast as Cathy and I were staring, shocked and speechless, at the television in the kitchen. The second plane had just hit the World Trade Center. It was now obvious that this was not just some incredible accident but a planned mass murder. We were worried that Ned would be scared, but we told him what was going on anyway. Not only was he not scared, he didn't even seem very interested. He was oddly calm and unaffected by the immediate events, or the later revelations of the Pentagon crash and the plane going down in Pennsylvania. A boy who has expressed such interest in tragedies and their human aftermath, like the *Titanic*, Mt. St. Helens' eruption, the Johnstown Flood, and a few others, acted as if the horrible tragedy of the World Trade Center was as trivial, and as usual, as a Mariners loss. Perhaps he simply didn't understand the enormity of it, the idea that in an instant thousands of people died. And maybe it was because it was happening now, happening to people who were alive just hours before, not like the disasters of the past. I told him that it would be a day he would remember for the rest of his life. But in fact that may not be true. He may not remember it, at least not as something he personally experienced, even if it was three thousand miles away and on television during breakfast. It is something that I will always remember, and so I almost envied him that day. I felt lousy for a week because of what happened, but Ned didn't. His indifference was bliss.

Putting him to bed that 9-11 night, I picked up a new poetry book, one Cathy had recently gotten at a library sale: *My Kind of Verse*, compiled by John Smith. I opened it at random, and a Siegfried Sassoon poem stared back at me. Cathy or I usually read three or four poems to Ned each evening, but

"Everyone Sang" is the only one I read on the night of September 11, 2001. I don't know whether Ned felt anything special about it or not. I'd like to think he did:

> *Everyone suddenly burst out singing;*
> *And I was filled with such delight*
> *As prisoned birds must find in freedom,*
> *Winging wildly across the white*
> *Orchards and dark green fields; on - on - and*
> *out of sight.*
>
> *Everyone's voice suddenly lifted;*
> *And beauty came like the setting sun:*
> *My heart was shaken with tears; and horror*
> *Drifted away...O but Everyone*
> *Was a bird; and the song was wordless; the*
> *singing will never be done.*

Wednesday, June 19, 2002

Dartmouth

Last night on board ship was the formal welcoming dinner. In the afternoon we found an invitation on our door to join the chief engineer at his table. When we arrived in the dining room I found place cards, with Ned seated across the table from me. He was between an aged English gentleman and a file clerk from Canada who spends all her savings every few years on trips she could not otherwise afford. So on vacation she's always surrounded by people who are a lot better off than she is, and she oozes the sense that she is very aware of that and resents it. At first I wondered what fool separated Ned and me, and then felt considerable appreciation for whichever Lindblad staffer decided to treat Ned like he was any other guest. I hope it was a conscious decision.

The elderly Englishman made valiant efforts to have a conversation with Ned. He probably learned a lot more than he wished to know about the Denny Party, and also the Siggins family. Ned is a Siggins on his mother's side. This hasn't mattered much in years past. The Dennys were just too powerful a force in his heritage. Then he learned that there were Sigginses at the Battle of Hastings. That one fact has put this trip around Britain in the kind of familial/historical context that is always important to Ned. He is going to the land his ancestors helped conquer. To the elderly Englishman he described his Siggins ancestors as "close personal friends of William the Conqueror." "Really!" said the Englishman, who survived the conversation with Ned, and maybe even enjoyed it.

The file clerk to Ned's left, however, spent much of the meal emitting whiffs of "They've stuck me next to the retarded kid. Typical." In a way, I could understand how she felt, like some kind of social outcast, with Ned to her right and the big, bearded Swedish chief engineer to her left. He was pleasant enough, but he was about as scintillating a dinner partner as you would expect a big Swede with limited English and diesel oil cologne to be. Engineers, in my experience—and I've been around a lot of broadcast engineers, as well as theater tech people, who are cut from the same cloth—usually don't enjoy conversations that drift too far from engineering. The only thing they enjoy even less is conversations about engineering with engineering-ignorant people, which certainly described seven-eighths of our table last night. "Hey, who's watching the engines!? Ha ha..." one of the others at the table said to Big Swede shortly after arriving. "I haff staff," he answered gravely, and then stared intently into his crab cocktail. For the rest of the meal, he looked like he wished to God somebody would come running in and tell him we'd hit a huge iceberg and he was needed below decks.

Madame File Clerk had no one to talk to, which you have to expect when you travel alone, but presumably less so at meals. Perhaps her resentment was class- and not Ned-related. As a file clerk, she got the Engineer's Table, which was bad enough, but she also got the "re-tard," which was insult to class injury as far as she was concerned. She gazed hungrily across the dining room, where the Captain, a suave German in his early sixties with impeccable manners, fluent English, and not a hint of grease under his nails, was regaling the "important" guests with tales of a life at sea.

(In Lindblad's defense, I don't think they care about class distinction any more than Ned does. If there were any real priority table assignments, I'd guess the captain got those people who have often sailed with Lindblad. Some of our fellow passengers have been on six or seven previous voyages, to Antarctica and elsewhere. Naturally, given the cost of the expeditions, they are also amongst the wealthiest on board. The cream rises to Table One.)

Ned did okay, even with me staring at him throughout the meal, praying he wouldn't suddenly fling an appetizer across the room. He has never flung an appetizer across any room in his life, but I was still nervous. It was the first night, the first big meal, and Ned was playing in a whole new league.

Today we spent in Dartmouth, near the Devon coast, a pleasant town of around seven thousand, with an impressive nautical history. The *Mayflower* stopped in Dartmouth for repairs before sailing west into the pages of a million junior high history books. More than four hundred ships left Dartmouth harbor for the D-Day invasion, and, in the twelfth and thirteenth centuries, ships assembled in Dartmouth for the Second and Third Crusades. So the original Palmers (they being Crusaders who returned carrying palm leaves to prove that they had been to the Holy Lands) probably walked Dartmouth's streets, waiting to sail. But unlike the present Palmers, they probably weren't looking for cheeseburgers.

I knew issues related to food would be one of our bigger problems on this journey. By his own choice, Ned has an extremely restricted diet. For breakfast he eats two peeled wieners, dry Cheerios, two pieces of white toast, orange juice, and milk. He has had this breakfast almost every morning for fifteen years. (If you're doing the math, that's 10,950 wieners to date. And just wieners. To my knowledge he has never eaten a hotdog bun in his life.) For lunch, at school anyway, he takes a lunchbox containing some fruit, a slice of cold pizza, celery sticks, a cardboard box of apple juice, a clutch of Cheerios, and two Chips Ahoy cookies, the only brand of cookies he has ever consumed.

We're fairly sure he eats the pizza and the cookies. Everything else is a toss-up. Or more likely a toss-out. After school, he has another wiener and two more pieces of white toast. (Total: 16,425 wieners; 21,900 slices of white toast.)

The Wiener Lobby in Washington, D.C. should hire Ned to tour the world as "Exhibit A" whenever they feel it necessary to respond to charges that hot dogs are injurious to your health. If tube steaks were that

Ned's smile in possession of a tube of Chips Ahoy Cookies hasn't really changed in twenty years.

toxic, Ned would have died years ago. But other than contending with the frequent colds and respiratory problems common to people with Down syndrome, he's quite healthy. I've been waiting fourteen and a half years for his pediatrician to call a halt to this parade of Ball Park Franks, but it hasn't happened. When I asked recently and for the hundredth time whether the all-dog diet were perhaps, oh, killing him, Dr. Dassel said bluntly, "He's healthier than you are." Point taken.

Ned's become more gastronomically adventurous in the past five years, especially at dinner time, but the fact remains that given the amazing variety of foods available in the world today, he will always opt for a cheeseburger, plain and dry, with a little ketchup. In London, before boarding the ship, we walked for many blocks in very hot weather to get to the McDonalds near Leicester Square. He wouldn't have done that hike if the Queen herself was standing on the corner handing out the Crown Jewels, but he did it for the burger. And today in Dartmouth, although he enjoyed the Town Crier officially welcoming us, and a bit of the walking tour to ancient and scenic buildings, what he really was in search of was a cheeseburger. We found it, he ate it, and all was right with the world. He was good to go for another few hours.

In fact he did go, back to the ship by himself, while I strolled a bit more through Dartmouth. It was a small but important moment for both of us. To get to and from the ship, we travel by Zodiacs, inflatable boats with outboard motors that seat nine or ten. These are the same boats Jacques Cousteau first made famous on numerous drippy television adventures. Zodiacs are hard to get into and out of, especially as they bounce in the waves next to the ship. But Ned did it, and he did it alone. He's becoming more independent as each day passes.

When I got back to the ship it was the cocktail hour. I found him sitting at the bar in the lounge, nursing a cold Coke and talking with the people. He barely acknowledged my arrival, and I took a seat some ways away. I've seen a lot of people over the years approach Ned with the assumption that he will be a drooling, monosyllabic village idiot type, good for a pat on the head and not much more. Initially they are pleasantly surprised at his gregariousness and social skills. For those who hang in there with him, there is a second surprise. It's that moment when they realize they are having an interesting conversation, usually for the first time in their lives, with a young man who happens to have Down syndrome. That's where we are now with many of our fellow passengers. It's a revelation for them, and a big treat for Ned.

We are surviving the meals. Fortunately, the ship's dining room has two regular entrees each evening in addition to that day's specialties. One of the regulars is a steak and baked potato. It's no burger, but it will do in a pinch. In the midst of plenty, Ned will not starve. But I expect the quest for shore burgers to continue.

E-mail sent from M.S. *Endeavour* Wednesday, June 19, 12:27 p.m. From Ned Palmer to Cathy Palmer (and exactly as written by Ned):

Hi Mom, right now its morning and we're in Dartmouth, and we're about to go ashore for a tour

of the town. It's sunny here and warm. We just
had breakfast, I had pancakes. *[He had one bite of a
pancake.]* How are my pets doing? Ned

Thursday, June 20, 2002, 10 p.m.

Crossing the Celtic Sea

This morning we visited the Isles of Scilly, a hundred hunks
of granite of various sizes plotzed in the ocean some thirty miles
off the coast of Cornwall. The Isles are our last port in England,
if you can call a slimy concrete jetty sticking out into the sea a
"port." The name of these Isles is pronounced "silly," which is
probably why the expedition staff is being very careful not to
call them the Scilly Islands. They don't want us to expect John
Cleese performing scilly walks along the jetty. The attraction
here, on Tresco, the biggest little Scilly of them all, is "the magnificent Tresco Abbey Gardens." They are magnificent because
the Scillys are smack in the middle of the relatively warm Gulf
Stream, which is here called the North Atlantic Drift. Because
of the warm winds, it is possible to grow flora on Tresco, such as
palm trees and Monterey Cypress, that one would expect to find
only in much balmier climes.

Alas, sometimes that warm wind to the Scillys comes in
off the Atlantic at gale force, so many shipwrecks have occurred
here as well. The most famous local naval disaster was the
1707 grounding of four "ships of the line," resulting in the
death of two thousand British sailors, including the Fleet Com-
mander, Admiral Sir Cloudesley Shovell. Admiral Sir
Cloudesley probably didn't get a lot of solace from the fact that
the wind that blew him to his doom was an uncharacteristically warm wind, and would some day nurture spectacular or-
chids for elderly tourists to photograph. But every Cloudesley
has a silver lining. Because of his and the sailors' tragic loss,
the British government was motivated to put up a 20,000£ reward for that person who could devise a way to compute longi-
tude at sea. The eventual winner, John Harrison, got the money
and, centuries later, a PBS Special.

None of these fascinating Scilly facts interests Ned in the least, however, not even the big death tally connected to the island. He's a one-shipwreck man, and that would be the *Titanic,* thank you very much. Perhaps when Leonardo DeCaprio plays the title role in *Warm Wind to Destiny: The Admiral Sir Cloudesley Shovell Story*, that will change.

Ned and I have never been garden people, either. That Australian plants are able to grow in the southwest corner of England is about as exciting to us as the fact that Australian plants are able to grow in Australia. So on today's outing to the magnificent gardens, especially as it requires a mile walk across Tresco to get there, Ned stayed aboard in our suite of rooms, listening to his CDs, playing with his toys, and preparing his patter for the cocktail hour. I went ashore, speed-walked through the gardens, and then sat on the jetty and stared out at the ship bobbing in the warm breeze five hundred yards away.

We are sailing across the Celtic Sea for Ireland all night tonight. It's a place I've always wanted to take Ned. I don't really know why. Perhaps it's because there's something kind of Irish about him, even though his ancestry is English/German/Italian and one thirty-second Iroquois, and his religion is Lapsed Unitarian. But like the Irish, at least the Irish I know, he loves music, poetry, and especially talking—what the Irish call "the crack." Like the Irish, family has always been important to him, and not just those he has contact with, but also those who were close personal friends of William the Conqueror. He can be obsessive about things that have little meaning for almost everybody else, and dismissive of things most people find important. He is usually happy and outgoing, and yet deep in his soul I think there is a sadness that is unreachable and immutable. Irish.

**E-mail from Greg Palmer to Cathy Palmer,
Thursday, June 20:**

His sealegs fine, tho complaining ocean swells
causing headaches. Left dinner tonight therefore,
seemed fine back in cabin. Much time spent there;
thank God for CD player; typically enjoys solitude,
own cabin. Came to Early Irish Monasteries

lecture today (we visit one tomorrow); sat at bar
with Coke, followed whole thing. Didn't go ashore
on Scilly Isles for mile walk to famous gardens.
Isles themselves most impressive. Weather gorgeous, but nasty-ing as we near Ireland. He
looking forward to Irish village visit tomorrow
afternoon. Has been eating okay, steak for dinner
every night, lotsa toast, OJ, egg in morn. No real
Cheerios in Brit. Almost all fellow passengers
most nice to him, even as they hear endlessly of
Denny party and relatives the Siggins...

Friday, June 21, 2002, 10 a.m.

Skellig Michael

The farther west we go, the rougher the seas are becoming,
even though the weather has been splendid. Swells that started
as a ripple from the breeze off a hummingbird's wing in Long
Island Sound are hitting us now like truck tires thrown against
the port side. Fortunately, the *Endeavour* was designed to ride as
smoothly as possible in heavy seas—Lindblad takes this boat to
the Antarctic—and Ned has never shown any propensity toward
seasickness. When we woke this morning I asked him how he
spent the night. He said the rolling had given him a little head-
ache, but his stomach was fine. He was standing on his bed at the
time, looking out our porthole. And there was Ireland, the gentle
green hills of County Kerry, a few miles off.

"That'd be Ireland you'd be watchin' there, Ned my boy," I
brogued. "The Emerald Isle, the auld sod. 'I'll take you home
again, Kath...'"

"Uh huh," he said. My son apparently does not share my
romantic response to Ireland, so I put my Barry Fitzgerald impression away for the duration. Perhaps what's really deep in
Ned's soul is the knowledge that he's descended from a long
line of Orangemen, not Irishmen.

An hour later *Endeavour* approached two huge rocks sticking up out of the ocean, eight miles from the mainland. They

were an odd sight, because they looked like they'd gotten the only snowfall this side of the Alps. But it's not snow.

Skellig Michael (also called Great Skellig) and Little Skellig are giant, phallic thrusts of red sandstone that would be impressive all by themselves, if one is impressed by giant phallic thrusts. We are told by the staff that "Skellig" means "rock," presumably in the no-nonsense Gaelic spoken by Irish mariners. These rocks are also renowned seabird nesting colonies, and not just for passing coots. Little Skellig reportedly has twenty-seven thousand pairs of nesting northern gannets. Frank King, the wonderful old Brit who is Bird Master on the *Endeavour's* staff, announces this fact at breakfast as if he personally did the counting. And he might have. That anybody did the counting I find amazing, and so very, very British.

Gannets are predominantly white. And what comes out of them, which includes but is not limited to eggs, is also white. And that's why the Skelligs look like snow has fallen. Ten thousand years of bird habitation can play hob with the carpets.

Those other birds that call the Skelligs home include fulmars, auks, Manx shearwaters, European storm-petrels, guillemots, razorbills, and puffins. For the ornithologically-challenged like Ned and me, these species all look more or less alike. Some are black, some are white, and some are black and white. Except the puffins. With their squat bodies, bright orange bills, and perky little faces, puffins look like they were designed by the Disney Studios to swim in Snow White's pond out in front of the Dwarves' cabin. That may explain why so many otherwise sane people go crazy for puffins. At breakfast some of our shipmates couldn't wait to jump into the heaving Zodiacs being readied beneath the dining room windows and head for Skellig Michael's puffinry.

Ned not only could wait, he could pass. For a long time now his interest in animals without major fur has been minimal. He is a dedicated dog and cat man. Other beasts leave him cold, and the smaller the colder. Insects? He and I agree that they should be immediately removed and killed, although he shares with me the desire to preserve and protect spiders. Spiders eat other, nastier insects, like mosquitoes, and also

E.B. White wrote one hell of a book about them which Ned and I have read together three times now. Charlotte-icide is not our way.

Ned is equally uninterested in reptiles, and for years now he's claimed a fear of birds, especially bald eagles. I've never really delved into where his fear of our National Predator comes from. Even living in the leafy green Northwest, and with the encouraging resurgence of North American bald eagle populations during the past few decades, I doubt that Ned has seen more than ten bald eagles in his life. And of those ten, not one outside a zoo came close enough to give him the evil eye. Yet he gets tense whenever there are eagles around. He's very patriotic, so I don't think this has anything to do with the bald eagle's symbolic role in our nation. I think it has more to do with very big hooked beaks.

Ned also hates smaller beaked chickens, but that's mostly because our otherwise genial next-door neighbor back home keeps chickens, even in an urban neighborhood. His chicken pen is behind his house but not behind ours, which means that at any given time we hear those three damned chickens a lot more clearly and loudly than he does. There are a lot of given times too, chickens being noisy, irritating birds. If they didn't lay eggs and fry up nice, chickens would be the usefulness equivalent of large feathered mosquitoes as far as Ned and I are concerned. And even though puffins and the other awaiting birds on the Skelligs are very un-chicken-like, for Ned the opportunity to go see them is the equivalent of asking someone if they'd like to see twenty-seven thousand nesting Rhode Island Reds.

So, given the choice of going ashore and walking around, including climbing more than five hundred "hand-hewn stone steps" to the top of Skellig Michael to see the ruins of St. Finian's Abbey, circa 560 AD, or staying in his cabin and occasionally going on deck and strolling over to the rail for sightseeing, Ned opted for the boat, especially after I said I thought I'd go ashore.

It's an hour later now. I climbed the first hundred steps toward St. Finian's, found a comfortable rock, and here I sit, waiting for a puffin to perch on my shoulder and trill. Apparently they don't do that. What they do is come barreling out of their underground burrows, and then try to look nonchalant while completely ignoring you. Our cat Max does the same thing, only he barrels through the cat door.

Off in the bay on the windward side of Skellig Michael, I can see the *Endeavour* at anchor, slowly wheeling around as the wind shifts. We've been aboard for five days now, and yet it still seems strange to think that Ned is on that ship, so far from home, so far from everything he's known before. Sitting in the bar on a boat full of Americans in Irish waters, even in the presence of twenty-seven thousand pairs of nesting gannets, isn't exactly pushing the "new experiences" envelope. It's not like we're camping in a yurt on the Mongolian steppes. But it's still a long way from the neighborhood. And it is very hard to sit here and not wonder if Ned will ever have the chance to do something like this again, after his mother and I are gone.

One of the regrets of my life is that I never slapped on a backpack in my early twenties and wandered around Europe for a while. Looking back from my now rapidly accelerating late fifties, it doesn't bother me as much as it used to. I've been around the world, from upcountry Ghana to downtown Taipei, from New Delhi to the Everglades, from visiting Dylan Thomas's grave on a Welsh hillside to shooting a movie in the Caucasus Mountains, bouncing from peak to peak in a Soviet military helicopter. I've met a lot of people who either were or became heroes of mine. For a college dropout who's almost always lived in Seattle, I've had a far more adventurous and interesting life than most people get to have. I've got no reason to complain. But I want my sons to have the same opportunities.

Ned's brother, Ira—three years older, college graduate—has already started having his own adventures. He's played football with the Carlton College team in Germany, been an exchange student in Japan, and traveled with me on a production trip to Britain. I don't worry about Ira having the chance to do what he wants to do. But when I think about the wonderful and enticing places I've been, I can't ever recall seeing people with disabilities there. Not one. I spent a month in Tbilisi, the capital of what was then Soviet Georgia, and never saw a person with an obvious developmental disability on the street, child or adult, resident or visitor. And the same holds true for almost every one of the two dozen other countries I've visited in the last twenty years. Are they not out among us because that's the way society wants it? Or is it simply logistical? They can't handle the myriad tasks that are part of doing interesting and exciting things? I don't know.

Once I got Ned on the *Endeavour,* with enough preparation he could be handling everything that's happened since then. But when Cathy and I are gone, who's going to get him on the boat? It's not a burden we can leave to Ira. He has his own life to live, and Ned is our responsibility. But it frightens and angers me that after we are gone, Ned might be doomed to a life without any excitement and adventure, a life where bowling on Tuesday nights and an annual trip to the county fair are the highlights. My idea of hell is being bored and alone. However hard Cathy and I work to make sure Ned has a variety of interesting experiences while we're still here, there are few ways we can ensure that his possibilities won't come to an abrupt end when we do.

Same day, 10 p.m.

During lunch today we sailed toward the mainland, to a town in County Kerry called Kenmare, where we were to board buses for a tour of the area. Ned was eager for this off-boat excursion, not because he felt like exploring, I think, but because he thought "town" meant "burgers." The Midsummer Swedish Lunch we'd just had on the boat was not a big hit with Ned, because the principal features were meatballs and objects that had once been fish. We took the first Zodiac to shore, and then walked up a country road to the buses. Ned fell asleep on the bus before the guide even had the chance to introduce herself, and he stayed that way for most of the drive. He can fall asleep faster and sleep more soundly than any non-feline creature I've ever encountered.

The big stop on the tour was Muckross House in Killarney, a Victorian mansion in Elizabethan style, built in 1843 in the center of what would become Ireland's first national park. Ned roused for a walk around the grounds and a look at the house, which wasn't nearly enough of a castle for him. Then it was back on the buses to where the Zodiacs were waiting. But Ned refused to board our boat when the time came. He insisted he wanted to ride back without me.

I was mad. We were holding up the line of our shipmates, breaking the Palmer family rule Cathy and I have always tried to follow: don't inflict your children on others. Just as our fellow passengers were starting to respect Ned and enjoy his company, I didn't want him suddenly to turn into an obstinate brat before their eyes. But I didn't want to force him into the boat, either, so I finally gave up and left him with the others on the jetty. When I got back to the *Endeavour,* I sat and waited for him in the small hallway next to the platform where the Zodiacs unload. He wasn't on the next boat, or the three boats after that. I started to get worried. A staff member told me he was okay; he was waiting to come back with Tom Ritchie, the expedition leader. Finally Ned and Tom returned, just the two of them in the boat. They'd gone on a Zodiac journey together, up a river near the jetty. Ned was exuberant, because of the special expedition he'd gotten and because of his developing friendship with Tom. The fact that defiance of me had worked out very well had something to do with it, too. And I let it go.

I found Tom later on, thanked him for his efforts, and said I hoped Ned hadn't been a problem.

"Not at all," Tom said. "He's a great kid, fun to be around. He's so enthusiastic." And then Tom told me that back home in Florida, he has an eleven-year-old son with Down syndrome.

It's reported by organizations that make such estimations that one out of every ten American families is directly affected by mental retardation. That percentage seems low to me. I've heard from a lot of people over the years about their aunts, their cousins, the siblings of their friends. And just when I think it seems as if everyone has had direct contact, I am around people whose sole exposure to a person of any age with disabilities is

my son. There are people on board who are like that. I can see it
when they meet him, first with curiosity, and, if all goes well,
eventually some respect.

Then there are people like Tom, who are all too familiar
with developmental disabilities. He told me that his son is nonverbal, so they communicate through sign language. I began to
understand his interest in Ned. My son has to be one of the first
developmentally disabled people to be a guest of Lindblad Expeditions. So at least professionally, Tom probably hasn't been
around many such folks, especially as young as Ned. Given the
amount of time he spends away from home doing his job, he
probably hasn't been around his own son much either, compared
to most parents. Now he's spending his days with an under-
standable, long-winded, engaging kid in the same situation, older
but not that much bigger than his own son. Ned's classification
of mental retardation is mild to moderate, whereas Tom's son's
is probably severe to profound. That's a world of difference Tom
may just be realizing. I know exactly how he feels because I've
felt it myself around kids with disabilities who are more "functional" than Ned. I've felt it around regular kids, too. It's a mixture of regret, anger, fascination, and encouragement. I hope
Tom's saying to himself that maybe his son can be a bit more
like Ned in a few years. And I hope he's right.

E-mail from Cathy Palmer to Ned Palmer,
Friday, June 21:

> Hi, Ned,
>
> How are you doing, sweetheart? I've been
> looking at the Lindblad web site for pictures of
> your expedition. Did you see the "graveyard" of
> ships that ran aground in the Isles of Scilly? Dad
> said in his last message that the weather was
> worsening a little. I do hope it stays nice enough
> to see those Cliffs of Moher. They were very
> impressive when Dad and I saw them from the
> land; I can hardly imagine what they would look
> like from the sea. When you get to Iona, say hello
> to St. Columba for me. Grandma Marcia and I

spent a very happy day and night visiting the
Abbey at Iona and collecting rocks on the beach. I
liked the rocks of Iona so much that I brought
home a bunch! I wish I had bought a little book
about the life of St. Columba; pick one up for me if
you come across a good one.

I went over to Grandpa John's and Grandma
Marcia's for my birthday lunch today: my favorite
celebratory lunch is always one of Grandpa's
salads...Lassie and Max and Harley *[the pets]* all
say "hi." When I was driving home from work
today, I saw a taxi cab that had crashed in the
intersection of 41st and Sunnyside: it ran up
against the wall of the house that is being so
carefully renovated. Good thing the portable
outhouse that had been there for so many months
had just been taken away, or we would have had
quite a smelly neighborhood. Glad I wasn't out
walking Lassie just then...

Love, Mom

Saturday, June 22, 2002

Aran Islands

In preparation for today's port of call, last night we gathered to watch one of the most famous documentaries ever made. Robert Flaherty's 1934 film *Man of Aran* shows the incredibly hard lives of Aran Islanders, eking out a bare existence by farming, fishing, and capturing sharks. In real life, the Aran Islanders stopped catching sharks about a century before Robert Flaherty showed up to make his movie, but as a director once said to me, "It looks great on film."

I first saw *Man of Aran* years ago in college, and found it deeply depressing. It's still depressing, but I forgot how boring it is. Flaherty shot the film over two years, and it seems like it's running in real time, with incidental music composed by Yanni's manic-depressive grandfather. And I am not one of those guys who insists that even a grainy black and white Depression-era documentary about starving peasants has to look like a Britney Spears video. I've done my time with grainy black and white Depression-era documentaries, ladies and gentlemen.

The other problem with *Man of Aran* is that you can't help wondering throughout why those stubborn Aran Islanders didn't catch the next boat to anywhere else and give up on their rock. I've made enough documentaries to recognize blatant staging, too. Although I'm sure the film is true to place (if not time), *Man of Aran* is about as real as *Ghostbusters*. I was just as glad Ned opted to go to bed.

Even in 1930s black and white, however, watching *Man of Aran* does lead to expectations about what the real place and people will look like. This morning we had our chance. The islands were out there when we got up at 7:00, these giant slabs of limestone on the edge of the Atlantic, just off the entrance to Galway Bay. We'd already learned that there is no indigenous soil here. For centuries local farmers have used sledgehammers and crowbars to cut up the limestone and smash it into a powder. Then they mix the powder with seaweed and sand to create their own soil. From Flaherty's film, you expect the three Aran Islands to be predominantly gray. From history, you expect them to be limestoney. In fact, they're quite green, possibly because soil is now imported from England, and possibly because Flaherty shot around the green places that didn't match his "vision."

We anchored off the main island, Inishmore, near the town of Kilronan. After a bus ride around and about the island, the planned excursion was a visit to Dun Aengus, a prehistoric fort on the high cliffs. It took some convincing, but Ned agreed to come along, even though seeing Dun Aengus up close required a mile hike up a hill.

Getting him to go also took some lying. I told him he could get a burger in Kilronan if he came, although I thought the possibility that the tiny village of Kilronan would have any burger joints was about as likely as a Kilronan K-Mart next to the *Man of Aran* Taco Bell. But I've about had it with Ned staying on the boat.

After a Zodiac ride to the town jetty, we boarded minibuses and were soon driving past nine thousand identical rock walls separating identical sheep standing on identical little patches of green. After an hour we arrived at the backside of a very high cliff. Leading off toward the top was a rocky, muddy road, at the top of which we could dimly see ancient rock walls. "Dun Aengus," said the bus driver. "Drive on up," said Ned. "Not bloody likely," said the driver.

With about twenty other Lindbladians, we started climbing. To his credit Ned kept up, although he's never been a happy hiker. When we got to the top, it was worth the effort. Even he agreed.

Dun Aengus was built anywhere from a few hundred years BC to the ninth century, possibly by the Danes but more likely by the Fir Bolgs, a Celtic race that came to Ireland from the continent. (It sounds like the description of an Irish race horse: Dun Aengus, out of Fir Bolg, by Continental Celt.) When Oscar Wilde's dad, Sir William, visited here in 1857, he reportedly said, "I believe I now point to the stronghold prepared as the last standing place of the Fir Bolg aborigines of Ireland, to fight their last battle if driven to the western surge...." Which is to say that if forced west from Dun Aengus, that first step is three hundred feet straight down off a spectacular cliff into the sea.

The fort consists of three semicircular stone walls, one of them thirteen feet wide and eighteen feet high, creating an almost square enclosure that is a hundred and fifty feet on each side. Like all children, Ned headed immediately for the edge of the cliff. My daddy-knee jerked, imagining he was about to become the first person since some careless Fir Bolg to take the short route to the bay. (I'm sure Oscar Wilde's dad felt the same way when little Oscar immediately headed for the brink.) But instead Ned stopped ten feet from the edge and sat in the short grass. Forty-five minutes later he was still sitting there, surrounded by the ancient rock walls, staring out at the sea and talking quietly to himself as he so often does. He had turned into Ned the Historian, oddly at home in this strange and miraculous place. He had no need to walk around, touch the rocks, listen to the lecture, or pose for snapshots on the edge of the cliff. He was feeling the place within him. He may actually have been mentally relishing the promised cheeseburger to come, but I don't think so.

I should say something here about Ned's conversation with himself. It started when he was a toddler, and may never end. When he was very young we thought it was gibberish, baby talk for a very old baby. We assumed he was mouthing meaningless syllables just to hear his own voice, almost as a way to keep himself company.

One Sunday morning, however, I was reading the newspaper and Ned was sitting on the floor nearby, babbling away. I suddenly heard him say, clearly, distinctly, and with feeling, "You're a very bad man. No, I'm a very good man. I'm just a very bad wizard." It's from the last Emerald City scene in the *Wizard of Oz*, when Dorothy first realizes the Wizard is a fraud and won't be able to get her magically back to Kansas, or do any of the things he's promised her friends. It's the moment she realizes that all the bad people in the world don't have green skin, magical powers, and armies of flying monkeys. Some of them look just like the man down the road, and their unintentional evil is confined to trying to be something they can never be. It's that instant when Dorothy grows up a lot, and adults stop being all-knowing and powerful in her life. So it may be the most important exchange in the entire film. Did Ned, even at five years old, realize the importance of the moment and so give it a little extra push? I don't know. But as I listened carefully that morning, I realized he wasn't talking gibberish at all. He was reciting the *Wizard of Oz*, all of it.

When he got to "Oh, Auntie Em, there's no place like home!" he started it again. I knew he'd watched the home video of the film at least fifty times, because half of those times I watched it with him. But it never occurred to me that he had memorized all of it, or was even capable of doing such a thing. By listening to him during the next few days, I learned he had also memorized the Disney *Snow White*, the *Snow White* and *Puss In Boots* I wrote for the Seattle Children's Theatre and subsequently videotaped, and three or four other shows in his collection of tapes. It occurred to me that Ned had never been just babbling. He was always reciting stories that he liked to hear.

As he grew older, the memorized pieces were first supplemented and then replaced by his own tales, inter-weavings of
the events and characters he has always found interesting, with
plots taken from books and films he likes. In Ned's imagination, I suspect Seattle pioneer Arthur Denny and *Titanic* owner
J. Bruce Ismay have fought dinosaurs on the slopes of Mt. St.
Helens to the music of Dick Dale and the Del-Tones. But I don't
really know for sure. Ned's private conversation is just that—
private. Approach him and it usually stops.

Cathy and I are so accustomed to it by now that we hardly
notice, but occasionally I'll see strangers looking at Ned when
he's off in a corner, slowly rocking back and forth and talking to
himself. A therapist once told us this was classic autistic behavior. He was surprised to see Ned doing it. "Usually autistics and
people with Down syndrome have exactly opposite personalities," he said. He told us not to worry about it, and we never
have. Some outsiders, however, seem to enjoy worrying about
it, and stare at the poor little retarded boy talking to himself
like he's playing with matches and why don't I do something
about it? They don't know the secret, and I feel no obligation to
explain that he's telling himself stories and not just babbling.
After all, I made the same mistaken assumption myself. I especially feel no need to tell Ned to stop, no matter where we are.
That endless monologue is so much a part of him, it would be
like asking John Muir to give up the Sierras, or Bonnie Raitt to
knock off all that singing. It's a manifestation of his memory
and his imagination, two of the real joys of Ned.

Halfway back down the hill from Dun Aengus, Ned produced an object from his pocket. History will never know for
sure who built the massive stone walls of Dun Aengus, but I
know for sure who made them infinitesimally less massive.

"Ned, where did you get that rock?"

"Up there."

"Please tell me you didn't take the rock from the walls."

"There were lots of them."

"You don't understand. I don't want you to tell me you took
the rock from the walls, even though I know where you got the
rock. I don't want you to tell anybody that."

"But…"

"Taking a rock from the walls is probably a felony in Ireland. If everybody took a rock from the walls, Dun Aengus would soon be a place on top of a cliff where there used to be a wall, and our bus driver wouldn't have any place to take people except the Taco Bell. So you picked up the rock from the ground. And you picked it up down here, not up there. Okay?"

"Okay."

"Especially don't tell the bus driver. Or Tom."

"Okay."

And he didn't. The bus dropped us back in Kilronan, where we had an hour to kill before the Zodiacs headed for the ship. While I looked at genuine Aran Island wool sweaters in the town shop, Ned strolled around outside. He found me a few minutes later, smiling happily. There was a restaurant in the lobby of the small hotel next door. It was open, and cheeseburgers were on the menu. His stroll of discovery had resulted in an important and unexpected reward.

I'll remember two things from this day for a long time: Ned sitting near the edge of a cliff, becoming for just a few minutes a Fir Bolg (or perhaps a Dane); Ned, just as alone, just as intrepid, sitting at a table in an otherwise empty Inishmore hotel dining room, eating a cheeseburger and fries, and looking out at the very spot in the sea where Robert Flaherty staged the shark hunt.

It's been a good day.

Sunday, June 23, 2002

Inishmurray, County Sligo, Ireland

Before breakfast this morning we anchored off a small island in Donegal Bay called Inishmurray. There are perhaps thirty roofless, deserted stone buildings along the length of the island. A community here has died or gone away. The buildings are their abandoned homes, meeting places and churches, with owners gone a hundred years or more because of the potato famine. No doubt there are Irish-American families today for whom the

name Inishmurray is a mystical, unseen place in the old country. It's where Granddad came from; where Great Grandma died
and is buried; where the hunger and suffering were intense and
unending; where escape was the only recourse.

The excursion to Inishmurray was to see wildflowers and a
ruined abbey. Ned stayed up very late last night, so he groggily
decided at 7 a.m. that he would pass on the excursion. Not a lad
for wildflowers or ruins is Ned. I thought he had gone back to
sleep, so I went to breakfast for the first time without him. A
half-hour later, dressed and grinning from having done it himself and alone, he joined me. These welcome flashes of independence are increasing as each day at sea goes by.

Our fellow passengers Crystal and her aunt were at the table,
and we talked of their previous trips to South America, including
Bolivia and Peru. Ned as usual found a family connection.

My Aunt Dorothy's second marriage was to a man named
Ed Heddy. His son by his first wife was Ed Heddy Jr., who
changed his name to Eric Fleming and starred in the 1960s
Western television series *Rawhide*–"Movin', movin', movin',
keep those dogies movin'," etc. At least he was the star until
the producers noticed that the show's second male lead, a
skinny twenty-one-year-old kid named Clint Eastwood, was
getting ten times more fan mail. Eric began to see more and
more episodes being built around Clint, so with that special
kind of insanity known only to actors, he demanded a raise.
The raise was denied, and Ned's step-cousin once removed quit
*Rawhid*ing. He saw his future as a star on the big screen. In
that he was in error. Making a television film called *High Jungle*
five years later, he drowned in the Huallaga River. And—here's
the connection at last—that river is in Peru. Currently, all Peru
means to Ned is that it is the place where step-cousin Ed—
who died decades before Ned was born—gave his life for his
art. In this tour around the British Isles, there is a lot to do
with family for Ned: where they came from, where they are
going, where they died.

Crystal is a very pretty twenty-one-year-old from Texas
traveling with her Aunt Gail, who is the best kind of Texas
blowzy, like the writer Molly Ivins. Crystal, not even pre-blowzy,

goes to Trinity College, where she's captain of the soccer team. We talked about soccer some at breakfast, and I mentioned Sue, a friend of mine who is also a soccer player.

During the conversation, Ned added the fact that Sue's cousin is Senator Patty Murray, Democrat of Washington. This led to a discussion of the United States Senate, which I compared to the passenger list of the *MS Endeavour*—old, wealthy, and white. Crystal said, "You noticed that too?" We are perhaps the only travelers to be aware that not a single guest on board is a person of color. There aren't even any Asians. The *Endeavour* passenger list is 100 percent Caucasian. Were it not for the Filipino housekeeping and dining room staff, it would be an all-white boat. It means that in the terms funding organizations like to use, Ned is the only minority present who isn't on the payroll.

In the general area of multiculturalism, some of our fellow guests are decidedly from a different era, or at least from a whole different part of America than I'm from. At dinner last night, a Southern gentleman was talking about Eleanor Roosevelt. He remarked offhand to the assembled, "They say she gave America two things: kudzu and niggers." I can't recall the last time I heard someone use that word in general conversation. Travel can be a broadening experience.

My breakfast over, I left Ned at the table and went off to send an e-mail home. Apparently, after Crystal and Gail also departed, Dennis the Waiter teased Ned that Crystal must be his girlfriend. Teasing little kids about their romantic interests, on the assumption they have none, is standard non-parent behavior. But Ned isn't a little kid. He's a twenty-year-old man, and he most certainly does have romantic interests, even if he doesn't recognize them for what they are. He was obviously pleased that Dennis would say such a thing—Ned takes the subject of romance, real or implied, very seriously—but he nevertheless told me he "almost blushed" and had to inform Dennis of his devotion to Lily back home.

I've heard a lot about Lily in these Irish days. Irish on her mother's side, or so Ned thinks, Lily is one of the ways Ned can make both a familial and personal connection to Ireland and

*Ned, Lily, and some middle school classmates after a canned food drive, with then
Seattle Mayor Norm Rice. Clockwise, from the Mayor's immediate left: Ned, Lily,
Kelsey, Santosh. Back row, right to left: Heidi, Matt, Sarah. Others unidentified.*

the Irish. We are also surrounded by couples, and having a girl
of his own back home is a way for Ned to think of himself as an
equal with the group. "I'm not just some single man traveling
with my father. I've got connections elsewhere," seems to be
the subtext here.

Lily has been Ned's girlfriend since middle school, when
they were classmates together for the first time. I distinctly remember Lily pursuing Ned most directly by informing him one
day they would be sweethearts from then on, but now he tells
me he decided to make her his girlfriend when he learned she
had seizures. "She needs someone to watch out for her and take
care of her and that's why I decided she should be my girlfriend,"
is the way he puts it.

Lily is a year or two younger than Ned, with developmental disabilities but not Down syndrome. Ned once described
her to me as "the most beautiful girl in the world." I was surprised by that, because he knows and is obviously attracted to
some girls of his acquaintance who are indeed beautiful. Also,

Lily's place in Ned's life seems to me to be far more symbolic than romantic. Always accompanied by a parent or two, they've been to many birthday parties together, plus a few movies and two dances. Nevertheless, their relationship is strictly platonic. Rarely have I seen Ned so much as hold Lily's hand, and though he eagerly tries to hug every woman under sixty years old he's ever met when he meets them again (unless I stop him, and sometimes I have to), he doesn't hug Lily, or if he does I've never seen it. At parties and in other social gatherings where you would expect Ned to hang with his girlfriend, they are almost never together.

Lily and Ned are alike in some ways. They both know how they want their lives to proceed right down to the smallest details, and can be forceful in maintaining personal control. And they've both been successful at it. Lily's parents are fine folks who give her what she wants whenever possible, just like Ned's folks do. From what I've observed, when Lily and Ned are together, she usually calls the play, and though he agrees, I don't know how much he likes it. Actually, I don't know how much he really likes Lily, but he very much likes and apparently needs to be able to say he has a girlfriend. In that sense, Lily serves a similar function in his life as those actresses who are married to gay male movie stars. It was a far more common practice under the studio system years ago, but I believe it is still known to happen. For public consumption, the men need to appear straight. But even in the old days, you couldn't get away with being called "Hollywood's most eligible bachelor" (Rock Hudson, 1958-1978) forever. So they marry "beards," women who pose as loving spouses. What the women get out of it I don't know, except that they are married to movie stars, and that's got to be helpful in some ways.

Ned came home from school a few years ago and mentioned that Lily had informed him they were going to get married as soon as she graduated. He said this without any particular emotional fervor. You might have thought he was talking about getting a bicycle. At the same time, he clearly accepted Lily's pronouncement as fact. A few days later I shamelessly sandbagged him. It was easy, really. I just asked him how he thought he'd enjoy living at Lily's house after they were married.

"What do you mean?" he replied, immediately suspicious.

"Well, Ned, Lily likes her parents a lot, and they like her and take good care of her. So after you get married, I can almost guarantee you that Lily will want to live with them, so they can continue to take care of her needs like they do now. As you know, Lily has some physical problems, seizures sometimes, and so I think it's pretty likely that she's assuming you guys will move into her basement and live there for the rest of your lives. Her dog and cat will become your dog and cat, you'll be eating what her mom wants to make for you, and you'll be saying goodbye to us, and your own pets, and your own bedroom and the family room. But you can come back and visit whenever you like. You'll probably be able to take some of your books and your videos along with you to Lily's, but they have a smaller house than we do, don't they? So you'll have to leave some stuff behind. Like two or three hundred action figures."

There was a very long pause. Ned finally said, "Oh," and departed for the family room, looking concerned. That was the last we ever heard about Lily and Ned getting married. I don't know if he said anything to her about it, but if he followed his standard procedure, he probably didn't, in hopes that the subject would just go away. I felt a little guilty about messing with him like that, even if all I said was true. But if I have any control over the situation, there are particular reasons why Ned won't be marrying Lily.

It's not because I think Ned shouldn't marry anybody. Working as a reporter in television news twenty years ago, I did a profile of a married couple with Down syndrome named Cyndy and Rod. I called a helpful woman at the National Down Syndrome Congress at the time to get some statistics on the number of married couples in America where both husband and wife have Down syndrome. "There aren't any," she told me. "Although there are many people with Down syndrome who are married, they aren't married to each other."

"Two of them are," I said, and told her about Cyndy and Rod. She was quite thrilled to hear it, and equally thrilled to hear I was doing a television news story about them.

Cyndy and Rod had their own apartment near a Seattle shopping mall called Northgate. They worked together in a sheltered workshop, were knowledgeable and experienced bus riders, bowled together on Tuesdays, and were very much involved in their church, getting a lot of support from the congregation. A few nights a week, a woman from a state-operated service came in to help Cyndy with the family budget and any shopping that needed to be done. But mostly they were on their own. They seemed quite happy, and they were certainly proud that they had been able to organize a life together. Rod didn't seem as bright as Cyndy—I suspect he doesn't read, for instance—but he was also a very macho guy, a true "I'm the king of this castle" type. One of the endearing things about them was how cleverly she made him think he was in charge when she really called most of the shots, as she should have.

Cyndy and Rod are dramatic proof that people with Down syndrome can be happily married if they are properly prepared and supported by a community of friends and professionals. I think of them often when I think of Ned's future, and I wonder how they are doing. I drove by a bus stop five years ago and they were standing there. I nearly stopped to say hello, but I know Cyndy and Rod have been taught to be very careful about strangers. It's been more than fifteen years since we met, so they might not remember me, and I would hate to frighten them.

The main reason I don't think Ned should marry Lily is that his romantic interest in her is minimal and because, physically and intellectually, she is just too high maintenance for him to handle. These days a lasting marriage isn't easy for anybody under the best of circumstances. I should know, because Cathy and I have been married for thirty-four years, a fact that many of the people we meet find shocking, bizarre, and unnatural. Far more of our friends and acquaintances are working on second or third marriages than not. For Ned to succeed as a married man, he needs to find somebody who is operating at more or less the same level that he is, and unfortunately that's not Lily.

He's met a few likely candidates. Some time ago, for instance, he took a dance class, and one of the other students was a girl with Down syndrome about his age. She was very cute, feisty, funny, and certainly at his level intellectually. I was nuts about her, and thought she was the perfect girl for him. He almost completely ignored her. When I did my "Dolly the Matchmaker" bit and asked him why he wasn't more interested in her, he told me, "My heart belongs to Lily." That's the frustrating thing about their relationship. Lily's presence in his life, her almost entirely symbolic role as Ned's Girlfriend, gives him comfort, satisfaction, and pride, but it also keeps him from considering other, possibly more suitable opportunities.

I think there are times Ned feels that frustration as well, but he isn't willing to let go of Lily. He likes girls, likes them a lot, and on one memorable occasion, he said so. Last year, in a high school English class, he wrote a poem, copies of which can still be found on some teachers' bulletin boards around the school. I'm told that thanks to e-mail they have also floated around the country. He wrote it entirely himself:

Girls
Girls are neat. Girls are sweet.
They're the kind of people I love to meet.
Teenage girls are what I love.
They're like angels from above.
I'm crazy for girls, I'm crazy for love.
Girls are like the wings on a dove.
When I grow up and am feeling old,
I'll find all the girls I love to hold.
I'd like to give all the girls a kiss.
If there weren't any girls, it's girls I'd miss.

As I write this, the romantic poet is asleep across the cabin, taking the morning nap that has become his custom on this journey, with his feet on his pillow and his head in amongst the deployed action figures. At 11:00, we are to haul anchor and push on to Donegal. Inishmurray will become the place neither of us went, the mystical tourist memory that at least for me represents massive death and loss and is therefore overwhelmingly sad, even in the bright sunshine of a Sunday in June.

E-mail, as written, from Ned Palmer to Cathy Palmer,
Sunday, June 23:

> Hi mom right now I'm off the small island of
> Inishmurray, where you can see from the ship maybe
> 25 abandoned stone houses that people who had to
> leave because of the potato blight used to live in. we
> decided not to go ashore, but to admire the view from
> the stern. This afternoon we're going to a real castle
> and a small fishing village in Donegal. Yesterday I
> took a long walk on the Isles of Aran up to a fort that
> was built around the time of Christ. I'm bringing
> back a surprise for you from there. *[It's a rock that
> looks exactly like the rocks that make up the fort, just a
> remarkable likeness, but of course, not actually from the
> fort, no indeedy.]* We cruised very close to the Cliffs of
> Moher and dad made movies of them from the
> seaside. Last night he went ashore in the village of
> Cleggen to sit in a pub for a while. I have recently
> been eating sausages, a new kind of toast, venison,
> lots of beef, and in secret been eating hamburgers in
> some of the local restaurants, like on Aran.

Monday, June 24, 2002

The Isles of Staffa and Iona, Scotland

Our first stop in Scotland is the Inner Hebrides. The Isle of Staffa is famous because it's composed of seemingly millions of hexagonal basalt columns. At water level, Staffa has sea caves, including Fingal's Cave, which was Felix Mendelssohn's inspiration for his 1829 overture *The Hebrides*. This morning we could either go ashore and walk on top of the basalt columns in the never-ending search for puffins and their pals, or go along the shoreline in the Zodiacs, peering into caves. Ned informed me that I was to walk the land, while he would ride in the boat, foregoing the opportunity to see the tops of a million hexagonal basalt columns dotted with puffins. An hour later I watched from a soggy cliff as Ned went by below, a tiny figure huddled in the bottom of Tom's boat. I could tell even from that distance that he was very happy, having his own adventure. Another goal achieved.

When I got back to the cabin, sopping wet from a light rain and a rough return trip, Ned was there, dry and content, listening to music, reading a songbook—still happy, and now even happier to see me soaking.

During lunch we backtracked south a short distance to Iona, off the western tip of the Island of Mull. It is one of the most sacred places in Christendom, the spot where St. Colum (or in Latin, Columba, "the dove") founded his church in 563 AD after being driven from Donegal. His goal was to convert the Scottish Picts to Celtic Christianity, and it was the Pict king, Bridei, who gave him the island.

I thought this excursion would be a tough sell for Ned, but once again he surprised me. The ship's bulletin this morning mentioned that perhaps as many as sixty Scottish kings are buried in a large mound in the graveyard just outside Iona's ancient abbey. Allegedly included in the assemblage are Duncan and Macbeth, together forever. (And where is Lady Macbeth? Out; out in some other damned spot, I reckon.)

If somebody had asked me whether Ned knew who Macbeth was, I would have said no. But he does, and he was eager to see where classical drama's foremost Thane is buried. So we went ashore, walked around the mound, pondered whether it was haunted, took pictures of it, and then went into the abbey next door. Once the church for the monastery/nunnery up the road, it's now a sort of generic peace-and-freedom religious edifice for the residents of Iona. Inside it felt a lot like a Unitarian church, if you happened to put a Unitarian church in a thousand-year-old abbey.

Afterwards Ned hit the gift shop. He was disappointed that there weren't any action figures of Macbeth or Saint Columba, but there were hymnbooks he felt he had to have for his songbook collection. They made up for the fact that even though Iona is called by some the Cradle of Christianity, it is not even the Diaper Pail of Burgers.

Most kids would probably pass by the hymnbooks in such a gift shop without a second glance. But not Ned, who has been a songbook collector for a long time. For his third birthday, we gave him a collection of children's songs. He carried it around for weeks, eventually read it over and over again, and started getting other songbooks. First it was children's material, works by Raffi, Red Grammer, Fred Penner, and especially the *Sesame Street* songs of the Muppets—all the things he was listening to for hours every day. Then came the old rock and roll collections, dozens of them, and after that big bands, American folk, *Love Songs of the 20s*, and anything Pete Seeger and Woody Guthrie ever wrote. Go to a bookstore with Ned now and he immediately heads for the music collection, and always finds something he just has to buy. (Like a lot of kids, Ned thinks it is practically criminal to enter a store and not buy something. I hope that belief diminishes significantly when he starts getting an allowance, and the money required for the purchase is his and not mine.)

His current songbook collection must be at least two hundred volumes, and he's read every one of them carefully. In 1997, I did a documentary for PBS about vaudeville. While we were in production, I wondered one day about songs that are standards now but were originally composed for the vaudeville stage, and how we needed to research that to demonstrate vaudeville's effect on contemporary life. Ned was present and immediately said, "'Take Me Out to the Ball Game' was written in 1910 by Jack Norworth for his vaudeville act." He said it the way another kid might say, "Peanut butter's the brown stuff." And he was right.

E-mail, from Greg Palmer to Cathy Palmer, Monday, June 24:

Just returned from afternoon at abbey; weather awful coming in, then brightened; now beautiful day. N enjoyed lots; forgot to buy Life of St. C, sorry, but bought religious songbooks and Iona video. N most excited about Macbeth burial mound.

> Only downer: No burger available.... N missing
> home now, asking when we get to Inverness;
> expected. Not problem yet; maybe never. Ship's
> doctor has 8 cats (+ 2 boas & other critters) 3 of
> cats Sphinxes—hairless. Very lively animal dinner
> discussion, N taking major role. Doc is from San
> Fran; surprised to meet real blind George Spelvin.
> Passengers now seeking N out for genuine conver-
> sation. Nice to see.

A word about George Spelvin. My brother is co-owner of the Vehicle Donation Processing Center, a Los Angeles-based organization that runs car donation programs for approximately three hundred charities and nonprofit organizations around the country. Some of these charities do radio and/or television ads, and I write, produce, and sometimes voice them. One of the charities is the California Council for the Blind. In the Bay area, a typical radio spot begins "Hello, I'm George Spelvin. I'm blind, and I want your car. But don't worry, I'm not going to drive it away myself. We've got guys who do that...." I play George Spelvin, a carefully chosen pseudonym. George Spelvin is the name actors have been using for hundreds of years when they don't want to appear under their own names for some reason. Versions of "George Spelvin" cover the dramatic map, from the porn star "Georgina Spelvin" to Laurence Olivier, who once was listed in the program of the National Theatre in London as "Lord Spelvin."

I feel no shame about pretending to be blind for the radio commercials, because they benefit a charity. It's not like we're trying to garner sympathy so we can unload a lot of cheap furniture or discount jewelry. But, as with the Ship's Doctor on the *Endeavour*, I occasionally meet Bay area people who have heard Spelvin and recognize his voice.

Tuesday, June 25, 2002

St. Kilda, Scotland, Outer Hebrides

The St. Kilda Archipelago is composed of the most remote islands in the Outer Hebrides, and the most important seabird breeding site in Europe. Sixty thousand breeding gannets and sixty-five thousand breeding fulmars, as well as oystercatchers, gulls, curlews, and of course the ever-popular puffin, all call St. Kilda home at times. It makes Capistrano look like a birdcage.

Ned opted for staying on the boat, while I went ashore on Hirta, the main island of the group. Two thousand years ago, Neolithic people lived here, but everybody gave up trying to survive the barren life on Hirta in the 1930s, so the British government moved the last residents to more livable places. Their little stone houses still stand and are maintained by the National Trust for Scotland.

When those houses were occupied, the locals survived by catching and eating birds and selling their feathers. This historical fact inspired the best Tom Ritchie moment of the trip so far. Riding back to the *Endeavour* in a Zodiac, one of my fellow travelers was pondering what the birds must taste like. She asked Tom if he'd ever tried a roasted fulmar or a fricasseed gannet in all his travels.

"No," Tom said, with an abruptness I didn't expect from so gracious a man. I know he loves these birds, and is clearly a man who has reverence for all living creatures.

"What, never?" she said, teasing him a bit. "Never tempted to see what they taste like? I would be."

"No," Tom said again, stronger. "And I don't eat whales, either."

Thank you, Tom.

E-mail, Greg Palmer to Cathy Palmer, Tuesday, June 25

    [A few days ago] We went ashore at Skillig Michael,
    N didn't, thank God. Wind rose while there; trip
    back to ship, especially transferring from Zodiac to
    ship, extremely hairy, N would have been terrified,

trying to jump from heaving inflatable to small platform. Hell, I was terrified. Fascinating place, took many movies. N also passed today at St. Kilda, sadly, while I walked around; equally fascinating. Sad story, remarkable feeling to place. Feral sheep. Afterward passed "stack" with 60K pairs of roosting gannets; looked like big rock covered in snow, but was birds, N enthralled. Seas extremely rough last night (bow almost going underwater), but N slept through; I was up most of night, felt seasick for the 2nd time in life, couldn't take the pills available because of other medicines. Okay now. N has developed many fans on boat, inc. bartender Anders, multi-millionaire Southerner John Proctor, President of Florida State (our most illustrious guest) and his wife, nice folks. N will make it, tho his interest in, A. ruined religious/prehistoric structures; B. birds; C. flora, has reached nadir. So he stays happily on board during said jaunts. Hope he's getting enough to eat, tho last night's Filipino buffet (entire wait/housekeeping staff F) not big hit, except for roasted pig, complete w/face. N has invited many guests to come to Seattle for "Chips Ahoy" party...

Wednesday, June 26, 2002, 11 p.m.

Orkney, Scotland

It was a great day for Ned. During breakfast we anchored at Shapinsay Island in the Orkneys. The morning excursion was a visit to Balfour Castle, built in the 1840s and once the ancestral home of the Balfours. Now it's owned by the Zawadski family, and is billed as the "Northernmost Castle Hotel in the World."

The castle itself is a mile from the pier, so we had the choice of walking through the gardens or taking a small truck. I walked while Ned went trucking, so he got there some time before I did. It's a measure of how much I think he's grown on the trip that I wasn't worried about him Balfouring by himself for a while.

When I got to the castle, I couldn't find him. It's a big place. The Zawadskis run the three room hotel on the top floor, and maintain the ground floor as much as possible as the Balfours had it. Searching for him in increasing panic, I finally charged into the main parlor. Ned was sitting on a couch chatting with Tom Heffernan, a Professor of Medieval Studies from the University of Tennessee who's one of the ship's historians. Tom told me he walked into the room a half hour before and found Ned, alone, sitting at Lord Balfour's one-hundred-and-fifty-year-old piano. Ned was playing *Lavender Blue (Dilly Dilly)* when Tom arrived. "It's probably the first time *Lavender Blue* has ever been played on that piano," Tom said pleasantly. "And he was playing it very well."

I've walked through enough National Trust Houses in the British Isles to know that if this house weren't privately owned, Ned would most certainly have been arrested. ("And this rock in your pocket," the bobby would say. "It looks rather like it's from the south wall of Dun Aengus.") Fortunately, the Zawadskis are a generous, relaxed, understanding family. Ned played the one piano in a stately home of Britain where he could get away with it.

But there was more. On our first night aboard the *Endeavour* nine days ago, Ned noticed the piano in the lounge and informed me that he intended to give a concert for our fellow travelers. I said no. We do not inflict our children on others. "And besides, Ned, your instrument is the guitar, not the piano." But Tom Heffernan was so impressed with *Lavender Blue* that he invited Ned to tickle the ivories tonight during the cocktail hour before dinner.

Ned planned a short program of his best numbers: *Lavender Blue,* of course; the main "Ode to Joy" theme from Beethoven's *Ninth Symphony;* and a gospel piece I'd never heard of before, *Standing in the Need of Prayer.* It's a song you don't encounter much in bars, but maybe you should. Tom Heffernan got on the ship's PA to invite our fellow passengers to "a special concert by Ned Palmer." When we arrived in the lounge, the house was full, although admittedly some of the crowd was composed of drinkers, not listeners.

I've found in these situations that Ned is at his best when I'm at my farthest away, so as he took his regular seat at the bar I went to mid-house and prepared the video camera. I was five times more nervous than he was—afraid he would embarrass himself, and even more afraid that he would embarrass himself and know it. And, yes, I was afraid he would embarrass me, too. It's not a feeling I'm proud of, but a fact, nonetheless.

Tom Ritchie graciously introduced the artist and the evening's selections at the conclusion of his regular announcements. Ned acknowledged the polite applause, stepped to the piano, and without a moment's hesitation launched into *Lavender Blue*, played with chords and both hands and far better than I knew he could play. He took four years of Keyboarding in high school, and apparently spent most of that time playing just a few pieces. The "Ode to Joy" was a one-finger exercise, and he seemed to get lost for a while in the middle of the gospel piece. But all things considered, it was far more successful than almost anybody in the

Ned tickles the ivories on the M.S. Endeavour. *(Still photo made from video.)*

room, except Ned, thought it would be. And it was over in ten minutes, which is always good when you're hearing somebody's kid, anybody's kid, play the piano. The applause from the two-thirds of the assembled who were paying attention was genuine, and Ned was shyly exuberant. Afterwards he stayed and worked the room until the last congratulator left for dinner.

He's asleep now, and I'm back in the almost empty lounge. Sometimes I have a problem with the family rule about not inflicting my kids on strangers. Too many of those strangers want to dismiss my son and those like him as useless, pitiable, and ignorable. It's not my job to change their minds even if I could. But if Ned and I can rattle their cages just a little through some judicious inflicting, we'll do it. A few minutes ago, a very nice guy from South Carolina named John Proctor told me that Ned's concert tonight was one of the best things about the whole trip as far as he was concerned. It was a very gracious thing to say, especially since I think he really meant it.

One other triumph of this day:
E-mail, from Greg Palmer to Cathy Palmer, Wednesday, June 26, 12:15 p.m.:

> Now it can be written, now it can be told. At 12:42 GMT, off the Orkney Islands, Mr. Ned Palmer had smoked eel for lunch, even though pizza was also offered. True, it was mushroom and onion pizza, and Mr. Palmer did not know the eel was eel until he ate some (due to a conspiracy entered into by his father and tablemates). But it is also true that after learning it was eel, he went back for more eel and ate all of that too. This morning we went to Lord Balfour's splendid castle in the Orkneys, did a nice tour. This afternoon Ned stayed on board digesting his eel (and, during the cocktail hour, nursing two Cokes in the bar with Anders the Floating Publican) while I went ashore and got wetter—in a driving, horizontal rain/wind storm—than I have in many moons. Saw many hotshot prehistoric dwellings and stone circles between gales.

E-Mail, from Ned and Greg Palmer to Cathy Palmer, Wednesday, June 26, 9:00 p.m.

> Hi mom. I'm right now back on board the Endeavour at Shetland islands. I've been out shopping

and bought an action figure called Daredevil. Last night I gave a concert piano recital to the whole crew aboard the ship (I played Lavender blue, ode to joy and Standing in the need of prayer) which turned out great. So How are things going with Lassie Harley and max. Tomorrow is my last day on the boat. I'll see you soon, love Ned.

Walked mile to get cheeseburgers, but nice walk in Lerwick. (Bought Ira a Scots rugby jersey. Declined to buy you Shetland sweater, looked like something Sonja Henie's great grandmother might have worn.) Took bus trip today to excellent Pict dwelling site, also saw pod of orcas off coast. Ned slept on entire ride—he does that—but together explored dwellings...Packing tomorrow; ship has bus to Inverness Marriott after docking, most convenient. Nessie awaits.

Greg

Friday, June 28, 2002, 10 p.m.

The grand expedition is over, except for pier-side farewells and getting home from Scotland. Right now we're traveling south aboard the *Endeavour* toward the Moray Firth and Invergordon, the Firth-port that serves Inverness, for an arrival at 8:00 tomorrow morning. I think Ned has been emotionally ready to go home since the concert in the lounge, although there have certainly been some moments of interest in the last two days.

We discovered there actually are Shetland ponies in the Shetland Islands. It's not like French fries in France, nor are all the ponies shipped in from Taiwan or New Jersey industrial parks. That's reassuring. You don't want to get too close to the ponies, however. Like all horses, the front end bites and the back end kicks, but you tend to forget that because they are so much cuter than your average nag. Then you get bitten and/or kicked and you say let the Taiwanese have them.

From the way he's been talking in the last few days, Ned's piano concert will become the high point of the entire trip, as far as he's concerned. It went well and I had nothing to do with it from start to finish. In fact, through his own efforts and the kindness of strangers, he did something I originally told him he couldn't do, and that made it all the sweeter for him. But for me, just as memorable as those ten minutes at the ivories was dinner last night.

Our table included Crystal and Gale, the aunt and niece from Texas; a staff member in his mid-twenties who is clearly smitten with Crystal; and Frank King, the British bird expert who now lives in Ireland—an erudite man in his sixties. The talk turned to his various activities, and Frank mentioned that back home he does a weekly radio program that has nothing to do with birds. He reads poetry. He recited a bit of Auden for us. The young staff member said he knew a poem too, and then recited a limerick that was both off-color and not very good.

I turned to Ned, because I knew what was about to happen. A few years ago, when he was mainstreamed in a sophomore English class, the teacher gave a last-minute assignment one Friday afternoon. "Next week," she said, "everyone has to recite a poem to the rest of the class. So start memorizing. And try to find a poem that means something to you."

Ned immediately raised his hand. She was about to tell him that he didn't have to do the assignment if he didn't want to, because she assumed that was what he wanted to ask. But before she could let him off the hook, Ned said, "I'm ready now." The teacher told him to go ahead. She made a second incorrect assumption—that the class was about to hear something of the "roses are red, violets are blue" variety. She sent a note home with Ned that afternoon to tell us what happened. And it's what happened last night at dinner.

In class three years ago, and again last night, Ned recited, word perfect and with ease and passion, *The Wolf*, written around the turn of the century by Georgia Roberts Durston:

> *When the pale moon hides and the wild wind wails,*
> *and over the tree-tops the nighthawk sails,*

the gray wolf sits on the world's far rim,
And howls; and it seems to comfort him.
The wolf is a lonely soul, you see,
No beast in the wood, nor bird in the tree,
But shuns his path.
In the windy gloom
they give him plenty, and plenty of room.
So he sits with his long lean face to the sky
Watching the ragged clouds go by.
There in the night, alone, apart,
Singing the song of his lone, wild heart.
Far away, on the world's dark rim
He howls, and it seems to comfort him.

It's a wonderful poem and he's loved it for years. For me it's always been a little bit about him. At least I hope it is. In the future, when his parents are gone and society is giving him plenty of room, his path may be shunned. He could be a lonely soul, but he will always be comforted by singing the songs of his lone, wild heart.

Our tablemates on the *Endeavour* were impressed, and the limerick reciter was a little embarrassed. Ned recited two more poems last night: Dr. Seuss's funny *Too Many Daves*, which always reduces him to hysterics, and perhaps his favorite poem of all, Carl Sandburg's *Buffalo Dusk*:

The buffaloes are gone.
And those who saw the buffaloes are gone.
Those who saw the buffaloes by the thousands
and how they pawed the prairie sod into dust
with their hoofs, their great heads down pawing
on in a great pageant of dusk.
Those who saw the buffaloes are gone.
And the buffaloes are gone.

Ned's concert was a gimmick, in a way. There are certainly far better pianists on the *Endeavour,* including an older woman who comes up to the lounge every morning before breakfast and plays Bach beautifully, usually for an audience of one—me. (Tom Ritchie thinks she's a retired concert artist.) And realistically, I think if Ned didn't have Down syndrome but was just a guy on the boat, he wouldn't have been asked to play.

Poetry at dinner was no gimmick. Ned wasn't showing off or trying to be the center of attention. He was holding his own in an adult conversation, getting into the flow of an adult world, and going with it far better than the limerick guy. His recitations were sincere and heartfelt, and like all good poetry reading, he revealed something about himself by his choice of poems and the way he spoke them. I don't think I've ever been prouder of him. And I was especially grateful to Frank King for his reaction. It didn't have even a hint of "Wow, the retarded kid has a good memory!" Afterwards he and Ned chatted like two men who share a love for words and their power to move the human heart. And if for Frank that means Auden, and for Ned that means Seuss, Durston, and Sandburg, it doesn't really make any difference.

This poetry event gives me the opportunity to boast about Cathy's and my parenting skills, and I'm going to seize the opportunity. We started reading to Ira every evening when he was just a few weeks old, long before he understood what he was hearing. In truth, this was no more a conscious parenting decision on our part than feeding him was a conscious decision. It was simply something we knew we should do and very much wanted to do for as long as our children would allow us to. She and I are readers ourselves, especially Cathy, who has a Ph.C. in English (which means she's done everything for a doctorate except write the dissertation). Thirty-eight years ago she took a paperback copy of *Jude the Obscure* on our first date, just in case things got dull. (I have never let her forget this.)

In our house, as in our parents' houses, there have always been books. Some visitors to Chez Palmer go wide-eyed if they get a chance to see how many books there are. Books line the walls of Cathy's office, my office, our bedroom, our basement, and every available space in between. We could turn the place into a small branch library tomorrow and not get many complaints about holes in the collection, especially in the areas of

past and contemporary novels, show-biz related works, reference, humor, travel, and art books. There's even some science,
although the engineering and mathematics shelves will always
have a lot of space.

When Ira and then Ned arrived, the twentieth-century
English novels, John Updike tomes, and biographies of obscure
comedians moved over to make room for hundreds of books for
kids. We started with the basics like *Good Night Moon*, Maurice
Sendak's wonderful stuff, and a series of books I still read to
myself now and then: James Marshall's saga of two hippopota-
muses named George and Martha (*Tons O' Fun*).

The children's book collection got ever more sophisticated
as Ira and Ned grew up. In the summer before his ninth grade
year, when Ira's communication with his parents had devolved
into the traditional monosyllabic grunts of most teenage boys,
Cathy read J.R.R. Tolkein's entire *Ring* cycle to him. It was the
end of their tandem literary journey, one that had begun a decade and a half before with *The Very Hungry Caterpillar*. From
then on, Ira read his own books, to himself. But he did keep
reading, and he and his mother did have that time together they
would not otherwise have shared in the tempestuous early teen
years. There's no question Ira is a smarter, more sophisticated,
better prepared man now because of the hundreds of books he
heard from us. All of the above—establishment of the joy of
reading, extended parental bonding, smarter kid—are reasons
to read to your children.

Ned has had a similar literary experience, only it didn't end
when he was fifteen; he didn't want it to and neither did his parents. We've had to spend more time at each intellectual level with
Ned than we did with Ira, but we still hit the same spots. He and
I even tried to read Tolkein's *Ring* cycle. We gave up only because Dad kept getting confused by all those needlessly similar,
cutesy-pie names, just as he did in high school forty years ago.

Ned's slower pace meant we spent more time on books I
loved to read (*Tons O' Fun*) and, unfortunately, more time on
books I loathed, like the appalling *Curious George* books. (I'm
sorry, George-devotees. The first and most famous *George* stories are okay, even if the Man in the Yellow Hat *always* goes

Cathy and Ned, Summer 1988.

away at the wrong time and George *always* screws up the moment he does and then *always* redeems himself by doing something right. But the quick-and-dirty sequels that grew out of the cartoon series are terrible.)

A few years later, we became equally mired in the uni-plotted *Hardy Boys* books. Ned and Cathy are still following plucky Frank and Joe and their corpulent friend Chet Morton down mysterious paths, but I couldn't take it any more. In between the dull books, or the ones we found dull, Ned has also been receptive to better works, and those works have become far more intellectually challenging as time has passed. When I was a kid, my mother and I read together everything the late Robert Lawson wrote or illustrated, wonderful books like *Rabbit Hill*, *Mr. Twigg's Mistake, Captain Kidd's Cat, Ben and Me, The Great Wheel*, and the perfectly illustrated *The Story of Ferdinand* by Munro Leaf. It was one of the true joys of being a parent to be able to read them myself to Ned a few years ago, and find him just as enchanted by Lawson's great heart and great eye. It was like introducing him to some very old but dearly remembered friends. Between the inevitable Hardys, Ned and Cathy have recently been reading biographies of his heroes—Martin Luther King, Jr., Woody Guthrie, Mahalia Jackson—and not all books written for kids, either.

Each night, after Cathy or I have read a chapter from the current book, Ned does his bathroom work and gets into bed. Then we trade off and the other parent reads him a few poems. I don't remember how this tradition started, but it's clear that Ned enjoys the poetry every bit as much as the story that precedes it. It could be the songwriter in him. He's a lyricist, after all, and so a poet himself. And though it is conjecture, I think one of the reasons Ned is so verbal is because of the reading we've done, both the prose and the poetry. It has been and continues to be a very important part of our lives together. Some of his favorite poems we've read dozens of times. But until that sophomore English class two years ago, I never realized he has memorized the ones he really likes.

Tonight's last meal on board was just as satisfying even without the poetry. As at the Captain's Dinner ten days ago, some guests received invitations to dine at specific tables with officers and crew. They were the guests who hadn't gotten invitations the first time. Because Ned and I had our evening with the Big Swede engineer, this time we were at a non-hosted, generic table. We were joined by Tom Ritchie and the ship's doctor, Gail Wagner. (From spending the last week and a half with him, I'd bet Tom doesn't host tables at these events because the whole practice is just a little too "Holland America" for him.) I think they sought us out because Tom wanted to spend his last meal on board with Ned.

We all talked about the things we had seen in the past two weeks, and what our plans were for the future. There wasn't anything special about this conversation, which is why it was special. It was a group of people who respect and like each other, talking of this and that. Ned was very much part of it, and was treated throughout like just another person at the table. Seeing if that would ever happen was one reason why we did this.

Tomorrow looks like it will be a very long day. We land at Invergordon, take a bus to a hotel in Inverness, try to get on a tour to Loch Ness in the five hours we have before we go to the Inverness airport, fly to Luton, and get ourselves and our bags to a Luton airport hotel. Then Sunday we get a bus to Heathrow, and British Air takes us home.

Sunday, June 30, 2002, 1:00 p.m., Seattle time

Over the Atlantic

Because Cathy and I have used British Air Visa cards for the last five years, Ned and I are flying home in business class. After the past two days, this is a Godsend. The BA business class seat isn't really a seat, it's more of an "environment," shaped like a large wooden bathtub. Passengers sit side by side facing in opposite directions, with their own personal television screens, magazine racks, and dinner trays. For privacy there's a foldable screen between the seats. It would be hard to imagine a seating design more to Ned's liking. He's sitting two feet away from me on the window side, with the screen up. He absolutely won't let me put the screen down so I might gaze fondly at my little man. Ned might as well be flying in his own private 747. The next time he has to fly Tourist there's going to be trouble.

Inverness was wet, dank, and unfriendly. In fairness to the burg, we got off to a bad start there. Ned has been looking forward to seeing Loch Ness for months. He's under the impression that a monster lives there, a monster that has been waiting at the bottom of the lake for centuries until just the right person shows up. It is her plan to then surface and pose for snapshots. Ned feels confident he is that person.

I booked the late flight from Inverness to London so we would have enough Nessie-time. But I didn't book a Loch Ness tour, because I didn't know exactly when we'd arrive in Inverness and I was assured by various authorities that this time of year we wouldn't have any trouble getting two last-minute seats on a tour. "Ach, nae problem," said the woman on the phone with the suspiciously drama-school Scots accent, "there's two grrreat companies that rrrun to the Loch every day, back and forth they go. You should nae worrry."

No, lassie, there *were* two big companies. Until two days ago, when one of them went out of business. So everyone who was booked on that company for a weekend tour switched to the other company. Ned and I were informed that all of the available Loch Ness tours were sold out, and why didn't we book ahead? And unfortunately Loch Ness is just too far from Inverness to take a cab.

Ned has always taken such disappointments well. He took this one so well I doubt that by the time we landed in Scotland he really wanted to go Loching. Where he wanted to go was home, and any planned activities before going home were an unnecessary interruption in that process. With one exception— the McDonald's burgers at Heathrow airport that have been a standing promise for a week now.

So there we were in wet, dank Inverness with six hours to kill, and no place to kill them. There wasn't even any place to sit down, because Inverness is one of those cities that doesn't provide many sidewalk benches, in or out of the rain.

(You can judge the quality of a city by the quality of its bookstores, according to many people, and I agree. But the availability of the most basic public conveniences—benches, whether covered or not, relatively clean toilets, explanatory signage, frequent buses, knowledgeable cops—is also a good way to judge if a city cares whether its visitors live or die.)

So, rather than visiting Loch Ness, we took the Highland Country Bus to Cawdor Castle, with a brief stop at the Battlefield of Culloden. Just five miles from Inverness, Culloden is where the last major land battle was fought in Britain, in 1746. British forces commanded by the Duke of Cumberland slaughtered Prince Charles Edward Stuart's army, thus ending the Jacobite revolts. That's about as far as I got in my Ned! You-are-there! description of Culloden before my sole student said, "Uh huh," and went back to sleep. He had fallen asleep two minutes after we got on the bus. Ned has fallen asleep within two minutes of getting on any bus in the last two weeks and so has missed huge stretches of scenery in County Cork, and the Aran, Shetland, and Orkney Islands. There's just something about tour buses that knocks the kid out, which is why I'm thankful that I opted for a boat cruise rather than a lengthy bus trip. Had we decided to tour Britain by bus, Ned would certainly have returned home refreshed, because he would have been asleep for eleven days.

He roused when we got to Cawdor Castle, because I told him the place was supposed to be haunted by two ghosts. According to the guidebook, there's a lady ghost who wears a blue velvet dress, and the ghost of Sir John Campbell, the first Thane of Cawdor, who does not wear a blue velvet dress. The castle looks haunted from the outside, too. It's a massive edifice, built in the late fourteenth century as a private fortress by the Thanes, long after erstwhile Thane of Cawdor Macbeth was in that big mound on Iona. Besides ghosts, Cawdor has everything you want in a castle, including a drawbridge, portcullis, dungeon, and very thick walls.

We took the guided tour of the interior, noted with disappointment (Ned) and relief (me) that the piano was roped off, and eventually ended up at the haunted bookshop. According to legend, the blue velvet lady was last seen in the retail trade area there, certainly a most convenient legend for building bookshop traffic. Then Ned and I caught the bus back to Inverness, a lovely drive through the Scots greenery, all of which Ned missed because he was, well, asleep again.

Getting from Inverness to Heathrow Terminal Four via Luton airport was a tedious and tiresome process, especially as it involved traveling on easyJet Airlines, a stunningly inept operation. Ned has always dealt fairly well with the tedium of travel, but perhaps as a result of the expedition, I think he's gotten better at it. He soldiers on through waits, lines, confusions, and crowds, and that's something some people, like his father, have never learned to do without working up a head of steam. The only problem we had was weaponry. Standing in a long security line at Heathrow airport being watched by plainclothes cops is not the ideal place to try to convince your son that nobody wants to hear about the gun in his backpack. The gun in question was plastic and approximately a quarter of an inch long, resting in the fist of an action figure. It took time and a lot of suspicious whispering to convince him that just saying the word "gun" around these people was a bad idea.

We've been flying for six hours now, in that odd east-to-west world where you leave and arrive at practically the same time and in daylight all the way. Perhaps that's why the young man who falls asleep so easily on buses when there are things to see out the window hasn't fallen asleep on this flight, when there's nothing at all to see. I can hear him over there now, talking quietly, continuing that endless conversation with himself that is so very much Ned. And it seems to comfort him.

Back Home

Monday, July 1, 2002

Students with disabilities are guaranteed an education up to their twenty-first year in our state. That age cutoff comes at the start of the school year, so that you're still eligible if you turn twenty-one during the nine months from September through the following June.

Shortly before we left for England, the school district notified us that Ned could not return to high school in the fall because his twenty-first birthday comes on September third, two days before school officially begins on September fifth. We protested, because the official guidelines we received clearly say that a Special Ed student who is twenty on September first, not September fifth, is eligible for another year. The school administration has finally agreed with us, which means that, by three days, Ned is still eligible to go back to Nathan Hale High for another school year. Were it not for this lucky break, on this first day back from the expedition, we would be planning the rest of his adult life. We would be struggling with where he will eventually live and what he will eventually do. And the "eventually" would be as soon as we set the wheels in motion.

He's going back to school, and we are all happy about that. We've explained to him that he'll be doing "graduate work" just like his mother did at the University years ago. His graduate work will be all that vocational instruction we've avoided for the past four years. Without any academic responsibilities, now is the time for it.

Tuesday, July 2, 2002

Mr. Sven-Olof Lindblad
Lindblad Expeditions
720 Fifth Avenue
New York, NY 10019   July 2, 2002

Dear Mr. Lindblad,
    Two days ago I returned from Lindblad Expedi-

tions' Wild Isles trip around Britain and Ireland.
My traveling companion, as his high school
graduation gift, was my son Ned, a 20-year-old
with Down syndrome.

I had a special reason for this journey. Ned is
entering the vitally important transitional period
between childhood—with the protection of parents
and teachers—and adulthood, when he must learn
to function independently, both economically and
socially, in a grown-up milieu. So it was the social
life of a Lindblad Expedition I sought, not the
ruins and rookeries necessarily, but the interaction
of a group of adult strangers who must quickly
form a community with a given purpose in a
particular time and location. I wanted to see if Ned
could become a viable and contributing member of
that community.

He did, I think. Ned is naturally inquisitive
and outgoing. With few exceptions our fellow
passengers were more than friendly, showing a
genuine interest in him. But they took their cue
from the staff. Neither Ned's gregarious nature
nor the other guests' kindness would have mattered were it not for the splendid and indeed
moving performance by the Endeavour crew. In
the midst of complex other duties, they took the
time to talk to him, listen to him, and teach him.
They encouraged Ned to go on adventures he
would otherwise not have considered, and stood
back and waited patiently on those occasions
when he needed to find his own way. In both
cases the experience was invaluable for Ned at
this time in his life.

This staff is obviously very well trained in the
care of passenger/guests. But without prior warning they went beyond their normal efforts to make
a young man feel, not just welcome, but an equal
part of a disparate group. They learned what he

could do, and then helped him to do more—they showed him respect, which might seem commonplace but is in fact rare in the world of the developmentally disabled.

I would pass on my appreciation to every staff member on board—expedition, hotel and ship's crew—but I'd like to particularly thank Expedition Leader Tom Ritchie, Historian Tom Heffernan, Physician Gail Wagner, and our principal two waiters, Chito and Dennis. Ned and I will never forget their kindness, compassion, and generosity of spirit.

Sunday, July 7, 2002, 5:00 p.m.

After being back home for just a week, Ned has reverted quickly and easily to his regular summer routine. He messes about in his room for a few hours, playing with action figures and listening to music. Then he comes downstairs any time between 9:00 and noon for that appalling breakfast of wieners, white toast, milk, and dry Cheerios. It's surprising how quickly I forgot the overpowering stench of two microwaved wieners first thing in the morning, and how fast it came flooding back.

Cathy and/or I and Ned try to do something in the afternoon, but if nothing's planned, he can amuse himself for hours. He's spent a lot of time looking at the official video of the cruise, which includes his piano concert and shots of us walking around the abbey at Iona. He tells me what he misses most from the Endeavour is the cocktail hour. Ned had never been to a cocktail hour before the trip, but we hadn't been on board for two days before he discovered the joy of going up to the lounge at 5:00, wrapping his fist around a straight-up frosty Coca Cola, and then spending the next hour discussing this and that with Anders the Bar Man and our fellow passengers. He even had his regular stool at the bar, and others would gladly move from it when they saw him coming. I realized that cocktail hours are ideal social events for Ned. There are people to talk to who usually feel like talking, there's Coca Cola on tap, and often somebody is playing show tunes on the piano. If he ever finds a bar that has little bowls of Chips Ahoy cookies rather than beer nuts, we may never get him home.

After this week back, it was time for his one other big event of the summer: Easter Seals Camp. Ned started going to a five-day session there a long time ago. The camp is in Vaughn, Washington, on Puget Sound, a two-hour drive south and west from Seattle, on the Kitsap peninsula.

For the first few years, Cathy and I worried about this very little boy away from us for almost a week. He seemed so small and defenseless. Most of the other campers were bigger and older, but often less socially and verbally developed than Ned. We were concerned for his safety, but also worried that the young staff wouldn't pay much attention to him. Many of their other charges needed help feeding and dressing themselves, and that doesn't leave much time or energy for the kid who wants to talk about Northwest history.

Even with these concerns, we thought it was important for Ned to have some kind of camp experience, for the same reasons it's good for any child to get away from home, be a little more independent in a controlled environment, try new things, and interact with his peers. I know the potential advantages a summer camp offers because I experienced them myself, starting in 1961 when I was fourteen. That was too old to begin going to a kid's camp, or so I thought at the time. Fortunately, where I went was the Henderson Camps, one of the best children's camps in America at the time, and certainly located on the best kid's summer camp site in America: four hundred and sixty acres on the southeast corner of Lopez Island in the San Juans. The Henderson camps, called San Juan for Boys and North Star for Girls, had a lot of waterfront, all the basic camp activities, a splendid staff, and tipis to live in. (This property is now one of billionaire Paul Allen's private estates, and how that came to pass is a shameful demonstration of arrogance, ego, and the power of money.)

After being a camper for two years, I worked for the inspiring Frank and Lucille Henderson for the last three years

Ned on board a Washington State ferry, heading for the San Juans (to hunt for ghosts on Orcas Island).

of the camp. They retired in 1966, and the operation was sold to like-minded people. Eventually it became Camp Nor'wester and moved to Johns Island, some fifteen miles to the north. Ira first went as a Nor'wester camper when he was nine, and was for several years a staff member. He's still involved with the camp, and quite a few of his former Nor'wester colleagues have remained good friends. I think Ira would agree with me that it's been a very important and beneficial part of his life, just as it was for me.

In the six years I was associated with the Hendersons and now the decades I've paid attention to Nor'wester through Ira, I've never seen a kid with developmental disabilities in the camp population. I don't blame anyone for that. First under the Hendersons, and now as Nor'wester, the camp just isn't set up for the intense monitoring some kids need. But Ned is not one of the kids who needs all that attention. If the Hendersons were still there and running the place, I would have gone to them long ago and tried to make some arrangement for Ned to attend for at least part of the four-week session. That might have required my going back to camp with him, just to be nearby in case he needed help, or hiring somebody else to be his helper in the unit. It would have been worth it to me, and I think worth it to the camp as well. Just as Ned's presence on the Endeavour was a positive learning experience for the wealthy whites who were his shipmates, it certainly couldn't hurt to show a camp-full of privileged young folks, who are used to the Special Ed kids being out of sight and mind, that someone with disabilities can function adequately amongst them. Who knows what the benefits of that would be twenty or thirty years later when they inherited their father's businesses?

That's the magnanimous reason I would have tried to get Ned into "regular" kid's camp. The selfish reason is that I don't want Ned to have just any camp experience, I want him to have my camp experience. I'll admit that part of this is my desire to have it again vicariously as well. Camp was the first place where I wasn't identified with my family, the first place where my success or failure was entirely dependent on me. That's the value of any out-of-family experience for a child. The Hendersons would probably have tried to take him in, but I don't know the current camp directors that well and I accept Ira's opinion that Nor'wester is a less supervised operation than its predecessor. It's probably true that a seventeen-year-old today is more sophisticated and independent than a seventeen-year-old was in 1965, and Nor'wester reflects that increased maturity by allowing its campers more unsupervised freedom to choose their own camp experience. Properly prepared and with backup systems in place, Ned could have handled the Henderson Camps, but maybe not Camp Nor'wester, although I will always wonder, and feel a little guilty that I didn't try harder to get him in. There are other regular kid's camps in the area that might have worked, too, but I was spoiled a long time ago by the San Juan island operation, so none of the others was really an option. The only option was Easter Seals Camp.

Our initial fear that Ned's ability to function would ironically be a disadvantage at Easter Seals camp was mostly groundless, because the staff so much wanted to be around Ned when time and duties permitted. After a few hours with a group of high maintenance campers, we got a sense that Ned was the camp equivalent of the Algonquin Round Table for these young college types. For years when I picked him up, it seemed like every staff member in the place knew him, liked him a lot, and told me jokes he had told them. Ned was clearly the Relief Camper for the staff, the kid you got to play with after working with the others.

This morning, driving him down to camp again, he didn't seem that eager to go. I assumed it was because he hadn't had enough time at home after getting back from the cruise. Plus the sky was gray and the weather drizzly, which is not a good omen for the pending summer camp experience. The farther south we drove, the wetter and nastier it got.

The worst part of camp in past years has always been the check-in process, because it seems endless. Many campers have medicines that have to be carefully logged, with precise dosages recorded so the staff can dispense the right meds at the right time. Photo IDs are taken, blood pressure checked. It can take hours to get through the whole group. It certainly did this morning, and they were especially excruciating hours for me.

The room was full of people with disabilities, almost all adults, and their parents. I'd seen it before a dozen times, but this time it was impossible for me not to compare the assembly with the people on the Endeavour. One of Ned's fellow campers this year, a man in his thirties who wears a red crash helmet to protect his head during seizures, spent the entire check-in period curled up in a fetal position on the floor. A young woman in a wheelchair drooled continually onto a soaking wet sweatshirt, looking around desperately for…what? The first person I saw in the room was a black man about Ned's age, continually moaning while a grandfather-type tried to feed him some brownish gray substance which could only be called gruel. It seemed like half of Ned's fellow campers this year are nonverbal and only vaguely aware of their surroundings.

These are the people Ned is expected to spend the rest of his life with: not the people on the boat, not Tom, not Krystal, not Anders the Barman, and not the Nor'wester kids either. The difference between this group and those other groups was so painfully obvious to me, and so depressing, that I couldn't

help thinking Ned noticed as well. I half expected him to run
back out the door shouting, "Been here, done this, never going
to do this again." He didn't try to escape, but he was certainly
upset about something. He balked at being photographed, at
having his blood pressure taken, even at the theme for the
week, which is Spaceman stuff. ("I don't care about outer
space," he said loudly and often.)

I'm not proud of having this reaction to a room full of
people with disabilities, but I can't help it. I think I can honestly say that if I were staff at this camp I could happily work
with these childlike adults without any problem. But we want
the best for our kids, and for Ned, this isn't it any more. There
are a few campers who seem to be as intellectually and emotionally functional as he is, and I hope in the next five days he
seeks them out. But I know that's not his style. In terms of
associates, he's always been happy to play the cards he's dealt,
finding whatever's useful in his classmates and going with it.
Or he retreats completely into himself. And the thing that bothers me the most is something I've noticed over the years, and
I've just had eleven days at sea to prove it again. His own intellectual and even physical abilities rise or fall depending on
the crowd around him.

We finally escaped check-in and were escorted by a nice
young English staff member named Corrina to Ned's A-frame
cabin. His bunk is wedged into the back of a dim room where
he will live with seven other campers and four staff members.
In the bed next to his is a man in a wheelchair named Geoff.
Like many adults with developmental disabilities I've met,
including my own son, he wanted to know everybody's name
and everything about them immediately. He talked a lot and
kept sticking his hand out to shake. Geoff has a very deep,
very loud voice, and paid much more attention to Cathy and
me than he did to Ned. Ned returned the favor by ignoring
him completely. He asked us for cookies and Cheerios. He knew
that he wouldn't be having either for the next five days, and
let that be the thing that upset him. With Geoff booming away
on the next bed, I quietly gave Ned the pep talk about having
a good time, obeying the counselors, and trying to make new

friends. I told him that when I pick him up next Friday, I'd bring along a fresh bag of Chips Ahoys. He smiled for the first time in hours.

Then we left him alone in that gloomy, noisy, uncomfortable room, and drove home. We've been doing this for years, but leaving this time was the worst, harder even than the first time, when he seemed so small and defenseless and lost. I think Ned knows now that there's another life out there. Whether he realizes that life may be unavailable to him most of the time, I don't know.

Driving home, Cathy said that one of the things that worries her most about Ned's adult life is the possible absence of friends he sees regularly. She wants to start setting up regular visits and activities with those friends, and find others. That makes sense and is probably something we should have been more actively pursuing for some time. Probably the only way to get Ned in with his functional peers and superiors is to set up gatherings and events ourselves.

One such event may be bowling, although it's become a cliché for groups of adults with developmental disabilities and so I automatically shy away from it. On previous bowling occasions, Ned never seemed to enjoy it that much. His actual bowling was perfunctory. What he really seemed to enjoy was sitting around talking with people between turns. Shades of the cocktail hour, the non-athletic activity bowling most resembles. But Cathy tells me that Ned recently proclaimed bowling to be his favorite sport, "because," he says, "you don't have to run around outside and get sweaty"—exactly the reason I took bowling at the University of Washington years ago.

Parents of kids with developmental disabilities rarely make "chip off the old block" remarks. We only want to see ourselves reflected in the admirable things in our children. But Ned is a lot like me, and I shouldn't be reluctant to say so. Nor should I be reluctant to say that there are a lot of ways where I could benefit from being more like him.

Cathy and I talked about something else on the drive home, a time that has finally come. Before he goes out into the world on his own, Ned must know or at least acknowledge that the world is going to make presumptions about him.

We finally have to tell him that he has a medical condition that will affect how he lives his life and how other people might let him live it.

Does he know already? It's hard to tell. The other day when we were walking along a city street, Ned dropped some money in a "Benefit the Disabled" collection plate. He told me that he always does that because he has some friends who are disabled, and then mentioned everybody he knows who is in a wheelchair. So, perhaps for him disability is exclusively physical, not intellectual. Have we waited too long to tell him there's another kind of disability and he's got it? Possibly. I dread the conversation, but it must take place, and we decided on the drive to do it right after he gets back from camp.

When we got home a few hours ago, there was a phone message for Ned from his old friend Heidi. She wanted him to call her as soon as he could. A classmate, one of the ones in a wheelchair, has died at the age of twenty. "Respiratory failure," Heidi said carefully on the answering machine. She was obviously in tears. Cathy called Heidi to tell her that Ned's at camp, so we'll have him call her back in a week when he gets home. It was a fitting end to the day.

Thursday, July 11, 2002

Pick-up day at Easter Seals camp. Although Cathy and I have always tried to take him down to camp together, for the past few years I've gone alone to pick him up. So it was this morning. I got there two hours before I was supposed to because I wanted to get Ned out of that place and I assumed he'd want to go as soon as he could. The camp seemed deserted when I arrived. No counselors or campers were anywhere to be seen. I walked down the hill and sat in the sun on a bench in front of Ned's cabin. Farther down the hill in the meeting hall I could hear a gathering going on, the final camp assembly probably taking place at that moment in a thousand different kids' camps across the country. And as at all those other camps, this one was the time to give out awards. I could just make out a name being called, and then a description of the achievement, and then great applause and cheering.

I knew from long experience that every single camper was going to be commended for something, and that can take a while. Finally the announcements and applause stopped, and there was a pause. Very faintly I heard a guitar playing and a soft voice singing. It was Ned. I couldn't tell what he was singing, but I knew he was all right and had survived the week. Twenty minutes later the doors banged open, and campers came streaming up the hill with ribbons and medals around their necks. Ned was one of the last to leave the building, carrying his guitar and walking with the staff, not any of his fellow campers. He was happy to see me, and happy to go. Once again the staff told me what a wonderful guy he'd been, after they got over a dispute about the cuisine. "Even the Aran Islands have burgers," he had informed them, with disdain.

As we drove away, I asked him what song he'd chosen to sing for the last gathering. "A song I wrote," he said offhand, but did not offer to sing it for me, because he didn't write it for me. He fell asleep very soundly not long into the drive, but roused enthusiastically when I suggested we might stop for a burger.

He's asleep in his own bed now. He told his mom he had a good time. When asked about any new friends he made, he named five people. They are all staff members.

July 17, 2002, Midnight

When I was six years old, one of our cats, a shy little Siamese named Tootoo, gave birth to seven kittens. For the blessed event my mother had prepared a nice bed for Tootoo in a low drawer of a bedroom dresser. But of course, cats are nothing if not perversely independent, so the miracle of life-times-seven occurred in my bed, between my knees, at three o'clock in the morning. I got up and went down the hall to get Mom. She assured me Tootoo's choice of maternity ward was not a problem, because I could just sleep on the floor until the young mother decided to move her kits elsewhere. I gladly sacrificed my bed and slept on a pad for a week, often waking up to watch the newborns for a while. Then at another three a.m. moment of inspiration, Tootoo picked up each tiny child by the scruff of its neck and jumped down onto first me and then the floor. She moved them one by one to a nest she had prepared in my closet.

We found homes for all the kittens, except one that stayed with us and became my constant companion. His name was Timothy Anne, because for a while we weren't sure of his gender and we needed a name. Timothy Anne died at the age of twenty-four. My mom took care of her cats.

She was even inspired to write about them, including a poem published in *Cats Magazine* in the mid-1950s:

> The dog I'm sure is man's best friend.
> His qualities are without end.
> He's patient, true, responsive, kind,
> His master's always on his mind.
> But as his mistress, I declare,
> With all his virtues, fine and rare,
> This paragon cannot combat
> The bathroom habits of a cat.

For this bit of, uh, doggerel, Mom was paid five dollars and received a year's free subscription to *Cats*. Since the day of the poem's publication, I have described my mother as a professional poet; that is, somebody who is paid for her poesy. And if she sold only one of her works of art in her lifetime, that's still enough to qualify. During his lifetime, Van Gogh only sold one of his works as well. So there.

Even if my mother hadn't been devoted to cats and my father to dogs, we would have had animals around the place. My parents believed it was good for kids to grow up with pets, and not pets like goldfish you just flush down the toilet when they pass on, but pets whose lives are important to the family. We had pets that could be petted. My parents thought nothing but good can come from raising a child to respect all creatures (okay, except insects) and care about the welfare of something else, even if it's small, down on all fours, and incapable of giving you anything but affection—and with a lot of cats, not much of that.

I agreed then and I certainly agree now. Even if I weren't my mother's son and a devoted cat person, I'd have had cats for Ned and Ira. And I think they are better people for it. Ned, for instance, first learned the nature of grief when his most beloved cat Peg died many years ago. Peg was the most irritating cat I have ever owned, but Ned loved her dearly, and in her own demented way Peg reciprocated. When she died after getting into some kind of poison in the neighborhood, he mourned her loss for years, and he still talks about her. He still talks *to* her.

When I did the documentary series for PBS about death a decade ago, I discovered that for many Americans the first death that had a real emotional impact on their lives was not the passing of a beloved grandparent or the loss of a friend. It was the death of Bambi's mother. This especially applies to a lot of us aging baby boomers. Major characters don't die in Disney movies, or if they die they are resurrected. Snow White, Sleeping Beauty, Pinocchio, Ariel, and other dead Disney folks all come back from the grave, sometimes literally. Death and resurrection are generally very common in most kid movies. *ET*, *Star Wars*, and *Wizard of Oz* all feature a faux death and real return. But in 1942, Walt's ominous, unseen hunters killed off Bambi's mom for good. It was a terrifying and unforgettable moment for hundreds of thousands of tots. It must have been even worse for the first kids who experienced it back then. Many of their fathers, siblings, and friends had just left for a war, or were preparing to go.

Peg was the equivalent of Bambi's mother for Ned, and it was a valuable learning experience for him. It was his first opportunity to begin to understand that nothing lasts forever.

For the last six years, our animal family members have been Lassie, a mostly Australian shepherd who's now about fourteen and beginning to show it, Max, a twenty-one pound black-and-white cat with affection issues, and Harley, a longish-haired black-and-white cat who is physically disabled in an interesting way. Our vet surmises that before he was born, Harley broke his right rear leg in the womb. The leg healed itself pre-natally as best it could, but now when Harley sits he must stick that leg out straight, or hang it down over the edge of a table or counter. When he lies on the floor on his belly, he sticks both hind legs out straight behind him, like he's Rocky the Flying Squirrel, about to take off and swoop around the room. The odd leg means he can't run quite as fast or jump quite as high as a non-physically challenged cat, so he's learned to adjust by being much more cautious around strangers. That must be hard on him emotionally, because Harley is by nature a very affectionate cat. Having to shun potential admirers for reasons of security is a sacrifice he makes for his condition.

I'm going into all this because Lassie, Max, and Harley are a big part of Ned's life. I peeked into his room half an hour ago and Max was sleeping with him on his bed. Max spends a lot of time in there when Ned isn't around, but occasionally he'll stay at bedtime and depart a few hours later.

I don't want to make too big a deal out of the following theory, because it's almost too precious for words and if I was reading it in somebody else's journal my bullpucky bell would start clanging. Nevertheless, I think Max, Harley, and Ned are kindred spirits in a way. Harley has a physical disability for which he's learned to adjust, and Max is, well, Max is kind of autistic.

I believe he likes us all very much. Whenever I'm puttering around the house, I can almost always count on Max following me and settling nearby, even if he's been recently fed. (He is at this moment lying on the floor five feet behind my chair, having come down from Ned's room a few minutes ago.) He will do the same thing with Ned and Cathy if I'm not around. This desire for proximity is one of the few ways he shows his devotion. Max's affection issues are simply that, like many people with autism, he doesn't know how to show affection. He has been our cat for a decade, and yet never once in that time has he crawled up in any of our laps. If placed in a lap, he will immediately bolt, and you should expect to get hurt if you try to keep him from running away. He has never let any of us pick him up or hold him, although being a very large and now elderly cat, he recently has started to let me to pick him up and put him on the counter by his food. The transfer must be directly from floor to food with no attempt at a mid-flight cuddle. He enjoys being petted, but only on the head and neck, and will invariably scratch or bite the hand that ventures aft of the shoulder blades. A much gentler biting is one of only a few other methods he uses to show you that he's fond of you. Walk by Max and expect to get a little nip on the shin. Or he washes you. Occasionally I've been awakened in the morning by Max diligently washing the top of my head.

For non-cat-lovers, Max's personality is irritating and they can't understand why we have put up with him for so many years. For cat people, Max is an amusing eccentric. But for the family, and I think especially for Ned, Max's inability to show the affection he feels is something more. It is a disability, a feline emotional challenge. A kid who has no trouble showing affection but has intellectual challenges to deal with understands and empathizes with that in ways the rest of us don't fully understand. Physically, I think Ned feels the same way about Harley. The stuck-out leg is certainly a source of amusement. It makes Harley look like a small, furry tripod. But it is also a disability that makes him special.

Of course, I could just be full of it.

Sunday, July 21, 2002

Week in, week out, the best non-fiction television program in America is *CBS Sunday Morning*, formerly hosted by Charles Kuralt and now under that puckish compère (a little too puckish for me, actually) from CBS radio, Charles Osgood. It begins at a sometimes ungodly hour. My local station often starts the show at 6:00 or 6:30 a.m. so they can run golf or even more despicably Ron Popeil info-mercials at 9:00. But it's worth getting up for.

Sunday Morning is practically the only program left on the commercial networks that regularly features lengthy, thoughtful pieces on the arts. It has well-produced news pieces too, cultural forays of various kinds, splendidly sharp profiles of interesting people, and commentaries and reviews. (God bless you,

John Leonard.) I'm told by a friend who's a photographer at CBS that hot shots in the news division consider *Sunday Morning* the CBS News purgatory, where unwanted stories and unwanted reporters go to barely live. There is no better evidence that the Professionally Crass have taken over television news. But I'm biased. While the rest of the family sleeps, I've been getting up for years to watch *Sunday Morning*, and have almost without exception found something on the show to make the early rising worth it.

This past Friday Alan Lomax died, so today *Sunday Morning* reran an old Kuralt story about Lomax and his contribution to American culture, which was massive and unparalleled. In 1932 he joined his father, John, on a legendary trip of musical acquisition. They traveled for four months and sixteen thousand miles throughout the South, recording mostly black singers on an early, crude machine. Huddie Ledbetter was discovered during that journey, as well as a lot of other people who would have been forgotten and their work lost had it not been for the Lomaxes. Alan Lomax didn't sing the Blues, but he is as responsible for the survival of authentic American Blues music as any other person alive or dead. And he didn't stop with the Blues and American folk music. In 1938 he was recording jazz and rediscovering Jelly Roll Morton. He worked practically until the day he died, so that in every field of real music performed by real people—in America and England—you will find that Alan Lomax was there first, respecting the people, respecting their art, and saving it in any way he could. He was one of the greatest Americans of the twentieth century.

As anyone can tell from the above, Lomax is a hero of mine. He is also a hero of Ned's, and not because I led him there. He found Lomax all by himself from a meticulous reading of his songbook collection. In his American folk music books, he started noticing Alan Lomax's name over and over again. Ned read a brief biography of the man, and from that time on he's been aware of this traveler who dedicated his life to music other people had forgotten. Often when we drive in the car, we listen to a CD the Library of Congress issued a decade ago of some of Lomax's field recordings, including Sonny Terry and Brownie Magee,

Woody Guthrie, Leadbelly, the Carter Family, and a lot of other wonderful people from the 1930s and 1940s.

Right after they teased the Lomax piece at the start of *Sunday Morning* today, I went upstairs to see if Ned wanted to watch with me. He was already awake, sitting on his bed with his headphones on, listening to music, and quietly singing along. He came down quickly and we watched the story together. I felt very proud. How many kids his age, disabled or not, have the slightest idea who Alan Lomax was and what he meant to American culture?

When you ask Ned what he really wants to be, he often answers that he already is a songwriter. We usually smile pleasantly at that answer and change the subject. More than once I've told him that there are thousands and thousands of songwriters in this world, and at best only five hundred of them who are making a living from their craft at any given time. But watching the Lomax piece with him, I had a twinge of guilt about dismissing his dream so cavalierly. On that first trip the Lomaxes took to the South they found and recorded men in prisons, including Ledbetter. They sought out men and women who were practically slaves, trying to eke a living out of nasty little parcels of land they didn't even own. In other words, they recorded many people who were just as disabled by their circumstances as Ned is by his. And over the years, some of those people became household names for millions of us because of their art.

Given the right circumstances, perhaps Ned could be a songwriter. And he's correct about being one now. He is especially a lyricist, forever writing simple, straightforward poems like his paean to girls. Some of these works he shows us, but there are hundreds more he's keeping to himself, buried in that mound of white papers up in his room. He needs a composer to work with, and more guitar lessons so he can start developing melodies as well. He needs less negativity from me. And he needs an Alan Lomax.

Saturday, August 10, 2002

Public school teachers in special education seem to break down into fairly obvious categories. I may be wrong, but I assume that most of those teachers who pick Special Ed do so because they really care about helping kids with disabilities. The Special Ed teacher has a calling that's a bit more than the one heard by other prospective teachers. Perhaps that's why there's a critical national shortage of qualified Special Ed teachers. These especially motivated people are usually young, eager, and quite splendid. Walk into their classrooms and there's always a lot going on, and they are right at the center of it. There's a kid in the teacher's lap, a book is being read, and art's going on in the corners.

I know it's rewarding, but I also know it is physically and emotionally draining, far beyond what most teachers in good schools endure. That leads to the second kind of Special Ed teacher, the one who's burned out and either doesn't admit it or isn't allowed to acknowledge the obvious by the school administration. They are required by law to have a Special Education program and you're it, honey, whether or not you want to be any more.

Exhausted teachers who still run Special Education classrooms are usually quite sad. They know what they should be doing and simply can't summon up the energy to do it any more. They're going through the motions and feel guilty about it.

At Hamilton Middle School, Ned had a teacher named Darol Reynolds who I thought was one of the burnt out ones. He'd been in Special Ed for more than twenty-five years when Ned got him, so I wasn't really surprised when homework started showing up that seemed to reflect a teacher who was just phoning it in while counting the days until his retirement. There were tedious worksheets that had to be filled out daily, in Math, English, and Science. Ned did one or two every night. He'd rarely seen a real school worksheet before, and a lot of the math was beyond him, so we helped in the beginning. But as the school year went on, Ned was more and more able to do the worksheets himself without us. And every worksheet came back graded and corrected. If something was wrong, this guy Reynolds said so. He obviously was not a person who thought that just because a student has Down syndrome, everything he or she does should be considered a wonderful, marvelous achievement. Darol Reynolds gave Ned some Ds and told him curtly to try harder. He didn't tell him while he was giving him a great big hug, either. In person, Darol was pleasant and professional, but he certainly didn't show much interest in being Ned's or any other student's good buddy. I suspect no child ever crawled into Darol Reynolds's lap.

I was wrong about Darol Reynolds. There's a third kind of Special Education teacher, and he's it. It's the kind who thinks touchy-feely is swell but eventually a child has to turn into a student, and be given specific tasks to do that involve learning. It doesn't make any difference whether that child has disabilities or not. And Darol Reynolds knows that middle school is the time a student has to get to work.

Darol retired last June after teaching Special Education for thirty years and never burning out—a truly remarkable achievement. This afternoon he hosted his own retirement party at his home north of Seattle, and we went. All of his former students and their parents were invited. *Seattle Times* staff reporter John Wolfson covered the event, and eventually wrote a long piece for the Sunday paper of August 25. It nicely shows how right Darol Reynolds has been for thirty years in the ways he's taught Special Education teenagers. An excerpt:

Special Redefined

We're used to stories like this: the teacher so beloved, who touched so many. But when a half-dozen parents in a single afternoon swear a teacher changed their child's life, or insist that he was one of the best things that ever happened, or acknowledge that he helped them better understand their own child's disability, it tends to leave the impression that something quite special was going on in Darol Reynolds's classroom all these years.

For 30 years, the classroom was where Darol Reynolds belonged. At a time when the growing demands of special education have driven many dedicated teachers from the field, Reynolds, 60, is something of a rarity....

He demanded work and effort and discipline from his sixth-, seventh-, and eighth graders, many of whom had rarely been challenged academically. Today, one of his former students works for the Postal Service, others volunteer at places like the Boys and Girls Club, and some have pursued the love of education he instilled and continue to study in adult programs.

When the school year ended in June—when his oldest former student was 44 and his youngest 11—so did Darol Reynolds's career....

As the retirement party begins, Emily Pope walks through the Reynoldses' living room, carrying a book and a card.

"Oh, is that what you're reading?" asks Heidi Burns.

"No, it's for Mr. Reynolds," Emily responds.

It's a natural mistake for Heidi, 19, who reads ravenously, especially anything by Stephen King, and assumes everyone shares her passion. But it was not so long ago that reading was more a source of intimidation than passion for Heidi. When she entered Reynolds's class as a sixth grader in 1994, she read only "little kid's books." So her mother, Mary, was more than surprised when Heidi brought home an adaptive version of "Moby Dick," written on a sixth grade level.

"I didn't think that Heidi was capable of being in his class," Mary says. Heidi had difficulty keeping up and Mary finally met with Reynolds to tell him that her daughter would be

*better off in another, less rigorous class. The
teacher disagreed. He demanded more. Heidi
could succeed, he insisted, if she worked at it.
Mary remained skeptical but agreed to keep
Heidi in the class.*

*When Heidi complained that the reading was
tough, Reynolds told her to work harder. "I had
problems following along," she recalls.
"Reynolds's response: "You need to follow
along." Eventually, with a sustained effort that
surprised both her mother and herself, she did.*

*"It was our first experience with that," Mary
says, "with someone pushing her. It was really a
breakthrough for her. It was one of the best
things that ever happened to her."*

The party at Darol's house was a refreshingly adult event, especially compared to the check-in at Easter Seals Camp a few days ago. People who are automatically written off by some parts of society sat around eating hot dogs and hamburgers that Darol had barbecued, drinking lemonade, and talking about their jobs, their apartments, and the world in general, just like the adults they now are. Darol was everybody's pal, just as he's always been, in his own way.

Monday, August 19, 2002, 9:00 p.m.

The Grand Canyon

A friend invited us to his wedding, and he was friend enough that we decided to accept, even though the wedding was to be held in Arizona in the middle of August. Why anyone sane would plan to do anything in Arizona in mid-August except leave for somewhere else is beyond me, especially a guy who actually lives in Arizona and knows what it's like. Seattleites instinctively avoid planning or attending mid-August events in the Northwest because it's too hot. Sometimes it gets as high as 80°—so hot you can melt an ice cube on the hood of your car in just a few hours. Although cooking a fried egg takes a lot longer.

When we landed in Phoenix three days ago it was 109 degrees. But don't worry, our friend had said, the wedding is in Sedona, two hours north of Phoenix. It's a lovely place and a lot cooler, he assured us.

Sedona, Arizona, is indeed a lovely place, with towering red mesas and massive, breathtaking rock formations. But a lot cooler? When you were born and raised to believe 80 degrees is sweltering and hellish, there isn't a lot of difference between 109 degrees in Phoenix and 92 degrees in Sedona. For a native Western Washingtonian, it's the difference between accidentally slapping your hand down on a burner that's 379 degrees and one that's 362 degrees. You suffer just about the same.

That's enough about the heat, which was the only irritating part of an otherwise splendid affair, as well as the beginning of an interesting journey. Each summer, Ned and Cathy have gone by themselves on a car trip to a national park. It all began with a memorable visit to Yellowstone in 1995. Cathy's mother's

Glacier Point, Yosemite National Park, 1996.

family is from Cody, Wyoming, east of the park, and that year she and Ned arrived just a few days after her Grandma Mildred died. What for other people might have put a damper on the whole journey was in fact a great piece of luck for Ned. He got to go to Yellowstone, but he also got to attend the funeral of a family member he didn't really know that well, so there was no real feeling of sadness or loss. A trip, a death, a family connection, a whole new crowd of people to chat up—no downside in there for Ned. To this day, his recollections of that journey start with the funeral and only incidentally mention Yellowstone. Since then, Cathy and Ned have visited Crater Lake, Yosemite, Mt. Rushmore, Mount St. Helens (of course) and a few other places.

There are both logistical and parental reasons I don't go along. Since it began in 1986, Cathy has been the Director of Education of the Seattle International Children's Festival, a week-long gathering in May that brings often wonderful performing companies to the stages of the Seattle Center. At any given festival, there are from ten to twenty acts, including dancers, singers, theater companies, clowns, and performance artists. I've always thought one of the reasons Ned is so artistically motivated is as a result of his almost lifelong exposure to the people who have appeared at the Festival.

For the first five days, the visiting Festival companies do shows for approximately fifty thousand school kids, bused in from all over the western half of the state. Cathy's in charge of practically everything to do with those schools and students except actually tearing their tickets in half. She starts hustling (she would call it advising) teachers in September as to which shows they should see, she makes the sale, she registers and ships the tickets, she gets the payment, and in her free time, she writes excellent, comprehensive study guides for every act at the Festival.

During the actual Festival week, Cathy leaves at dawn and comes home exhausted long after dark. In other words, from September through May she has one of those six-days-a-week, ten-hours-a-day part-time jobs in the arts. So for most of the year, and especially since 1990 when I became self-employed and only punched my own clock, I've spent more time with Ned than she has. I'm usually the one who meets him at home after school, spends Saturday and/or Sunday with him, and takes him to the various places he needs to go. Cathy and Ned still have time together, but it is usually in the evening. The exception is during July and August, when Festival work is over for the year and she is home. That's what led to the summer national park trips, and why they do them without me. Ned and Cathy's summer jaunts give them valuable time alone together, and give me time to work more intensely on various projects. I also get a respite from the Ned-caring I do the rest of the year.

By the time their trips started, Ira was already firmly established at summer camp in the San Juan Islands. So he doesn't go on the trips either, not that he would even if he were home. Spending a week in a small car with his brother wouldn't appeal to him at all.

I suppose I should say something here about Ira and Ned's relationship, except that there isn't much to say. Ira is almost exactly three years older than his brother. In most ways they are completely different types. Where Ned is outgoing, talkative, and a ham like his father, Ira is quiet and more reserved, like his mother, with a small circle of loyal friends. Ira would no more sing in a choir, act in the theater, or publicly play a musical instrument than he would jump off a bridge into crocodile-infested waters. Many years ago, our one attempt to get him to take piano lessons was evil, mean, brutish, and short. He is artistic, but his artistic efforts have for a long time centered on drawing, painting, and now carving in the Northwest Indian tradition. As a kid, he spent a lot of time doing excellent drawings of monsters, and he greatly enjoyed the cartooning classes he took. He is an excellent artist, but I have never heard him sing a note.

Physically, where Ned is quite small—about five foot two— Ira is very large, well over six feet tall. He easily fills a doorway, and has recently been working hard to take off weight, now that he's done with college football. Cathy has always said he's very handsome, and though I didn't disagree with her, I didn't see him that way. But as he's gotten closer to his fighting weight, I've noticed that when he walks into a room the women present clearly take notice and perk up a bit.

The major difference between Ned and Ira is that Ira is very smart, a National Merit finalist who took every science class his high school offered and maxed them all. We were told a long time ago that he's "gifted," and never let that go to our, or his, head. At the same time, we realized it would be shameful to waste such a gift, so we sought the best possible educational opportunities for him. A few years after Ned was born, a counselor type said to us one day, "It's interesting how many retarded kids have gifted siblings, far above the law of averages. It's one of God's little jokes."

Last year Ira graduated from Carleton College in Northfield, Minnesota, one of the best small liberal arts institutions in America. He went there originally to study Biology, although we didn't think that would last, and it didn't, once he ran into all those doctors-in-waiting. His degree is in Sociology/Anthropology, and he now works as the head of Internet marketing for my brother's advertising agency. This isn't just a nephew job. Ira's good at what he does and my brother needs him.

Given their differences, it has always been unlikely that Ned and Ira would become best pals. They were never going to be the kinds of brothers who sit around in each other's bedrooms chewing the fat. Ira is almost always nice to Ned, although he hasn't developed the thick skin his parents have for those occasions when Ned does something eccentric in public. Ira is easily embarrassed. He will take Ned to the movies or on an occasional outing, but usually only if asked. Even when they lived in the same house, they lived completely different lives. The only times I've ever seen Ira act like a traditional big brother is when someone outside the family is bothering Ned. In Ned's freshman year of high school, a senior in Room 104 named Christopher bullied him almost daily. For weeks when he got home from school, the first thing we heard about was Christopher's latest outrage. Ira, then a very large offensive lineman, eagerly volunteered to go up to Ned's school, find Christopher, and put the fear of God and Ira in him.

I wish I could say they were close. I wish I could say that Ira liked being around Ned as much as Ned would like to be around Ira. But it's naïve to expect that, and it would certainly be unfair to Ira to blame him for the fact that it hasn't happened. In one way, I'm grateful that Ira doesn't resent Ned any more than the occasional twinges I've seen during the past twenty years. We tried very hard to give Ira as much attention as Ned, but it was a different kind of attention, less

Ira and Ned at the family farm in central Washington, swimming in the Teanaway River, 1988.

focused, less intense. Fortunately, I think Ira has always been smart enough to realize that's just the reality of the situation. He doesn't take it personally. Although his reticence precludes his saying it, I think in his heart Ira knows that Cathy and I love him deeply, and are extremely proud of what he's achieved already. He's become a very fine young man and a pleasure to be around.

Ira's no fool about the future. Cathy and I have worked hard for a long time to make sure Ned becomes a self-supporting, independent adult if at all possible, in part so he'll never be a burden to his brother. But Ira knows that there's only one way Ned won't be a major factor in his life. Ira would have to turn into a complete heel and abandon his brother after we're gone, something he would not do. So if he doesn't want to spend a lot of time with Ned now, he knows he may have no choice when they are the last of the Palmers together.

Meanwhile, back at the Canyon, it's one of the national parks Ned and Cathy had always planned to visit some summer. The Grand Canyon happens to be a relatively short drive from

Sedona, so we brought Ned along to the wedding, although he wasn't invited, even after we told our friend he was coming.

For a while I had a problem with Ned's not being asked to attend the ceremony or reception dinner. One of the dangers that goes with being the protector of a child with Down syndrome is that you almost immediately acquire an acute sensitivity to your kid's being slighted for who he is. I claim that I'd be satisfied if Ned is treated just like everybody else, but there are certainly occasions when I want and expect him to be treated better, without my even realizing that's what I'm doing.

That was certainly the case here. I thought Ned should be invited because he was in Sedona with nothing else to do, but also because he was "special," and how dare they exclude my special son. In addition, the bride and groom had to know that if Ned didn't come to the service and reception afterwards, they would be forcing us to leave him alone in a strange motel room for quite a few hours.

Which is exactly what happened. Ned stayed happily in our room watching the tube. It was the anniversary of Elvis's death, and to honor that event, the local television station was showing *Loving You*, Big E's semi-autobiographical second film. Cathy and I left Ned with The King, and went off to enjoy ourselves.

The wedding was an intimate affair held in a simple little church with an amazing view of Cathedral Rock, a spectacular red formation somewhere out there in the desert. There weren't any children present except for the ring bearer, a cute little girl who is the bride's cousin. Ned's never even met the bride and groom, and had no business at an adult wedding. And the newlyweds had much more important things to deal with than what I did with my kid during their festivities. I was wrong to feel any kind of resentment about Ned's not being involved.

The next morning we drove northwest to the Grand Canyon, stopping over in Williams, Arizona. There is absolutely nothing to recommend visiting Williams, Arizona, and the Williams-ites seem to know it. They are trying to survive on the historical fact that their main street was once a couple of miles of fabled Route 66. Good luck.

I have to admit to a certain prejudice against Williams after spending a day there. Each evening a group of fake cowboys stages a gun battle on Main Street, in front of all the Route 66 souvenir shops. This hokey little drama is well attended by tourists, because what else is there to do in Williams, Arizona, on a weekday evening except drain the tanks in the camper? Cathy, Ned, and I walked down from the motel to watch, but five minutes before the gunfight was to begin, a cowboy fired off a shot to attract everyone's attention. That was all Ned needed. He's always hated loud noises, and this pistol was *loud*. Ned and his mother headed back for the motel before the real shootin' began, and I stayed to watch, having a lifelong (some would say perverse) interest in hokey little dramas.

After an initial flurry of shots, the cowboys shouted at each other for a few minutes. Most of the "dialogue" was based on one cowboy calling another cowboy an idiot and a third responding that they were both morons. I left when a tall thin cowpoke called a hairy old cow-man a "re-tard," to the amusement of the crowd. The cowpokes were clearly proud that they were able to adlib such biting wit.

I was glad Ned had already gone, and sorry the cowboys weren't using real bullets on each other. Once again I found it interesting that people who wouldn't consider using racial or ethnic slurs or mocking people with physical disabilities see nothing wrong in being offensive about intellectual disabilities. It's not just hick amateur actors in small towns, either. Big time comedians, politicians, and movie and television writers do it all the time. Someday I should write *The Complete Idiot's Guide to Intellectual Bigotry*, except those for whom the book was intended wouldn't get the joke.

We left Williams early this morning and have been here at The Grand Gully for about nine hours now. I'd visited before, nineteen years ago, on a movie junket for *National Lampoon's Vacation*, where Chevy Chase told me for the third time in three meetings that I looked just like his old prep school chum, the actor and playwright Wally Shawn. Those who know what Wally Shawn looks like will see that Mr. Chase was not exactly paying me a compliment. Which is why the third time he did it I told him, "And you remind me of an aging golden retriever."

What I remember from that first visit to the Big Ditch is that unless you're a geologist, anthropologist, artist, Havasupai Indian, or tour bus driver, the Grand Canyon ceases to be all that compelling after a few hours. You stare in awe at its, well, grandness, the canyon-ness of it all, how big and colorful the thing is. ("And you're only seeing a very small part of it!" — Park Ranger, a hundred times a day.) But after a while, if you don't plan to hike down or ride a donkey or run the Colorado rapids, a little voice in your head says, "Is that all it does?" You start wondering if your lodge room has cable television, and eventually you are pleased to discover that it does. Nineteen years ago it didn't even have a television. We were tougher people then, real pioneers in the Great American West.

I feel a little guilty about this reaction to one of the world's most spectacular scenic wonders. I know it must indicate a lack of something in my character. But I prefer to think of it as a natural consequence of Falling-In-It Phobia.

If one goes to the ocean, one can sit happily on the shore and watch it for days, even though All It Does is go out and come in. However, the only way to enjoy the Grand Canyon is to stand at the edge and look across and then down. And not only is that view missing the diverting movements and relaxing sounds of the seashore, but there is always the possibility that you will fall in it, whether because of your own clumsiness, loose dirt, the push of a murderous companion, or the slightest little earthquake.

If you accidentally fall into the sea, you get a little wet, but the Miracle of Evaporation eventually makes everything right again. If you accidentally fall into the Grand Canyon, you get immediately dead after an especially terrifying two or three seconds. Way down there at the bottom, it is your vital organs that are affected by the Miracle of Evaporation. That's why, for my money, Sedona is a more interesting place. Sedona's gorgeous rocks are up, not down. This far too lengthy analysis is brought to you by the fact that there's not enough to do at the Grand Canyon.

I don't think Ned shares my concern about falling into the Canyon. He doesn't approach the edge in the many places where that's possible, but that just seems to be common sense. I would have said he doesn't have a fear of high places, except for an extremely frustrating experience in Hawaii a few years ago. We were on Maui, visiting Cathy's stepsister Julie, who lives in Hana. Mostly because Ned was in the midst of his fascination with volcanoes, we made the tricky drive up to the top of Haleakala, the Maui volcano that's ten thousand feet above sea level. When we got there, Ned refused to get out of the car. He claimed he was afraid of how high we were. After considerable coaxing, he finally emerged, peered into the spectacular crater, and immediately went back to the car and sat there for an hour while the rest of the family wandered about. In retrospect, I think this nasty little moment of obstinacy had more to do with control than altitude. We had it, and he wanted it. Historically, he has always been very interested in volcanoes, especially Mount St. Helens, the family volcano, which he has visited many times. It was the subject of one of his best poems a few years ago:

> Before the mountain blew there was a valley
>   with a lake.
> Spirit Lake looks like it's touching the mountain.
> When the mountain blew a powerful wind
>   knocked down the trees as it flew by.
> 57 people died and their blood is under the icy
>   brown mud.
> Ever since then the lacing trees still lie.
> And all life has died.
> People sing to remember friends by the way
>   they lost their lives.
> Yet they cry.
> The wild animals return like the birds in the sky.
> They open their wings and they fly.

If it is a character flaw to find the Grand Canyon kind of dull, then Ned and I share it. Late this afternoon we trudged down the path to Hermit's Rest at the far left end of the South Rim, to stand on yet another promontory sticking out into yet another spectacular, multi-colored, striated abyss. Ned kept asking me how much farther it was, in the way he has that implies that no matter how much farther, it's too much farther.

"Had enough of looking into the canyon from promontories, Ned?" I asked him.

"For the rest of my life," he answered immediately.

Ned's facility with phrases I never thought he knew brings me up short sometimes. Once we were watching Ira's high school football team get slaughtered by an opponent. Right after the other team made a touchdown and the score hit 38 to 3, Ned said casually, "This is like watching the carnivores against the herbivores." He didn't overhear it from somebody else in the stands, because there was hardly anybody else there. I certainly don't think he read it anywhere. It just occurred to him, a summation of the game that any sportswriter would be proud to claim. Although his brother found it less than amusing the five or six hundred times I repeated it during the next few years.

Ned and I agreed on the rapidly diminishing attractions of the Grand Canyon. As he gets older, I'm seeing more ways we are alike, and a "like father, like son" moment is oddly satisfying, even when the shared trait isn't necessarily positive. He's like me, and just as I would be of any other son, I'm proud of that. And if I'm doing okay as an adult, maybe he will too.

Thursday, August 22, 2002, 2:00 p.m.

Oak Harbor, Washington

Ned's fascination with death is almost always an interest in the deaths and death accoutrements of people he never met and certainly never knew well. In fact, I think he prefers that. He rarely mentions his grandmother's death last New Year's Eve, or the memorial service he attended for her, and she was the person he knew best who is now gone.

There are exceptions to his exclusive interest in the passing of the unknown. Here in the small, unkempt Fircrest Cemetery in Oak Harbor is one of those exceptions, Ned's Great Aunt Dorothy. She was my father's older sister, and until her passing in 2001, Pop's last surviving sibling. Dorothy had a long, interesting life in Seattle and Los Angeles. One of her high school chums was the actress Frances Farmer, whom she taught to sew. In L.A., she sang in vaudeville under a different name so her parents back home in Seattle wouldn't find out. At age ninety-four she could still describe in detail the night Bing Crosby was in her audience. According to Dorothy, Der Bingle told her she had "nice pipes." Mostly she was a shop girl down there until she married a big, ebullient LA county sheriff named Ed Heddy. From a prior marriage, Ed was the father of Eric Fleming, star of the television show *Rawhide* until Clint Eastwood stole it from him and he made that ill-fated trip to Peru and an early death. By all accounts Dorothy and Ed adored each other, although neither of them had much time for Eric. Dorothy used to describe her movie star stepson as "full of himself."

After Ed died, Aunt Dorothy came back to Washington and eventually married a man who was as unlike Ed Heddy as possible. Grady Hopkins was a quiet, shy, gentlemanly cobbler. That's when we became part of her life again, and she a part of ours. From the day they met Ned, Dorothy and Grady were exceptionally kind to him and interested in his doings. I always suspected that somewhere in his past Grady had a relative or friend with a developmental disability. If so, he never mentioned it. He just obviously liked Ned a lot.

They lived here in Oak Harbor, on Whidbey Island, eighty miles north of Seattle, where Grady had a shoe repair shop and Dorothy worked her nice pipes in the church choir. After Grady died, Dorothy moved into a local nursing home, which she hated. Dorothy always liked her eats, and the home seemed to specialize in tapioca-centric cuisine. So, first with my father and then with Ned, I would drive up and take her out for a good breakfast once a month or so at a joint up the road called Mitzel's. For her, that meant a lot of white toast with strawberry jam, eggs over easy, hash browns, and three or four strips of unappetizing, nearly raw bacon. "I love bacon," she'd tell the same waitress using exactly the same words every single time, "but I don't have the teeth for the hard stuff anymore. If it isn't soft, don't bother bringing it to the table." By then she was this slightly crazy old lady with bright orange hair, nearly blind and still sharp as a tack in her mid-nineties.

Dorothy had been a first-class pisser all of her life. She once accused the nursing home staff of stealing her medications. The institution's administration and her relatives, including us, put it down to the paranoid fantasy of a dotty old woman. More to shut her up than for any other reason, the Oak Harbor police finally installed a hidden camera in her room. They probably saw it as a training exercise. Two nights later that camera recorded a staff member sneaking in early in the morning and stealing medications, just as Dorothy had been saying for months. My aunt was polite enough not to gloat about it, while the nursing home administration acted like it was somehow her fault. Dorothy's experiences in that place are one of the reasons Ned will never be in an institution as long as I can do something about it.

For Dorothy in her last few years, Ned was this voice in the darkness, a barely seen presence who would come and talk to her happily about all his interests and just as happily listen to her stories about the family, about her life, about Ed and Eric and Grady. She was exceedingly generous to him as well. She gave him family pictures, sheet music, recordings by forgotten dance bands of the forties and fifties, and a lovely Martin mandolin. It was still in its original packing, accompanied by the 1964 sales slip from a Los Angeles music shop. She'd never even tried to play it. I don't think she ever took it out of the case once she got home with it decades before. Dorothy was just the kind of person who thought a girl should have a mandolin around, if only to give to her great-grand-nephew when the time was right.

Ned was a pallbearer at her funeral, a job he took very seriously. And he brought something with him that day, a small American flag he'd carefully drawn the night before. He put it on her grave, where I assumed it would end up in the cemetery trashcan within the hour. When he wasn't looking, I pocketed the flag. It's been over my desk at home ever since. If he's noticed it there, he hasn't mentioned it.

Today he brought her flowers, pink carnations he thought she'd like. This is the first time we've visited since the funeral. The stone is up now, the simple marker she ordered before she died to make sure her stone matched Grady's. Some headstones—and I've seen a lot of headstones—tell the story of the deceased's life, but Dorothy's is very simple: Dorothy Palmer Hopkins, 1905-2001.

At this moment, Ned is sitting at her grave next to Grady's. I'm fifty yards away across the brown lawn, because one of the things I've learned about Ned is when he wants to be alone. He's been there for more than half an hour now, and shows no signs of leaving.

I know what he's doing. He's talking to her, just as he always did, telling her about his birthday coming up, about his trip to England, about the songbooks he's gotten recently, and the songs he thinks she'd like.

He can stay as long as he wants. We're not in any rush.

Tuesday, August 27, 2002, 6:00 p.m.

Ned starts school a week from tomorrow. And for the first time in his life, his schooldays will be totally devoted to preparing him for adulthood, learning the skills he'll need to survive independently. As part of this vocational training, he'll have a job of some kind in the community. Right now he's holding out for singer/songwriter, although what's offered is scut work in a hospital, nursing home, or veterinarian's office. When he's not working, we hope he'll be learning about making change and riding buses and keeping a budget. So we decided that it was time for Ned to confront the reason he needs such special instruction. We decided to tell him he has a disability, and try to do it as simply and straightforwardly as we can. As I surreptitiously recorded, this is what was said this afternoon, sitting around the kitchen table:

MOM: Ned, are there any kids in Room 104 who have Down syndrome?

NED: Well, no, but I do know for a fact the only people who are in Room 104 who have disabilities are my friends Lacy, who has cerebral palsy, and Sergei, and he's autistic. And of course Sharon has allergies, and Lily's the only one who's blind. *[This isn't Lily his girlfriend, but a wonderful young woman named Lily Vang.]*

MOM: Isn't Dani in Room 104?

NED: Actually, in a word, yes.

DAD: The girl on your bus.

NED: She used to be on my bus...

MOM: I think Dani has Down syndrome. Do you know what that is?

NED: Not really.

MOM: Well, you know we talked about kids in Room 104 as having different kinds of disabilities, and a lot of times disabilities are a combination of having physical challenges with your body, your body doesn't work the same as other people's...

DAD: Like being blind...

MOM: Or you have cerebral palsy or something like that.

NED: I see. That was one of the reasons I came up with being a teacher, what I meant by being a teacher was not only to help other kids, but to help the kids who have disabilities, you know, work with them, show them how to use the educational stuff, and transfer them to the swimming pool and back...

MOM: Well, I think there are lots of things you could do to help.

NED: And especially getting to the lunchroom...

MOM: There are kids in room 104 who also have other kinds of disabilities besides physical disabilities, that are called developmental disabilities...

NED: Yeah, of course...

MOM: And that has to do with different ways in which you learn, and different challenges that you have in learning, not just academics but also practical skills. How to get along all by yourself in life. Cerebral palsy can be a disability like that—it can be both physical and developmental; in fact, most disabilities have some physical elements and some developmental elements as well. And Down syndrome is a pretty common disability to have.

NED: Yeah, true. The reason why I didn't know anything about the Down syndrome part is because I think that Dani kept that from me as sort of private.

MOM: It doesn't have to be a secret, and in fact it's usually pretty apparent to most people if somebody has Down syndrome because they have certain physical characteristics that indicate that they have Down syndrome. Do you remember the other day when you were telling me about your friend in the choir who was playing around with you and laughing with you about your long tongue and the things you could do with it....

NED: Oh, yeah, that was Miss Kerrigan. One little problem. She's not Down syndrome.

MOM: No, she isn't. And you remember that I said that I knew that she was your friend and she was nice to you but that it didn't seem to me that that was the kind of joking around that was all that appropriate. Ned, do you know that Rob has Down syndrome?

NED: Not really.

MOM: I'm sure he's talked about having Down syndrome....

NED: To tell you the truth, I don't remember him talking to me about that.

MOM: That's probably true. I've just heard him when we used to spend more time over at his house. He would occasionally mention having Down syndrome and various things being hard for him. I think this was when he was learning to read, and it was hard for him, learning to read, because he had Down syndrome.

NED: Oh, yeah, of course...

MOM: You're turning 21 now, and people are concerned about your ability to begin to learn to do things that will help you live independently and have a job and things like that. I think it's very nice that you're looking to help other people, but people are also looking to help you, sweetheart. Do you realize that you have a disability as well?

NED: I find that a little hard to believe.

MOM: Well, you do. You have Down syndrome, something that you were born with.

NED: *(almost whispering)* I didn't actually know that.

MOM: Really?

NED: Though I find that a little hard to believe.

DAD: It's true, though. Just like Rob does. Jack does. Dani, some other people we've met...There are things you have difficulty doing. There are things that everybody has difficulty doing...You need to develop the skills you need to live an adult life. Have a job. Probably live independently, or with some other people, not necessarily always live at home, and those are the kinds of things you're going to be learning at Nathan Hale this year. You're already a graduate, so this is sort of graduate study in Life Skills. The job you do will be one of those things, but I think you'll be doing other things to learn how to live. You already have done some; you learned how to handle money. I think you'll be learning more about how to ride the bus, to get to places you want to go. Things like that.

NED: Oh, yeah. That.

DAD: That okay?

NED: Yeah...

DAD: What we're saying, Ned, is that you're somebody with a disability. Fortunately, your disability isn't physical...

MOM: Primarily...

DAD: Primarily. But your disability has to do with how you learn things. You're very lucky because you talk very well and you have an extremely good memory, and those two things are going to stand you in good stead for the rest of your life. Some people with Down syndrome aren't so lucky. Remember Tom on the cruise? He has a twelve-year-old son with Down syndrome who can't talk. He talks in sign language. So you're very lucky, and of course you worked very hard to be a good reader, and a good guitar player, and to do all kinds of stuff. But there are things that you have trouble doing, and in the next few years you're going to start learning how to do those things at home and at school. Because you want to be independent some day, don't you Ned? More or less? One of the things I couldn't help noticing on our cruise around the British Isles is that you seemed happiest when you were sort of on your own, whether it was sitting in the bar, going out in the Zodiacs with Tom or the other staff, when I wasn't around…You seemed really happiest on our cruise when you were doing things independently and that was just fine with me. Isn't that true?

NED: Well, yeah.

DAD: And so we want to help you, and Tim *[Hilton, his principal teacher]* and the school want to help you, become more independent. There's still some things you can't do, that you need to learn how to do before that can happen.

MOM: You have many skills, Ned; that's undeniable. We're going to have to leave it to Mr. Hilton to figure out the best way to help you learn some independent skills this year, Ned. This is your last year when the school district is responsible for providing an education or a program for you during the daytime. When you were born, Dr. Dassel came to our house and told us about the fact that we had a baby with Down syndrome and that we would have to do a lot of things that we hadn't been expecting to with a new baby. One of the things you do when you have a baby with disabilities is that you register with the State Department of Developmental Disabilities. So that the state can keep an eye on you and make sure that we're doing our best to take care of you. That's why, when you were a very tiny baby, only two weeks old, you started going for lessons at the University of Washington and worked with a physical therapist to help your muscles and…

NED: What I remember of that was meeting my old friend Matt.

MOM: That's right. That's when you first met Matt, who's another fellow who has Down syndrome. You met him in the toddler program at the University of Washington, when I think you guys were two years old. And then when you were three, you started going to what's called Special Education at Seattle Public Schools and remember, that's when you started with Debbie Bush. And you were at Wedgwood for a long time with a whole bunch of different teachers and then you went and spent time at Hamilton Middle School with Mr. Hilton and Mr. Reynolds and then on to high school. But that comes to an end after this year. So we've got to help you learn as much as you can this year, to help with your transition into adult life. And after that, we'll probably figure out some kind of program with a job coach or whatever to help you get a job, start looking around for social activities that you'd like to be involved in, where you'd like to live. None of these things is going to happen immediately. You're going to stay with us for a while, right?

NED: Actually, I prefer staying in this place for as long as I can remember.

DAD: You know Ned, I think some day, maybe sooner than you think, you're going to want to go and maybe live with some guys—two or three friends—and live in your own place. Do your own stuff. I think you're going to want to. I understand that you don't want to now, it seems like a big step, but some day, you may.

MOM: Yes. Just like Ira has moved out on his own...

NED: Uh, I intend to go to the family room for a while.

MOM: All right, sweetie.

NED: *(to himself, leaving the room quickly)* My guardian angels are going to kill me for this....

Cathy and I didn't talk much afterwards about the conversation we had just had. It seemed to go as well as could be expected, but it was still painful, and probably more painful for us than for Ned. We know we're telling him that he'll be challenged for the rest of his life in ways most other people aren't. We're telling him that there are some things he will never be able to do that other people take for granted. But I don't think he realizes that. He didn't refuse to believe us, at least not openly, and after twenty years of ignoring the reality of his situation, that wouldn't have surprised me.

We once consulted with a counselor about Ned, and our principal question was whether we were making a mistake not discussing his disability with him. After talking to us for an hour about Ned and the life he was living, this counselor said we shouldn't be in any rush. "When Ned needs to know, you'll tell him," he said. And so we didn't worry about it. I'm glad we finally had the discussion, although given what he said leaving the room, I'm terrified Ned thinks this is something he's done wrong, something that could have been avoided, something we blame him for. That would indeed be a tragedy.

September 3, 2002

Advice to Future Parents: When planning for children, avoid planting the seed, so to speak, on or about December ninth. If you do conceive then, it will mean your child will be born on or about Labor Day the following September. For years thereafter you'll go through hell trying to organize birthday parties during the last three-day-weekend before the start of school. It is a time when not only you don't want to mess around with your child's birthday, but other kids' parents don't want to either. And it is very difficult to convince your six-year-old that he has been born into a family that doesn't celebrate birthdays for religious reasons. (Read your Bible. After that very first one, Jesus never had a birthday party. He had to make that myrrh last a long time.)

2002 is the last year we Palmers will have to deal with the Labor Day/Birth Day dilemma. Ned turned twenty-one today. His life still has a lot of kid things in it, but as far as the State is concerned, he's a grown man. And as far as his mother and I are concerned, Exchangius, the Roman God of Birthdays, is a State employee. So Ned's next scheduled birthday party is September 3, 2021. It will be one of those ghastly "ha ha you're an old man now" events when he turns forty.

He certainly tried to make today's celebrations a big deal, but then he's always tried. Exactly as he has prior to sixteen previous birthdays, Ned spent weeks preparing for an elaborate party of his own creation. At this day-long gala affair he imagines every year, the Coca-Cola flows like water, chocolate cakes magically appear on festively decorated tables, and presents fill the room.

This year, as before, he first composed the guest list, which included almost everyone he's ever encountered in his life, from blood relatives to one-meeting-only shopkeepers. Ned is an inveterate writer of lists, including hundreds of numbered white sheets full of the songs he likes, famous people he admires, and his official "Friends" list. The highest I ever got on that one was #2, right below his cat, Peg. This honor was diminished somewhat for me by the fact that Peg had been dead for six years when he wrote the list.

After composing the guest list, Ned then turned to the second and more important birthday list, an elaborate catalog of the gifts he desired. To our delight, that list has changed over the years. As he has gotten older, it's included more books, CDs, and sheet music. But at the top there are and always have been action figures.

For as long as I can remember, Ned has had in his hands, or very nearby, a selection of four-inch-tall posable familiars. Originally they were *Star Wars* characters and He-Men, playthings he liberated from big brother Ira's Cardboard Box of Forgotten Childhood Effluvia. Later on, when he started making his own action figure selections, he was drawn to horrific-looking monsters and their equally horrific nemeses, creatures from comic books and films he's never read or seen. Most of these buff little men and drooling fiends have been supplemented in the last few years by extremely healthy young ladies, who are usually wearing nothing but studded thongs, tiny fur brassieres, and big swords on their ample hips. Apparently female action figures live in a fantasy world that is very violent but always quite balmy.

At Christmas a few years ago, I accidentally gave him his best present ever from me. The man in the action figure store said this particular healthy young lady came in two versions. In Japan you could buy her with a removable bra, but the American edition I was holding was more chaste, with permanently installed undergarments.

Ned came up to thank me that Christmas afternoon, wearing a smile that was both gracious and lewd. It turns out there is only one version of the young lady, the Japanese version. I know it's hard to believe, but an action figure sales representative had led me astray. I probably should have taken the time to tug on the lady's top before making my purchase, but she was deeply encased in form-fitting plastic, and through it that bodice looked solid. Also, investigating the underside of doll clothing is an activity I haven't engaged in since I was eleven.

A few days later I found the bra on the family room floor. I still don't know where Ned has hidden the girl. That was the week I made Friend #2.

When strangers trying to make conversation with Ned ask him to identify his figures, he always seems a little confused by the question. As far as he is concerned, the names and contexts of the little plastic fellas and gals are immaterial to his enjoyment of them. The people asking the question usually assume he isn't smart enough to know where they come from, poor little boy, and change the subject. He knows all right; he just doesn't care. His action figures are for companionship and manipulation, not necessarily character-related fantasies that would require some kind of distinct persona. If they do require character traits, Ned is perfectly capable of making up stories himself without benefit of their comic-book reality.

Every night before going to sleep, he lays them out on his bed in tight rows, shoulder to shoulder, so they look like those old drawings of Africans tightly packed in the holds of eighteenth-century slave ships. Some of the first figures he acquired have been handled and shaken for so long that the paint has worn off and limbs have broken away. That doesn't make any difference to him. They are friends, and you don't toss a friend in the garbage just because his arm has fallen off. Ned probably has four hundred action figures now. That's a lot of immediately available friends.

Ned collects new action figures whenever the opportunity arises, like Christmases, birthdays, and walking within five blocks of a store that sells them. The actual physical manipulation of each figure has decreased in the past few years. Previously he would sit for hours with a figure in both hands, rhythmically shaking them while talking to himself. This could happen anywhere in public or private. But now that activity happens almost entirely in the family room or his bedroom, while he's watching television or listening to his CD player.

I'm not sure what the decreasing manipulation of the figures says about their changing role in his life. He knows that it drives me crazy when he doesn't have a hand free to help with groceries because he's holding at least two action figures. And he knows I think he carries around far too many of them at home. Every morning he used to lug a cardboard box and two bags full of figures down from his bedroom, and then carry them all back up every night. Out of curiosity I once weighed this movable community. It was forty-four pounds combined, and included at least a hundred-and-fifty figures, or 37½ percent of the entire collection. He might only play with five or ten in the course of a day, but he wanted them all handy. The heft of this morning and evening load has decreased, but he still moves a whole lot of little men and women around daily. It's one of the reasons he's so strong.

We've never told him not to play with them in public, unless doing so prevented him from performing some other necessary activity. If strangers want to pity the kid because they think that's all he can do, I could care less. I suppose I found it a little embarrassing a long time ago, but those days are gone. I've asked him why he likes action figures so much and why he always wants at least a few around. He looks at me as if I've just asked him why he breathes so much. Action figures are just part of who he is. But their power is declining, and some day the birthday will roll around when he doesn't want any of them. But not yet.

The birthday party Ned envisioned this year didn't happen, as it hasn't happened for a decade. Ned's twenty-first birthday was the forty-third offspring birthday we have been called upon to celebrate. Long ago Cathy and I packed away the noisemakers, Happy Birthday plates, and contact information for Deeno The Clown/Birthday Parties and Special Events/Hourly Rates.

Ned keeps trying for the lavish party. Just like everyone else in the holiday-observing world, he wants to be treated as an adult, except at birthdays and Christmas, when he wants to be treated as a six-year-old. It's only fair to say that he never complains when the hundred-and-fifty guests don't show up, the big celebration fails to materialize, and the bottom seventy-nine items on his gift list are not forthcoming. He happily accepts whatever does happen, as long as there's a cake. Ten months later, he begins planning again. He knew his twenty-first would be a very special occasion, so figures of national importance were included among the guests. And if Mick Jagger and the Clintons had arrived this afternoon in a limo, I don't think Ned would have been the least surprised.

Ned doesn't know that this week marked the end of Birthdays As He Has Known Them. I have at least two-hundred-and-fifty days before he starts compiling the guest and gift lists for next year, when I must tell him his work is for naught. And I'm going to take every one of those days. Procrastination: the chicken dad's best friend.

For his twenty-first, we had good times yesterday and today. Ned actually had two birthday parties, the first for adults and the second for his school friends. My colleagues Sue and Rosemary, who respectively produced the *Death* series and the *Vaudeville* special I wrote for PBS, coincidentally have birthdays the day before and the day after Ned's. So for some years we've all met at our house for a joint celebration. This year, Ned's being twenty-one and an experienced veteran of that adult delight known as the cocktail hour, we had the party as a lunch at the Two Bells Tavern in downtown Seattle.

The Two Bells is an eclectic place. At any given hour, the crowd might include grunge rockers, ad men, television news anchors, reporters, secretaries, and artists in all media. This is partly due to the Bells' location near the television stations and the artsy part of Seattle known as Belltown, and mostly due to a wide selection of beers, plus excellent soups and sandwiches. I've spent a lot of time there, but because it's a tavern, Ned couldn't come in until yesterday.

Out back in the sunny Two Bells Beer Garden, all the family (including my father, Ira, and beloved Auntie Maralyn), Sue, Rosemary, and ten others gathered at noon to celebrate Ned. The guest of honor had his traditional Coke and burger on a regular hamburger bun I brought along, because the Two Bells encases its outstanding burgers in French bread. This is an indefensible breach of burgeriana as far as Ned is concerned, and the joint's only failing. I didn't even waste my time offering him a beer, now that he could legally have one. Long ago Ned developed a strong moral aversion to alcohol. I doubt he's ever ingested any liquor, in any form, in his life, but he talks about the evils of drink like a fifth generation member of the Women's Christian Temperance Union. Cathy and I hardly drink at all and there aren't any heavy drinkers elsewhere in the family, so we haven't the slightest idea where or why this anti-libation crusade began.

Among the attendees at the party was Bob Newman, an ex-Marine (is any Marine really an "ex" Marine?) who is Seattle's foremost female impersonator. Since the early 1960s, Bob has played "Gertrude," the girlfriend/sidekick of J.P. Patches, Northwest television kid's show legend.

J.P., played by Chris Wedes, was "the retired circus clown who lives down by the city dump." For more than twenty years he hosted the kid's show on the local CBS affiliate, where Bob worked as a floor director when he wasn't in drag. The show eventually died, as local kid's shows died all over the country, when the Federal Communications Commission decided that hosts and sidekicks couldn't do commercials any more because they might actually sell some product. Advertisers wanted to see J.P. holding up their product, not Mr. Announcer Man. When that wasn't allowed any more by the F.C.C.'s stupid and short-sighted decision, the advertisers deserted local kids' shows.

J.P. and Gertrude soldiered on, working parades and fairs, selling videos of their old shows, firmly establishing themselves as beloved icons who were always available to help those trying to relive their childhoods. Bob has tried to hang up his taffeta frock and orange fright wig many times, grow a mustache, and become a real boy. But Chris, the kids, and their nostalgic parents keep calling him/her back.

(My late mother, who really was named Gertrude, hated Bob from the other side of the screen for finding something comic about her name, even though she herself loathed it. She could never get anybody to call her anything but Gert. She thought that "Gert" sounded crude, but she just never was a Trudy. When we got a copy of her birth certificate so she could get a passport, we were surprised to see her first name had been miss-typed back in 1915 when it was entered in the county records. Officially, she was "Gert<u>ur</u>de." And that explains it. Her friends would have had to call her Turdy. And she never was that, either.)

None of the "Gertrude" legacy means anything to Ned. He's only seen Bob en travesti a few times. Their principal contact is in the green room at KCTS, when Bob comes in to do makeup on the host and guests of the public affairs and money shows. (In the credits he's listed as "Raoul Broadbent" or "Sneed, from the House of Hearn.") They are friends, and they talk a lot about this and that. Bob has probably worked enough kids to last him for eternity, but his affection for Ned and interest in his affairs is obviously sincere. Perhaps part of it has to do with Bob's own disability. He has multiple sclerosis, walks with a cane, and knows something about overcoming all kinds of challenges. He's one of Ned's few friends who is more interested in what Ned is going to do than what he's done. Second only to the immediate family, Bob Newman wants to know that my son's future is going to be a happy one. He's a fine guy.

The Two Bells Cocktail Lunch and Birthday Party was a great success, and so was the burger dinner today with Ned's friends. Most of them are going back for another year of school, with a concentration on vocational training. Like Ned, they don't see much difference in what they've been doing in school before. Like Ned, I think they're in for a surprise, and it won't necessarily be a pleasant one.

Ned is twenty-one now. Given the shortened life expectancy of people with Down syndrome, he's just a few years away from middle age.

School

Ned's Wedgwood ID photo, 1989.

Thursday, September 5, 2002

Today Cathy and I went up to Wedgwood Elementary, Ned's alma mater, to help set up part of his vocational training. School has started, and for now Ned goes with a teacher and some other students to The Theodora, a large home for adults with various disabilities, including the disability awaiting us all—old age. Run by Volunteers of America, The Theodora gets a lot of Nathan Hale High vocational students because it's just up the bus route from the school and the staff is willing to be part of a training program. It's traditional work for a Special Ed vocational program, and there's nothing inherently wrong with Ned's working there. But our general discomfort with large institutions and belief that Ned has particular skills that might be better utilized elsewhere led us to suggest alternatives. The best possibility is working as an aide for his former Wedgwood fourth and fifth grade teacher, Marcy Wynhoff.

Marcy taught Special Education classes for quite a few years. When she realized that she didn't have the energy for it any more, she switched to teaching a "regular" combined first and second grade class at Wedgwood. Special Ed lost one of its best teachers, but it is to Marcy's credit that she saw what was happening to her and got out before she had to get out. She is still a very good friend.

This morning we met in the teacher's lounge with Marcy, Ned's high school teacher Tim Hilton, and Jim Spoor, who has been teaching Physical Education at Wedgwood and elsewhere for twenty years. Because all these people know Ned, like him, and know his capabilities, setting up the deal was easy. Starting in a few weeks, instead of going to The Theodora with others from his class, he'll get off the city bus four blocks from Wedgwood, walk to the school, and work for half an hour helping Jim set up equipment and teaching his first class. Then Ned will go to Marcy's room and help her. Then he will come back up the stairs to work with Jim for a last half hour. Work over, he will walk four blocks to the bus stop to catch the bus back to Nathan Hale.

I know he can handle the classroom stuff, but riding that bus and making that walk each way alone scares me. Ned has never been alone on a city bus in his life. I have this memory to contend with: Ned climbing on the bus in Inverness, Scotland, and falling asleep before we pulled away from the curb. What's to keep him from falling asleep again, missing his stop, and waking up alone in Tacoma?

Something like this actually happened once. On the first day of middle school when he was twelve, Ned was riding the school bus home and fell asleep. Eventually he lay down on a seat near the back of the bus. This was Special Ed transportation, so the bus driver had personally signed him onto her bus. But when she started for our house after dropping off all the other kids, she glanced back in her mirror and didn't see him. Apparently she then concluded he wasn't on the bus. Perhaps she thought he magically disappeared while performing the Indian Rope Trick in the back seat, or maybe he disguised himself as one of the other kids on the bus and snuck off that way. Maybe he was doing that dynamite impression he does of an empty school bus seat. Or it could be that the driver was just as dumb as a box of rocks. Whatever the reason, she headed for the bus barn, thinking her work was done for the day.

I called home around 4:00 to see how Ned's first day at middle school had gone. Cathy barked into the phone, "Ned's-not-home-they've-lost-him-somewhere-I-have-to-keep-the-line-free!" and hung up.

A few moments later, I made a dent going through the metal KING newsroom door that was still there five years later when they threw me out that same door. A drive home that usually took ten minutes I accomplished in four. When I got there they still hadn't called to tell us they'd located Ned. So I called the bus folks myself. They seemed infuriatingly unconcerned about the whole matter.

"Oh, he's somewhere, he'll turn up," a school bus bureaucrat told me pleasantly. "First day, you know, things are a little screwed up. It's just too bad the radio is broken on that particular bus, or we could call the driver and ask her if she's got him."

That's when I started screaming. There are times in one's life when it's handy to be a lawyer's kid, and this was one of them. I informed the gentleman that the young man in question was developmentally disabled and was missing through the obvious gross negligence of the school system and the contract bus company my listener represented. I mentioned that the missing young man's grandfather was one of the top personal injury litigators in America. (My father specializes in trusts and estates and is now the house counsel for a property management company. He hasn't stood up in court in fifty years and has probably never handled a personal injury case in his life. But I made it sound like he was the Oliver Wendell Holmes of ambulance chasing.) I informed this blasé, smug bureaucrat that he should be prepared for a massive lawsuit in which he would be personally named as a co-defendant. "Or," I concluded, "do you want to get off your ass and find my son right now?"

We got a call back a few minutes later. The bus driver had pulled into the bus barn and parked her bus in the midst of fifty other identical busses. She was just getting off to lock it up and go home for the night when Ned sat up and said, "Am I home yet?"

"He's fine," they told us on the phone. "He's sitting in the office. The driver will drop him off on her way home."

"No," I said, "the driver will not. I'm coming for him. The driver will wait for me." I was running out the door when Cathy said, "Don't say anything to his bus driver." I had been planning a few remarks that would eventually delve into the nature of her true species, but Cathy said, "He's got to ride with her for the rest of the year. Leave her alone."

The hardest thing I had to do that day was pick Ned up twenty minutes later and listen without responding while his bus driver told me that everything was okay and I needn't have worried. She never did apologize for being stupid and inept, and I never did ask what might have happened had Ned not woken up when he did, but instead awoke a few hours later to find himself locked in a bus in a deserted parking lot in the middle of the night while the police combed the city looking for him.

The incident bothered me more than it did Ned. When I picked him up he had obviously been crying a bit, but was otherwise fine, and eager to get home. Perhaps my concern about his solo bus riding is misplaced, or needlessly exaggerated. We'll see.

Friday, September 20, 2002

Ned continues to work at The Theodora Retirement Home while awaiting the Wedgwood Elementary deal. This morning I went along with him and a few others from his class. His job at The Theodora is to go with a cook to the food storage area in the basement, get the supplies that will be needed for dinner, and bring it all back up to the kitchen. He has a list, and I can see that, given time and more familiarity with where things are, he'd be able to do it all by himself. But for now the accompanying cook does the real work while Ned and his classmate Terry mostly watch, or lift and carry. He likes the job because he's with kids he knows. But at present he's certainly not providing any useful service. The cook could do it more efficiently and quickly without him. It's to the staff's credit that they take the time to work with Ned and his colleagues. But it bothers me. I know this is vocational training and that's the principal reason he's doing it. Still, I'd like to think that even in these early days, Ned isn't doing work that's been created so he can do work. Somebody once defined one kind of success as doing work that has a positive benefit on somebody's life other than your own. So far, The Theodora isn't it.

After he did his work this morning, Ned gave a guitar concert for the residents in The Theodora lounge. He engineered this presentation and has been preparing for it for weeks. He even wrote up an invitation and stuck copies of it around the building:

Volunteers of America Presents "Kidsongs":

With a special guest appearance By Nathaniel Palmer

Appearing Live at the Theodora
Little kids are invited to attend

Song list made for your listening pleasure
1. Hello in there
2. Bingo
3. Last Night I had the Strangest Dream
4. If I had a Hammer
5. Tingalayo
6. Let's Hear it for America
7. Sodeo
8. We're a Family
9. Piano Medley (Lavenders Blue) (Ode to Joy)
   (Standing in the Need of Prayer)
10. America the Beautiful

Not many residents showed up. It was mostly a concert for the other Nathan Hale students who work there. Ned played well, and I was pleased to see he knew enough to make the program ten minutes long even if the song list indicated a two-hour show. He's naturally developing a stage presence and stage smarts, something a lot of people never manage to do.

Tuesday, October 8, 2002

The past three days have had their moments, from death to war to crime. I could probably find a theme in there somewhere but it would require a lot of running around the Bush.

When Ned was away at camp last July, his former classmate James Williams died of complications from muscular dystrophy. He had just turned twenty. Although James and Ned were in school together for years at various times, I didn't remember the boy until I saw his picture, and then only vaguely. He was the quiet, smiling kid in the wheelchair. I remember he always seemed very fragile, and apparently he was.

Because he died in the summer, the word didn't get out about the memorial event. Only six people attended his funeral, including his mother and older brother. A funeral director shouldn't compose one-sixth of your mourners. This really bothered one of those who did attend—Glenda Feyes, a Teacher's Aide in the Special Ed program at Nathan Hale. She had known James for a long time, both in school and in Young Life Open Door, the Christian gathering for teens with developmental disabilities. She thought more attention should be paid to his passing, and also that those who knew him needed a chance to say goodbye. Ned and his classmates needed closure.

Glenda decided to organize a "Remembering Ceremony" at his grave as soon as the stone was installed. That turned out to be last Saturday. Her most devoted helper in this enterprise was Ned. I didn't think he was that close to James. Certainly his name hasn't been mentioned as much as those of a dozen other classmates and friends during the past fifteen years. But Ned was stunned when he heard of the death from Heidi right after getting back from Easter Seals camp. James's death affected him in a way quite different from the deaths of his great aunt Dorothy, his cousin John, even his grandmother. He isn't a kid who cries much, but he cried for James. So during the past few weeks he's been preparing intensely for this remembering, working with Glenda on who should speak, what should be sung, how the announcement should read. Like the artist he wants to be, like the artist he is, Ned's response to the ceremony was principally artistic. He decided to lead the gathering in "Amazing Grace." And he wrote a song for his friend; a simple farewell.

> *Goodbye, my friend, well it's time to go*
> *Goodbye, my friend, well it's time to go*
> *It's sad to say goodbye, but we really must go.*
> *Goodbye, my friend, goodbye.*

Acacia Memorial Park is a big, well-maintained facility, founded by the Masons but now owned by a national corporation. All the graves must be flat to the ground for financial rather than religious reasons. It's odd how our monuments to the dead have been impacted in the last fifty years by the invention of the riding lawn mower, coupled with cemetery owners' desires to cut maintenance costs with it. A good mortuary mower driver can do the whole property in a few hours now because he doesn't have to work around all those cumbersome, stick-up headstones that make less controlled, less cost-conscious graveyards such interesting places to visit.

James's service was scheduled for 2:00, but as usual we got there an hour early. During the drive north we listened to *John Denver's Greatest Hits* in the car. Ned sang along and played air guitar. I could tell his mind was a long way away.

Instead of waiting in the office for the others to arrive, we walked up the hill to the Cyprus Gardens section to find the grave. I think Ned wanted to be there for a while without a crowd around. I also think he wanted to check out the venue, like any artist about to do a performance in a new place.

Ned discovered from reading James's gravestone that Glenda had gotten the dates of birth and death wrong in the printed announcement of the ceremony. She was only a day off on each side, but as someone dedicated to death facts, Ned found the errors to be a shocking mistake. He could hardly wait for Glenda's arrival to tell her, even though I argued that it wasn't a big deal and he shouldn't bother her with it. I even tried to convince him that perhaps the grave was wrong and Glenda was right. "Just because it's written in stone doesn't mean it's, uh, written in stone, Ned," I said. But for a long time now Ned has been reading gravestones and believing every single word carved into them. Every woman was a wonderful wife and mother; every man loved his family and was a great provider. As far as Ned is concerned, human beings are fallible but a tombstone never lies.

On the way back down the hill to the cemetery office, we strolled through the huge mausoleum that dominates Acacia. In there we found the grave of Emil Sick, owner of the now-destroyed Sick's Stadium, where the late Elvis Presley made his final appearance in Seattle. These are the kinds of progressions one goes through walking around a cemetery with Ned, death historian of the stars.

Shortly before 2:00 the rest of the celebrants arrived, these friends Ned has known for so long: Santosh, Heidi, Tanyss, Patrick, Jacob, and three or four others, plus a few parents and teachers. I suppose everyone has seen groups of people with mental retardation on outings, in bowling alleys, swimming pools, and museums. I certainly did before Ned was born. Back then I remember finding it hard not to stare at these strange people, hard not to feel sorry for their parents and sorry for them too. But looking at that group Saturday afternoon, I realized all those ancient, ignorant feelings are over. Because I've come to know them. Here they had gathered to remember their friend and to grieve, and yet they were enjoying themselves too, enjoying each other's company as any group of old friends would. They're all in their twenties now, mostly out of high school and adjusting to new and sometimes completely different lives. They are from different races, different cultures, and different kinds of families. What they have in common, the wellspring of their camaraderie, isn't disability. Simply put, it is a profound and trusting friendship. If you told them you felt sorry for them, they wouldn't have the slightest idea why.

We walked up the hill again as a group and gathered around the new stone. Glenda spoke, and then invited others to share their thoughts of James. Most did. Ned did at length. We heard stories of James's sense of humor, of his courage confronted by sickness and pain, of his faith in God. We sang *Amazing Grace*, Ned performed his song, we prayed, and it was over. Heidi sobbed through most of the ceremony. On the way to the parking lot, every single young person went to her, hugged her, and comforted her as best he or she could. Nobody had to tell them to do that. They are friends. Because of the tendency these friends have to die young, most of them have been through this before. And most of them know they will do it again.

On the way home, Ned and I listened to John Denver again. No more air guitar, just listening.

> *Love is why I came here in the first place*
> *Love is now the reason I must go.*
> *Love is all I ever hoped to find here,*
> *Love is still the only dream I know....*

On Sunday, Cathy, Ned and I went to Volunteer Park to protest President Bush's proposed war with Iraq. We took a city bus up to Capitol Hill from downtown. To the driver's surprise, his bus was jammed with protestors.

"The police told me they only expected two or three hundred people to show up for the whole damned thing," he whined. "I've driven three hundred people up there myself!" We apparently drew the only Republican bus driver in Seattle.

There were maybe two thousand protesters in the park by the time we arrived. The crowd included everybody from pre-teens to a lot of the people I used to see at anti-Vietnam War protests more than twenty-five years ago. Some of them had broken out their old protest duds: tie-dyed peace symbol tee shirts and ancient ventilated jeans. For a moment, swept up in nostalgia, I didn't notice the number of these "hippies" who suspiciously had haircuts that said "small business entrepreneur." But they were there, and that's what mattered.

Ned wanted to get down front. He and Cathy found a spot on the grass right in front of the stage while I paced around the back of the crowd. (I find as I get older I get more claustrophobic in large groups.) A chorus sang a few songs, a few people only a little older than Ned spoke, and then it was time to march down the hill to the heart of Seattle, a town square of sorts called Westlake Center.

One of our failures as parents is not encouraging Ned to get involved in sports, organized or otherwise, nor scheduling some other regular physical activity for him. He had P.E. classes in the school gym but they were never much. For two years, he satisfied his high school P.E. requirement by swimming daily in the community pool next to Nathan Hale, the same place where he took swimming lessons a long time ago. I'm not sure that he enjoyed the high school swimming that much, and we were less than pleased that it was always the first class of the day. We'd get him up early to make sure he was neat and properly dressed, and then the first thing he did at school was take all those clothes off and then put them back on again an hour later with far less attention to sartorial detail. He also spent half the day with wet hair. When the opportunity came for him to drop swimming, we didn't object.

Recently Cathy and Ned started making a weekly visit to a nearby public pool for an hour of aquatic fun. I don't go on these trips, being a drowning victim just waiting to happen. But generally we have allowed him to become sedentary, rather like his father. His brother was the same way until he shocked us the summer before his junior year in high school by announcing that he was going to turn out for football in the fall. Ira made the team. He was then around 325 pounds, and that fills a pretty large hole in a high school line no matter how inexperienced you are. After a first week of practice that nearly killed him, he enjoyed the gridiron experience so much he also turned out for football in college.

Ned had no such opportunity, not that he would have taken it if he had. The result is that he's surprisingly strong from carrying around forty-pound boxes of action figures for fifteen years, but he has little stamina or endurance. He's chubby, too, which is partly the cause and partly the result of his inactivity. On those occasions when we have to walk any significant distance, he will slow to a crawl after only a few blocks and then start complaining that his feet hurt.

For that reason I had considerable trepidation Sunday about the protest march from the top of Capitol Hill to downtown Seattle. It's downhill all the way, but it's also two miles. On national park trips with his Mom, Ned has done a seven-mile-round-trip hike, and hiked two miles up Yosemite, but this was still a long way to go on pavement. Not once in the entire march did he so much as say he wanted to rest. He was swept up in the event, in the crowds, in being surrounded by signs and passionate people.

We didn't stay long to hear the speeches at Westlake Center. We'd taken our stand, and Ned took it with us. It was time to catch the bus home. I don't know if he really understands what it was all about. The intensity of his interest in current events varies widely with the subject, and politics is usually not very compelling for him. Other than being aware that his parents think George W. Bush is a man whose only real accomplishment has been to pick his parents well, Ned has ignored him. (Would that we all could.) But maybe he did realize what it was all about and that's why he marched without complaint. Whether he did or not, I was proud he came along, and proud to be with him.

The next morning, the front page of the *Seattle Times* had a picture of our congressman, Jim McDermott, walking along in the parade. Besides being one of the brightest people in Congress (not a difficult achievement, unfortunately), Dr. McDermott is also one of the most liberal, and represents one of the most liberal districts in America. If they found him in bed with a goat and two choir boys tomorrow, he'd still get reelected the next time around. Electoral invincibility gives Jim the freedom to speak and vote his convictions, one of which is that the proposed war in Iraq is foolhardy bravado, America at its worst, and sure to go horribly wrong. So it wasn't a surprise that he joined his constituents in the streets. You can see a few of them behind him in the Seattle Times' photograph.

One of those pictured, blurry but unmistakable, is Mr. Ned Palmer, concerned citizen and voter.

The final event of the weekend happened yesterday morning. I left on my morning walk at 6:45; Ned got on the school bus at 7:10; Cathy left for work at 7:30. When I came back from walking at 8:00, a burglar was strolling through our living room with my backpack over his shoulder. If I'd thought about it for a moment, I wouldn't have given chase. I had no idea whether he was armed or not. But the mixture of adrenaline and fury is a powerful force. The burglar took off out the back door and I took off after him. Fortunately he dropped the backpack, which contained our cameras and other electronic things, and a few spare credit cards. And he didn't have time to stop and pick up my laptop computer or Ned's leather jacket, which he'd already stashed on the back porch. He jumped over the fence into the neighbor's back yard, and I assumed he was gone. Two minutes later I saw him still hiding back there, and he saw me, so he took off for the street. Turns out he had parked his car right in front of our house.

The police arrived a few minutes after he drove off. I described the perpetrator and gave them a partial license number. To my considerable surprise the investigating officer asked me if my burglar had a mullet, that famous hairstyle that is very short on top and hangs to the shoulders on the sides and back. (The only uglier hair in America can be found on top of Donald Trump.) I said he had at least half of a mullet, but I couldn't see the top of his head because he was wearing a hat. I've been wondering ever since whether the Seattle police make the assumption that all burglars have mullets. Maybe universal burglar mulletheadedness is the contention of a police department profiler.

Too much television for me.

Thursday, October 10, 2002, 2:30 p.m.

Flying to Oakland, California

Ned has a four-day weekend from school, so we decided to fly down to Oakland and visit my brother Pete, who has lived in the Bay area for a long time. Ned's never been to Pete's home and he's always wanted to go. We're flying on Southwest Airlines, just passing over Crater Lake at the moment. Southwest has a "no assigned seating" policy which apparently saves them money. We boarded early and grabbed the front row window and aisle seats. Ned likes the window and I am an aisle man. Which means there was an empty seat between us.

Five years ago, I gave a speech about Ned called *The End of Cute*. The premise was that when he was a little boy, people were drawn to him. He was talkative, friendly, and cute. But as he reached his late teens, I noticed that strangers who only a few years before would have taken a step toward him now seemed to be taking a step back. He was a Retarded Adult, and Retarded Adults scare some people. I said it back then, but I had never had any obvious, direct experience with the fact that for some of the population, Ned is someone to avoid.

I got that experience an hour ago on this plane. Our flight was completely full, so as the final twenty people arrived in the cabin, they looked around for somewhere available to sit. Five of them saw the empty seat in the front row and started for it eagerly. Then they saw Ned. They stopped, looked apprehensive for a moment, and then went down the aisle to the back of the plane. Just as the doors were about to close, the flight attendant tried to direct a woman who appeared to be in her early sixties to the empty seat between Ned and me. She looked at Ned, said haughtily, "Well, I'm certainly not going to sit there!" and marched on past. I glanced over at Ned. Looking out the window at the ground activity, he was oblivious to what was going on inside the plane, thank God. He was also not drooling, playing with himself, leering at women, or slowly removing his clothes. He was just looking out the window.

Practically the last guy through the door took the available seat happily. Right now he and Ned are having a nice conversation about this guy's work in computers, the likeable things about Seattle, and why Ned and I are going to Oakland. The latecomer told me a few minutes ago that he was surprised to find a seat available in the front row when he got to the plane at the last minute. "Usually on these Southwest flights I'm crammed into the middle row of the back seat."

"It's because there are a lot of crapheads on board," I explained.

Sunday, October 13, 2002

We're back on the plane coming home from Oakland. Exactly the same thing happened with some entering passengers that happened on the way down. When offered the seat between Ned and me, even though it was in the front row with more legroom and a quicker exit at the other end, they got a look as though there were a bad smell on the plane and took off for the back rows. I can see I'm going to have to get used to this. I'm going to have to suppress the urge to go back there and pass among the bastards with a baseball bat.

Ned had a nice time in Oakland. My brother, Harvard, Jr. but called Pete, lives in a tan, Mediterranean-style house he calls The Compound (not entirely facetiously), located on a large lot in the hills above Oakland, with a view of both that city and San Francisco. There's a county park directly in front of The Compound, so in theory his view will never degenerate into vistas of housing developments. For being so close to two major cities, it's a nice, almost rural sort of place. Small deer occasionally come wandering out of the park and gambol in his front yard, coyotes are heard nightly, and I once saw a cougar working its way down the park hill five hundred yards away. Nobody believes me on that one, but I did.

In the past, Pete rarely left home, and he still doesn't spend much time away from the place. His advertising agency staff comes to him every day. When he ran his business out of an apartment on Cathedral Hill in San Francisco, he was once described in a *San Francisco Chronicle* article as "The Adman from Hell," because he would call on his various clients—a list then leaning heavily toward discount jewelry, furniture, and stereo stores—on a Harley, or driving his gold 1970 Cadillac DeVille. The license plate of this vehicle is "Pitchem," as he was also known as "Pitch 'em Pete." He still has the Harley and a Norton, the Caddy, and a few other vehicles, but since moving to The Compound, he hasn't found the need to go many places, and he never had the desire. Instead he works the phone and wanders around The Compound dealing with his staff and his pets, not necessarily in that order.

The pets are a big attraction for Ned. For weeks he's been talking about visiting them, and only incidentally visiting his Uncle Pete. When my brother bought the house a few years ago, just around the corner from the kitchen was a glass-enclosed cage of sorts. That's where the previous owner (and the house's builder) planned to keep his pet iguana, if he ever got a pet iguana. Pete felt something similar should fill this space, something cold blooded but not necessarily an iguana. (I should explain that although we are the sons of a cat woman, my brother is a bit fastidious for cats. To own a cat, you have to be able to watch it walk purposefully toward the new couch and not immediately start yelling and throwing shoes. This is not my brother. I think it is not coincidental that every pet he owns cannot wander but is encaged in some way.)

The Bay area's most noted reptile man was summoned and he brought along a sampling of his stock, including tortoises, lizards, geckos, and one snake. Pete gathered his staff together and let them pick the reptile they liked the best, or disliked the least, depending on their personal feelings about such beasts. (He didn't want any ophidiophobes turning up later on. Look it up.) And though he didn't necessarily want the snake, it was the snake that won the hearts of his almost-all-female staff. (See *Genesis,* 3:1.) The result was the purchase of Adman and eventually Boopsie, Adman's mate presumptive. They are carpet pythons, black and yellow and now about six feet long, so not terribly large for snakes but not so small as to get lost in the furniture.

The first problem with live snakes as pets, besides the fact that they can't crawl into your lap for a little cuddle, is that 90 percent of the time they might as well be dead snakes. They don't do anything but lie there, unmoving and unmoved. An occasional and incredibly slow slither from tree to rock is about all you can hope for. Unless it's feeding time, and they only eat once every three weeks.

Feeding them is the other problem with snakes as pets, or at least Pete's snakes. He can't just go to the supermarket and pick up a bag of Purina Snake Chow and dump a little into a bowl now and then. What these snakes eat are mice. Since Adman's arrival, a section of my brother's refrigerator has been taken up with mouse carcasses purchased from one of those big, open-all-night mouse stores that dot the Bay area. And trust me on this: as a houseguest, coming across a baggie full of cold dead mice in the fridge can give you quite a start in the middle of the night when you're just looking for a snack.

The feeding process, which Ned and I watched the other day with a mixture of fascination and horror, involves taking two pairs of tongs, each holding a deceased white mouse. (Adman and Boopsie have not yet embraced the concept of sharing.) Said mice have been slightly reactivated in a pot of hot water, which is why you always decline a cup of tea at Pete's. Slowly the tongs are inserted through the door into the snake enclosure. Adman and Boopsie initially fain disinterest, even as they casually start sliding toward the tongs. After a minute or two of this, they suddenly snap into action, grabbing the mice in their coils with such speed you can easily miss it if you blink at the wrong time.

The final part of the process, which Ned and I agreed is the most disgusting thing we've ever seen in an otherwise normal home, is the snakes' slow insertion of the dead mice through the unhinged jaws of their unbelievably wide mouths. They use their coils like big, thick fingers to shove the carcasses in. It's only a matter of minutes before the mouse-shaped lumps inside the snakes lose their structural integrity and become just lumps, working back toward the tail, undergoing the miracle of digestion. During this digestive process, Adman and Boopsie are, if possible, even less animated than usual. Apparently it takes a lot of energy to digest a mouse, and they eat four or five mice at each feeding. The snakes probably feel like a human being would feel if he ate two whole turkeys in one gulp.

Pete's other pets aren't as Old Testament fascinating, but at least they're a little more lifelike. In his office he has the most impressive fish tank I've seen outside a pediatrician's waiting room, featuring both tropical fish and living coral. The fish are all named, and Pete insists they have distinct personalities. To the untrained observer, however, they have about as much personality as the coral does.

Finally on Pete's Pet Parade, in a concrete pond out in front of the house, live Mama and Buster, Red Eared Slider turtles. Mama came with the house. Her PCV (primary care veterinarian) estimates she is sixty-five years old. Buster arrived in 1999 as a companion for Mama. Although Pete has had these turtles for years now, they often dive in terror to the bottom of their pond whenever he or anyone else approaches. They even do this at feeding time, demonstrating conclusively that turtles are supremely dumb.

When you add up all the dumb turtles, moribund snakes, colorful fish, and enthralling coral, my brother owns twenty pets, and not one of them makes a sound. The snakes don't even hiss. And not one of them can be touched by a human being, either, until it is dead. (Pete insists that the snakes are touchable, but who wants to?) Every single Pete pet has only two personality characteristics: It is either terrified and running away from you, or dead-like because it hasn't noticed you yet. This is not my idea of a pet. It is also not Ned's idea, and if a stranger had snakes, turtles, fish, and coral, Ned wouldn't pay much attention. He and I have visited the Woodland Park Zoo in Seattle many times, and never once has Ned expressed an interest in seeing our zoo's impressive reptile house. They aren't *our* reptiles. But these are Pete's pets, very much a part of his life. So they're family, and just like so many of his other interests—the Denny family, old rock and roll, the Battle of Hastings—Ned is drawn to anything with which he can make a family connection, even some damned dull animals.

Pete's menagerie has recently become slightly more traditional. Last March his fiancée, Patricia, moved into The Compound and brought along her beloved Miniature Schnauzers, Sabine and Vesta. These two small dogs are allowed to run around the property, which is why nobody believes me about the cougar. They don't *want* to believe me, given the equation that small dogs plus one cougar plus a little time and inattention equals zero small dogs. For the rest of the family, the fact that Pete has let these two little beasts take up residence in his quiet, previously pet-urine-free compound is solid evidence that he is gaga for Patricia.

For a lad devoted to his own dog, Ned has a fear of other dogs, especially noisy ones. Barking drives him mad, a trait he inherited from his mother. So I don't think he cared much for Sabine and Vesta, who have a tendency to yip. But we endured.

Saturday we took Bay Area Rapid Transit (BART) into the city, hopped an E-train (lovely old trolley cars from around the world) down to the waterfront, and then grabbed a cable car back to the BART station after a long walk through the tourist dens of the piers. Ned fell asleep on BART both ways. He fell asleep on the E-train. And in what I suspect is a first in the annals of San Francisco tourism, he fell asleep on the famous cable car within two minutes of boarding, and stayed sound asleep through all that bell clanging. There's something about this kid and public transportation, at least public transportation on the ground. He never falls asleep on planes, and isn't asleep now. But the minute the bus wheels start rolling, he zonks.

Monday, October 14, 2002

This was Ned's first day as a Teacher's Aide at Wedgwood Elementary School. Tim Hilton had to be elsewhere with other students, so I did the route with Ned and will again tomorrow. Everything went well. We rode the bus together from the high school up to the intersection nearest Wedgwood. Tim and Ned's classmates stayed on board for the trip to The Theodora, while Ned and I got off and walked four blocks up the hill to the school. It was a beautiful, warm day today, which is odd for Seattle in October. It can frequently be sunny this time of year, but rarely balmy. So it was a good day to begin, though I dread his doing this walk in January when it will be dark, dank, and cold.

At school Ned worked with Jim Spoor in the first P.E. class while I sat in the lobby, and then I went with him downstairs to Marcy Wynhoff's first/second grade class. Marcy knows how much Ned enjoys reading. She immediately put him together with a small, pretty second grader named Mary, who has that kind of shining blond hair that made every guy I knew in 1965 fall in love with Mary Travers of Peter, Paul & Mary. Ned and his Mary went off into a corner to read a book together, alternating chapters. Ned took to the role of reading instructor instantly. One of my lasting memories of this day will be peeking around the door of Marcy's room and watching Ned with this sweet little girl, who immediately and easily accepted him as her teacher. They were smiling together at the book, and it was obvious that Ned was not only providing real value but also enjoying the opportunity. He was making someone else's life a little better through his work.

After another stint with Jim, we walked back down to the bus stop, getting there just as the bus did. Ned's classmates coming back from The Theodora will be on the next bus, so he and I rode back to Nathan Hale alone together. I dropped him at school and took off for my own work. Ned still says he'd rather be at The Theodora with his friends, but I can tell he is at least a bit more receptive to the idea of helping teachers and working with kids. It's a natural for him, and I hope he accepts that fact soon.

Friday, October 18, 2002

For the last two days I told Ned he was on his own doing his Wedgwood job. As far as he knew, he was. But I got in the car and watched him, following the bus, sneaking up side streets when he did the walk to and from school, sitting outside waiting for him while he was inside working. I didn't want him to think I had doubts about his ability to do the route. At the same time I wanted to be ready in case there was any problem. Occasionally he knew I was there, especially on the walk back down to the bus, but he enjoyed ignoring me. He did everything as he was supposed to do it.

This morning I had to be elsewhere, and he knew it. Cathy drove up to Wedgwood at 11:00 to shadow him down the hill after work. Instead of waiting for the bus back to Nathan Hale, he went into the supermarket that's near the bus stop, something he's been told not to do. Cathy watched the bus come and go and still Ned didn't come out. Finally she went in to find him. He was in the checkout line trying to buy a bag of Chips Ahoy cookies with money he'd filched from me. But he didn't have enough cash and the checker was trying to explain that to him as Cathy arrived, I suspect with steam coming out of her ears.

It was the first day when he knew for sure I wasn't watching him, and he took the opportunity to be sneaky. This was not good.

Monday, October 21, 2002, 10:30 a.m.

Wedgwood Elementary School

I had originally planned to let Ned go about his business on his own this week. No more secret observation. But after last Friday, I told him that from now on he could never be sure when I was or wasn't watching him, and he should behave accordingly. This isn't at all the way I wanted this to happen. I dislike doing a John Ashcroft impression even more than I dislike John Ashcroft. I wish I could just trust Ned to do what's right. But the plain truth is, I can't. So once again this morning I took up my position behind some trees to see him get on his bus. I followed the bus up the hill, drove through back streets watching him do the walk, and at this moment I'm hunkered down in the car outside the elementary school playground where he's working.

We've changed his schedule a little so that he now catches the same bus back that his colleagues are on, coming from their Theodora jobs. That meant giving him something more to do at Wedgwood so he isn't waiting for the bus for a half hour next to the lure of the supermarket. Now, after helping in the gym the second time, he goes down to his old Special Ed classroom and helps with the little kids at recess. I'm parked on the street outside the playground fence watching him, and he's doing fine. The only one likely to get into trouble is me. Old guys who hide in their cars outside grade school playgrounds watching the little kids frolic end up on the teevee news being led into the courthouse in ankle chains. If that happens, the only consolation I'll have is that Ned will find it extremely funny.

Wednesday, October 23, 2002

Cathy leaves this evening for a twenty-two day business/ pleasure trip to India, so Ned and I will be on our own for much of a month. Whether he knows it or not, I've been secretly observing him at school and work since Monday. During that period I'm most pleased to say he's been right on the money about everything. I look forward to not having to do this any more. Perhaps he has learned a lesson about trust.

Tuesday, November 5, 2002

After the supermarket incident, Cathy and I decided it was high time Ned had an allowance, first so he can have his own money and stop seeing his parents as a never-ending source of cash, and second so he develops some sense of what that money is worth. We've been far too lax about this. We should have given him an allowance years ago, but for some reason never got around to it. So we established an allowance, with one special condition: if he lies to me about anything, it costs him a dollar.

A week ago Saturday, I gave him his first ten dollars, and then another ten spot three days ago. He spent a little over the weekend, and had seventeen dollars in his wallet on the family room shelf yesterday morning.

We still don't want him wandering into supermarkets or with loose cash in his pocket at school, so the rule is that he can't take his money out of the house without our permission. Yet when I looked in the wallet this morning, it was empty.

Ned came home from school at 2:45, and I asked him what happened to the money.

"I don't know," he said immediately. That cost him a dollar. He didn't know two more times—two more dollars—and finally he said that he took it to school, hidden in his shoe so I wouldn't find it in his pockets when he left in the morning. That cost him another dollar for breaking the rule, and a dollar for being sneaky.

"And what happened to it at school?"

"Mr. Hilton has it."

"If I call Mr. Hilton and ask him if he has your seventeen dollars and why he has it, what will he tell me?"

"Uhh, he doesn't have it." One more dollar down.

"And what happened to it?"

"I lost it." We had a long discussion about how that might have happened. I wanted to make sure he hadn't given his money to another student or spent it on something. I finally believed what he said, that the money was somehow lost. It was a chat neither of us enjoyed at all, especially my having to tell him that because he has Down syndrome, all his life there will be people who think he's stupid and will try to take advantage of him. "I'd sure hate to think you're being cheated already, Ned," I said, and he assured me he isn't. I don't think anybody bilked him out of the dough, but I also think it's not too early to warn him of the possibility.

Ned's allowance this coming Saturday is down to a dollar. I don't think he yet realizes what that means and probably won't until he wants to buy something. My real concern is the ease with which he lies to me and his obvious lack of concern about breaking rules. Just as with the Chips Ahoy incident of last week, he's not sorry that he did it, but only sorry that he got caught. Most kids go through a larcenous stage, but Ned's lack of honesty at the age of twenty-one is a considerable concern. From now on I'll be frisking him every morning when he goes out the door to school, something I will hate to do even more than he will hate my doing it.

Wednesday, November 20, 2002

A lot of people with developmental disabilities end up as fast food workers. The McDonald's Corporation, for example, has been excellent about hiring adults with disabilities for their stores, although it would be nice just once to see one of them behind the counter taking orders or at the grill cooking meat rather than in the john wielding a mop. Still, they are working at real jobs, and doing those jobs where the public can see them making a worthwhile contribution.

The availability of fast food jobs for the developmentally disabled means that anybody running a vocational program has to consider that their students' future might involve handling food. In our state, that means passing the test to get an official Food Handlers' Permit. Without it you can't get a job anywhere around eats.

Tim Hilton called a week ago to tell us one of Ned's classmates was going to take the Food Handler's test today, and he thought Ned should take it too. I'd rather not consider the possibility that Ned will spend his adult life cleaning McDonalds' bathrooms. In years past he's often talked about how he'd like to work for the Golden Arches, the near proximity of burgers being the principal attraction for him. He never wants to wield a mop, however. Ned sees himself working as The Owner. Actually he sees himself working as Ray Kroc, the sales genius who took the McDonald brothers' cheap eats concept and conquered the world with it. I doubt if Ray ever had a Food Handler's Permit—Ray handled the money, not the food—but Ned should have one because you never know what's going to happen.

Tim sent the study booklet home a week ago and we all ignored the upcoming test until yesterday afternoon. Then Ned and I went through the information. I found it far more complicated than I'd remembered from the summer of 1965, when I had to take the test to flip burgers at the Samoa Drive In on Mercer Island. I guess handling food has become more involved, or possibly there are just a lot more lawyers around now who are eager to sue restaurants on behalf of the litigiously nauseous.

Ned and I tried as best we could to learn the material. We memorized the Food Temperature Danger Zone (45 degrees to 140 degrees, when bacteria grow so rapidly in eats you can practically hear them procreating) and took note of the fact that the State insists restaurant workers must wash their hands thoroughly every time they so much as breathe heavily. After we were done going through the booklet I thought it unlikely Ned would pass this test. He just hadn't had enough time to study it. I didn't think Tim would even drive him down to take the test if he realized how little effort we put into studying the booklet and how little of the material Ned retained. Sitting in the car out in front of school, all I could do was tell Ned that on the multiple choice test the State would be giving him, always pick the answer that involves killing germs as fast as possible and washing your hands as much as possible.

Tim called from school half an hour ago. Ned got thirty out of thirty-three correct and is now officially allowed to handle food. After he washes his hands. I think my last minute advice helped, but mainly this is Ned's achievement. He figured it out.

Thursday, November 21, 2002

Nathan Hale Little Theater

Another opening, another show. I'm not sure how this afternoon's *Unexplored Talents* production came about. I gather that some Regular Ed students at Nathan Hale decided to produce a Special Ed talent show with the people from Room 104. Perhaps this was in response to the all-school talent show coming up soon, a production for which Ned has auditioned every year but has never been chosen to perform. He is always disappointed, but he gets over it quickly.

Every 104 student was welcome to do something in the show today. Many did, after performers and audience members stood around in the school halls and ate pizza together. The quality of performance varied widely. Jacob was in the choir with Ned for four years and has a fine voice. He sang a Spanish song, in Spanish, beautifully. Terry, a boy with autism who was Ned's partner at The Theodora for a while, nicely played that Celine Dion hit from *Titanic* on his trumpet. That was a big surprise for me because he hardly ever speaks. Who knew he had the chops for brass? Ned played guitar and sang *I Don't Want to Live on the Moon*, one of Ernie's lesser-known numbers from *Sesame*

Ned Palmer, artist. (Photo by Rowland Studios.)

Street. Afterwards a couple of parents asked me if Ned had written the song, which I thought was the best compliment they could have given him.

The rest of the performers made up in enthusiasm what they lacked in ability. The closing act was my favorite. New in the class this year is a Somali girl named Randa. She has osteogenesis imperfecta, so-called brittle bone disease. Randa has endured dozens of surgeries in her few years on earth. She'll be in a wheelchair as long as she lives. She is one of the most beautiful children I've ever seen—tiny, dark, with soulful eyes and a gleaming smile, which makes her situation all the more heartbreaking. Tonight she danced to the music of her native country, spinning and swooping around the stage in her motorized wheelchair, stopping here and there to perform what I assume are the traditional hand gestures of Somali folk dancing. She seemed a completely free spirit, ignoring her handicap and expressing nothing but pure joy.

The educational numbers crunchers who consistently cut or kill school arts programs are shortsighted fools.

Wednesday, November 27, 2002

I picked Ned up at school today, because I was in the area and school got out early for the Thanksgiving holiday. While I was waiting for him to gather up his stuff, I played around on Room 104's computer, and found the following essay Ned wrote last year for a class assignment. Over the years I've been accused of doing his homework for him, or at least providing too much help, by people who don't realize how creative Ned can be. On occasion I probably have helped him more than I should. But I've never seen this essay before. He did it entirely on his own, based on his own research, and it is the essence of him:

The Age of Music
By Ned Palmer

Way back in the 50's when Rock n Roll got started the main people whom created Rock "n" Roll were actually Black people. This phenomenon began in the south a few years after World War 2. It was around that time when we were segregated, meaning that we are separated by color (The Black folk, The White folk). Those times were rough in those days. But that was when the 50's rolled in.

It started in the south with the black folk. At the time when this music first began it was called Rhythm and Blues meaning it's the blues up-tempo that is what Rock n Roll was called. The first mention of the R. n. R. was by a man named Alan Freed who called it Rock n Roll black slang for sex. Through out the 1950's scores of people began playing that kind

*of music like Elvis Presley, Little Richard,
Jerry lee Louis and many others (including my
cousin John Felten). Rock N Roll was centered
around love, woman, and the pursuit of happiness including courting the ladies around in
cars and going to movies. They were also some
songs of sorrow like The Everly Brothers with
their song called Bye Bye Love and Elvis
Presley with Blue Moon.*

*Those people were very smart especially with
the idea of giving a girl (50's term "Chicks") a
Ring. Yep that's what the 1950's were. As the
50's were reaching toward their end Rock n Roll
was expanding all across the United States.
Though some Rock stars had died during the
1950's like The Big Bopper, Buddy Holly,
Ritchie Valens and Eddie Cochran. There was
also the Payola scandal that Alan Freed suffered
from losing his job as New York's famous Disk
Jockey. Year's later Don McLean will recall
"The Day when the music died" in his song
called American Pie.*

*Since that time Rock N Roll is still popular
even over in Briton. The 60's were a time of
rebirth of the music. The first notice of rebirth
of Rock music was dance music like The Twist
by Chubby Checker and the Bristol Stomp. This
was around the time when Elvis returned from
the army. Elvis stared in what the 60's invented as the idea of Rock movies (Bye, Bye
Birdie in 1963). This was also the time of the
Vietnam War that placed America in to a
tailspin of chaos. New kinds of Rock music
were created like Surf music thanks to advent
of The Beach Boys and others like Dick Dale
and the Del Tones (Dick Dale was called King
of the surf guitar). And of course Folk Rock like
Bob Dylan and others like Peter, Paul and*

*Mary and of course Pete Seeger. Those folk
Artist started their careers in folk music only to
send two words across the globe, "Peace and
Love". This was also due to the Black civil
Rights that were led by none other than Martin
Luther King and others.*

   *The biggest form of Rock N Roll was British
Rock that began in Liverpool, England with
four young men better known as The Beatles.
Through out the 1960's the Beatles were the
main Rock group of that era. The Beatles had
scores of songs (Please Please Me, She Loves
You, From Me to You). Many others, due to the
Vietnam War, started doing weird things to
themselves. The Rock N Roll of long ago was no
more. Even though the artists of that era are
still around many of them died (Elvis Presley
died in 1977). Rock n Roll became psychedelic.
The end of the 1960's was horrifying due to the
assassinations of Martin Luther King and
Robert Kennedy.*

   *Rock N Roll became sinful with riots and
drugs (especially a drug called LSD). Those
were the dark times. A lot of Rock stars died
including those years like Mamma Cass and
Jimi Hendrix. My cousin John Felten died in
1982 in a plane crash just like my other Heroes.
But Rock N Roll is still around. In other words
Rock N Roll is here to stay.*

   *This story is dedicated to their memories and
to their heroic effort for entertaining our ancestors long ago.*

Thursday, November 28, 2002

   Tim Hilton, Ned's teacher for some years now, is first generation Welsh/American, and very proud of it. The pictures on

his office wall are of the Welsh national rugby team, which once included his brother. Because he's extremely fond of Tim, Ned is most intrigued by his country of origin. Ned also knows his own parents have been to Wales a few times and love the place. Some day I hope to take him there myself, to the border country and to the sea.

Yesterday was Tim's birthday. We didn't know it at the time, but Ned gave him a gift—a poem, and not just a knock-off job done in a spare moment. Clearly Ned thought about the work for some time and then researched it before writing. He has a video tour of Wales he's watched many times, and there's also a hint of one of his musical favorites, Pete Seeger's recording of *The Bells of Rhymney*, that describes the church bells of Wales. When Tim told me about the gift today and showed me the poem, he was clearly moved by the effort and the result. It's a fine poem, and what makes it especially interesting to me is that Ned wrote it not from his point of view but from Tim's. To a proud dad, that demonstrates a literary sophistication I didn't realize he possessed. I should have known. The young man who reads poetry, listens to poetry, and recites poetry is clearly a young man who can write it as well.

Hail to Wales
To Mr. Hilton from Ned Palmer

Hail to Wales, my pride and joy and my native land,
And hail to its wonders that are so grand.

Hail to the old miners of Rhondda and Swansea,
And hail to the old castles of our ancient history.

Hail to Dylan Thomas whose poems were so grand,
Especially Under Milkwood, in tribute to our
   Mother land.

Hail to the rocky slopes of Mount Snowden that
   rises so high,
And hail to the valley of the River Wye.

Hail to our heroes so brave and fine,
And hail to this old Welsh heart of mine.

Hail to the towns where my people live,
From Blaina and the capital city of Cardiff.

Hail to our highness the Queen and
Hail to her reign, which we are celebrating.

Hail to my people and my home so glorious and free.
Hail to Wales, you were good to me!

Friday, November 29, 2002

Ned and I went to the movies this afternoon, fighting our way through the post-Thanksgiving holiday crowd to see Disney's space age *Treasure Island*, called *Treasure Planet*. The film is that rarity, a true Disney stinker. Incorrectly thinking that there would be a big crowd at the theater, we arrived a half-hour early and had time to kill in the lobby. Ned allowed as how playing the many available video games would be just the thing to do while we waited. I've generally tried to dissuade him from video games, because I dislike video games and I am cheap. I don't see much value in dropping half a buck into a machine for a few minutes of killing time while killing people.

(I once suggested in a television essay that video games should be prohibited from places where you have taken your kids to do something else. There are video games on the Washington State ferries, for instance, as well as at the top of the Space Needle. When you've already paid good money so your children can see tossing seas, lush islands, and/or sweeping vistas, you shouldn't have to watch the scenery by yourself because Junior is inside playing the kind of video games he could just as easily be playing in a Newark bowling alley. Nor should you have to endure a big fight with Junior—"Give me a quarter, Dad" "No! We did not come here to play video games, goddam it!"—and force him to watch the scenery with both of you angry and resentful. I did the piece, and dozens of parents wrote in to agree and inquire when they could expect legislation. We parents don't have a chance on this one, however. Too much easy money involved. The manager of a pizza joint with two video games clogging up his small waiting area once told me why they were there. "Because I don't have to do anything about them, but I get half of the money that goes into them," he said. "It's pure profit." And there you go.)

When Ned asked for quarters to play the games today, it was the first time this has happened since he started getting an allowance. So I said that if he wanted to use some of *his* money to play video games, it wasn't any of my business.

"Would you like me to take a few dollars from your allowance for video game playing?" I asked. He thought for a moment and said, "No."

"So you're only interested in playing video games when you're doing it with my money?"

I'm still waiting for the answer to that one. But I was happy to see that at least some understanding of the value of money has begun. A quarter into a video game is a quarter you won't have when you need it.

Monday, December 16, 2002

Ned has been working every morning as a teacher's aide at Wedgwood for two months now. Before Christmas vacation—or as it's known in the public schools, winter break—Tim Hilton thought it might be a good idea to gather together those involved to discuss how it's going. We met around the same table in the teacher's lounge where this all started.

Ned's routine at Wedgwood has changed in the last month. P.E. teacher Jim Spoor is a fine guy and an old friend of Ned's, but Ned is not a P.E. kind of person. His heart really wasn't into ball bouncing, rope jumping, and calisthenics, and so his head wasn't into it either. Jim found Ned's attention wandering, and then everything else about him starting to wander. Now he works in the library for half an hour a day.

His duties are to re-shelve books, do other library scutwork, and help with classes that come in. It's a harder job for him than assisting Marcy or helping out in his old Special Ed class, because Ned loves to putter around in libraries. When he's in there, he acts more like a student than an employee. The librarian doesn't particularly need a freelance student asking about songbooks and videotapes; she needs what my father calls a "pilot," somebody to pile it in the corner. We vowed to help reinforce the idea that even if he is in the library, Ned is a worker, not a customer.

The other classes seem to be going well. Marcy's room was always a lock. He's providing a service there he enjoys and she knows how to handle him as well as anybody besides us. Sometimes she knows how to handle him better than we do. She is one great teacher and friend, is Marcy.

Of the teachers in the Special Ed classroom, one is our old friend Kathy Schaeffer, and the other is Marcy's replacement and therefore new. She told us Ned's doing okay there too, with the only problems happening at recess. When he's asked to gather up the class on the playground to head back into school, Ned does okay with all those who want to be gathered up. But he finds it very difficult to turn into a cop, and is completely unable to deal with any child who challenges his authority. One child in particular, a boy with autism, is an almost daily trial. So they've learned not to force Ned into any kind of disciplinary role.

We learned today that there is a side benefit to Ned's working in the Special Ed first grade classroom that doesn't do much for him but apparently does a lot for others. The teacher told us that even though most of her students are six or seven years old, many of their parents are just coming to terms with the fact that their children have mental retardation. That doesn't surprise me. It's possible to overlook or ignore your child's preschool lack of intellectual development. But put that child in an academic environment for the first time, where even in Special Ed there are assignments to do and goals to achieve, and what you're facing for the rest of your life can suddenly become much clearer and more daunting.

"But having Ned there," the teacher told us today, "when parents come in they see a young man with Down syndrome, a graduate of this very room, who's actually doing a job, who's very verbal and functional. For some of them, I think Ned renews their hope for the future for their own children, just when they need it."

I'm glad Ned's doing valuable work as a teacher's aide, even if his success is in one way frustrating. It's perfect work for him, especially with Marcy, but it is work he will probably never get the opportunity to do again. The Wedgwood job is strictly a high school vocational position that ends when high school ends. Given school funding and the many qualified teacher's aides out there looking for work, the chance that Ned will find paid employment as a teacher's aide is nil, unless some special program is created. We certainly can't count on that, nor could we count on any program lasting longer than the next school funding crisis. We could probably hustle volunteer work for him somewhere, maybe even at Wedgwood. But once he's out of high school and living as an adult, Ned should have a real job, not a volunteer position. Volunteering is what you do, and what you should do, when you've taken care of the rent money and the three-squares-a-day. To be a functioning adult, Ned needs to get a paycheck, as much for psychological reasons as financial ones. I don't see that paycheck ever coming from a school district.

Saturday, January 4, 2003

We lost a good friend this week. For eight years Ned's been taking singing lessons every Saturday at the Washington Academy of Performing Arts in Redmond, fifteen miles away across Lake Washington. Redmond was a forgettable bedroom community for Seattle until our local software company settled over there. It's called Microsoft, and I hear they're doing quite well.

The Washington Academy was founded more than a decade ago by Deborah Hadley, once one of the most spectacular dancers in the Pacific Northwest Ballet company. Debby is one

Ned and Charlotte Garretson at the Washington Academy, 1996.

of America's best ballet teachers as well. One of the first things she did at her new school was start a program called *Into the Arts* for kids with developmental disabilities. Maybe such a program was a priority for her because she has a stepson with a disability, and maybe it's because that's the kind of person Debby Hadley is. But it was a great opportunity, run by excellent people. *Into the Arts* kids gathered in a studio at the Academy every weekend to learn the rudiments of dancing and singing, but principally to enjoy themselves leaping about and making more noise than usual.

Ned joined up when he was in the sixth grade. He didn't much care about the dancing, but he loved the singing. *Into the Arts* has two or three instructors every week. The vocal teacher was a woman in her late fifties from Tennessee named Charlotte Garretson. Although she spent most of her working time at the Academy as a ballet class accompanist, Charlotte was herself a noted soprano. She had a Bachelor of Fine Arts degree from the University of Tennessee, a Masters in Voice Performance from the University of Illinois, and was working on a doctorate at the University of Washington's music school. She had studied in Vienna and Florence, and had performed all over America in opera and musical comedy, as well as the church choir of whatever city was her home at the time. She was one of the most talented, experienced, and accomplished musicians on the Academy's faculty, but you wouldn't have known that to meet her. There was nothing pretentious or arty about Charlotte. In her heart she was still a small-town country girl from the South who was kissed once by Elvis back when she was a teenager and he was still sane. (Ned found her report of this encounter quite staggering.) Charlotte exuded a quiet, friendly, down-home grace and style.

I don't know whether she had been around kids with developmental disabilities much before *Into the Arts* began, but she was wonderful with them—patient, creative, and kind. She was especially great with Ned, who was probably the only *Into The Arts* student who took his music and his singing seriously. Soon after he started, we signed him up for private lessons with Charlotte after the regular group session was done.

Each Saturday morning Ned would gather up a dozen of his songbooks and we'd drive to Redmond. He and Charlotte would go over the books, choose that day's selections, and then retire down the hall to a tiny rehearsal room with a piano. Ned most definitely didn't want me sitting in. I usually waited in the Academy lobby, passing the time by watching Microsoft mothers herd their pink-leotard-encased prepubescent daughters into Beginning Ballet classes. During the lulls I could just barely hear Ned and Charlotte working away. Over the years they sang everything together: 1920s vaudeville numbers, 1940s big band hits, 1950s rock and roll ballads and show tunes, and more recent efforts by the Beatles and the Muppets.

Ned had one of the few singing teachers in America who was just as enthusiastic about his doing covers of Kermit the Frog as she was about his take on Sinatra standards. He wasn't preparing for the regional auditions of the Metropolitan Opera, after all. He was there to enjoy himself, and with her he certainly did. No matter how much they like the subject, kids who have regularly scheduled lessons almost always have a time or two every year when they have to be talked into going. During the brief period Ira was a piano student, we usually had to start talking him into going two or three days before every lesson. But not Ned. Never once in all these years has he not eagerly gone to meet Charlotte.

I think she has been just as eager to meet him, because besides being enthusiastic about all kinds of music, Ned really can sing. This comes as a surprise to people, especially parents, who have been told that those with Down syndrome are automatically tone deaf and incapable of carrying a tune. That may be the case for the majority, but not for Ned. As long as he is accompanied or singing with a recording, Ned is usually in tune, or close enough not to send his audience screaming from the room. He has a sweet, soft tenor/baritone voice with a little scratch in it.

When he accompanies himself, however, his ability to carry the tune goes right into the dumpster. I had a director once in a musical who told us at the first rehearsal that 90 percent of being in tune isn't how well you can sing, it's how well you can concentrate. I didn't believe it at the time. I've always thought that you can either carry a tune or you can't, and no amount of concentration or training will change that. Training, rehearsing, and concentrating can only improve your singing if you can already sing. But Ned is a clear example of the importance of focus.

Years ago he took guitar lessons from a friend of a friend named Joe. Joe had never formally taught guitar to anyone, but his credentials to be Ned's teacher were impeccable. He liked Ned, he was enthusiastic about teaching him, and most important, he had played in a rock and roll band for years. His guitar case was covered with stickers from heavy metal rock bands. That case looked like it had been dragged cross-country behind a Volkswagen bus. He and Ned had a great time together, and Ned learned a lot because he was so eager to do so.

Joe eventually moved away and the guitar lessons ended, but not before Ned had learned all the basics. Using his songbooks, he plays now for hours most days, carefully following the songbook directions for chords. He also sings while he plays, but his concentration is directed entirely toward the proper fingering. He sounds on these occasions like the Singing Mayonnaise, nowhere near the tune and completely unaware of its absence. But take exactly the same song, have Charlotte play it on the piano while he sings, and he's right where he should be.

How Ned escaped tone deafness I don't know. Maybe it's because he comes from a long line of musical people and has been surrounded by music all his life. My father sang on the radio, in churches, and with the University of Washington Choir, Men's Glee Club, and Madrigal Singers. He worked his way through college and law school singing professionally and driving a bus. My mother was a high school music teacher and pianist. Though I don't play an instrument, I've written, directed, and performed in musicals. Because of her association with the Children's Festival, Cathy has worked with musical performers from dozens of countries and developed an extensive collection of ethnic music that she often plays at home. So perhaps Ned inherited not only a love of music but also the ability to perform it. On those rare occasions when he does get a chance to sing in public, the relief in the audience after the first few notes is palpable.

There weren't many opportunities for performances at the Academy. At the end of the first year, Cathy and I, with Debby Hadley, crowded into the small rehearsal room down the back hall and listened to Ned sing "Edelweiss" from *The Sound of Music*. It was soft, and sweet, right on tune, and at the end the only one of us who wasn't crying was Ned. He did some Academy performances with Charlotte's son, too, a fine young man in his twenties named Craig, who has a beautiful tenor voice. And last spring, as part of an Academy recital by all of the private music students, Ned sang "The Rainbow Connection" from *The Muppet Movie* for an audience of parents and fellow students. He closed the first half of the show and stopped it cold. The only thing missing from the performance was Charlotte. She had always been frail and was home recovering from a small stroke. Someone else accompanied Ned, but it was Charlotte's work we were hearing. Her friendship, support, and encouragement have been a part of his music for a long time now.

And now no more. Charlotte died December 30th, at the age of 62. The death was sudden and surprising, although I will always suspect she had a premonition. I talked to her for the last time two weeks ago when she called to apologize for not showing up that Saturday for Ned's session. She told me she was still recovering from a fall but thought she'd be back in January. Then out of the blue she said, "I want you to know how much I've enjoyed knowing Ned and working with him." She told me what a great young man he was, and how he'd brought her a lot of happiness in the last few years. And then she was gone.

Today we went to her memorial service at a Presbyterian church in Bellevue where she was a member of the congregation and, of course, sang in the choir. Charlotte was a very religious person, with an encyclopedic knowledge of church music, especially the old gospel hymns she used to hear in the Tennessee churches of her childhood. The hymn we sang today at her memorial service wasn't that obscure, but it was her favorite. It was a hymn she and Ned had done together many times over the years—"Amazing Grace." Ned wanted to sing something special at the service in her memory, but with the short notice and the nature of the event, that wasn't possible. When the time came for Charlotte's friends to stand up and say a few words about her, he was too shy. But there were others there who knew he was her last student, and how much they meant to each other, and said so.

I should have told my favorite Charlotte story at the service, but I waited too long and the opportunity passed. So here it is now. A few years ago, we decided to record Ned's singing professionally, as a gift for the young artist. Charlotte graciously agreed to come to Seattle from Bellevue and accompany him. The recording studio we booked isn't far from our house, and survives financially by making demo tapes for garage rock bands. The technical equipment is adequate but the rest of the place is a dump, full of ratty chairs and couches teetering on floors covered with haphazardly placed, filthy rug samples. It's a tossup which is dingier, the lighting or the staff.

When Charlotte arrived, Ned was already recording a few numbers on his guitar, a painful experience for all present except the artist. She waited patiently in a far corner, sitting on a couch that looked like a thousand grunge rock musicians had crashed on it for long periods of time. Just before her opportunity came to play, Charlotte sidled up to me and said, by way of information and not complaint, "Greg, I think a cat has peed in that corner." Then she paused, looked around, and said, "At least, I hope it was a cat."

Tuesday, March 4, 2003

The past few months have been relatively uneventful. Ned continues to work in the mornings at Wedgwood, only now I drive him up there at 8:45 so he doesn't have to take the city bus up the hill.

That is partially a lie. I really don't mind the fact that he takes the bus and neither does he. But if he takes his regular school bus to Nathan Hale, it means he gets there in time to go swimming, and we don't want him spending the rest of the day with rumpled clothes and wet hair. This is also partially a lie. What we really don't want to do is get up at 5:45 in the morning.

Because of a finite number of school buses, elementary, middle, and high school starting times have to be staggered in Seattle. A group of elementary school parents apparently got the ear of the school administration many years ago and presented their concerns. In the winter months, they whined, their little babies would have to wait for the bus in the dark. Little tots standing by the side of the road in the dark? Never! Our wise educational leaders announced that elementary school would begin at 9:00 a.m. (when it's still dark for at least two months) and high school would start at 7:45. The administration was apparently not swayed by the argument that little kids naturally tend to get up earlier than teenagers. They also chose to ignore the fact that high school kids have after-school jobs and far more homework and so usually have to be up much later in the evening.

"We have spoken," said the Supreme Educators, and so for nine months of every year the Palmers have been rising at 5:45 a.m. to put first Ira and then Ned on the bus. (This is another partial lie. There were many mornings when we let Ira fend for himself, and got up after he left.) I find some consolation in the knowledge that those elementary school parents who first created this lunacy are now high school parents. I do so hope they are enjoying the dawn and seeing their offspring exhausted all the time.

Thursday, May 9, 2003

Ned has one month more of state-sponsored, high school-organized, vocational training. After that he's on his own, ready for whatever the world has to offer him, and what he has to offer it. I'm just not sure that he now has or ever will have the ability to seek, find, and benefit from those world offerings.

Just as frightening right now is a contemplation of what he is about to lose. In a month Ned walks away from most of the social contact that has been so important to him for the last fifteen years. The teachers are going to disappear, not just those like Tim Hilton and Glenda Feyes who have worked with him directly and become his friends, but a dozen others he regularly visits, knows, and cares about, and who care about him. Ned's been at Nathan Hale for five years. He's worked those halls for a long time. There are a lot of wonderful teachers and administrators at Hale who have made an effort to know him and encourage him. Even as his student comrades in the regular school population graduated, went off to college, jobs, or the military and were never heard from again, the teachers were a constant. They were the people he looked forward to seeing again every fall.

Walking down the Hale hallway with Ned for the past few years, I'm always surprised at the greetings he gets from most of the students and practically all of the adults. It's usually a lot more than just "Hi, how are ya?" stuff. Adults and kids have specific conversations about their dealings with him. One rarely gets away with a stock "How are ya?" greeting to Ned anyway. He exploits all openings, boring in on the greeter with whatever's on his mind. And except for chance meetings in public places, starting a month from now he will never see most of these people again. I don't think he realizes that yet. When he does, it might break his heart.

Losing touch with high school friends and acquaintances is hardly exclusive to students with disabilities, of course. I've made the effort over the past forty years to keep in touch with a few good friends and two or three teachers from high school days, but there are dozens of teenage acquaintances of mine I've seen no more than five times in the last thirty-five years. And three of those times were class reunions. For the first few months I missed them and the milieu in which I knew them, but they were replaced by people I met in college, people I met in the various places I worked, and people I met through my spouse and my kids.

For Ned, however, the opportunities to meet others won't include college, the military, or PTA meetings. Ned will never have to go to a fundraising pancake breakfast with little Ned, Jr. If his life does eventually include a spouse, I'm guessing the Ned Palmers won't hit a lot of neighborhood cocktail parties. So other than job-related associations, the traditional ways most of us acquire new friends and acquaintances won't be available to him. And is it likely that whatever job he gets, he'll be part of the social scene outside the workplace? Everybody will be his pal from 9 to 5, but the intimate dinner party with coworkers is unlikely to include Ned Palmer, the retarded guy on the loading dock, in the mail room, or sweeping up the sales floor. And when the boys from sales gather at Joe's house on Sunday afternoon to watch the Seahawks game, are they going to ask Ned Palmer to drop by and bring some brew? Not likely.

Unless he joins a large and active church group or some other established social setting for adults, I'm afraid it will turn out that these years in elementary school, middle school, and high school provided one of the few and one of the best opportunities for him to be part of a group of friends, especially friends who are not in Special Ed. That is ending soon, and there's not a damned thing we can do about it. If we aren't proactive about finding alternatives, losing the school connection is going to be a lot more harmful to Ned than just losing a few acquaintances.

Working the halls of high school is more than just an amusement for him. It is a core element of who he is, and how he sees himself. Almost exactly a year ago I got a call from a producer at Edge Media, a video production company based in Atlanta. Edge had been commissioned by the publishers Holt, Rinehart and Winston to produce a series of five educational videos, under the title *Lifetime Health*, on various subjects of personal interest to teens. Each piece was going to be shot at a different American high school. The last one was being done at Nathan Hale and was called *Building Self-Esteem*.

The producer who called told me that the Nathan Hale administration had given him a list of students who might be good interview subjects. Ned wasn't on that list, but when the producer told the first three kids who were on it what the video was about, independent of each other they all responded, "You should really talk to Ned." So he did seek out and talk to Ned, and as a result of that conversation he decided to build the whole piece around this little kid who, without knowing it and certainly without trying, was apparently serving as a self-esteem role model for many of his fellow students. The producer was calling us for our permission, which we gave. The title of the video became *Building Self- Esteem: Graduating Ned*.

> *"He's none of those things society says we ought to be. He's not cool enough, he's not good looking enough, he's not smart enough. He's not any of those 'enoughs' from society's perspective."*
> (John Morefield, Educational Consultant.)

The completed video opens with one adult and three students on camera, talking about Ned. We don't see him yet, so we don't know why they are singling him out until near the end of the opening sequence.

> *"He's very good about showing his happiness. When he's scared, he's good about showing that too."* (Kelsey, a student.)

> *"He's so open, you know? If he wants to ask you something, he's not going to be scared, he's*

> *going to come up to you and talk to you,*
> *and...socialize."* (Netsonet, another student.)

> *"He's the living embodiment of being okay with*
> *yourself."* (Alex, another student.)

> *"He would be called our poster young man for*
> *self-esteem, because he in fact believes so*
> *strongly, inside, in his own worth, that he lives*
> *it out so that other people and everyone around*
> *can see it. If all of us felt as good about our-*
> *selves—if all of us had the kind of high self-*
> *esteem that Ned has—what an extraordinary*
> *world we would have."* (John Morefield)

The bulk of the video doesn't directly reference Ned. John Morefield, Kelsey, Netsonet, and Alex talk about the self-image issues they've encountered in high school and what methods they've used to deal with the pressures. Intercut with them are short scenes of Ned doing things like introducing friends to the camera and signing people's annuals. It ends with the Nathan Hale Class of 2002 graduation last June. Ned looks very small and very happy. We watch him walk around the track in the opening procession, and then wait through the speeches to get his diploma. The last video of the graduation shows Ned's classmates standing and cheering as "Nathaniel Palmer" steps up, shakes the principal's hand, and sits back down again. Then we hear Ned's friends talking specifically about him again:

> *"I'm not even his parents, and watching Ned*
> *graduate, I'm just proud of him. He's probably*
> *had to overcome a lot more adversity than I ever*
> *will."* (Kelsey)

> *"When I watch Ned go up there, I'm going to be*
> *thinking, he's the one who deserves this more*
> *than any of us."* (Alex)

"You know he's not trying to hide behind, like, a façade of someone else. It's really Ned that you're looking at. I'm not sure you can say that about a lot of people." (Kelsey)

"Ned represents, for all of us, that many of the external trappings that societies say are so important don't count as much as we think they really do; that what really counts is the heart and the compassion and the belief inside. And Ned's got it!" (John Morefield)

Nathan Hale High's Class of 2002, with Ned Palmer, front and center. (Still photo taken from video.)

For those of us who really know him, *Graduating Ned* is an odd, and even disturbing presentation. For some reason, they chose not to interview the title character. It's almost like one of those cheap movie star biographies on cable television, where the subject refused to be involved and they didn't have any production money to buy clips of his movies. The whole show becomes the same black and white stills, panned and scanned in increasingly uninteresting ways, interspersed with generic file footage of the star walking around while childhood friends, ex-agents, and distant relatives talk about him. You can't help wondering why the "tele-biographer" didn't find another subject to profile when Brad Pitt or whomever suggested he get lost.

Certainly Ned would have been eager to be interviewed. My kid's no moody Brad Pitt. But as far as I know, the producers never tried. It's ungracious of me to complain. *Graduating Ned* is generally a wonderful and inspiring piece, and I'm proud they chose to build it around my son. But I suspect that the producers assumed Ned's "too retarded" to have anything worthwhile to say about his self-esteem and where it comes from. In that assumption they were wrong, although I admit the interview wouldn't have been easy. It would have taken time and finesse. Plus, it's always hard to interview somebody when you're clinging to preconceptions about them that are incorrect. It can lead to embarrassing surprises for the interviewer. (I once did a live radio interview with a candidate for state auditor while under the mistaken impression she was running for the United States Senate. She must still be wondering why I think Roe v. Wade will have an impact on Washington State's accounting system.)

Ned also does not deal well with abstracts. "Why do you eat hot dogs every morning?" he can answer. (Hungry.) But if you asked him, "What's the secret behind your healthy self-esteem?" he might very well answer, "I have white toast, too." That's if he understood what "self-esteem" means, and he wouldn't try real hard to figure it out.

He's also not given to easy slogans and inspirational cant, so he wouldn't spout the kinds of encapsulated self-esteem boosting sound bites an interviewer would be looking to present to his viewing audience. I once read a book co-written by Jason Kingsley, the man with Down syndrome who practically grew up on *Sesame Street* because his mother is a writer for the show. (She is also an advocate for people with disabilities, and much of the excellent stuff on the *Street* relating to physical and intellectual challenges, like the pieces with Itzhak Perlman, was due to her influence and her talent. Thanks from a lot of us, Emily Perl Kingsley.) I think it was somewhere in that book that Jason Kingsley says "We don't call it Down Syndrome! We call it Up Syndrome!"

Although I admire the young man's enthusiasm and positive outlook, this is the kind of thing Ned would never say. I've always been leery of canned slogans, like "Be your own best friend," and "Today is the first day of..." etc. I don't consider Tony Robbins and Wayne Dwyer among our great philosophers, and Ned is like me in that.

(I was driving along one day trying to think of a title for this journal, and suddenly it hit me: *Been Downs So Long It Feels Like Ups to Me*. Ned the punster would love this title, if he understood it. And that would make two of us who were for it. Many, many other people took the time to tell me I was making a huge mistake, even though I was never serious about it. Really.)

Besides the "I'm Okay, You're Okay" sloganeering of "Up Syndrome," the historian in Ned would never allow it. It's called Down syndrome, he would point out if he knew the facts, because in 1866 the physician-superintendent of an English asylum for the mentally retarded first identified a specific type of retarded people. Unfortunately, he called them called Mongoloids, because he thought they looked like Mongolians. At the time, Mongolians were considered intellectually inferior by people who had never been within ten thousand miles of a real Mongolian. (They're actually remarkable people, the Mongolians.) That physician's name was John Langdon Down.

So, Down syndrome has nothing to do with the opposite of Up, any more than Lou Gehrig's disease has to do with baseball. This is a point Ned would most certainly make, but then he wouldn't use such boosterism in the first place because he wouldn't see any need for it. I haven't given him a rousing pep talk about anything for a long time, because whenever I did it was unsuccessful. Eventually I realized it was unnecessary, too. Ned keeps his own council. He doesn't need the "You can do anything if you really, really try, buster" speech because it's never occurred to him that he can't do what he wants to do. When he realizes that he is incapable of something, he lets it pass and moves on to the next thing. There are exceptions, like his undiminished wish to be a professional singer/songwriter or a teacher's aide at Wedgwood or in Room 104, but one of the reasons Ned is usually happy, and certainly one of the reasons he doesn't have big self-esteem issues, is that he believes he can do what he wants to do. And when he can't, he's able to forget it and try something else. If more people had this ability we wouldn't need 90 percent of the psychiatrists we have now.

I've mentioned before that we're frequently amused by some of the adults Ned meets for the first time, because they're surprised and even shocked that he's as happy and outgoing as he is. They want to demonstrate what compassionate people they are by showing us how sorry they feel for the poor little re-tard, and they want the poor little re-tard to help in this effort by feeling sorry for himself. It is the subtext of their reaction— "The kid's so stupid he doesn't even understand how awful his life is"—that is infuriating. Even if Ned acknowledged that he had a developmental disability, it wouldn't change who he is and his general happiness one bit. His bliss isn't based on ignorance. It's just bliss.

Kelsey's wrong when she says Ned has had to overcome more adversity to get where he is. In one sense, he's probably had to overcome less than she has, because the genuinely good people he's been around all of his life have cut him a lot of slack when he needed it, certainly more than the average kid gets. John Morefield is correct. Ned has never worried about a date for the prom, bad hair days, the hipness of his clothing, or the random viciousness of friends and enemies.

Made-for-television movies may love the plot of a Special Education kid being mistreated by students in the mainstream population, but that has never happened to Ned in eighteen years of public school. Or at least I don't know that it has happened, and I think I would. The only kids who have ever bullied him or treated him meanly have been a few of his colleagues in Special Education, and in one case that still appalls and angers me, the parents of one of his best friends, whom I'll call Ronnie. With no warning or prior discussion, these people we thought were our friends called one day and informed us that they had decided Ned could no longer come visit their son, "because Ned is a bad influence on Ronnie." Their real reasons for this disgraceful act are complex and not worth going into now. They not only had the nerve to terminate abruptly a friendship that was then a decade old and very important to two nice young men, but the audacity to blame Ned for it. I was furious and still am. All I can think is God help Ronnie. His parents are willing to jeopardize his happiness so they can feel better about themselves. Unless Ronnie is the only person on the planet with both developmental disabilities and too many real friends, which I doubt.

If the producer/interviewer of *Graduating Ned* had asked my son how he maintained his self-esteem in the face of all that nonexistent adversity, Ned wouldn't have known what to say. "Adversity? You mean like my father only letting me have three Chips Ahoy cookies at one time? That kind of thing?" *Graduating Ned* seems odd because the premise of the piece wrongly assumes that besides the additional difficulties of having mental retardation, Ned also faces the challenges of his normal classmates, including academic achievement and social acceptance. I don't think Ned worries for a moment about academics. While it's true that he wants to complete individual assignments successfully, in the main he learns things because he wants to know them, not because they will be on the test. Like every other human being on the planet, he hopes the people he's around think he's smart, or at least knowledgeable, but compared to the people he's around most of the time, he is. And he is so much smarter than the rest of the population expects him to be that in his presence they act like he's the brilliant one.

He does deal with social acceptance, but not via the accoutrements of traditional high school life. He doesn't drive a hot car or wear hot shoes, he doesn't have a piece of clothing any high school kid would find remotely cool, he isn't a star student/athlete/actor/lover/comedian/musician, he doesn't have a great looking girlfriend, and I don't think he's ever kissed the girlfriend he does have. He's a short, chubby, comparatively weird-looking guy, none of which bothers him. Social acceptance for Ned means being an equal in the group. It means being part of the conversation, both listened to and talked to. He's unhappiest, and his self-esteem probably suffers the most, on the rare occasions when he's not part of the conversation because he's not allowed to be, or he doesn't want to be. I think that's what happened on that awful day he checked into Easter Seals camp. He realized emotionally, if not intellectually, that he wasn't part of that group any more. He had seen an attractive alternative just a few days before.

I wouldn't claim to know all the reasons Ned's self-esteem is as healthy as it is, and I shouldn't think anyone who watches *Graduating Ned* will know either. But I know that it has something to do with his creating the world he wants and learning to function in it. And I know there have to be people in that world for it to work, people he can call friends.

That's why *Graduating Ned* is disturbing for me and I have a hard time watching it. "Graduating Ned" also means "Goodbye forever, Ned." In five years of high school, he has never once been invited to the home of one of his "normal" high school buddies, nor have any of them ever been in our home. It would be naïve and unrealistic to think that any of those friendships will survive after June. But that doesn't mean they weren't real friendships, and I certainly don't blame any of those young people for not making the effort to be closer to Ned and stay that way. On the contrary, I can't thank them enough. The simple fact is that they could have ignored him, but instead they made him a part of their lives as something far more than a pet or a curiosity. It's not their fault that it couldn't last forever, or that uniquely among them, Ned doesn't have nearly as many friendship options from now on. It's just the way things are.

I'm wrong. It's not going to break Ned's heart to lose all that. With any luck he'll do what he has in the past. He'll accept the situation, take from it what he can, and move on. It's my heart that's going to break, because I know what he is losing. The last bus is going by, and he's back at the side of the road.

Saturday, May 11, 2003

In our family, this weekend in May has been the calm before the annual storm for seventeen years. The Seattle International Children's Festival begins early Monday morning. Many thousands of school kids, ranging in age from six to sixteen, begin arriving at the Seattle Center to spend a week being culturally enlightened by world music, theater, and dance, whether they want to be or not. At the start of the week the Festival staff facetiously says, "This would be a great children's festival if it weren't for all these children." At the end of the week they say it for real.

There are hundreds of major and minor hassles that arise when you are trying to bring world performers and fifty thousand school kids together in one place at one time. Years ago, for instance, an acrobatic company from the People's Republic of China (where they seem to turn out identical acrobatic companies by the dozens) was coming down from Canada and got stopped at the Blaine, Washington, border crossing. A U.S. customs official at the border took it upon himself to declare that the company's costumes were not costumes at all but were really "textiles" being brought into the United States for resale. He demanded thousands of dollars in duty before he would let the company cross the border with the exact same costumes they had carried into many other countries. Until many frantic phone calls were made, it looked like the company would be performing in Seattle in their skivvies.

Some years before, a different Chinese acrobatic company charged more than eight hundred dollars to the Festival, buying M&Ms at the grocery store next to the Center. Chinese folks want to go home with as many American dollars as they can possibly acquire. So instead of spending the daily stipend they were given for food, the members of this company put the cash in their pockets and lived for a week on snacks, especially the chocolate they loved. That was the last year the Festival had an open account at the grocery store.

As the Festival's Director of Education, Cathy has more school- than artist-related hassles. There are always children who should not have been let out of their cages. There are always teachers who arrive an hour late with fifty-eight kids in tow and think they can either totally disrupt a performance in progress by just walking in with their charges, or automatically get fifty-eight seats for a later performance. Others with reservations don't show up at all and assume they will get their money back, not understanding that the Festival can't just automatically resell the seats they reserved. Teachers are not alone in their complete incomprehension of the fact that theater seats are a finite commodity, but you'd think they would figure it out.

Starting this coming Monday morning, Cathy will have to deal with these kinds of problems and dozens more, so it's no wonder Ned and I are mostly on our own for the week. Our consolation is we get to go to a lot of the Festival's shows, and over the years we've seen some great performances. The big act this year is a can-can dance company from France, here to show that far from just being an opportunity for Maurice Chevalier-wannabees to see underpants in action, can-can is a legitimate artistic dance form.

The weekend before the Festival begins, all the acts arrive and try to get one technical rehearsal completed. It's a madhouse, or a series of madhouses, and Cathy works hard. So she wasn't able to make what may become a very important journey with Ned and me today.

Cathy saw mentioned in the newspaper a few weeks ago that there was going to be some kind of symposium on work opportunities for adults with developmental disabilities, to be held today on Mercer Island. The events included instructional sessions, speeches, and a vendor display area where companies that do job finding and training for people with disabilities would be available to chat. Ned and I drove over this morning. We weren't interested in the instruction or the speeches, but it seemed like a perfect opportunity to check out potential counseling/job placement services, especially since we're doing this part on our own.

A few weeks ago Cathy met with Tim Hilton at school for a last official conversation. If Ned had followed the normal progression and left school at age eighteen for three years of at least half-time, away-from-school job training, their meeting would have involved reviewing job training options run by the Seattle Public Schools. But because Ned was about to be out of the public school business entirely and would no longer be the district's responsibility, Tim just gave her some pamphlets about education programs around the area, as well as various check-lists for signing up with the state's Department of Vocational Rehabilitation and Department of Developmental Disabilities. Tim did what he could, but because of the decisions we've made, there wasn't much else for him to do.

My interest in driving to Mercer Island to talk about job counseling far exceeded Ned's. He still clings to the idea that he will be a teacher's aide in Room 104 at Nathan Hale, and any-thing else is just a waste of time. But he was also intrigued by the process, and came along with enough curiosity to make the journey valuable.

We arrived just as the vendors were setting up in the gym-nasium of the middle school where the symposium was being held. Representatives from five organizations stood around card tables covered with literature, mostly brochures that invariably had a picture of a developmentally disabled person on the cover grinning into the camera at some work site. I noticed that all of these happy workers were people with Down syndrome, I as-sume so any passing reader would immediately know that the person pictured had mental retardation.

We visited all the tables and chatted with the people stand-ing there. Some of them seemed a little surprised that Ned was part of this visit, which in turn surprised me. It's his life we're talking about; he should be there. Others were happy to see him, I think, and rightly spent more time talking to Ned than to me. Not that they got much out of it. He told every one of them that he was going to be a teacher's aide at Nathan Hale, thanks very much.

Three of the companies were operated by religious organi-zations. I didn't spend much time with them. Although it's fine that churches offer such services, I'll take people with no par-ticular agenda to promote every time, if there's a choice. Fortu-nately, the first company we came to is operated by old friends, and in Cathy's case, old employers. The organization is the University of Washington School of Medicine's Employment Training Program. This is how they describe themselves and their services on their website:

> *The Employment Training Program (ETP)*
> *is a national leader in developing and imple-*
> *menting support services for adults with dis-*
> *abilities. Our goal is to provide resources to*
> *individuals with a disability seeking to establish*
> *themselves as independent, contributing mem-*
> *bers of their community. ETP was the first*
> *training program in the nation designed to*
> *train and place adults with developmental*
> *disabilities into competitive employment. We*
> *made our first successful placement in 1976.*
>
> *Our Employment Specialists look for jobs in*
> *the community that match the skills and needs*
> *of the individuals in our program. They provide*
> *on-the-job training once a client is hired and*
> *gradually reduce their presence as the person*
> *becomes increasingly independent.*
>
> *While they are still at the job site, the Em-*
> *ployment Specialists provide consultation to*
> *supervisors and co-workers to help make*
> *everyone's adjustment to the new employee*
> *more comfortable.*

Standing behind the ETP card table today was a tall man named Peter Simonson, with prematurely gray hair, a quiet smile, and a nice, calm manner. He told us how they do a complete assessment of the client's skills. For Ned that would include not only interviewing him at length but also talking to his teachers and any other employers he might have had about his strengths and weaknesses. For me one of the most attractive parts of the assessment process is that Ned would spend a week or so at the University doing a variety of jobs. ETP plants him for a day or two each at worksites within the University's massive medical center, as well as other places around campus, and watches how he does at a variety of tasks. After all that is done, they go out and find him a job, train him for that specific job, and then after he's hired, stick with him on the job site until they're sure he can do it, and he's sure he can do it.

It sounds very straightforward and efficient. It would also be a miracle to me if we didn't eventually go for these University people. One way or another, the University of Washington has been a part of our lives for decades. All four of Ned's grandparents are graduates of the U Dub. We live five minutes from campus and have for thirty years. I walked out of the place in 1967, but Cathy graduated from there and then did graduate work in the English department before getting a job teaching UW writing labs. I suppose if Peter Simonson had said how proud ETP is that so many of their clients now have good jobs down in the coal mines or working in slaughterhouses, we'd consider going elsewhere. But at this moment it seems historically and emotionally right that Ned puts his future in the hands of a division of the University. Cathy and I talked about it tonight when she got back from Festival fun, and she agrees.

Friday, June 27, 2003

While I was at work today, Cathy called Peter Simonson to tell him that we have chosen to put Ned's occupational fate in the hands of the University of Washington. It wasn't a difficult decision for us for the reasons already stated. The real decision that took some thought over the past few months has been whether to pursue a job for Ned or get him into a post-high school education program. Some of his fellow graduates of Room 104 are in such programs at community colleges in the area and are doing well. We investigated some of these opportunities for Ned, and certainly could have found classes that would have benefited him. But one of the main goals of such programs is continuing intellectual stimulation, and that's not something Ned needs, at least not in a formal setting. His own voluntary reading and researching serve that purpose and serve it well. He did fine as a student in school, but we think that now he's more comfortable and accomplishes more on his own and with our help. He lives in an intellectually stimulating environment that in part he created and in which he seems to thrive, with no indication that it will end just because he doesn't have to trot off to school every morning. What he needs is a way to support himself, and that means a job.

ETP has three or four case workers, but we think Peter will be our guy. That's good, because Ned says he likes him. We'll see whether Ned will like the process of being assessed every time he turns around before he actually starts working somewhere.

Adulthood

Friday, September 19, 2003

Having seen many books where people who are supposedly writing about their kids end up writing about themselves, I admit that today's exercise starts with too much about me. Eventually it's about Ned. Trust me on that.

In the summers of 1967 and 1968, I had my only experience as a professional actor. Saying that Lord Olivier and I were in the same profession for those six months is the equivalent of saying Mario Andretti and the guy who runs the kiddie cars at Play-Land are doing the same thing. Both men work with vehicles, but that's where the comparison ends. So while Lord Larry was doing *King Lear* at the Old Vic in London, I was doing Sample Switchell in *Ten Nights in a Barroom* at the Potlatch Playhouse, Bainbridge Island, Washington, a ferry ride across Puget Sound from downtown Seattle.

In the midst of my second summer at the Potlatch, I played "The Irish Cop" in *Betsy Green the Cannery Queen*, a play I wrote over the winter. I had a falling out with the theater's owner/operator, and as they would say in *Variety*, "Palmer Ankles Potlatch Playhouse." But before I left, the boss had already told me that given the way I looked, I wouldn't get any decent parts as a professional actor, at least for a while. "Nobody wants a twenty-year-old guy who looks fifty, when there are so many fifty-year-old guys who have been in the business for years and have credentials. Wait till you're fifty or so, get some time and experience in your face, then try." And I believed him.

Many years later, my friend Lucy Mohl and I did a television news series about people from the Northwest who had gone to Hollywood to find fame and fortune. We talked to some who had succeeded, including Kyle "Dune" MacLachlan and Jean "Designing Women" Smart, and many who had not, like Bill "Crowd Scenes" Stoner. The biggest star we interviewed was Robert Culp. After a bumpy half hour—not a cheery man, Robert Culp—I finally said, "Mr. Culp, there are kids in Seattle watching you right now, kids who'd give a lot for the career you've had. What do you want to say to them? Should they come down here and give it a try like you did?" And Culp responded, "If you can't think of anything else in this world, sure. If literally nothing else on earth will make you happy, then come ahead, try it. But if there's anything else you want to do, do that instead. Because down here it's murder." And I realized that he was talking about me. There were other things I enjoyed doing in 1968 and thereafter, so I left acting and went and did them. I'm still doing them. But over the years I've noticed that whenever I stand on a stage I get a little jolt, a jolt that's part excitement at the possibilities and part regret at opportunities lost. Especially now that I'm a fifty-five-year-old guy, give or take a year, with a face absolutely sagging with time and experience.

Six months ago I read that the twelve-year-old Seattle Fringe Theatre Festival was looking for companies to appear on its stages in September. In a moment of foolishness/egomania, I signed up. I chose to do a one-man show not only to see if I could write it, but also to see if I still (or ever) had any acting chops. Starting tonight, there are going to be seven performances in a forty-nine seat auditorium with the lilting theatrical name Union Garage.

Part of the reason I signed up was to do some material I wrote a decade ago that I've never been able to get anybody else interested in. The real reason I decided to do this, however, is that tingle I've always felt standing on a stage. Ham, sir? Yes, sir!

Figures of Authority is a series of four brief monologues. The first speaker is Dato Shalikashvili, who is the Chairman of the Moscow May Day Parade Central Organizing Committee. The second monologue I'll get to in a minute. The third is Helmut, the Swiss border guard who confronts the escaping Von Trapp family in the Alps in 1939 and drives them mad filling out his forms and asking his required questions. He has trouble understanding why an unemployed sea captain is refusing sea captain work and is instead escaping to Switzerland, where there is no sea. And the fourth speaker is Darrin Stevens, a few minutes before he is executed for murdering his wife, Samantha, because she was a witch he thought was trying to kill him.

Finally, back to Ned. The second monologue in the piece is called "Grumpy," and has its origins in an adaptation of *Snow White and the Seven Dwarfs* I wrote for the Seattle Children's Theatre in 1986. They wanted me to do *Sleeping Beauty* but I talked them into Snow instead, because *Sleeping Beauty* is a drag, and for a long time—well, since Ned was born—I've wanted to respond to the 1937 Disney version of *Snow White*.

In show biz tradition, certain characters were standard figures of fun, and especially ridicule, for their lack of intelligence and sophistication, or sometimes their venality. In order of appearance on the American stage, especially but not exclusively in vaudeville, these stereotypical fools included the Yankee, then the Jew, the German (or Dutchman), the Irishman, the Italian, and the Asian. And throughout that progression, the African-American. As each ethnicity's numbers increased in the general population and thus in the audience, they stopped being maligned because the performers could no longer get away with it. There were Irish acts in vaudeville, for instance, that were very successful in 1910, and booed off the stage in 1920, especially by the ever-increasing Irish audiences in New York and Boston.

The most obvious category of stereotyped rubes was blackface acts. Every comedian in vaudeville, including Jack Benny, George Burns, Bob Hope, Fanny Brice, Eddie Cantor, Ed Wynn, Bert Lahr, Milton Berle, and all the others who went on to fame in other media, slapped on the cork at least once early in their careers. They thought they had to, to keep working.

Ironically, real black vaudevillians also had to wear blackface on stage or they weren't allowed to perform. Perhaps the greatest comedian in American history, Bert Williams, never appeared on stage in his too-short life without corking up. Blackface characters lasted on stage a lot longer than derogatory Irish, German, Jewish, and Italian stereotypes because blacks weren't allowed in the audience, or were relegated to the balcony and forgotten. But there was another group that was also never found in that main floor audience but certainly found on that stage. That was the fool, the funny simpleton, the laughable moron, the modern village idiot.

In other words, Disney's Dopey. By including in the seven dwarves what is obviously meant to be a nonverbal mentally retarded adult (and it was a Disney inclusion, because the Grimm Brothers dwarves are unidentified by name, gender, or character), Disney was relying on a known and still acceptable comic character in 1937 when the film was made. I would argue that the character is still acceptable to audiences, when the dope is played by Jim Carrey, Adam Sandler, and loathsome others. Watch *Saturday Night Live* for a while and see how many painfully unfunny sketches include a "comedic" retard. It's a goddamned disgrace, and not offset by such films as *Forrest Gump* and *Rainman*, where the simpleton is both lovable and/or does remarkable tricks. The former is insulting and the latter is condescending.

Drooling Dopey in *Snow White* is always screwing up and his brothers are always beating the hell out of him for it. Sometimes they just slap him around for laughs. I once tried to count the number of times Dopey gets hit by someone in *Snow White*, but I gave up at fifty, with the film far from over. If you're sensitive to the treatment of people with developmental disabilities, and you recognize Dopey for what he is (the name's a clue), then watching much of *Snow White* is excruciating.

In my version of *Snow White*, the Dwarves are a regular-sized family whose name just happens to be Dwarf. I did that partly because I wanted the play to be about a family and partly because finding seven dwarf actors in Seattle would have been impossible. I certainly didn't want kid actors dressed as dwarves, either, because I didn't think they could handle it. At the first meeting between virgin and dwarves, Snow complains that the dwarves are supposed to be little people. Rose Dwarf, the earth mother amongst the Dwarves, responds, "I know a family named Green and they're not green at all. And what about the Lurkenmüllers? There's absolutely nothing Lurkenmüller about them."

My Dopey equivalent is a twenty-year-old woman named Peg, the baby of the family in more ways than one. She's cute and verbal and always questioning. When I wrote the adaptation of *Snow*, Ned was just four. In retrospect I think I was hoping that Peg was what Ned would become, and also how he would be treated when he was twenty, with respect, kindness, and compassion by the family and by strangers like Snow. And generally that's happened.

At the end of my play, when Snow is trying to decide whether to ride off with the very handsome but very vain and self-centered Prince, it is Peg who jumps up and says, "You don't love him! Do you love him?"

Snow, in despair: "Oh, Peg, I don't know...."

Peg: "If you're going to get married, marry someone you love. Someone you care about. Marry someone who cares about you."

Snow thinks about it for a moment, and then turns to another person on stage and says with some surprise, "Elliott, I...I love you!"

Elliott is my Grumpy. (Disney owns their dwarf names, and they can have them.) During many performances, I would get down on the side of the theater so I could see the audience's faces during this last scene. Invariably there would be little girls, and some moms, whispering up at Snow, "Elliott! Pick Elliott!"

They got it. And they're getting it was one of the most satisfying successes of my professional life. But when I was thinking about what to do in this one-man show, I realized that there were still some things I wanted to say about the story of Snow White, the dwarves, and especially Dopey. So I decided to present Grumpy late in his life, telling the real story from his perspective and talking about his brother. I think it's the best piece in the show, in no small part because it's the piece that really means something to me. But I'll find out tonight if I have the script and the ability to make an audience feel what I feel. A costume designer made some short legs for me, so I have to sit throughout the piece with the legs in my lap. But at least in rehearsal it felt comfortable.

Here are the pertinent parts about Dopey, and so in a way they are the parts about Ned. This section follows an opening designed principally to pull the audience into the tent both emotionally and comically, trying to get them used to seeing Grumpy as a real human being and not just cartoon comic relief.

Grumpy

...You probably want to hear about Snow.
Everybody does. That very first night we found
her asleep in Doc's bed, I tried to give her the

bum's rush. I said to the others, "Don't you know what's going to happen here?" But they ignored me. They were already gaga over her. So they offered her a deal. We'd protect her from the Queen, and in return, she'd do all our cooking, cleaning, washing, ironing, knitting, sewing and gardening. And she agreed, which told me right off that she was desperate, and dumb. But nobody ever went to Snow White for intellectual stimulation....

The next afternoon we came home from the diamond mine whistling like idiots. We were all happy, which was kind of confusing to Happy, but that was his problem....

...We'd always gotten along okay. We had everything we needed, and we didn't need much. Sneezy drove us crazy, and I had a problem with Happy. Try being around a guy who's happy all the time, and see if there aren't occasions when you just want to bust him in the mouth. But generally we were satisfied. We didn't have anything to fight over.

And within hours after Snow got there we were snapping at each other, competing for her attention. She was a very sweet kid—then, anyway—but she started playing us against each other. She couldn't help herself; probably thought it was fun, it was a game for her. She was too young to see she was tearing us apart.

We were all infatuated with Snow, so it may seem odd to say that only one of us really fell in love with her, real love. That would be me. I came back from the mine early the next day to check on Dopey. He wasn't feeling well, so he'd stayed home. With any of the others I would have thought it was a trick to be alone with Snow, but not Dope'. He's never been sneaky in his life. Wouldn't know how.

*I went up to the sleeping porch, and she was
sitting in his bed, with his head in her lap,
softly stroking his shoulders, telling him a story
about faraway kingdoms and magical beasts.
When you have a brother who's retarded, you
tend to judge strangers by how they treat him.
You hope for kindness; you insist on respect. But
Snow was already beyond all that. She realized
instinctively what it took his brothers years to
see, something outsiders never understood.
Dopey's the best of us.*

*Seeing the two of them together like that was
like getting hit in the head with a mallet. I was
in love, and I knew it. At the same time I was
ashamed of myself, because I wanted to grab
Dopey up and throw him out of his own bed and
take his place, so I could lie there with her
forever. I was jealous of Dopey. Jesus!*

*That week was kind of sublime agony for
me. We were together, all the time. I could
watch her and hear her laugh and dream about
a life with her. And it was agony seeing my
brothers fawning over her.*

*One day she had a little cold. Doc immedi-
ately went into his chiropractor routine. He was
knocking the furniture over to get behind her
and grab on. But before he could I jumped him,
and we fought. I think I would have killed him,
but in the middle of it I saw something out of the
corner of my eye. I thought it was some big
animal that had crept in. But it was Dopey,
curled up on the floor in the corner. He was
terrified, sobbing, staring at me like he didn't
know me. And still not making a sound.*

*I...I just ran out the door. I walked for
hours in the forest that night. I realized that
the only way I could have Snow to myself—if
she wanted me, which admittedly was a big*

*if—was to destroy my family. I couldn't do that,
even for her. I decided to get as far away as I
could from all those people. I'd come to
America, and start again.*

*The next morning we marched off to the mine
as if nothing had happened. I apologized to Doc,
to all of them, and they said they understood.
But they didn't. That was the afternoon we came
home and found Snow lying on the floor with
that apple in her hand. We tried to revive her,
but it was hopeless. She was stone cold—there
was nothing we could do. Yeah, I know, people
think we chased the queen over a cliff. Nonsense.
That bitch was long gone, back in her palace,
back to being a queen. And royalty could kill
anybody they wanted to.*

*It was my idea not to bury Snow, to build
the glass coffin, to keep her with us that way.
And by not putting her in the ground to rot, we
finally did save her life. Because pretty soon the
tall handsome prince rode in on his big white
horse, and without so much as a word to us,
gave her a big kiss full on the lips. She jumped
up, patted us all on the head like we were
goddamned children, and rode away with a
guy she'd never even spoken to before. The
whole process took fifteen minutes. I guess
she'd had enough of small furry animals and
small furry men. I lost her again, and this time
I lost her for good.*

*... A few months later the Prince national-
ized our diamond mine. Apparently Snow had
told him all about it. Soldiers showed up, and
gave us twenty-four hours to get out. We spent
the time gathering up all the diamonds we
could, and killing all the soldiers, with a feroc-
ity that was as big a surprise to us as it was to
them. Then we <u>all</u> escaped to America.*

...We became cowboys, riding around on horses—well, ponies—helping folks out. We called ourselves The Magnificent Seven...Dwarves. But that's a whole different story. Some other time, maybe.

...We dwarves eventually split up. The others wanted to marry, settle down, have kids of their own. And they did—great kids. But that wasn't for Dopey and me, so we lit out together. I couldn't ask for a better man to ride with. Some nights, though, we'll be sitting around the campfire, out there in the middle of nothing, and I'll look across at Dopey and he won't be there anymore. He'll have tears in his eyes, and that goofy smile on his face. And I know he's thinking about her, about that week we had together. The best week of our lives. And the worst.

She broke his heart too, but he still loves her. He'll always love her.

What's good enough for Dopey is good enough for me.

Heigh ho.

There are a lot of things wrong with the Disney version of *Snow White* besides the presentation of Dopey. Snow wins in the end, but for the wrong reasons. She wins because the Magic Mirror is correct. She is the fairest in the land, so beautiful the dwarves can't bring themselves to bury her, and then so beautiful the handsome prince hears about it and sweeps her up without a word exchanged between them. For kids and especially girls, the Disney *Snow White* sends exactly the wrong message. It reinforces the idea that your success in life depends on how you look, and especially how you look to men.

One of the most moving moments I've ever had occurred after a performance of *Snow* at the Seattle Children's Theatre. Ten young people from a nearby children's hospital were in the audience. They were all cancer patients, all undergoing chemotherapy, and so they were white-skinned, with completely bald heads and big, frightened eyes. After the show, the cast stayed on stage to talk to them. I was standing with Annajo Trowbridge, a beautiful young woman who played Snow, when one of the adults accompanying the group approached us.

"I just have to thank you for doing this," she said. "You probably don't realize how important it is for these kids to hear that what you look like doesn't matter, how much they need to hear that it's what's in your heart, and in your mind, that really says who you are. We organized this trip just to get them some entertainment, something to take their minds off what's going on in their lives, but, well...." By then she was crying, the other parents and caregivers were crying, Annajo could hardly stand up, and everybody else associated with the show was losing it too. These ten ghostly kids stood and looked at us weeping and hugging each other and they probably thought we were nuts. Because underneath it all, they were still kids.

The other problem with the Disney *Snow White* is the finish. It's great for the virgin, but what about the little guys who have saved her life once in the film and three times in the original story? She really does just pat them on the head and ride off. And we're supposed to think they're happy about that? We're to assume that because they're little people, their love for Snow isn't real and so how can they have broken hearts? That's exactly what some people think about adults with developmental disabilities. And that's why *Grumpy* is ultimately about Ned.

I've heard far too many people tell my son and his parents how "cute" it is that he has a girlfriend. Ned's a twenty-two-year-old man. He may be part of a cute couple, but there's nothing cute about his desires. They are strong, and adult, and they aren't going away. His sexuality can't be diminished or dismissed just because he has Down syndrome, or because he may never know the physical part of love. Far too many people have the mistaken idea that people with mental retardation are scary, oversexed, predatory creatures. They conjure up televised mug shots of drooling predators and don't know, or want to know, about people like Cyndy and Rod, the married couple with Down syndrome I mentioned before. But all of the adults with mental retardation I know are like all of the *other* adults I know. They want warmth and tenderness in their lives. They want someone to share those lives with. They just want someone to love who will love them. They want Grumpy, not the Prince.

I hope *Grumpy* says to people that just because you are dopey—or sneezy or sleepy or bashful, for that matter—it doesn't mean you can't love in every way. It doesn't mean you can't be devastated when you lose that love. Dopey is as human and as emotionally vulnerable as Grumpy, his smartest brother. Out there in the middle of nothing, they are kindred spirits, with far more in common than either of them realizes.

Ned's not coming to opening night tonight. I don't go on until 9:45, which is a bit late for him. That's good. I want to see how it works before he sees it.

Saturday, September 20, 2003

Opening night went well, but then on opening night in a forty-nine-seat theater, almost all those seats are filled with friends and relatives. Unless you're doing a one-man show called *Josef Goebbels, A Hell of a Guy!* you'd have a difficult time laying an egg. It was also a learning experience after all these years off stage. "Grumpy" is obviously the strongest of the four, while the Parade Chairman is the weakest. That's odd, because a month ago writing the piece, I would have predicted it would be exactly the other way around.

I guess it goes to what I've always said about passion. Any art that is successful has at its core one person's passion for the work, whether it's a David Hockney painting, a Tony Kushner play, or a Sherwood Schwartz television situation comedy. Sherwood Schwartz had a passion for a slapstick comedy about some people stranded on an island. It was a way to get laughs, but for Schwartz it was also a way to look at a microcosm of society, even if the societal members in the show were all blatant stereotypes. Everyone told Sherwood Schwartz he was nuts and that his pilot episode stank. His passion survived. He recast a few roles, made another pilot, and added a title song he wrote in one day that gave the background for the whole show. He was told it still stank. "Experts" kept telling him that for the four years it was one of the top television programs in the world. Sherwood Schwartz stank all the way to the bank. The lead character's name was Gilligan.

The "May Day Parade Chairman" is a bit, a sketch I've wanted to do for a long time. So are the Swiss border guard and the doomed Darrin Stevens. But because of Ned, I have a passion for doing "Grumpy." Of course it's the best of the lot.

Ned comes in a few days, but he has a major and much anticipated event to enjoy first.

Sunday, September 21, 2003

One of the things that has come from Ned's connection to the Washington Academy of the Arts is his friendship with a young lady named Vicki Noon. Originally Vicki was just another one of the dozens of people who ran around the Academy halls being as artistic as a pre-teen can be. It took us some time to see that Vicki was a little different. She was one of the few young ladies running around on Saturdays who had more on her mind than how she looked and how she danced and how other people thought she looked and danced. She was a studious type then; glasses, fully clothed, sensible shoes—a very likable young lady.

One day Charlotte asked me if I would be interested in appearing in an Academy stage production as Guest Artist. She was asked by the Academy management to approach me, because they didn't know how the "former minor local celebrity" that I am (Ira's phrase, very accurate) would respond. The Academy was doing *The Wizard of Oz* and needed a Wizard. Kelly Willis, the director, didn't relish the prospect of casting the part with a twelve-year-old female ballet student, even though there were many twelve-year-old female ballet students available. For a variety of reasons, including Ned's great love of the material, a minimal rehearsal and performance schedule, and my own deep strain of ham (these reasons are not in order of importance), I agreed. After three decades, I would return to the stage in a school production surrounded by youths ranging in age from five to seventeen. I saw that as just the right dramatic challenge. I may be a mediocre actor, but I can still wipe the stage with a ten-year-old kid wearing a lion suit.

They let me skip a lot of the rehearsals. When I finally attended one, I was surprised to see that the young woman cast as Dorothy had apparently decided on her own to play the role as Britney Spears might play it, with all the subtle nuance of a stripper in the second worst joint in El Monte, California. Dorothy also didn't know her lines when everyone else did, and didn't seem to care that she didn't, even though we went into dress rehearsal in a week's time. I think she thought her personality would win the day.

Kelly didn't care to present a *Wizard of Oz* in which Dorothy and Toto were on the same intellectual level, so she invited the young lady to seek new challenges in the theater, somewhere else. At the next rehearsal, I was introduced to "the new Dorothy," Vicki Noon. Although she got the part five days before opening night, the difference was magical. Vicki was obviously extremely talented, hard working, and without being too saccharine about it, properly virginal. She also knew all of her lines, which I always think is important when you're in practically every scene.

The next rehearsal I attended was the first performance in costume, in the theater of a high school fifteen miles down the road from the Academy. The suburbs in that area have a lot of newly rich people in them, including a lot of Microsofties, and this high school reflects its upwardly mobile clientele. The place is huge, immaculate, and has a theater that is better equipped than some of the Broadway houses I've seen. It's a real theater too, with a fly loft and adequate backstage area, not the cursed "multipurpose auditorium" of most high schools. Because it's a real theater, the school hired an experienced union stagehand to run it.

The memorable moment of that rehearsal for me was the first time I heard Vicki really sing. That opening number is "Over the Rainbow," of course, and I watched this fourteen-year-old kid walk to the front of the stage and belt it out. The pro stagehand came out from the wings a few moments later and stood staring up at the sound booth. He told me later he was trying to figure out why they weren't letting Vicki sing the song herself, why the director was playing a recording by some thirty-year-old professional singer.

Vicki was singing the song. She has a remarkable voice, in the same way the then sixteen-year-old Judy Garland had a remarkable voice. Both women sound twenty years older than they really are, and fifty years older experientially. The difference between them is that Garland perfected her style during a decade in vaudeville as part of the Gumm Sisters, whereas Vicki just has this incredible natural instrument and an innate musicality to go with it. Needless to say, she owned the show as Dorothy, and I was proud to share the stage with her.

Ned, Vicki, and I became friends. I had a small hand in getting her a role at Seattle's Act Theatre, a real big time Actors Equity stage, and she did very well with it, especially for someone who had never acted professionally before. We went to other shows she did after that, including a second production of *Wizard* produced by the Academy. To give somebody else a shot at Dorothy, Vicki played Auntie Em, and Mr. Ned Palmer was a citizen of Emerald City. I watched.

To say that Ned was smitten with Vicki would be an understatement. She's about his age, she's very talented, and she has grown up to be a very attractive young woman. Whenever he spotted her at the Academy, he would light up like a pinball machine, and she and her mother, Liz, have always been wonderful with him.

We lost track of her for a while after the two *Wizards*. We stopped going to Redmond after Charlotte died, and Vicki had a falling out with the Academy and transferred to a regular high school. Then she invited us to her high school graduation party, where we had a fine time and I enlisted her as a volunteer worker on the PBS documentary about video games I'm still staggering through.

Vicki was just about to start at Seattle Central Community College. She was going to live at home with her folks, twenty miles away, and commute. It's not an easy thing to do, because you're fighting rush hour traffic in both directions, and once

Treat-or-treating with Vicki Noon and friends, 2003.

you get into the area of the college, you're competing with ten thousand other people for the limited parking available.

At the same time, Cathy and I were considering finding a student to live in our basement in exchange for afternoon help with Ned. Ira is out now and has his own place, so there's a nice apartment down there. I suggested making the offer to Vicki, and Cathy agreed.

Vicki moved in today, and Ned couldn't be happier. She will pal around with him three afternoons a week while I stay at KCTS and Cathy is at the Children's Festival. It should work out fine, although I have some concerns about the effect on Ned. He's never said so, but he is most certainly attracted to Vicki. Having her so close, so often, might be hard for him, especially as she will and has every right to continue her own social life while living here. Ned understands that the basement is now hers, and he is never to go down there without her permission. My concern isn't that he'll bother her. My concern is that she will, unwittingly, bother him a lot. She will become his Snow White, eventually to pat him on the head and ride away with a prince.

Late this afternoon, he came up to me, looking concerned.

"Dad," he said conspiratorially, "I've decided. I'm not going to tell Lily about Vicki."

Thursday, September 25, 2003, midnight

It hadn't occurred to me that it would be difficult to perform Grumpy this afternoon with Ned in the audience, but it certainly was. It may take me a while to figure out why. It wasn't because I thought he might be embarrassed. Even after hearing the word "retarded" applied to him, I don't think he makes the slightest connection between himself and the Dopey I talk about in the piece. No, that connection is made entirely by me and those in the audience who know about Ned. At this moment I'm glad he doesn't see the point I'm trying to make doing Grumpy, the point that Grumpy and Dopey are on different intellectual levels but are emotional equals. They can fall in love with the same person, and have their hearts broken the same way, and never forget, but find comfort and solace in each other. But there was something about saying that in front of him that was excruciating. It's a small theater so I could easily see him out there. But I couldn't look at him without losing it, except for one line, a line I wrote months ago, especially for him. And I said it right to him.

"I couldn't ask for a better man to ride with."

Sunday, September 28, 2003

The Fringe Festival is over, and I did all right. The script was okay to good and the performance was adequate. A friend who's a fine actress and director actually told me how surprised she was that I did so well. I can live on that for a few years.

Ned hasn't said much about the show, but to my surprise his reaction to the whole enterprise has been minimal from the beginning. *Figures of Authority* did not become one of his obsessions; far from it. He enjoyed checking the theater out with me a few weeks ago, but he didn't insist on coming to opening night and didn't ask me much about the script or the audience reaction. He was almost blasé about attending last Thursday, like he was just going to another movie and not to something starring his father. Perhaps I am not the continually fascinating person I think I am to him. I'll survive.

Wednesday, October 8, 2003

In the summer of 1997 I was working at KCTS on a show for the PBS *American Masters* series. The show was called *Vaudeville*, and it was the first and so far only documentary about the dominant form of working class entertainment in America for more than twenty years. Vaudeville was also a precise and revealing mirror of American society from the late 1800s through 1930, more so than any entertainment that came before or since.

It still took us years to get the funding to do *Vaudeville*, but perseverance and passion for the subject eventually paid off. Working with three talented women—producer Rosemary Garner, Associate Producer Shannon Gee, and photographer Valerie Vozza—we went into production and eventually traveled all over America interviewing surviving vaudevillians. We talked to more than forty people. In the eight years since that trip, we have sadly lost almost all of them, and I will forever be proud that because of *Vaudeville*, America got one last chance to see and meet these remarkable talents.

One of the hard parts about doing television production on the road is that sooner or later you have to come back home and actually create the show, which includes a lot of irritating, tedious administrivia. The summer of 1997 was a long gauntlet of arguments and adjustments for me. While I was stressed, Ned was having a great time working just down the hall at KCTS. I had negotiated a deal with the KCTS management for a paid summer job for him in the station's mailroom. The fact that Cathy and I donated the exact amount he was going to be paid is inconsequential. At sixteen, Ned had summer employment and his first experience getting a paycheck in return for his labor.

Ned's supervisor in the mailroom was a bright young woman named Merritt Klarsch. A few years later she left KCTS to go to Chicago and work for Oprah, and not in the mailroom either. But back then, she was just out of college and still pondering a career as a television producer. She and Ned hit it off, in part I think because Merritt's father runs an excellent private school in Tacoma, so she's been around lots of kids, likes them, and knows how to show it. It was also close to the perfect job for Ned. The actual work wasn't much of a challenge. Matching the names on letters and packages with the names on mail slots was hardly daunting for as good a reader as he is.

The principal joy he found in the job was the social interaction. As in many businesses, the mailroom at KCTS is the hub of the operation. Everybody goes through many times a day, and chatting with Ned became an enjoyable part of the day for a lot of them. It certainly was the most enjoyable aspect for Ned. He already knew half the staff from hanging around with me, and they knew him, so there was none of the nervousness he might have caused somewhere else. In fact, his only real problem at work was too much socializing. If Ned was asked to deliver something directly to someone's desk, the trip could take an hour and a half, not because he got lost (the original assumption by some) but because he was working the room, checking in with his friends, telling what became Ned's Joke of the Day. After Ned had been on the job for a few weeks, I quietly told my colleagues that they shouldn't hesitate to cut him off if they had things to do and he was going into hour two on the Denny party or any of his other interests.

Ned worked in the mailroom for two and a half months before he went back to school. Toward the end of that time, a committee of workers and managers named him the KCTS Employee of the Month. Part of his selection had to do with the fact that he could perform the job required, which came as a surprise to the KCTS folks who didn't know him and his abilities. As usual, some folks had little or no previous experience with developmentally disabled people, and for them Ned was a revelation of sorts. Ned in the job and able to do the job made a lot of KCTS workers just a little bit happier to be at

the station. Because of him, Channel Nine wasn't just presenting public affairs discussions about a community issue like
meaningful employment for people with disabilities; Channel
Nine was actually doing something substantive about it, one
mailroom clerk at a time.

I didn't find this reaction at all surprising. It's my experience that those who are involved with the media coverage of
public issues feel a certain frustration, especially if their work
focuses on people in trouble. At least those media folks with a
conscience are frustrated. They gather together people in the
community with an interest and expertise on the subject, shoot
videotape of programs in action, ask questions about what the
public can do to make things better, and, after the program's
over, those guests go off to do something real while the producers and reporters get ready for next week's issue. A public affairs producer/reporter eventually starts feeling like a parasite,
deriving sustenance from the woes of embattled people without
ever doing something to alleviate those woes directly. They usually react in one of two ways. They either lose the conscience
and don't care about their subjects anymore, or they walk away
from the newsroom and end up directly involved in a supportive
agency. The ones who like money and power with their social
conscience run for office.

Part of Ned's award as KCTS Employee of the Month had
little or nothing to do with his disability. It was because he was
a pleasure to have around. Even though there were a lot of worthwhile candidates, Ned got the nod because he was about to leave,
his spirit would be missed, and the other possibilities could wait.
And most everybody agreed with those reasons. Choosing Ned
was a popular decision. It was certainly popular with Ned.

Vaudeville aired on PBS in October of that year. Not only
was it the second highest rated *American Masters* to date, but
at the end of the year *People Magazine* said it was the best entertainment special of that television season on any network,
thanks almost entirely to the people we talked to, and the clips
we had of their work and the work of their fellow vaudevillians.
In the list of names at the end of the show, among the research-
ers, is "Ned Palmer." It is a legitimate credit for the work he did

scouring his songbook collection for vaudeville-related items, like the origin of "Take Me Out to the Ballgame." He is very, very proud of that credit and mentions it often.

Today Ned started working for KCTS again, but this time as an unpaid intern in the marketing department. I'm back in the building every day producing and writing two national projects: the video game history (*The Video Game Revolution*) and a travel/historical piece about the Inside Passage, that thousand-mile-long body of water, islands, rocks, and trees that runs from Puget Sound to the Alaska panhandle. My difficulty at least at the beginning of work on these programs is that I don't know much about video games and what I do know I don't like, and even though the family's been here for a long time, I've never been farther north on the Inside Passage than Vancouver, B.C.

There are various things Cathy and I need to take care of both financially and logistically before we start working with Peter Simonson to find a real paid job for Ned. Cathy suggested that in the interim Ned might intern at KCTS, as long as I was there every day to help if need be. It would give him on-the-job experience and also give him something to do three days a week.

So it was set up, thanks to Jay Parikh, an old friend who is now in charge of marketing, new business development, and practically everything else sales-related at KCTS. Tuesdays, Wednesdays, and Thursdays Ned will work directly for Marcie Finnila, who does double duty at the station as Jay's associate marketer/salesperson and as the other producer of the video game show. (She's the one who actually knows and cares something about video games. Although it is a stretch to say Marcie is the one with the passion for the subject, she'll do for now.) So from working with both Jay, his supervisor, and me, his father, Marcie's in the perfect position to oversee Ned's internship.

Her suitability for the role of Ned's supervisor is more than just proximity. Like Merritt Klarsch years ago, Marcie started at KCTS in an entry-level position, as the receptionist. She rapidly moved up to something more substantive. But the first time I really met her, she was still running the front desk and I was looking for a woman from the South to read a letter in the show I was working on.

The Perilous Fight: America's World War Two in Color is a documentary series about the American experience in the war that uses only color footage shot at the time. We didn't have an original frame of film in this four-hour epic, nor did we do any interviews with aging vets. The story is told through narration and a reading of letters written to and from those on the war fronts in Europe and the Pacific.

Perilous Fight's executive producer, a brilliant British filmmaker named Martin Smith, may be the only person in broadcasting today who has too much integrity. Actually, he may be the only person in broadcasting today who has any integrity at all, but that's a different book. For the letter readings in the show, Martin insisted that something written by a woman in Virginia had to be read by a woman from Virginia, or at least from somewhere south of the Mason Dixon line. He didn't care to hear any Seattle actresses doing their best drama-school-Southern-belles. This restriction about voices meant that as the writer/producer of the third program in the series, which covered the war in Europe from D-Day through V.E. Day, I spent months trying to find Seattle-area people with authentic Brooklyn, Mississippi, German, French, and other accents. (Almost as a respite from this effort I searched for one decent letter from a Norwegian to include in the show, but only because in Seattle I was and am surrounded by people with slight Norwegian accents but few authentic Mississippi drawls.) I chafed a bit at the regional accent requirement, but as usual, Martin was right; it was worth it. And Marcie was the proof.

While I was searching for a young Southern woman, I heard that the new KCTS receptionist was from Virginia. I approached Marcie at her desk one afternoon and inquired if it was true. She said yes, in what sounded to me like a slight Norwegian accent.

"But you don't have a Southern accent," I said. "I don't want you to fake what you don't have."

"No problem," she replied. "A Southern accent is the way I talk normally. I'm faking *not* having a Southern accent now."

This was true. Marcie learned after coming north that too many people on the winning side of the Civil War assume somebody with a Southern accent has possum fritters and hog jowls for breakfast, drives a pickup with a gun rack, and is at best dim. So she spends her day faking the no-accent Northwest accent. When she goes home to her husband and two-year-old daughter, she lets the drawl hang out. That sweet little drawl can be heard on *Perilous Fight: Wrath* as Mrs. Jackie Greer, writing to her fiancé the night after he landed in Normandy on D-Day:

"All America had been asked to pray, so I slipped out of bed and knelt in prayer for a few minutes. I prayed for all the boys over there. But mostly, I prayed for you."

It is the best line reading in the show and one of the most moving, in large part due to Marcie's delivery. Martin Smith's genius was to have people read these letters who were geographically legitimate, but also people who were emotionally legitimate. Marcie, the young wife and mother, could easy imagine what it must have been like for a woman around her age to sit at home listening to the radio, knowing that the person she loves could already be dead and lying in the sand on a beach three thousand miles away. You can hear her compassion and fear—her identification with Jackie Greer—in those three simple sentences.

Marcie's Southern accent is not the only reason people might make incorrect assumptions about her. With pale skin and bright red hair, she is very pretty in an unconventional way, with the striking figure of a model. There is still something little-girlish in her voice which you might assume is an affectation if you didn't know better. In other words, Marcie could be and has been mistaken for a bimbo, a twinkie, someone who's all hair and no brains. (I believe there are such people in broadcasting. The men are called "meat puppets.") Marcie's look and sound is very deceiving. She's one of the sharpest people I know.

Marcie knows from firsthand experience what it's like to have people make quick, false assumptions about your intellectual abilities. Besides her compassion, good humor, and intelligence, she brings that sensitivity to her relationship with Ned. She's asked me about his skills, but is as interested as I am in expanding those skills.

In the first hour of Ned's first day as a volunteer marketer, he got his own desk, which is near mine but not next to it or even in sight of it. That's as it should be. Ned isn't here to work for me or be around Dad. He also got an ID badge with his picture, his own computer, and his own password to get into it. All of these things he found cool, topped off by the coolest thing of all for him. He doesn't have to take directions from me; he takes them from Marcie, and he's crazy about Marcie.

His first assignment is to take the hundreds of business cards Jay has collected in his sales travels, alphabetize them, and put them in plastic sheet pockets in a three-ring binder. It's pretty basic work, but Ned has never done anything like it before. I doubt that he's ever paid any attention to a business card in his life. The job requires not only basic alphabetizing but decisions about whether to put someone under their name or the name of their company. Marcie and I sneak around and peek at him occasionally, but mostly he's on his own and seems to be doing fine.

November 11, 2003

> From Jennifer S. Lee, Treasurer
> Seattle Fringe Theatre Productions
> Dear The Just One Old White Guy Company,
> c/o Greg
>
> Thank you for your participation in the 2003 Seattle Fringe Theatre Festival. As you are aware the Fringe is currently in a cash flow crunch that has left us unable to make full payments at this time. We apologize.... Please know that the board is aggressively fundraising to generate the money to pay you in full....

They can make that check for my cut of the box office out to "Blue Boy," because I'll be holding my breath until it arrives.

Friday, November 17, 2003

This morning while I was otherwise engaged, Cathy and Ned drove up to the Washington State Department of Vocational Rehabilitation office in the far north end of Seattle. They met with Louise Goodman of the Department and Peter Simonson of the University of Washington's Employment Training Program to formulate a plan to assess Ned's employability and review the terms for Peter's work with Ned. The state is picking up part of the tab, and we get the rest.

Since Ned was three weeks old, we have attended 14,365 meetings with various school or governmental officials to formulate some kind of plan or another. What's different now is that Ned is at the table and not messing around out in the hall while his fate is being decided. That's a good thing, although Cathy tells me he didn't participate much. No matter how many times we tell him it's not going to happen, he still clings like a pit bull to the idea that this is all wasted time until he assumes his duties as a teacher's aide at Nathan Hale High or Wedgwood Elementary. (He would accept ownership of a McDonald's as an alternative.) But even if he chooses not to participate in all the preliminary events, he has the idea reinforced that these are plans being made for his life. He can and should have a say in them, even if his say so far is, to quote the succinct movie mogul Samuel Goldwyn, "include me out."

Monday, December 1, 2003

Let the assessment begin. This morning we trotted over to the University to meet with Peter and Susan and have our first real meeting to determine who Ned is, what he wants to do, and what he's capable of doing. Slowly but surely Ned is getting more involved in this process, as a participant rather than as just an observer. Peter and his colleagues wisely don't reject any employment possibility, including the teacher's aide dream to which Ned still clings. They let Cathy and me tell him how unlikely that is, so that Ned may even see them as allies in his cause. Now that he's talking more in meetings, I think Peter is getting a much better idea of how capable Ned is, and that may lead to a wider range of job possibilities.

This afternoon Peter went to Nathan Hale and talked to Tim Hilton about Ned. We resisted the temptation to ask many questions of either person about that conversation. We know Tim has a high regard for Ned and his prospects, and didn't need to intrude on the process. I'm sure in his job Peter has to deal with many parents whose assessment of their child's abilities is either too high or too low. Best at these early stages to shut up and let him do his job.

Friday, December 5, 2003

I took Ned to the Young Life Open Door Christmas Party this evening. I haven't said much about his involvement in Young Life, which he's been attending since the first year of high school. I haven't said much because the organization gives me the whimwhams, or at least our local manifestation of it does. Ned goes to the weekly meetings and we encourage him to go, because Young Life Open Door (the club for teens with disabilities) provides a regular out-of-school social experience. Such opportunities are rare and we take advantage of them whenever we can, even if the philosophical/religious views of the organization differ from ours. If the Klan, the American Nazi Party, the National Rifle Association, or the Bill O'Reilly Fan Club suddenly started sponsoring weekly *Coffee and Disturbing Flags Night for Our Friends with Developmental Disabilities* we'd probably pass, but Young Life Open Door is acceptable.

The organization describes itself in its national website as:

> *...a non-profit organization committed to making an impact on kids' lives and preparing them for the future. Young Life leaders leave the comfort of their adult worlds and enter the arena of high school and middle school life. You will find Young Life leaders sitting in the stands*

*at football games, walking the streets of inner-
city neighborhoods, driving carloads of kids to
the shopping malls or tutoring students in study
centers after school. In fact, you will find them
almost anywhere you can find kids. Young Life
leaders model trust, respect and responsibility to
their young friends, and they do it within a
meaningful context, within the context of a
teenager's world.*

This is just the first paragraph of the website's home page:
it covers the basics, except that it fails to mention that Young
Life's stated mission is to "Introduce adolescents to Jesus
Christ." And introduce Him not, as the title of my Unitarian
Sunday school textbook claimed, as *The Carpenter's Son*. At
Ned's Young Life Open Door, being introduced to Jesus means
being told repeatedly that Jesus is It, the one and only God, the
Big Deal, all you'll ever need to have a fulfilling life. This strikes
me as odd for an organization that claims to be nondenominational. If it's nondenominational, it's nondenominational in a
very denominational context, excluding as it does Jews, Mus-
lims, Buddhists, Hindus—approximately 70 percent of the
world's peoples. I think it also effectively excludes us Unitarians (all right, lapsed Unitarians), especially those of us who
don't believe every human being on earth is wallowing in sin.
(Just conservative Republicans. Only kidding. Sort of.) At this
moment, I can imagine a Young Life leader reading this and
saying, "We don't exclude anybody. We just expect everybody to
eventually wise up and opt for Jesus." Granted.

My reservations about Young Life go back a long way. Every Friday when I was in high school this guy in his thirties
would show up. He'd stand in the front hallway during lunch
and after school, working the crowd, introducing himself as
"Ray from Young Life" and encouraging us all in a very caring
and hip way to come check out his club. I never heard him
mention Jesus once, and in fact it was some time before I realized that Young Life was a religious organization and that Ray
was in fact a hip, very with-it evangelist. Mercer Island High

School must have been a real challenge for him, because (and I say this with pride) it was the most wise-ass school in the Northwest, full of guys who couldn't fight their way out of a tub of yogurt but could verbally reduce an opponent to tears without much effort. Imagine trying to sell guys like that on the concept that sin would be our downfall unless we attended meetings on Tuesday nights. At the time many of us were actually seeking sin, and admired our peers who had already found it. That could be why Ray went light on the Jesus stuff around us. But he was still working the halls of an American public high school for the Nazz, as the comedian Lord Buckley used to refer to the Man from Nazareth.

My Unitarian/lawyer's kid knee jerked at this clear violation of the separation of Church and State. So after a few months of avoiding Ray and enduring a surprising number of converts singing his praises, I went to the Vice Principal's office and inquired as to whether they were aware that a minister was in the school selling Jesus.

"That's not a minister," the Vice Principal chortled. "That's just Ray from Young Life. Heck of a guy!"

I responded that if good old Ray were allowed to operate in a public school then I was going to get my Unitarian minister down every week to pitch his youth group. And as long as I was at it, I was going to call the Catholics and the Mormons and Rabbi Levine and why don't we get a few people in here selling the Watchtower at lunchtime and do baptisms in the football team's whirlpools? That was Ray's last day inside Mercer Island High School. (School administrators on Mercer Island were deathly afraid of being the subject of Mother's Marches, because at least some of our mothers—and fathers— were lawyers who knew their way around the Constitution.) Thereafter, he'd stand on the public sidewalk across the street and wave at us in a very caring and hip way, trying to lure potential Young Lifers to cross. And to the Cross.

Ned's experience in Young Life has shown me that he can't be easily proselytized, which is encouraging. From the very beginning five years ago, when the leaders were directing the assembled in prayer, Ned was the only one who didn't look down. He looked up, and continues to do so during the prayers. When I asked him why, he explained to me that he figured God was up in heaven, and therefore you should look up when praying because it is impolite not to look at someone you were talking to. This may sound too cute to believe, but he really said it, and he said it sincerely.

In the personal characteristics list Ned wrote a while ago, the very first item on the list was that he is "very religious in my own way." That's fine with me, and if Ned becomes a devout Christian or a devout anything else and it makes him happy, I've got no objections and would certainly not try to talk him out of it. The only exception I'd make is if he became enamored of some sect or faith that militantly believes everybody else is wrong and isn't shy about saying so. Maybe that's my problem with Young Life. They come far too close for comfort to the "You're wrong, I'm right, you're doomed" school of proselytization.

For now, I think that Ned's interest in Young Life is almost entirely social. Last September the weekly meeting was split into two sections. The first hour was given over to the boys in one room and the girls in another discussing religious matters, or discussing their problems in a religious context. Actually, I'm not sure what they talk about in these gender-specific meetings, because to my surprise Ned opted out of attending this first hour. He chose to come solely for the second hour, which is the regular Young Life meeting and begins with generally nonreligious games and singing.

The religious pitch, and a strong pitch it is, comes in the last fifteen minutes. Each week Ned hears how he's a sinner no matter who he is or what he's done, how God created everything over a long six-day week, and that Darwin's theory of evolution is bunk. (I thought saying that to a roomful of high school students was shameful.) It's been suggested to Ned by the Young Life leaders that if he just takes Jesus into his heart everything will be dandy. Ned mentions none of these blandishments to me afterwards. I really think he ignores them, rather like the way he ignores the infield fly rule when baseball is on television. We've never really discussed religion at all, and he's never asked the traditional kid questions: What's God look like? Is there really a heaven? Is there really a hell? Do I have to go this Sunday?—that kind of thing. And it could be he hasn't asked the questions because he's already figured out the answers that work for him. It is entirely his decision to resist taking Jesus wholly into his heart, leaving room for other possibilities.

At the same time, the irony is that Ned knows more about the Bible and Christian religious facts than any other kid in Young Life. Indeed, he knows more than either of his parents, who are victims of that sparse religious training known as Unitarian Sunday School. One of Ned's favorite books has been a compilation of stories from the Bible, purchased years ago at the county library's annual book sale. He also has a video tour of the Holy Lands that he's watched many times, and because of Charlotte's influence and his special fondness for Mahalia Jackson, he knows many lovely old gospel songs, too. Thanks to his awesome memory, he's retained a lot of the information from these sources. When a Young Life leader asks a Bible-related question, Ned's hand invariably goes up, and frequently only Ned's hand goes up. I've seen from my chair way in the back that this causes the leaders some distress. They are well aware that, since Ned's Jewish friend Jacob left Young Life last year, Ned is not only the sole pagan among the multitudes, but the kid who over the years has been the most reluctant to take Jesus (or anybody else) into his heart. They would prefer that one of the more devout give the answers, but they are stuck with the only kid who knows.

(On one delightful occasion last year, a leader asked the group to describe God in one word. "Loving," said one kid; "Old," said another. The leader finally and reluctantly called on Ned, who said "Omnipotent." "Yeah, right," said the leader dismissively, as if Ned had just suggested that "overrated" is a good word to describe God. "Anybody else?" The very next kid said, "God is all powerful." "Right!" beamed the leader. "That's very good!" It occurred to me that this college graduate in charge didn't know what "omnipotent" means. Unlike Ned, who did.)

The Young Life Christmas Party is one of three or four yearly YL events, none of them as religious as the last fifteen minutes of any given meeting. Tonight we ate spaghetti and sang a few carols, with "Jingle Bells" and "Rudolph" holding equal standing with both of the "Nights," "O Holy" and "Silent," and all the other carols where the swaddled Babe actually makes an appearance. And there were games, in one of which a kid stands very still while his team decorates him like a Christmas tree. This year Ned was the tree.

I don't know how much longer Ned will do Young Life. It's meant for high school teens. High school and teenagerhood are over for him, and yet many of the others in the room are his age or older. They may just change the name to Middle-aged Life, and then Old Life, and keep on going forever.

Saturday, December 6, 2003, 10 a.m.

Nathan Hale High School Cafeteria

J.S. Bach wrote what's called *The Coffee Cantata* ("Schweigt stille, plaudert nicht," or "Be quiet, stop chattering") around 1731. It contains a memorable line which translates from the German as, "If I can't drink my bowl of coffee three times daily, then in my torment I will shrivel up like a piece of roast goat." That the immortal Bach composed a piece about coffee, with references to goat roasting, comes as a surprise to those unfamiliar with classical music, people who in their ignorance think that when the organs, harpsichords, and cellos come out, the subjects are almost exclusively Jesu, Joy, Man's Desiring, and "Hey, Wotan, Here Come the Big Girls."

These are the thoughts that rise up when eating breakfast to live music: in this case, my fifth, and (I hope) last visit to "Pancakes and Performances," one of the two big fundraising events of the Nathan Hale High Music Department. So at present I am sitting in the cafeteria at a table sticky in many spots and littered with the detritus of the pancake eaters who came before me and have now moved on. The walls of the room are festively and permanently decorated with the names of outstanding wrestling team members, plus exhortations to "Go Hale Raiders!" without any indication as to where they are supposed to go. At the end of the cafeteria opposite the kitchen, the Nathan Hale Jazz Ensemble is playing a Dizzy Gillespie piece. That seems appropriate. Dizzy Gillespie always looked like a guy who could pack away the pancakes and had already consumed way too much coffee. Listening to the Jazz Ensemble at that end of the room are the parents of the jazz players, while the parents of musicians in other Hale musical groups sit in this end of the room ignoring them completely while trying to choke down the cakes.

I hope the person who invented the pancake breakfast as a way to raise money had to go to hundreds of them. No other punishment would fit the crime. To begin with, the pancakes are always cold, and where eats are concerned, nothing is colder than a cold pancake. The thick postage stamp of equally frigid butter just squats on them, like a tiny square brick dropped on a concrete floor.

They are also quite elderly pancakes, or at least they are at Nathan Hale's annual pancake-o-rama. I know this because I was the volunteer cook for this event for the previous three years, having exactly the right qualifications for the job: I am a sucker, and I am handy with pancakes. I always worked the first shift, which meant that I got to the school kitchen around 6:00 a.m. The doors opened at 8:30, so that by the time those early arrivals sat down to their paper plate with "three pancakes, two pieces of sausage, seasonal fruit, and coffee," the cakes were two hours old, flatter than a manhole cover, and cold. Like a piece of roast goat, as Bach would say, only a roast goat that lost an encounter with a steamroller. In Alaska.

Nobody attends a pancake breakfast for the pancakes, although this fact seems to escape some people. In Ned's freshman year, the woman who volunteered to run the pancake breakfast decided it was going to be a "gourmet" pancake breakfast. "No Krusteaz," she said proudly. "We are going to make the batter from scratch, with real buttermilk and fresh eggs." She made this announcement at the first Music Supporters meeting I ever attended. A few of us present suggested that perhaps she was completely out of her mind. "Scratch pancakes will be very difficult to pull off," I remember saying, trying to speak with the voice of pancake experience, "and besides, nobody will care anyway, because nobody will be there for the food."

Her response wasn't as direct as I might have wished. "Isn't your child a freshman?" she asked me, "and a singer?"—the implication being that the father of a freshman singer can't possibly have the pancake expertise of the mother of a senior second-chair trombone player. And before I could answer, she huffed, "If we don't do it my way then I refuse to be involved." It was the perfect stand to take, because ten times worse than attending a pancake breakfast is running a pancake breakfast. She kept the job.

When Ned and I arrived that year around 9:00, the line to get pancakes came out the kitchen door, through the cafeteria, and down the hall outside. I think the end of that line was somewhere near Tacoma, but I don't know for sure because I never went looking for it. Many people who had paid the money for the breakfast that year, including me, never had a gourmet pancake or any other kind of eats. We never even saw an available pancake, because we declined to wait. However, I couldn't resist peeking in the kitchen door. One single dad was standing at the smoking grill with nothing to cook, while five guys in the back hovered over home mixers and bowls, frantically cracking eggs, throwing flour around, and spilling buttermilk onto themselves and the floor. (Interesting that it was all fathers back there. I suspect the mothers knew a lot more about kitchens, cooking, and making a few thousand pancakes from scratch, and so happily sacrificed their husbands on the altar of volunteerism.) It looked like a Ritz Brothers routine with no laughs. The pancake breakfast director was running around trying to motivate her troops, all of whom looked like they would have killed her for a single box of Krusteaz. I believe I had identified their problem, supply-wise.

Her kid graduated that year, thank God, so she disappeared into the miasma. (I hope she's doing the Pancake Breakfast at Notre Dame now. We don't like Notre Dame here in the Northwest.) The next year, people who understood the true pancake breakfast concept took over, including me. I had five hundred cakes cooked before the first one was eaten, and nobody had to wait more than ten minutes. The pancakes were mediocre, but the line to get them was nonexistent, which I thought was the point. (It's a variation of the old Woody Allen joke, "The food here is lousy but the portions are big.") People come to pancake breakfasts like Hale's because they have to, and sitting and schmoozing with each other over cold cakes and slightly warmer coffee is the only real activity they have a chance of enjoying.

In other words, it's a perfect event for Ned, who doesn't eat pancakes, sausage, or seasonal fruit, but is a schmooze-meister of practically Congressional quality. I can see him now on the other side of the room, sitting with a clutch of his old choir colleagues, discussing I don't know what—sex, drugs, and rock n' roll, possibly. He has told me my job is to "guard" his untouched plate of food, which is his way of saying I'm not to leave the table, not to come near him, not to cramp his action. My reward is that I get to steal his sausage, a mission already accomplished. In a few minutes the choir is scheduled to perform and I assume he and I will move to that end of the room to listen. He may allow me to sit with him. Then we will get the hell out of here. For good.

For good. This will probably be Ned's last contact with a choir that has been very important to him for a long time. When he first enrolled at Hale, the school choir seemed a natural choice for a boy who loves music and singing as much as Ned does. It was also a very good way to get him out of Room 104 and in with the regular school population for an hour a day.

We talked to the choir director, an ex-Marine trumpet player named Rich Sumstad, and explained about Ned. We told Rich how Ned had taken singing lessons for years but had never been in an organized group. With his permission, we said, we'd like to give it a try. To Rich's credit, his first question was not, "Can he carry a tune?" He was immediately supportive, and continued to be so for the next four years.

I think Rich decided that he'd find out for himself whether Ned could really sing, and then take action if action was needed. He'd give the kid a chance, which is all we've ever asked of anybody. Rich wouldn't have hesitated to drop Ned if it wasn't working, either. He supports an inclusive music program, but he is also a professional musician and knows the emotional and educational dangers of a lousy group. He told me a few years later that he'd just had one of his worst days as a school music director. He'd had to call the parents of one of Ned's Room 104 friends who had just joined the choir and tell them that their daughter would have to transfer out. "She simply can't sing," Rich said, "and she tries at the top of her voice. It's not fair to the others."

Ned did the full four years with Rich, standing in the center of that group and singing his part. We could occasionally hear his voice in the ensemble, but rarely, as it should be in a choir. And when we could hear him, he was always on tune and on time. With the choir, he traveled to a competition in Victoria, B.C., and a high school musical celebration in Honolulu. I went along as a chaperone on both occasions, but didn't really need to be there for Ned. In most situations he

Ned's final appearance with the Nathan Hale choir, performing the "Hallelujah Chorus" *from Handel's* Messiah. (Still photo from video.)

was just another member of the group, and acted like it. He met many of his non-Special Ed friends at Hale in choir, including one of the interviewees in *Graduating Ned*. Getting him in choir was certainly one of the best things we ever did for him.

I don't know about taking him out of it. When he started his vocational training at Hale last year, we made a very tough decision. Even though Rich was amenable to having him in the choir for a fifth season, we wanted Ned to understand that he had already graduated and was no longer a high school student. So we told him he couldn't be in the choir, or do most of the other student things of years past. He was to concentrate on his student job and on picking up some of the simple skills of an independent life. I think he was very disappointed and I know he was furious. At this moment, watching him across the room yucking it up with his former chorus mates, I'm not so sure about the decision. It was probably right to get him thinking toward the future and what he needed to learn to survive. But we automatically eliminated an opportunity for the kind of social interaction that he so enjoys. There's no changing that now.

Friday, December 12, 2003

I suppose if somebody had asked me any time during the last twenty years if there would come an evening when Ned and I would double date, I'd have said no. He's Ned, for one thing, and Cathy and I have been married for thirty-five years, for another. I haven't really "dated" anyone since the Johnson administration. (That's the Lyndon Johnson administration, not the Andrew Johnson administration.)

Last night, however, Ned and I double dated. Sort of. His companion was the lovely Ms. Vicki, I escorted my old friend Lucy Mohl, and the event we attended was the opening night of *The Wizard of Oz* at the Fifth Avenue Theater. Cathy declined the opportunity to follow the yellow brick road, being a person who wouldn't get caught dead at a stage musical based on *Wizard of Oz* unless Al Pacino were appearing as the Tin Woodman. She's Italian, is Cathy.

The Fifth Avenue in downtown Seattle is a huge old barn built in 1926 as a vaudeville house with movies. The Chinese'y interior was modeled after the Forbidden City, the Temple of Heavenly Peace, and the Summer Palace in Olde Cathay, which is why to this day the Fifth is an acoustic nightmare. None of the structures that inspired it is a theater, which should have given someone pause for thought back in 1926. All that kitsch *eats* sound.

Like practically every other giant movie palace in America, The Fifth fell on hard times in the 1960s and '70s. It was rescued from the wrecking ball by a clutch of Seattle deep-pocket business types who got grants to restore the building. Avoirdupois-wise, that restoration was a revelatory experience. The 1926 seating capacity was near three thousand, but after the restoration, it dropped to twenty-one hundred. The change wasn't because the seating area shrank. It's because people's butts were a lot smaller in the 1920s. All the Fifth's existing seats had to be replaced with wider versions. I blame Tater Tots, first introduced in 1958.

Ned, Vicki, Lucy, and I were putting our modern big butts in those expanded seats last night for two reasons. First, Vicki and I have done this show together, so we were eager to see the big time Fifth Avenue production. There's nothing actors enjoy more than going together to see a show they've done themselves, so they can make nasty remarks about their equivalents.

Second, the new Fifth Avenue production features Lucy's and my old friend Laurence Ballard as the Cowardly Lion. Larry is the best actor I know—nationally, locally, stage, or screen. During the past twenty years I have seen him do remarkable work: as Roy Cohn in *Angels in America*; as the French diplomat in *M. Butterfly*; as a variety of Shakespeare characters; and in at least two dozen other productions. Once he did remarkable work for me as an old Georgian storyteller. I've seen him in leads and I've seen him in walk-ons. I've seen him miscast, misdirected, sick, and angry, but regardless of part or play, I have never seen Larry anything less than compelling.

Last night was the first time I've seen him in a Dog Suit Role, which is how another actor friend dismisses any part in which you find yourself playing an animal, whether the beast is in fact a dog or the Bird of Paradise. Nor have I seen Larry in a musical, which is all they do at the Fifth Avenue now. (Someone I know describes it as America's largest community theater; not a compliment.) I assumed Larry was doing the show for the money, this very serious and accomplished actor taking the musical stage in a dog suit, playing a role that is very hard for a good actor because it was created entirely for somebody else.

Specifically, the part of the Cowardly Lion was hand tailored for burlesque and vaudeville comic Bert Lahr. Ever since Bert, any actor doing the lion in this show has to decide whether he's going to do a two-hour Bert Lahr impersonation, or fight the Lahr and create something new. The stage script doesn't help because it's a very faithful adaptation of the screen play, with all the Lahrisms intact. Choosing to create something new may sound like the obvious choice for an actor with artistic integrity, but maybe it isn't when you have to fight the script from the first "Put 'em up! Put 'em up!" to the last "Shucks folks, I'm speechless!"

Thus my interest, but only Lucy's and mine. Ned could have cared less whether Larry felt forced to do Bert Lahr, Bert Lance, or Bert and Ernie. He was out on the town with Vicki, going to a show he loves so much he memorized the entire film a decade ago. And he was hanging out with the bigs in a theater where he once scored a personal triumph.

Some years ago, the touring bus&truck production of the musical *Titanic* played at the Fifth Avenue. My friend Erika Warmbrunn, late of Seattle who works on Broadway as a spotlight operator, had done the New York production quite a few times and got us ducats, right at the height of Ned's obsession with the ship. In the lobby when we arrived was a huge placard listing everyone on board that fateful night and what happened to them. Ned the Historian was drawn to this placard like a bee to a sunflower. He studied it carefully and then began telling me about the survivors who were listed. "She lived in Colorado and died this year; she's still alive and living in Louisiana"—that kind of thing.

A few people were eavesdropping on our conversation. This frequently happens when Ned and I are out and about together, because people hear a few words from him and can't believe he's as well-spoken as he is, and also because I am a former minor local celebrity they vaguely recognize.

Eventually a good-sized group gathered around Ned in the Fifth's lobby. I think these people were genuinely amazed that anyone, especially Ned, would know so much about the *Titanic* survivors. Ned went easily into lecture mode, and for a good five minutes entertained the crowd with *Titanic* trivia. He even took questions and answered all of them. Ned and I both remember that lobby event much more than we remember the musical we had come to see. *Titanic* has one good effect—a boat sinks—and that's about it. Ned enjoyed it, although he was shocked by the historical inaccuracies.

For our double date at *Wizard of Oz*, we two couples had dinner in a semi-fancy place across the street from the downtown library. I knew Ned was going with the flow last night because he didn't object when the cuisine eschewed burgers. Then we strolled a few blocks down the street to the Fifth, took our places, and watched the show.

When Larry first entered in the dog suit I felt an immediate wave of pity. Here was my friend, this consummate artist I am proud to know, all furry and be-tailed. But I had underestimated him. Larry wasn't doing Lahr, and he wasn't doing un-Lahr. He had found a compromise that must have been very difficult to sustain but worked like a charm. It worked so well that Larry stole the show, dominating every scene he was in and making you wish he was in every other scene. For the dramatic good of the presentation, shows usually shouldn't be stolen by the third comic relief. I think Larry was actually holding back in some ways for just that reason. But the Fifth's production was built around a Dorothy who was simply not up to the task. Vicki didn't have to say it, because I did: she was a lot better in the role, in a cheesy little school production, when she was fourteen. So the show had to be stolen by somebody. Larry did it without even trying.

The best part of the evening for me, and the reason I've gone into all this here, was the conversation on the drive home. Ostensibly with Lucy and Vicki, but really for Ned's benefit, we talked about Larry's performance. It was for me a shining example of professionalism in action, and so allowed me to do my professionalism speech.

The wonderful novelist and poet Peter DeVries was once asked how important inspiration is in his work, whether he had to be inspired before he could write. He answered, "It's true, I only write when I'm inspired. And I make sure I'm inspired every morning at 9:00 o'clock." Being a professional means making the job you do your first priority, something that's easy to say but for many people very hard to do. It applies whether the task at hand is filing papers, delivering mail, being a cowardly lion, or being Lear. Larry Ballard is a person of unparalleled talent and he has been for a long time. But talent and experience are only part of his success. You have to be ready and willing to do it, every day. And you have to work hard at it, too. You never phone in the part no matter how strong the temptation is to do so. As an actor Larry works so hard he makes it look like he's not working at all.

And this is important. For Ned, Larry isn't some magical person up there on stage or screen. I could tell Ned all about actors I admire, like Tom Hanks and Harrison Ford and older folks like Audrey and Katherine Hepburn, Spencer Tracy, Stan Laurel—people who are as obscure and remote to Ned as Tom Mix and Francis X. Bushman are to me. But Ned knows Larry, not well but certainly well enough to see him as a real person.

When Ned gets his job, whatever it may be, chances are good his employers won't expect professionalism. They will hope for at least a modicum of competence and that's all. I hope Ned will surprise them, as he has surprised so many others in so many ways. I'm not sure if he was listening to our conversation. He certainly didn't contribute in any significant way to it. But on previous occasions when adults were talking, Ned has been paying far more attention than he's shown at the time. Months and even years later, something will bubble up out of him and you realize he is indeed a little pitcher with big ears. I may have to wait a while to see if that was the case last night. But even if it all went past him, it was still a nice evening for four friends, watching a fifth do his stuff.

Monday, December 15, 2003

Peter Simonson visited Wedgwood today to interview the teachers with whom Ned worked. We assume they told him the same things they told us almost exactly a year ago, but we didn't make any calls to find out. If they did tell Peter essentially the same information, we can assume he won't be looking in the field of law enforcement for a job for Ned. I don't see a young man who has trouble rounding up first graders at the end of recess wearing a badge, although it's an interesting prospect.

Officer Palmer: Where were you on the night of November 13...

Perp: I was...

Officer Palmer: ...1851?

Perp: I beg your pardon?

Officer Palmer: November 13, 1851, when the Denny Party landed at Alki. Don't play dumb with me.

Perp: Uh...

Officer Palmer: Who are your famous ancestors?

Perp: Uh, well, my mother told me once that Clint Eastwood is a distant cousin, but...

Officer Palmer: Hah! You know what that bum did to my step cousin Eric Fleming? Stole his show, that's what he did. *Rawhide*. Do you ever watch *Rawhide*?

Perp: Is it still on?

Officer Palmer: I'll ask the questions around here. Who wrote "Unchained Melody"?

Perp: Uhh...

Officer Palmer: You know, "Unchained Melody," big hit for the Righteous Brothers in 1965. Who wrote it?

Perp: The Righteous Brothers?

Officer Palmer: They sang it, I said. Hy Zaret and Alex North wrote it. In 1955. I can see it's going to be a long night. Cookie?

Tuesday, December 16, 2003

Today Peter and his colleague Susan Loggins visited KCTS to observe Ned at work and talk to Marcie. We made sure Ned had something to work on so the visitors had something to watch. Shortly after arrival, they were standing at Ned's desk. I came around the corner and asked if they needed anything from me. In unison, both Peter and Ned said, "No," although Peter may have said "No, thanks." And that was that. Later Marcie told me they had a nice chat about Ned, what she had him doing, and what other things she thought he might be able to do.

I don't know a thing about Peter's work and how much prior experience his other clients have, but I should think there's more information and opinion available about Ned than what he usually learns. Peter hasn't talked that much to us because he doesn't have to. He's had Marcie Finnila at KCTS, plus Tim Hilton, Marcy Wynhoff, and the other Hale and Wedgwood teachers. Being friends and fans of Ned's, they aren't completely objective, but they're all bright people and know that Peter needs to make the most realistic assessment he can to do the best possible job for Ned. Having outside "employers" to interview has to be better than relying solely on the opinions of parents or caregivers.

Tuesday, January 20, 2004

Cathy drove Ned over to the University this morning for the beginning of Ned's on-the-job assessment. Originally I thought this part of the process took a week or two and involved Ned working at different kinds of jobs at various places around campus while Peter observed. Now it appears it will only be three days total and that all of the jobs will be at the University of Washington Medical Center—what we old-timers used to call a "hospital." Peter's employer, the Employment Training Program, isn't housed at the Medical Center, but it is part of the Department of Rehabilitation Medicine in the School of Medicine, so it makes sense that they have good job connections in the University's massive medical operation. The hospital/medical school combination makes the University's complex on the Lake Washington Ship Canal the largest medical building in the world, which explains why, until recently, I've never been in the place without getting lost. I'm glad Ned's going to have Peter to lead him around.

The fact that he will be working at the hospital was good news for Ned. One of his girlfriend Lily's vocational jobs in high school was there. She sorted and delivered linens, I think. Lily enjoyed it and enjoyed the people with whom she worked. She may still be a hospital volunteer. We also have a close family friend who is a UW Urology doctor, and in the past few months Ned has been in the place quite a few times visiting his grandfather after various surgical and medical procedures. So I think he feels comfortable with the institution, and I know he now feels comfortable with Peter. He left this morning like he was going off on an interesting adventure.

He returned this afternoon describing that adventure. Most of his time was spent wheeling a cart around, picking up medical supplies, and delivering them to the appropriate places. The only problem he had with the job was that he found some of the objects he had to pick up and deliver "disgusting."

"Like what?"

"Like needles and syringes. Disgusting."

"But they were all wrapped up in bags, right? It's not like you were actually touching them."

"Yes. But still. The bandages were all right."

"So basically if it goes on the body it's okay, but if it goes in the body you'd rather not get involved."

"Yes."

So on the list of jobs we can be pretty sure Ned wouldn't enjoy, after "Police Officer" add "Surgeon."

Wednesday, Feb 18, 2004

The first big question to be answered by all the assessment of Ned that's been going on is whether he has the functional ability to be employable on the open market, in a commercial, competitive business. If Peter and his colleagues don't think he does, then our goal switches from finding him a competitive job to finding a sheltered workshop of some kind where the environment is as important as the job.

Years ago when I did the news story about Cyndy and Rod, the married couple with Down syndrome, I spent half a day in the operation run by the Mormon Church where they both work. With forty other developmentally disabled people, their jobs involved sorting and cleaning donated clothing for the stores the workshop manages. There was a lot of camaraderie around the place, which was very nice to see. Cyndy and Rod took considerable good-natured ribbing from their coworkers about the television camera that was following them everywhere. The managers, with a few exceptions, were pleasant and professional. Their goals were safety—the room had some big cleaning and pressing equipment—and keeping the employees on task. As long as the workers kept at their jobs, the management didn't pressure their charges, no matter how long it took them to complete a specific task. But they had to keep doing it and only stop during lunch hour and the numerous breaks. Cyndy and Rod were happy to be there, and especially happy to be there together. It looked like a good operation.

But if that is the kind of workplace where Ned ends up, I would be disappointed. Other than occasional contact with the managers on duty, Cyndy and Rod spend their entire day in the company of other people with disabilities. For the whole workweek, they are cut off from mainstream society except for the ride on a city bus to and from their place of employment. That's why it's called a "sheltered" workshop, I guess; the workers are sheltered from the real world. (And the real world doesn't have to think much about the workers, either.)

In an environment like that, Ned would do what he's done for years at Easter Seals camp. He would gravitate toward the managers, competing for their attention with everybody else in the room. For their part, the managers would like him, but they would also do their job and tell him in a kind and caring way to get back to work. About the twentieth time they had that conversation with him, they'd call us about the "problem." Eventually Ned would either accept the situation and adjust to it—as he has so many times in the past—or he'd hate the whole operation and tell us so. Or he'd hate it and not tell us, which would be even worse. And if he came to me and told me he was miserable, could I really respond, "Sorry, Ned, that's your lot in life, so back you go?" Not a chance.

There is in the heart of many fathers the unyielding belief that their sons should be the starting pitcher, quarterback, or center and never warm the bench or be relegated to the second or third team. Such fathers convince themselves that it's only politics and favoritism, and never ability, that keeps their little chips-off-the-old-block out of the big show. I've been around fathers like that and I've pitied them because they can't curb their misplaced ego and pride. I've felt especially sorry for their sons, usually kids who just want to have a good time doing something with their friends and wish dad would shut the hell up. I remember going to Ira's high school football games and on many occasions wondering why my son was still sitting on the bench when his team was down by thirty points. It was very difficult to resist shouting at his coach, "What, he's going to make it worse?" What stopped me was knowing how mortified Ira would be.

So it would be hypocritical not to admit that some of my feeling about Ned's employment potential comes from my own ego. I want the best for him, and from personal experience I truly believe that he is happiest and most functional when he's around people without disabilities. But it's also true that I am happiest when he's around such people. I suppose it's part of a twenty-two-year-old dream that has never died, even though sometimes I think it has: the hope that Ned can be "normal," or near enough to pass. I want him to be me, and with people like me, while at the same time I know how much he enjoys being with those school friends he's had for so long. The group that showed up for James's memorial gathering is made up of some very nice, loving people. I hope they will be his friends for the rest of his life, and so does he. So maybe he would be happy to be almost exclusively with them, plus those new friends he'd find amongst his fellow employees in a sheltered workshop. I have to admit that possibility.

I don't think Ned is any better than Cyndy and Rod and their workmates, but because of his abilities, the experiences he's had, and the friends he's made outside the developmentally disabled community, I think he is a little different. Because of that difference, he has a wider range of opportunities before him. It would be a shame not to pursue those opportunities. But I am his dad, and my perceptions of my son are bound up not only in my years with him, but in my years with me.

At a meeting today with Peter and others to get the results of the assessment, we heard the good news. They think Ned can be a player in the real world. Peter will start looking for a job for him, and so will we. He told us that although the Employment Training Program has a lot of resources in the community, most of the jobs they find for their clients come from private connections outside ETP. In other words, us. We never planned to sit back and let Peter do all the hustling, so the fact that there's a burden on us to look around for an employer for Ned is not, in fact, much of a burden at all. We have resources, too. My family has been in the Seattle area for five generations on my mother's side and three on my father's; Cathy's family has been in the state practically that long as well. We have naturally developed a lot of contacts in the area from our backgrounds and our own work over the years.

At this moment we have a connection to, or history with, Boeing, Nordstrom, Microsoft, Starbucks, the University of Washington, three television stations, the *Seattle Times*, the *Seattle Post Intelligencer*, two weekly newspapers, Puget Sound Consumers Co-op, a hotel, a movie theater chain, four legitimate theaters, and one radio production company, plus friends who own or operate book and record stores, gift shops, travel agencies, museums, festivals of various kinds, non-profit organizations, construction companies, and car dealerships. We should be able to find something appropriate for Ned somewhere in that list. And I certainly hope those aren't famous last words.

Friday, February 20, 2004

Ned's been working at KCTS as an intern in the marketing department for a few months now. His jobs have included a lot of filing, preparing marketing sampler tapes to go out, and doing a little research on various projects, all under Marcie's supervision. She already has too much to do, but to her great credit she has worked hard to find tasks for Ned and help him accomplish those tasks.

Alas, today was Marcie's last day at KCTS. A few weeks ago she was offered a much better-paying job at Gas Powered Games, a company on the east side of Lake Washington that made its fame and fortune with a video game called *Dungeon Siege*. They are now preparing *Dungeon Siege II*, and Marcie is to be a producer on that and subsequent projects. Publicly we've kept her new job quiet, because she's also the co-producer and co-writer of *The Video Game Revolution*, the PBS documentary about video games it seems like I've been working on since before there were video games and everybody played the piano or Parcheesi in the evenings. It was through making the documentary that she met the Gas Powered people and they got to know her. Because *Dungeon Siege* appears in the program, it might look to some as if Marcie was hired as a payoff for including the game in the show. This is nonsense, but we take precautions nonetheless.

Ned's going to miss her, but perhaps not miss her efforts to keep him busy. He's happy just sitting at his computer doing his own death/rock and roll research and making lists of people and their birth and death dates. Making such lists is one of the principal things Ned does when a computer's handy and there's nothing else to do. He can spend hours at it. It's obviously one of the main manifestations of his fascination with the trivia of death, and therefore—cheap layman's psychology here—a way to trivialize death and so diminish it. I don't know why he feels it is necessary to laboriously copy the name of the deceased and his or her birth and death dates, but it's certainly part of the experience. In his bedroom at home there must be hundreds of sheets of paper with handwritten lists containing names and dates. At any moment, his KCTS desk is covered with dozens more. It may be as simple as an aid to memorizing the information.

Recently Ned's started getting old movies from the library. I came home the other day and he was watching Busby Berkeley's *Gold Diggers of 1935*. It occurred to me that Ned was the only human being in the entire universe who was at that moment in time watching *Gold Diggers of 1935*, and singing along with its Oscar winner for best song, "The Lullaby of Broadway." I don't know if he was enjoying it, but I do know he enjoys looking up the dead cast members afterwards and writing down their names and dates. In a sense, he's worked his way through all the dead rock and roll stars and moved on to dead movie stars. (*Golddiggers* gave him the late Dick Powell and Adolf Menjou, who plays a producer in the film bragging about his production of *A Midsummer Night's Dream* "with an all-Eskimo cast.") Ned's traded Jim Morrison and Janis Joplin for Nelson Eddy and Fifi Dorsay.

Someone who gets concerned about these kinds of things is probably reading this right now and thinking we have a problem with Ned's death fascination/obsession. Maybe. But we prefer to think of it as research, and so does Ned. At KCTS, such research falls a bit short of good work experience, unless Ned gets that newspaper obituary researcher job for which he's been training most of his life.

Saturday, February 21, 2004

Ned and I seem to go to a lot of birthday parties. Today's was for a young lady named Caroline Leedy. Her parents have been my friends for a while. Their only daughter is a quite beautiful child with big eyes and a sweet, inquiring look, now three years old.

A few weeks ago she was hospitalized for an onset of diabetes. She's always seemed delicate to me, and now there's little question that the rest of her life will probably revolve around visits to the doctor, injections, glucose tests, and an intense concentration on what she eats and when she eats it. Eventually she'll have an insulin pump and learn to do the complicated dietary measurements before each meal that I've seen adult diabetics go through. One can only hope that given her young age, the new concentration on diabetes research, and the potential for stem cells to assist in finding a cure, eventually Caroline will be able to throw away the pumps and glucose testers and just live her life.

For now, her folks seem to be handling her condition well. For the outside world they are very "We'll soldier on" about it all, although I suspect in the privacy of their home they are frightened and in pain. We knew Ned's situation when he was two weeks old, but other than doing some research, there were no particular actions we had to take immediately or regularly because of that knowledge. We could and did sometimes just ignore it and do what we would have been doing if Ned didn't have Down syndrome. But Molly and Tom Leedy have daily insulin injections to give and blood tests to take from a little girl who was afraid of needles long before this medical crisis occurred. Their opportunities to just forget it don't last for weeks or even days, but for just a few hours at a time. To have to inflict fear and pain on your own child on a regular schedule must be excruciating, and something you never get used to. You just pray to God your child gets used to it.

Although the Leedys have to do a lot more right away than Cathy and I did, I'm watching them go through an emotional readjustment that's the same as ours was at the beginning. They know now Caroline is going to have a far more lasting and profound effect on their lives than most kids would. For the rest of their days, they will never be able to relax completely where their daughter is concerned, never watch her go out the door without the fear that she could have trouble and not be around someone who knows what to do.

Caroline's health has already started affecting everything in the Leedy household. Molly recently left a job as a book editor with a company she liked, and took another job she's not too sure about, because the medical benefits at the new company are much better than where she was. (Her old company's plan paid for four doctor visits a year by any member of the family. Now and for the foreseeable future, Caroline can easily have four or more doctor visits a month. It was as simple as that.)

But there is a personal price to pay for the better coverage. Her new employer is much more driven to succeed. It's the kind of company with managers who think a forty-hour work week is just the beginning for an employee. Molly was careful to tell them about her family situation before she was hired, and they are good people and sympathetic to her needs. They sincerely promised to help where they can. But there's little question that at the very moment in her life when she needs more time at home, Molly's had to go to work for a company that will allow her that time for only so long before she gets the "this isn't working out" line from a manager whose own job is dependent on staff productivity. To provide adequately for her daughter, Molly will have to leave her daughter far more than she wants to. The fact that every American doesn't have medical coverage if need be through some kind of government plan is a national disgrace.

Ned's relationship with Caroline is interesting. He is very fond of her, and showed it a long time ago by loaning her all of his *Sesame Street* records. They don't make many of those records any more, at least as records and not CDs, so they are irreplaceable. Ned has listened to them hundreds of times since the 1980s. I suspect they are among his most prized possessions, and he certainly wouldn't loan them to just anybody who asked. But he did so with Caroline as soon as he heard she was a big fan of the *Street*. It's true he keeps asking Molly about them. "Is Caroline enjoying them? Is she done with them?" But that's just standard collector anxiety. As far as Ned is concerned, Caroline can have those records for as long as she wants, with the understanding that the day she's done with them, they immediately return to her benefactor.

Caroline is a girl, three years old, and her challenge is medical and not intellectual. She and Ned have little in common. Yet in ways I don't think he realizes, Ned sees her as a kind of colleague, another person whose life will be outside the mainstream not by choice but by chance. In the same way he's shown care and concern for his schoolmates with disabilities, albeit always defining disability solely as the need for a wheelchair, Ned feels he has to support and befriend this nice little girl. He is eager to do so. Today at her birthday party, he assumed the role of beloved uncle, leaping up to answer the door when new guests arrived and uncharacteristically sitting back and watching Caroline open her presents.

At previous birthday parties we've attended together, Ned usually volunteers to open a few presents for the guest of honor and begins ripping into packages if somebody doesn't immediately say no. Today, for the first time at any child's birthday party he's ever attended, Ned was much more on the adults' side of the room than the kids'. He shared Caroline's happiness without trying to be part of it. I hope that in the years to come, he can go to her high school graduation, be the beloved uncle at her wedding, visit her first child in the maternity ward, and drop by her office on the thirty-sixth floor. I hope that they can be good friends for the rest of their lives.

(A note: There is no Molly, Tom, and Caroline Leedy. This family exists, but in the preceding I have disguised them in various ways at the mother's request. She was advised not long after "Caroline" was diagnosed to keep her daughter's medical condition quiet. Apparently there are still public and private agencies, schools, and businesses that discriminate in nasty and hidden ways against people with medical conditions. This family wants to have control over who knows and who doesn't, and I certainly respect that, although the reason I have to do it makes me furious.)

Friday, February 27, 2004

Since the day he walked out of Nathan Hale High for the last time as a student, Ned has wanted to go back to Room 104 and hang around. Other than his continuing insistence that the only job he wants is as a teacher's aide in 104, I suspect this desire to do an alumni schmooze is the manifestation of an intense longing for that place and the life it represented. He misses the social milieu that was so much a part of his existence for so long, as well as the scene of his biggest successes.

Room 104 was and is a combination classroom, computer room, counseling center, and rest and staging area for all the Special Ed activities at Nathan Hale. I once overheard a student in the regular school population refer to it as "Area 52." It was in Room 104 that Ned created wonderful things on the computer when he wasn't wading through Find-A-Grave. In 104, he expanded his reading skills and helped those others who needed it, both physically in the case of his blind friend Lily Vang, and scholastically, in the case of students he advised on their work. From 104, he left for choir and his other regular classes. Perhaps most important to him, it was there that he worked with the adult staff, especially Tim Hilton and Glenda Feyes. I think it's fair to say he was, for five years, one of the stars of Room 104. He certainly thought he was. So it's not surprising that he wants to go back and relive the experience.

Since last September, we've told him that just dropping in isn't allowed, especially in these days of heightened security, but that some day we'd set up a visit. We haven't actively pursued it, however, because we thought it was best to make the break clean. In my experience, absence does not make the heart grow fonder, but just the opposite. I've hoped that the more his high school experience fades in his memory—even that prodigious memory—the more easily he will turn to plans for the future and not the joys of the past. So far it ain't workin'.

I must also admit to having vague memories of my own high school days, and encountering the graduates who found any excuse to come back and walk the halls. They struck me as kind of pathetic, the first real "get-a-life" folks I can remember. They always seemed a little disappointed by the experience, too. After just two years, half the student body didn't know who they were, and the other half didn't care who they were. The teachers who once seemed so interested in them now had a whole new crop of kids to be interested in. What these wandering alumni wanted to hear was, "How wonderful to see you again! We've missed you terribly and needed you here!" But what they usually got was some version of, "What are you doing here?," no matter how popular or successful they had once been. With Nathan Hale's beloved Principal Benson now retired and gone, and other significant changes in the school, I thought Ned might have the same disappointing experience.

Today I had to go to the school to do some prep work for the Nathan Hale Music Department Auction. The Music Department used to do a little off-the-cuff, low-yield silent auction as part of its traditional big spring fundraiser, Casino Night, an event held in the school cafeteria. When Ned was still in the choir, I suggested at a parents' meeting that if we were going to go through the hassles of an auction anyway, we might as well do it right, make it an auction-only event, and not in the midst of the plastic tables and "Go School!" friezes. We should make an off-campus evening out of it.

I've done a lot of auctions for Ira's various schools over the years, and long ago learned that the best way to get people to bid foolishly on donated items is to get them liquored up first. Once as auctioneer I got two tipsy macho types to bid against each other on a baseball autographed by Mickey Mantle. About the time the bidding reached $500, the guy who donated the baseball snuck up beside me on stage and whispered in my ear that what I was doing was wrong. The baseball, he hissed, was acquired at a sports convention for six dollars, from the very hand of The Mick himself. The man just did not understand auctions, and further proved it by going to the winning bidder after the auction and telling him the same story. The chump then refused to take the ball or pay the $700 he bid to get it. (I have occasionally used this story to demonstrate the subtle difference between a schlemiel—the ball donor—and a schlimazel—the guy who refused to pay for the ball.)

So it came to pass last year that for the first time the Music Department auction was off-campus and included a bar, so there weren't all these inconvenient teenagers underfoot. And for a premiere effort, it was a moderate success. We made about ten large, which was more than any other Music Department fundraiser had ever taken in. My co-auctioneer was Pat Cashman, an old colleague from KING, a gracious and funny man who is now a talk radio host (the good kind, who uses wit rather than hatred to attract listeners). Ned attended along with his beloved cousin-once-removed Jere Felten, so of course we could have sold bupkis and Ned would have been happy. Jere— singer, musician, preacher, and brother of rock and roll great John Felten—is one of Ned's true heroes. He could go to a myocardial infarction with Jere and enjoy it.

I agreed to do the auction one more year even though I no longer have a kid in the school. It occurs to me at this moment that the only thing more pathetic than an alumnus still hanging around school is the parent of an alumnus. But it was in a good cause. So with the auction tomorrow, I had to go up to the school today to check out the live auction items and prepare descriptions of them. I invited Ned to come with me, and he was on his way to the car before I finished the invitational sentence.

We got there early. I get everywhere early. It's one of my irritating habits, but less irritating than getting everywhere late, in my opinion. Since we had some time to kill, I told Ned we could go down the hall to Room 104 and say hello. He took off like a shot. Unfortunately, most of the students had already gone home. Terry, Ned's fellow-worker from The Theodora old folks home, was the only kid left in the room, and he had just had some kind of trouble—missed his bus, I think—and was not in the mood for reminiscing with Ned or talking to anybody about anything. Ned's old teachers were still there, including Darol Reynolds, out of retirement to replace a teacher who had to leave earlier in the term.

All the adults were waiting around to leave. Ned had a nice chat with them, which is what he wanted to do in the first place. But he has changed. There was something different about what he said, how he said it, the way he carried himself. It was a subtle difference, something I wouldn't have noticed had I not spent a lot of hours in that room with him in years past. It took me a while to realize what the change was.

In that place where he was always one of the kids, he came back as an adult, and talked with adults as an equal. Perhaps if the room had still been filled with students, it would have been different, but I think not. Whether as a result of his experiences on the cruise, or working at KCTS, or just the natural process of growing up, Ned will never be one of the kids again. He still carries action figures around—he may always do that—and though his diet has expanded some, he still regularly eats many of the things he ate when he was six. But in most other ways he's a grown man now. It took a visit to the center of his kid life for me to realize that.

Saturday, February 28, 2004

It's been one of those occasions when Ned spent time on both sides of his current life. During the day he was a kid with the disabled kids, and in the evening he was the only disabled adult in a roomful of other adults. More and more as time goes on, he seems happiest and most comfortable being part of the latter, but that may be wishful thinking on my part.

During the day he participated in a fundraiser for Young Life Open Door, an annual event at which Young Lifers bowl for dollars. Ned hustled Vicki and her mother for a donation and they graciously pledged twenty cents for every pin he could knock down in three hours. I knew better than to go for the per-pin deal. In developmentally disabled Bowling for Dollars the gutters are filled with big blue cushions, so pins fall on every ball no matter how bad a bowler you are. Somebody who averages fifteen pins a game suddenly is in the hundred and fifty pin range. That's why I kicked in a flat twenty bucks.

One could do an interesting research project on how many Americans had their first contact in a bowling alley with coveys of people with disabilities. That was certainly the case with me. Forty years ago at Bel-Lanes in the suburb of Bellevue, I was actually in a league and went off on Saturday mornings to be athletic for an hour or so. It was my sole venture into organized sports, if a bunch of teenage guys rolling balls around for a few hours and making fart jokes can be called organized sports. And every week, at the last two of the thirty-two Bel-Lanes lanes, five to ten teens with developmental disabilities would be bowling.

In the 1950s, and maybe now for all I know, it could get very busy on Saturday mornings at a suburban American bowling alley. Bel-Lanes was usually packed. But I still remember how isolated the guys at the end seemed to be, as though there were a wall between lanes thirty and thirty-one, invisible but very solid. If so, it was a wall they created and observed as much as we did. People weren't unpleasant to the end group, but nobody was particularly friendly either. The rest of the Bel-Lanes Saturday morning crowd—mostly spotty, unattractive youths such as myself—treated them with mild curiosity. Their reactions to a strike or a spare—and really any time more than four or five pins fell—could be spectacularly exuberant, probably because they weren't encumbered by the need to appear cool that affected everyone on the other side of the wall. So, naturally, we laughed at them for their celebrations. But mostly they were ignored. When we found ourselves standing in line for eats with one of them, words were never exchanged. Nobody on either side said, "Hi, how ya doin'?"

My own interest in bowling waned after graduating from the bowling program at the University of Washington in 1966. You had to take three quarters of Gym in your freshman year. Bowling 101-103 were the only P.E. courses available that didn't require changing into different underwear after shagging it down to Clarence C. "Hec" Edmonson Pavilion. You could bowl fully clothed, in the student union, fifteen yards from a snack bar. For me, that made it the ideal required sport. I signed up.

Vince, my UW bowling teacher, was no muscle-bound unemployable ex-Husky-football player like most of the U's P.E. instructors. He was a real big-league bowler who wore a robins-egg-blue shirt that had bowling balls stenciled on the back and "Vince" embroidered over the pocket containing his Luckies. Thanks to Vince and the ambience of the student union, Bowling 101 was also the only course on campus in any discipline, except perhaps Philosophy at the post graduate level, where you could smoke and drink beer during class. "It's all part of the bowling experience," said Vince, who smoked and drank prodigiously during class, and gave you an A if you showed up on the days he showed up. (I am a 4.0 University of Washington Bowling Program graduate, the only course I ever maxed on the college level.)

I digress. After 1966, it seemed pointless to bowl for no class credit and without the tutelage of Vince. ("Just bowl and leave me the hell alone.") So I packed away the bowling shoes I forgot to return and didn't regret it for a moment. Nor did I regret the fact that Ira disliked bowling as a little kid. So it wasn't until Ned was about six that I was forced to return to the lanes on any regular basis.

Bowling is apparently the dominant sport for people with developmental disabilities, or so Special Populations Program Directors seem to think. I've seen newspaper articles about disabled skiers, mountain climbers, shot-putters, golfers, weight lifters, extra point kickers, surfers, and practically every other sport. These articles are usually written in the same "holy cow!" style as are stories about such activities performed by cats, dogs, horses, and chimpanzees. They aren't as common or as offensive as the allegedly uplifting stories about school teams adopting a Special Ed kid as a mascot, but they're close.

But as a regular activity, society apparently assumes kegling is it for the dumb kids, just like shuffleboard is for old folks, ice hockey is for Canadians, and that bizarre, lethal Australian football is for bizarre, lethal Australians. Perhaps it's because bowling is so simple. You roll the ball down the alley and try to knock down the pins. It doesn't have all the intricate subtleties that are part of knocking a little white ball across a lawn into a hole. That obviously requires a lot of brains. And though bowling is often performed by teams, it's not really a team sport. You are up against yourself and ten lumpy sticks. If you fail, you can't blame the teammate who didn't pass you the ball, or set up your shot, or block out the big kid. Bowling offers useful aggression-relief (heavy ball, pins, noise) but only through the deployment of sacrificial inanimate objects and never other living creatures, like the opposing team in football or small defenseless animals in hunting and fishing.

I assume that for all these reasons, somebody decided a long time ago that bowling, not baseball, was going to be The Great American Pastime for Persons with Developmental Disabilities. And they may have been right. It drives me nuts to see the stereotypical cliché of such groups bowling, but I have to admit that they almost always appear to be having a good time.

Ned and all his friends have been carted off to bowling for many years. It started a decade ago when he was a weekly participant in Saturday Activities, an opportunity for social interaction, physical activity, and just darn fun provided by the Seattle Parks Department "Special Populations" office. Each Saturday morning I'd drop him off at the gathering point, which for many years was a bowling alley. He'd board the green Parks Department van and be off to visit a playground or a movie and then come back and bowl before I picked him up. I'd always get there early—part of my aforementioned irritating charm, but also because I've always had an inordinate fear of Ned standing alone on a sidewalk waiting for me—and so I've had many chances to watch him bowl. Though he says it's his favorite sport, I think his enjoyment of it is almost entirely the social aspect, not the game itself. He'll be chatting with the others in his immediate group or those on the lanes on either side and invariably have to be told when it's his turn.

He takes that turn as quickly as possible. He walks to the line, drops the ball from waist-high, and gives it a little forward shove as he does. Then he frequently doesn't even wait to see if he's hit anything before running back to his chair to continue the conversation. I've tried being the Vince to his me and giving him a few pointers, but he makes it clear that he doesn't need or want my advice.

Today at Young Life Bowling for Bucks it looked at first like he was again paying more attention to the company than to the competition. I signed him up while he worked the room. The site of the Nathan Hale auction was only a few minutes' drive from the bowling alley, so I ran off to check out the venue where I'd be working tonight. When I came back to the lanes a few hours later, I finally found him in the middle of the hall. He was sitting on the bench, staring off into space, not talking to anyone. He stayed that way for a long time. This particular Young Life event was sponsored by two different Open Door groups, and with only a few exceptions Ned's regular crowd didn't show up. Most of the other kids were strangers, including everybody in his immediate foursome. But I don't think that was the reason his normal social interaction was missing.

When he's around adults, Ned usually enjoys strangers. They are both fresh meat to hear about his various interests and new research possibilities for his current quest. Recently he's taken to asking people he meets who their famous ancestors are. The question is very Ned. It's not "Do you have any famous ancestors?" but "Who are your famous ancestors?" He assumes everyone has them, and the weird thing is, he's usually right. Even if people aren't absolutely sure of a connection somewhere, almost everybody can conjure up memories of their mom saying something about a famous relative. In the last six months we've met people who say they are related to Thomas Jefferson, Miles

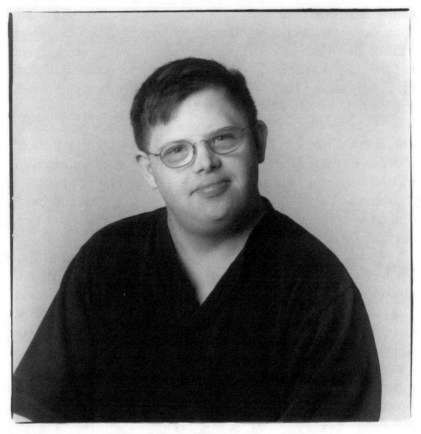

Ned Palmer, historian. (Photo by Fred Milkie.)

Standish, John Rolfe (Pocahontas's honey), Martha Custis, and Dan Quayle. Ned listens to these stories with great interest while at the same time using the opening to tell about his connection to the founders of Seattle, his late rock 'n roll cousin John, and those on his mother's side who were tight with Bill the Conqueror. But with only a few exceptions, these exchanges of the famous are limited to his meetings with adults.

Ned didn't behave this afternoon as he has in previous bowling encounters, and I think it's only partially because his bowling mates were strangers. It's mostly because he doesn't have much to say to these people any more—or he thinks he doesn't. With friends like Heidi, Santosh, Tanyss, and Lily, he has a history. They can and do talk about what they've been up to recently, and their shared experiences. With most strangers with disabilities, however, his limited conversational openings—Seattle history, famous relatives, rock and roll—don't work. Ned knows and cares about a lot of things that most other people don't care about at all until he brings them up. Like the crowd on the *Endeavour*, the "normal" ones have the ability to run with the conversation, because it's just like a million other conversations we've all had that begin with new topics. The only difference for our shipmates was that the kid with Down syndrome started the ball rolling. But as I've seen many times, when Ned approaches people with developmental disabilities in the same way he approaches other adults, they often look at him as if he's speaking a foreign language. It's like he's too old for them.

At the same time, Ned has learned that he can hold his conversational own in an adult, "normal" social milieu. He's discovered that they enjoy him and he enjoys them, and nobody looks at him like he's nuts. They often look at him with astonishment. That Ned doesn't think he has much left to say to people who can't hold up their end of the conversation isn't that strange. It's no stranger than a sixteen-year-old not having much to say to a ten-year-old. The frightening question is whether society will let Ned be sixteen, or force him to be ten, whether he wants to be or not.

He told me driving home that he had a good time bowling today, and if the opportunity came up to do it again, he would. I wonder.

I left a few hours later to get set up for the auction. Ned came with Vicki and cousin Jere when there was already a good crowd on hand. He spent the next hour dragging Vicki around, introducing her to everyone he knew, beaming with joy. She is his dream date and he is immensely proud to have her beside him, proud of their friendship. And she is splendid with him, patient and interested. But sometimes it's hard for me to see them together. If he were a normal kid and he brought her home one day to introduce her to us as his girl and the future Mrs. Nathaniel Palmer, I'd be thrilled. But that will never happen. Some day, probably some day soon, she will go off and find somebody and eventually they'll marry and have kids of their own. I hope she and Ned will always be friends, no matter where either of them is or what they are doing. But they will never be what he wants, even as he doesn't really know what that is.

The auction went well. The last item was a turn as guest conductor of the Nathan Hale Wind Ensemble at the final concert of the year in June. To my surprise, I couldn't get anybody to bid on it, even though last year it sold for relatively big money. Rich Sumstad, the real conductor of the ensemble, finally bid on it himself. Suddenly there was another bidder—Ned. He got it for sixty dollars, or the equivalent of six weeks' allowance. So on June third, Ned will step to the podium and lead the wind ensemble in John Phillip Sousa's *The Liberty Bell* march. With Rich leaving at the end of this year and Tim Hilton probably retiring too, there won't be any reason for Ned ever to go back to his old school. That concert is going to be his last hurrah at Hale.

Monday, March 1, 2004

E-mail, from Cathy to our families:

Dear family members,

Ned has recently completed the first phase of job training through the Department of Vocational Rehabilitation. The first phase involved observing him at his current (volunteer) job at KCTS, talking to people who have seen him in a volunteer work situation, and testing him (3 days, 2 hours a day) at a "job station" at UW Hospital. Completion of the first phase resulted in his being judged eligible for competitive employment, that is on the open market instead of in a sheltered workshop.

Now comes the hard part. We're working with an Employment Training Program based at the Dept of Rehab Medicine at UW, specifically Peter Simonson. He will be trying to develop a job for Ned, but, as he has told us, most jobs for developmentally disabled persons come through private contacts. That's where you all, I hope, can help.

Among us all we have a wide range of connections, not only with some of the biggest employers
in the region but also through networks of friends
and acquaintances, with much of the life of this
community. Greg and I would really appreciate
your putting the word out with anyone likely to be
helpful (obviously, any contacts in HR are especially useful) in finding a job. Ned's strengths are
his articulateness and sociability (also a potential
weakness, as those who've heard countless rendi-
tions of the Denny story can attest!), good work
ethic, filing and some computer skills; weaknesses
are limited stamina and math (not good at a cash
register). He does best with consistency and clear
expectations. A smallish office or department in a
larger company would be ideal; manual labor
(janitorial, etc.) is probably not a good fit, but
restaurant work (except as cashier) might be (he
does have a foodhandler's permit). Right now
we're looking for part-time work, 4-5 hours a day,
3-4 days per week; benefits are not important
now. Peter would work with any potential employer to develop the job, and would provide
ongoing support services to Ned (job coaching and
shadowing), as needed.

Thanks for any help you can give. If you have
any leads to share, you can call or e-mail me or
Greg, or contact Peter Simonson directly.

Love to all,

Cathy

Sunday, March 14, 2004

Our Story So Far

Yesterday was one of those rare occasions when Ned was
looking for something to do and not having much success, so I
asked him to write down whatever he cared to record about re-

cent events for this journal I'm keeping about his life since high school. The journal makes him nervous—a logical reaction as far as I'm concerned. "Who are you to be writing about my life?" is a perfectly valid question. He eagerly took up the assignment of "setting the record straight" (his term) and handed me the result a few minutes ago, written out on long yellow sheets. I've cleaned up the punctuation and a little spelling here and there, but otherwise this is it.

Since Graduation
By Ned Palmer

1. I went on a British Cruise on the M.S. Endeavor and I visited strange places like Iona where Macbeth is said to be buried. While on the trip I discovered cocktail hour, meaning drinking a Coke and talking to the barman. I even tried new types of food like smoked eel. I also visited some places that are said to be haunted like the Tower of London.

2. After my British cruise I returned to my high school and had a job as a tutor to some little kids up at Wedgwood Elementary where I was a student from 1984-1995. The teachers that I worked for were Marcy Wynhoff, Paula Peterson, Kathy Schaefer, Janice Israel, Mr. Spoor the Gym teacher, and the librarian (I worked in the library).

I had a lot of fun teaching the kids. I even made friends with some of them like Austin Curti, Laura Lustig (1993-2004) and of course some of the kids in Marcy's class.

Adult Life

1. So far I have recently turned 22 and because of that I have been working at KCTS where my father Greg Palmer has been working.

I got my first desk and computer for me to surf the web but not the whole time. During my time [at] KCTS I had many adventures like

- *Helping my dad on his shows about the "Inside Passage" and V.G., "Video Game Revolution."*
- *Helped my dad's friend Jay Parikh organizing cards and putting them on the computer.*
- *Helped my friend Jeannie Cunningham provide music for her show "KCTS Connects."*
- *Sometimes my dad and I like to go down to the Center House, Seattle Center, to have pizza.*
- *I also went to some parties like*
  - *Marcie's farewell party and other farewell parties and celebrations*
  - *Business parties*
- *I also helped get information for Marcie from the computer, sometimes Find-A-Grave of someone.*
- *I also met some Indian people, some of them Lummi. I even helped my dad to rescue two cats, meaning kittens, which we named Lummi (alias Tippacanoe) and Lulu (alias Tiffany).*

I'm right now still working [at] KCTS even though my boss Marcie Finnila left to find a job in the video game industry. I was also present at Pledge with Bob Newman (Gertrude the Clown) and Chris Wedes (J.P. Patches). They actually appeared on a pledge show as a promotion for a book about Patches and Gert and their friends and fans, including famous celebrities.

During most of my year at KCTS I mostly had other adventures that didn't happen in KCTS like

- *Having fun with my recent new housemate Vicki Noon who now apparently moved into the basement of my house and ever since then both me and her had so many adventures together. We recently went and saw the grave of Jimi Hendrix.*
- *Recently one of my students that I once tutored back in the year of 2002 had died. Her name was Laura Lustig who died on January 17th of a brain infection. When I received the news of this I was emotionally crushed. I didn't know that this happened. And not only that I didn't receive any phone call about it so I never got to go to the funeral service and that made me mad.*
- *I also recently got a new singing teacher named Andy Shaw who was impressed by my singing ability...*
- *I also went to the 50th Birthday of Wedgwood. I even ran into some of my old friends there including Mr. and Mrs. Lustig. I told them that I was sorry about their loss.*
- *I have been going to some new movies recently like "The Haunted Mansion"— totally neat though creepy. "Brother Bear"—totally funny and exciting.*
- *I recently have been working at the University Hospital with my job coach Peter Simonson. I liked wheeling a cart down the aisle picking up a lot of stuff for the doctors and nurses though some of those objects scared me, Yikes.*
- *I have also been going to Young Life Open Door every Monday night. I usually hang with some of my friends there but my favorite is Tanyss Banks to whom I like hanging with. I'm going to that club for a long time,*

since high school. The man in charge is my
old pal Blaine Clyde to whom I respect.

What's missing in this list is just as interesting as what's included. No Grand Canyon. Vicki, but no Lily. In fact, very little mention of any of his former classmates and friends.

Thursday, March 18, 2004

This evening, Ned and Vicki went to the Fifth Avenue Theatre without dad tagging along to see *Thoroughly Modern Millie*, which Vicki says is one of her favorite musicals. I doubt that Ned has ever heard of *Millie*, but he would have gone eagerly and happily even if the show were *Thoroughly Modern Podiatry*. They made a very nice looking couple, and he was walking about two feet off the ground when I picked them up out front afterwards. Tomorrow she leaves for Mexico for a week, and then it will be only a month or so before she's gone for good, or at least gone from the basement for the summer. There was a time when I thought that departure would bother Ned a lot, but he's grown up a little. He's still very devoted to her, but he is beginning to understand that she has her own life and will soon be off to pursue it without him.

Saturday, April 17, 2004

We drove to Renton this afternoon for yet another birthday party. Vicki's half sister Natalie is two years old today. The crowd on hand was a gaggle of very little girls and their slightly older siblings, plus parents and adult friends of Vicki's mother and stepfather. Once again Ned was in the middle. He wasn't one of the adults in the eyes of most of the adults, and certainly not one of the kids, either, especially not to kids that young. In these situations Ned usually tries to be part of both groups. He told a lot of people about his ancestors, and to my surprise, informed one woman that he was going to be a teacher's aide at

Nathan Hale. I thought we were over that, but we may not be over that until he's five years into some other job.

When the time came to belt the piñata, Ned wanted to be in there with the bat. Then he was eager to get down on the floor and help Natalie open her presents, whether she wanted his help or not. His odd-man-out status in these situations doesn't seem to bother him, even as I find his behavior dealing with it sometimes infuriating. Every time the doorbell rang, Ned ran for it as if he were the host, just as he did at the "Leedy" birthday. But this time, the new arrival at the door, who had come for the birthday of a two-year-old girl, was confronted by this unknown adult person introducing himself as "Nathaniel Palmer, great great grandnephew of Arthur Armstrong Denny, the founder of Seattle." It was confusing for the newcomers, and God help them if they then inquired further. They got the whole story unless I jumped in and cut him off, which made Ned furious.

Sunday, April 18, 2004

When I was eleven, my mother and I went to McCann's Men's Store in downtown Seattle to buy my first suit. (The first of four suits I've owned. Not a suit person. Although for television appearances I once had the world's largest collection of ugly corduroy sport jackets, or so a colleague claimed.) I forget why it was decided I needed a suit at that particular moment in my life. I do remember hating the experience and hating Mr. McCann, who looked like Warren G. Harding and had the habit of talking about you as if you weren't there. I'm sure Warren G. Harding did the same thing. I especially hated that suit. The coat was hot, the pockets were sewed shut so you couldn't put anything important in them like your hands, and the pants itched in hard-to-reach and embarrassing places. The pants were also designed to be worn so the belt buckle nestled a few inches below the wearer's chin. To this day I don't understand why suit pants are cut so that they can't be worn at the same altitude as jeans and every other pair of pants one owns.

The only other thing I remember about suit-buying day, besides hating it, was that my parents thought this was a very big deal event. It was some symbolic rite-of-passage thing for them, a throwback to the old days when a young man's clothing maturation was charted and significant: from diapers to no diapers to short pants to long pants to first hat to first suit. All of those events were plateaus in the assault on manhood. I suppose that's why Mom and I had to go downtown. You couldn't get your virgin suit in a suburb. It wouldn't be proper. That first suit had to be a downtown suit.

It was far from a big event for me, however. Mostly it was a spoiled afternoon. So I felt considerable pangs of guilt today when Cathy and I spoiled Ned's afternoon. We went downtown and bought him his first suit, just one city block from where McCann's used to be. All I could do to improve the experience over my own 1958 agony was to not make it some big symbolic deal. That was easy, because Ned certainly saw it as nothing but a pain in the tush, even as he supports the reason he needs a suit. The first time he'll be wearing the suit is for his upcoming appearance with the Nathan Hale Wind Ensemble as guest conductor, leading the boys and girls in a rousing rendition of Sousa's *Liberty Bell*.

Originally, I thought I'd rent him a tux with tails for the event, something very Maestro Palmer. The guest conductor appearance in the past has usually been played for laughs, on the assumption that the one-time-only maestro hasn't the slightest idea what he or she is really doing and the band doesn't need a conductor anyway. If you get them all started at approximately the same time on the same song in the same key, your work is done. You'll be lucky if any of them even looks at you for the next five minutes. Last year the guest conductor was the departing head of the parents' music support group. As I recall, she conducted with a magic wand, complete with streamers, glitter, a star on the end, and big yuks all around.

I hope it won't be that way this year, because conducting the band is no joke for Ned. He's told everyone about it as if he were being paid for the gig, including every guest at the birthday party we went to yesterday. He has also invited everyone he's had any contact with for the last few weeks to come to the concert and witness his maiden appearance on the podium. That's why no tuxedo with tails. Anything that makes him look like a comedy act would be a disaster. Laughter when he comes out or starts to conduct or takes his bow at the end would confuse him and hurt his feelings. He needs to look formal and serious—hence the suit.

I wasn't present today at the Bon Marche for the actual suit selection. Ned and Cathy did that together, a moment in his life I don't regret missing at all. It was relatively easy, though, because George the Salesman said the store's "best tailor" wasn't around, so Ned didn't have to endure being measured. (I remember Mr. McCann himself grabbing at various parts of me for what seemed like hours.) So they just picked the black suit they wanted—or more accurately Cathy wanted—and Ned has to go back and be measured in a week or two. That should be just puddles of fun.

I met up with them an hour later for the selection of accessories, like shirts, ties, and shoes. It was one of those extremely irritating occasions when Ned immediately and without warning turns into a stubborn six-year-old. He glared at us or stared at his feet, and we had to ask him any direct question three times before he'd grunt an answer that was usually unhelpful. When he's in this mood and forced to answer something simple, like "Do you like this tie or that tie?", for instance, he will automatically say "Yeah, okay," even if one of the ties being offered features hand-painted dogs playing poker.

In one way, this reaction to clothes and the tedious rituals involved with their purchase is our fault. We've always taken the line of least inconvenience regarding his attire, never asking him to wear anything that wasn't very comfortable and easy to put on.

Like pants. If Ned has a pair of regular, zipper-up-the-front, belt-around-the-waist long pants, I've never seen them. Since getting out of diapers, he's almost always worn sweatpants in cool weather and shorts in the summer. The shorts do include some standard zipper-and-belt loop configurations, but the majority of them have elastic waistbands. Even then he never wears a belt with the looped ones. I don't think he even owns a belt. Although he has some shirts that button up the front, including the white shirt he was required to wear for Nathan Hale Choir performances, his top choice daily is either a tee shirt, if it's warm, or a sweatshirt, if it's not. Thanks to the miracle of Velcro he's never had to tie a shoe in his life and so has never learned how. At least, we haven't tried to teach him. Perhaps in elementary school and unknown to us, some occupational therapist showed up one day with traditional sneakers and did the whole shoe-tying bit with Ned. If so, he never mentioned it and he certainly never learned anything from it. My suspicion is that this never happened.

I'm not kidding about the miracle of Velcro, as well as the godsend of elastic. With all that teachers have to worry about, especially Special Ed teachers, if little Neddy Palmer's shoelaces never dragged in the mud because they never existed, I'll bet the principle of "If It Ain't Broke, Don't Fix It" kicked in.

Ned isn't the only one among his friends whose parents wrap their kids in sweatpants and slip-ons. When you've got only so much time and energy to teach a child to read, write, count, and make it to the bathroom in time, why take some of it to teach him how to button a regular shirt when he never wears one in the first place? How much easier to just button that shirt for him on the four occasions a year (the choir concerts) when he has to wear it?

We are paying for this missing element in his education now. On an otherwise lovely Sunday afternoon, his parents are suddenly asking him about ties, suspenders, belts, and shoes that are heavier and harder than anything he's ever worn. He's being confronted with all manner of clothing that most people his age have been enduring for a decade. No wonder he wants nothing to do with it. It's like suddenly asking a native Hawaiian to pick among an assortment of mukluks and anoraks.

Eventually he'll have to upgrade what he wears if the job he gets is anywhere other than a gym or a sweat suit factory. So I suppose it's best to go through this clothing catharsis now, when the upcoming event—the concert—is something he wants to do so much. Who knows how much he'll want to go to work on the first day, whatever that work may be? At one point this afternoon I actually said that if he didn't give us more help picking stuff out he could forget about the concert. I'd call Rich Sumstad and tell him that I was replacing Ned as conductor du jour. Ned was facing insult—not conducting himself—and injury—watching me do it. I would never actually make good on such a threat, unless he insisted on appearing in his jockey shorts and a tube top, but it worked instantly today. He was as helpful as he could bring himself to be, which wasn't much but was more than the nothing we had been getting.

My fear is that for most of his life we have been too lenient and forgiving with Ned about some of those necessary skills that are a big part of growing up and operating in adult society. In the daily trivia of existence, Ned eats, dresses, and lives as he has for almost his entire life. He exists in a child's universe, with hot dogs for breakfast, sweatpants for almost any occasion, and toys forever at hand. We, and especially Cathy, have always tried to make sure he's clean, neat, and presentable in public, with his hair cut, his face washed and shaved, and his clothing, no matter how basic, in good shape. It fits and it's washed. Just because you have a developmental disability doesn't mean you should be shabby, grubby, or inappropriately clothed.

One of Ned's acquaintances is a girl with Down syndrome I'll call Millie. She's a few years his junior and is grossly fat, yet she always wears tee shirts and pants that are at least two sizes too small. Millie spills great rolls of pink fat out of her clothing in many unfortunate places, and seems proud of it. If the young lady didn't have Down syndrome, how she dresses wouldn't be accepted for a moment by her parents, her peers, or herself.

If dressing her in spray-on clothing is her parents' choice, then it's a bizarre, cruel thing to do to her. Her folks seem to be nice, normal people who love her a lot and wouldn't consciously do anything to embarrass her, so I have to assume that what she wears and how she wears it is her choice. If so, then she should be discouraged and indeed prohibited from doing it. But I can hardly criticize, because we're doing much the same thing with Ned, letting him wear what he wants and finds most comfortable. We're just lucky that most of the time he lets us pick the comfortable clothes. Millie's folks probably don't get that break from her.

Ned's clothing doesn't challenge his skills. By not requiring more of him now we may soon pay the price when circumstances are such that he quickly has to become more adult. Until now we haven't concerned ourselves much with age-appropriateness. And if he were going to spend the rest of his life in our home, or some Home, perhaps it wouldn't matter. I don't want him working in a place where they allow him to slack off in any way just because he has Down syndrome. If the dress code or company style where he's going doesn't allow for sweatpants and sweatshirts, then I'll be damned if they make an exception for him. So we may be exacerbating what might already become a difficult situation. Just when he's nervous about starting his first adult job, he will also be upset about starting a new way of living. There's not much in his life he can control, but at least he's had a say in the comfort of his clothing. What happens when that control disappears so he can do something he's going to be ambivalent about doing in the first place?

After haberdashery frolics, Ned and I went to Merle Carey's house. Merle's a jack-of-all-trades crewmember at KCTS, sometimes lighting, sometimes running a camera, sometimes pulling cable. Today is his sixtieth birthday, and he invited station folk to stop by. When we arrived, there were ten people sitting around a large table. Besides Merle and one other staff member, Ned and I didn't know any of them. Nevertheless, Ned listened quietly to the conversation, joined in when he had something to say, wished Merle a happy birthday, and we left after a half hour. Nothing special, except that Ned was just another person at the table, and accepted as such after the strangers got over their initial "what's this all about?" reaction to his arrival.

Suit-buying aside, he's grown up now. These days when he switches emotionally from being a six-year-old kid to a twenty-two-year-old adult in just a matter of moments may whip his mom and dad around like crazy, but he seems to be able to do it easily. The good news is that the six-year-old moments are diminishing.

Saturday, April 24, 2004

This afternoon I drove Ned over to Heidi's house in Ballard for, you guessed it, her birthday party. Heidi will be twenty-one in a few days, a fact that seems as unbelievable to me as the fact that Ned turns twenty-three in a few months. We've known Heidi since she and Ned were toddlers together. She's as functional as he is, and in some ways more, but Heidi is also more emotionally fragile. I don't know what her particular condition is called, but she has unnamed dreads that can lead to very anxious moments in otherwise benign situations. Some years ago at a social event I happened to glance over at Heidi and was surprised to see she was clearly terrified about something. Staring off into space, her eyes were as big as silver dollars and filled with tears. I asked her what the problem was and she couldn't tell me, but clearly she was having a powerful anxiety attack. "Let's go for a walk," I suggested. She said, "Okay," very quickly and jumped to her feet.

We hit the sidewalk. Heidi and I walked for maybe an hour that day, around the block again and again, chatting of various things. Like Ned, she is a devotee of rock and roll, but her rock interests start where his end. In George Lukas's film *American Graffiti*, the character John Milner says, "Rock and roll went to hell the day Buddy Holly died." Ned isn't quite that restrictive, being a large fan of the Beach Boys, Beatles, and some other post-Holly acts, but he's close. I doubt that Heidi would give you a dime for the Beach Boys. Her rock musical tastes seem to start with Heavy Metal and move out from there. Or I think they do. I haven't heard of most of Heidi's favorites, believing as I do that rock and roll went to hell the day Buddy Holly died. But on this day and this walk my ignorance was useful. All I had to say was something like "Black Sabbath. Now that's a band, right?" Heidi, being like Ned in a lot of ways, immediately and happily went into instructional mode. When we came back to the party she was calm again, she was Heidi again, and we were even better friends than we had been before.

She's a big kid who's been going through a punk period for the past few years, with black lipstick, black nails, and tee shirts celebrating rock bands that make Black Sabbath look and sound like Guy Lombardo and the Royal Canadians. But she still seems like just a kid to me, a nice kid, and now a twenty-one-year-old nice kid.

It's the natural tendency of most parents to think of their offspring and their offspring's friends as perpetual children. Sometimes such thoughts are good, like mothers lovingly describing their two hundred and fifty pound, thirty-five-year-old sons as Sweetie. And sometimes they are bad, as in "When is that big oaf going to learn how to pick up his underwear?" The tendency to infantilize our offspring, regardless of their age, seems stronger when it is closer to the truth—when there's a disparity between their chronological and intellectual age. So it's something of a shock to see them grow up physically.

The other night at Young Life Open Door I was sitting in the back of the room staying out of the religious flow, watching a group of kids I've known for a long time. And I realized that they didn't look like kids any more. Most of them wouldn't be carded in the strictest bar in America. They don't even seem like young adults, but just adults. Like Patrick, who I first remember from elementary school days as a friendly, loopy, noisy little kid. He's still friendly, loopy, and noisy, but now he's also very large and balding. For the last year he's sported a perfectly hideous mustache. (Sorry, Patrick.) Wrap him up in a Men's Warehouse suit and he'd look like the second best insurance salesman in Kansas City.

Because he's smaller than most of the other young men, Ned can still pass as a kid. That's over forever for Patrick. But it's been years since I've walked Ned into the movies as an "under 12." (Not that I ever did that, because that would be wrong.) There are a few restaurants where I still order the "under twelve only" junior cheeseburger for him, but never when the counter person can see him.

Although that's an interesting phenomenon. Even when he can be seen, even when his sideburns reach down his face to his jaw and he is clearly too old to qualify for the kid's price break, nobody has ever challenged me when I claim he's a pre-teen. I could ascribe this to my honest face, or to a counterperson's intuitive understanding that "under twelve" doesn't have to be a chronological distinction, it can also be developmental. But I think the real reason is that nobody wants to mess around with a kid with disabilities, or his dad. If they challenge Ned and they're wrong, it would lead to nasty recriminations. And if they challenge him and they're right, big deal. If Ned looked "normal," I don't think I'd get away with it. But he doesn't, so the guy taking the orders lets it slide. Why make a confrontation out of it, especially if you're wrong and some of these "retards" actually look a lot older than they really are? You don't own the business anyway, so what do you care if the short guy gets a burger for a buck or two less?

In one of our regular restaurants I now order for me from the Senior Menu and for Ned from the Children's Menu. This means we both get a cheaper meal, but also a meal that's just about the right size, which makes sense all around for two guys who are personally too big, uh, all around. As I get older and feebler, I see the day is coming when they bring us both a cup full of crayons for drawing on the menu. That's the day I stop going back. We seniors have our pride.

Watching the Young Life Open Door crowd, it's especially interesting to see the way they react to Tanyss and Santosh. She's black and he's Indian. They're nice, personable, articulate kids (they don't have Down syndrome) and are cuter than a box of fluffy ducks together. They've been a couple for years, but now they really look and act like it, always aware of each other's presence but no longer giggly teenagers about it. They're also no longer concerned when they develop friends and interests apart from each other, which has always seemed to me a major advancement in any relationship. (Heidi told me at her birthday tonight that her ex-boyfriend's inability to trust her was why she dropped him after years together. "I just hadda do it," Heidi said, sounding like a character on *Sex in the City*. "It was just getting to be too much.")

In the social hierarchy of our particular developmentally disabled crowd, Tanyss and Santosh are the "old marrieds," like that couple your parents knew who lived in the big house down the street, hosted lovely parties and had successful children, three cars, and an income just a little bit better than everybody else's. Like them, the developmentally disabled neighborhood respects Tanyss and Santosh, seeks their company and opinions, and envies them for having and holding on to each other. In most other social hierarchies, that envy would come with some resentment, but I've never seen it with these kids. They sincerely and genuinely enjoy the successes of their friends.

When I went to pick Ned up from Heidi's, a spirited round of karaoke was going on, using the diabolical machine Heidi had just received as a birthday gift. Ned has always been a fan of karaoke, partly because he knows how much I dislike and avoid the whole concept. Tonight at Heidi's he seemed happy to let the girls—and all the other guests were girls—do it by themselves.

Waiting for Ned to leave, I had a nice chat with a young woman I'll call Renee. Ned's known her since middle school, although they went to different high schools so we only see her now at parties like Heidi's or at the weekly Young Life gatherings. I often spend most of that hour in the back watching her. She has autism, or at least I think she does. Usually Renee seems very normal. She hasn't any obvious physical or mental disability, and in fact strikes me as a sharp young woman.

I'm sure that parents and other adults who drop by Young Life Open Door initially assume Renee is one of the leaders, not one of the followers. But it only takes a few minutes around her to realize that Renee, if not developmentally disabled, is emotionally disabled. She will be laughing and happy one moment and sobbing or furious the next, with no obvious reason for the change and no reason for the change back a few minutes after that. Renee dashes in and out of the Young Life meeting room a dozen times during the evening. And when she's in, she's often standing in the back near me, shifting back and forth on the balls of her feet, looking nervously around the big room as if at any moment some monster is going to burst through the door and carry her off. When that fear becomes too much, she rushes forward and grabs one of the leaders (never one of the other teens), wrapping herself around that person and holding on as if her life depended on it.

There's a demon inside this fascinating woman. The only time I've ever seen her completely at ease with herself and her surroundings was at the Young Life Halloween party last October. The event took place in a big church gym. It was relatively dark, and very noisy, and after a few minutes sitting on the sidelines I spotted Renee. She was off in the darkest corner, dancing alone, her eyes shut tight, a slight smile on her intense face. She's a very good dancer, I suspect because she's a very good athlete, currently playing on two different softball teams. A few minutes later she was sobbing again, and ran from the room.

Tonight she and I talked about her family situation, which isn't good, and her current problem at Young Life. Renee decided a few years ago that she's a lesbian. Whether she acts on that decision in any way I don't know, and it's none of my business anyway. Most of the people she knows don't take her choice seriously, and that drives her crazy. When she tells them, they react as if she's just announced she's going to be an astronaut when she grows up and fly to Mars. But even worse are those Young Life leaders who grab for their Bibles when they hear of her sexual preference and start lecturing her about sin. We are all of us just oozing sin, according to the Young Life leadership, but Renee's sin is now a Born Again Top Priority. It's in the newspapers and everything. Homosexuality is the Sin of the Moment for the intrusively devout. Renee is afraid the leaders have made her conversion back to good traditional developmentally disabled asexual heterosexuality their personal cause. And she doesn't need or want to be a Young Life Leader's team project.

The leaders should spend their time comforting her, not condemning the choices she's made that give her some kind of peace. That's what the Christ I've read about would have done. But Renee's not my child, and it's not my place to tell them that, as if it would do any good. I'm just glad that tonight at Heidi's we got a chance to talk. For months in the back of the Young Life meeting room she has been eyeing me with suspicion and then dashing out the door again. I hope now Renee's decided that I'm not one of her demons, Christian or otherwise.

Because Ned has Down syndrome, everyone he meets can tell he has a disability. There is one benefit to that. People tend to make allowances for him, allowances he sometimes needs. He can wear his sweatpants when everybody else is a bit more formal. He gets the kid's cheeseburger. He has the opportunity to surprise people with what he says and what he knows compared to their expectations. If some people immediately avoid him because of his obvious disability, I can easily convince myself that they're probably not people we'd want to be around anyway. I may have detested those folks on the flights to and from Oakland who declined to sit by him, but sitting with one of them between Ned and me would have been worse. In brief, for those who choose to avoid my son because he has mental retardation, the hell with you.

Whenever I wish he looked like just another kid, I can think about Renee. She's tall, thin, and rangy, with short, spiky hair, an intelligent look, and a wonderful smile that's all too rare. She looks normal, and probably all of her life the strangers she meets will assume she is. When they find out what she's really all about, she's likely to scare them off far more than Ned scares off those he first meets. Renee is the highest functioning person in Ned's teen world, so logically she should have the best chance to be productive, successful, and maybe even happy. But ironically she is probably doomed to a more lonely, frightened life than any of the others.

Wednesday, April 28, 2004, 9:00 p.m.

Chelan

Ned and I got up about 3:30 yesterday morning to drive almost two hundred miles east to Lake Chelan, a deep, glacial body of water surrounded in ascending order by motels and high cliffs. We're here for the cliffs, not the lake or the motels. Chelan is the site of the 2004 Speed Gliding Nationals. With my former colleague from KING, Bill Fenster, we've come to shoot a KCTS documentary of the event in High Definition television.

Speed gliding is a special kind of competitive hang gliding. Most hang gliding is up up and away, jumping off a high place, finding thermals to gain more altitude, and then either cruising around up there or seeing how far and how long you can go. Conceived in England a decade ago, speed gliding is in some ways just the opposite. Competitors hang glide down a slalom course marked by pylons and altitude gates. They don't want thermals taking them higher, because, comparatively speaking, the whole enterprise is done low to the ground. At the altitude gates a hang glider pilot has to fly below twenty feet, which is mighty close to the turf when you're moving around sixty miles an hour, suspended by a strap or two from a big wing. If you make an unanticipated one-point landing, that one point is going to be your nose, and it's going to hit the ground hard.

It sounds as spectacular and as dangerous as it is, which may be why when we arrived early yesterday morning there were only three competitors present. And they weren't competing, because the wind at the top of Chelan Butte was gusting to sixty miles an hour across the face of the cliff.

"We don't go up in this," the competition co-organizer, Aaron Swepston, shouted to us over the wind. Aaron is forty-five but looks younger. He's one of the best in the world at his sport, which he and co-organizer Steve Alford have been doing for twenty-six years. They've hang glided (Hung glided? Hang glid?) all over the world, and are particularly known for developing acrobatic hang gliding, which makes speed gliding look like a walk on the beach.

"Take off in a cross wind like this and you can get slammed back into the ground," Aaron said with the authority of someone who knows what that's like. Being slammed back into the ground certainly sounds like a good reason not to fly. An even better reason not to fly is that there isn't a plane under your rump to keep you from falling to your death. That's just one coward's opinion. When I first called him a few weeks ago, Aaron said we could cover his event if we promised not to present hang glider pilots as Extreme Sport daredevils. That was never my intention so it was an easy promise to make. It's a relatively safe sport if the proper precautions are taken. But it is certainly true that the overwhelming majority of human beings worldwide take the best precaution available, which is not to do it in the first place. And especially not to do speed gliding, which is a lot closer to the knuckle than basic gliding.

Having gotten up before dawn, come a long way from home, and driven up a long, tricky, steep dirt road to get to the launch site on time, we spent the entire day doing nothing but eating lunch and watching the wind blow hard. Everyone assured us such gales were not typical for the Chelan area this time of the year. Apparently they were right. I called Cathy last night and the same odd windstorm had belted Seattle, with power lines down everywhere.

Ned spent most of the day in our motel room, doing what he loves to do in motel rooms—listen to music and watch the tube. (I fear the day when he discovers room service, that moment of Ned ecstasy when he learns that in some lodgings his father is usually to cheap to take, there are people whose sole job is to bring Coca Cola and cheeseburgers to your bedside at any time of the day or night.)

We hoped for calmer winds today but it was still blowing hard. The first speed-gliding pilot took off between lessened gusts at 6:00 p.m., thirty-two hours after we arrived. Such is the glamorous world of documentary film production.

Acquiring and maintaining control over yourself and your equipment is the hard nut of every sport, but hang gliding is one where the penalties for inattention are deadly. Lose control in bowling and your ball goes into the gutter. Lose control in golf and the worst that can happen is that you brain the personal injury lawyer teeing up on an adjacent fairway. But lose control in hang gliding and you spiral down into the ground from a long way up. It's not surprising that hang glider pilots are very control-oriented types, and not just when they're in the air.

They especially dislike surprises. This dislike centers on, but is not limited to, surprising winds. Yesterday morning, besides that wind, Ned was the surprise. In our exchanges of e-mails I hadn't told Aaron anything about him or even that I was bringing my son along. So when we all met for the first time at the top of the butte, I think Aaron and the other pilots' reaction to Ned was one of mild confusion and concern. As I've now seen many times since my son crossed that invisible but distinct border between cute kid and "different" adult, the strangers took a step back, not a step forward. Without asking directly, they wanted to know why he was there and what role he was going to play in our coverage of their event. I suppose they even contemplated the possibility that I was one of those irritating parents who insist on bringing their children everywhere they go and then further insist on inserting said youth into the event, no matter how inappropriate. Was I going to suggest that we let the boy go up and give it a try? That may sound nuts, but I've seen daddies make sillier suggestions.

So far, Ned seems unaware of these moments of hesitation around him, whereas I am perhaps too aware of them. Most of the time they pass quickly, because Ned steps right up and isn't a bit Boo Radley. This moment was soon over, as much for the all the other things going on (wind, wings) as for any other reason. Ned didn't have the opportunity to work the crowd as he usually does. I still don't know if Aaron, Steve, and the others have famous ancestors or an abiding interest in the history of rock and roll, but I suspect that will come. Ned is warming to them and they are warming to him. For now he's just one of the television crew, and that's the way it should be.

It's a very nice, small crew. My friend Bill Fenster, besides being one of the best videographers in America, is also one of the nicest guys. That not only makes life pleasant on the road but is of inestimable value when photographing strangers doing whatever it is they do. People just naturally like Bill and are eager to do things for him. And do them again, and again, and then just a couple of times more, only can you do it with this hand?, as Bill keeps moving the camera around to make a one-camera shoot look like a three-camera shoot.

Together Bill and I created news stories, feature pieces, arts reviews, and short documentaries at KING, the Seattle NBC affiliate, from 1977, when we both arrived, to 1990, when they threw me out. He stayed for a while as chief photographer, and I became an independent writer/producer, mostly for public television. So this is the first time we've worked together in fourteen years, but it doesn't seem like that. It seems like just yesterday that we covered the royal wedding of Chuck and Di, the fortieth anniversary of D-Day, and made a children's movie in the Caucasus Mountains of Soviet Georgia a year before that country declared its independence. I don't think Bill and I have changed much in the time we've been working on other things with other people. He rides a big white Harley now, but there was always a bit of the biker in his soul. Perhaps that's why the only people who aren't immediately fond of him, and he of them, are police officers and other uniformed officials.

The other member of the Chelan crew is our volunteer grip/ sound person/grunt, a woman slightly older than Ned named Dara Horenblas. She's from Portland, where her father is an ER doctor. Dara walked into KCTS a year ago and volunteered to be an unpaid intern on the video game show. Public broadcasting, and especially program production, survives on the exploitation of eager young people, especially women, who are willing to do menial tasks in exchange for experience and a credit to put in their résumés. I've worked with dozens of these folks since 1990, almost all of whom have far better educational credentials than I have. Dara's one of the best, with more experience in production than a lot of interns, and an easy nature. I suspect she thinks Bill and I are a couple of weird old bald guys who finish each other's sentences, but so far she's hiding that well.

Ned's reaction to Dara is further evidence that slowly but surely he's maturing. He likes being around her. For sure he likes it more than being around a couple of weird old bald guys. But he's not gaga and gushing. In the past he's practically swooned around young women, like his reaction to Vicki and Marcie Finnila. He certainly wants Dara to be his friend, but there's little or no romance to it as far as he's concerned. They are just friends, and that's nice to see. Falling slightly in love with all the possibly available women you meet can lead to a very lonely, creepy life.

Friday, April 30, 2004, 11:00 p.m.

We're driving home from Chelan after a long but fruitful day shooting speed gliding. The wind finally died down and some more pilots showed up, so we spent all day today getting the quite spectacular shots we hoped to get all week.

I'm glad I brought Ned. There's no telling how many chances he'll have in his life to go to interesting places and meet interesting people doing uncommon things. If he gets those opportunities through my work, it's worth the minor hassles of people wondering why he's there, and his cheeseburger obsession, which can be such a drag when we're on the road with people who don't make their dinner plans based on which restaurants have burgers.

It was also most encouraging to see how the hang glider pilots, especially Aaron, warmed to him. They spent a few minutes this afternoon running around in a park together, my kid and this world-class athlete. It reminded me of the cruise around England, of the people on the boat who were having their first real encounter with an adult with developmental disabilities and were enjoying it, often to their surprise. I don't believe in forcing Ned on people; I believe in just the opposite. But it's nice when it works out well.

Tuesday, May 4, 2004

After weeks of not hearing from Peter Simonson about the Ned job search, he called today and talked to Cathy. He says they are developing ideas. They've talked to a nearby movie theater complex, the same one where Ira worked ripping tickets years ago. The owners hire adults with developmental disabilities, but currently they have no openings. Peter also talked about Ned stocking and shelving in a bookstore, which we suggested in the first place because it seems like such a natural for a young man as devoted to books as Ned is. The problem is that bookstores are in trouble, especially the small, independent booksellers most likely to hire Ned. Cathy told him that we've sent inquiries out to family and friends but haven't followed up because at present we don't feel any urgency. The summer is almost here, and after the Children's Festival next week, Cathy will have free time to do things with Ned. When he really needs a job is in the fall.

Wednesday, May 5, 2004

E-mail from Aaron Swepston
...By the way, I thoroughly enjoyed Ned. What a
complete pleasure he was, and I was amazed at
how brilliant he is. If only I could retain as much
information as he can. I'd be happy to be able to
retain even half as much! I hope that he can
accompany you next time around; I enjoyed his
company and hope that he also had a good time
playing with us kids!

Saturday, May 15, 2004

Ned and I went downtown today to do a fitting for the suit
we bought a month ago. It's a basic black suit, but so different
from anything he's ever worn before he looks practically ancient
in it. To my surprise the pants wouldn't go around his stomach
where suit pants are usually worn, so the tailor measured them
for his waist. And why they couldn't do that for me forty-seven
years ago, I still do not understand. I was dreading the whole
fitting experience, but Ned was quite pleasant about it all.

Saturday, May 22, 2004

I believe that there are certain seminal cultural experiences
one should have if at all possible, and I've been lucky to have
some of them. Mine have been especially musical, including hearing in person Ray Charles, Ella Fitzgerald, Miles Davis, Simon
and Garfunkel, and Lena Horne. I've been to a Yankees game,
seen Yul Brynner and Carol Channing in the roles that made
them legends, and been in Laurence Olivier's audience twice
and Dame Edna's once.

To be a true collector of important cultural experiences,
the experiences can't always be what you would otherwise do. I
actually attended half of a Wayne Newton concert. My friend

Marilyn Raichle and I stayed long enough to be amazed at the theatrical magic Wayne dropped on us for his big first-act finish. He took off his coat and showed us his belt buckle. From Row M it glittered like the altar in a small Catholic church. That was it, the big curtain dropper. The room went up for grabs, while I and the hysterical Ms. Raichle went up the aisle to the exit. We had the experience. We left.

In the spirit of cultural-experience-gathering, today Ned and I went to Hooters. Hooters, for those who read the *Christian Science Monitor* and watch religious cable and so are unaware, is a restaurant chain that started in Florida and is now based in Atlanta. At Hooters the food is secondary to the person who serves it. ("The food's awful," Ira told me on the phone this morning. "And how would you know?" I asked.) That crucial serving person is a Hooters Girl, and she is carefully designed to be hot stuff. All Hooters Girls wear orange satin gym shorts of a size more appropriate for a five-year-old, plus tee shirts that say "h O O ters" on them. The word is surrounded by a drawing of an owl, as if "hooters" is not a synonym for breasts, but has to do with the sounds made by an owl, wink wink. Needless to say, these are all very healthy young women.

When Hooters first opened, there was such negative huffing and puffing about the restaurant chain's obvious exploitation of women that to this day the Hooters website (yeah, I've done a little research here) defends the female staff. From the website: "Claims that Hooters exploits attractive women are as ridiculous as saying the NFL exploits men who are big and fast." (But wait! It does!) "Hooters Girls have the same right to use their natural female sex appeal to earn a living as do super models Cindy Crawford and Naomi Campbell." (Isn't that also the argument for the legalization of prostitution?) "To Hooters, the women's rights movement is important because it guarantees women have the right to choose their own careers, be it a Supreme Court Justice or Hooters Girl." I'm sure Ruth Bader Ginsberg would be interested to know that she and Misti and Tammi and Bunni and Brandi are socio-political soul mates.

Anyway, I can honestly say that I would never enter a Hooters unless there was some legitimate reason to do so. I think the places do indeed exploit women and it doesn't make that much difference to me if the women want to be exploited or not. I also have no desire to spend an hour or so over a plate of lousy food feeling like a leering old creep. In essence I reject the Hooters idea because of the way it makes *me* feel (slightly despicable) more than the way it must make the girls feel to work there. But Hooters is certainly an American cultural experience that for educational reasons is worth having, just like attending a Wayne Newton concert, or a monster truck rally, or listening to Rush Limbaugh just once for as long as you can stand it.

My reason for going to the Hooters on Lake Union today was that a Hooters Girl there may be in a television program I am producing. Her name is Kristin. She is an old friend of Dawnelle, who works in the accounting department of KCTS. When I mentioned to Dawnelle a few days ago that I was looking for a young woman to ride in a car while we filmed a travelogue of Seattle from that car, she suggested her friend. Kristin is apparently eager for the opportunity, but I wanted to meet her personally and tell her about the show. This may be a sexist reaction, but I wanted to make sure Kristin can do something other than serve chicken wings whilst shaking her "thang." Walking and talking at the same time would be a good start. Dawnelle says Kristin is also in cosmetology school, works as a receptionist, and in the evenings delivers eats at another Hooters up north, so she's sort of "torn between two Hooters," in the lyrics of that old country classic. Given that schedule, going for a weekend Hooters lunch was the best way to meet her.

I took Ned along because it was something to do on Saturday, I knew he would find Hooters fascinating for a variety of reasons, and why not? One could argue that it's insensitive to present him with a room full of unobtainable objects, but don't unobtainable objects surround every guy in the place? Though I have no direct experience, I'd guess that the quickest way to go flying teeth first into the street from a Hooters would be to lay hands on a member of the wait staff.

I didn't tell Ned much about the place in advance. I just told him we had to go to this restaurant and meet this girl. If he knew ahead of time the Hooters story, the raison d'étre of Hooters, so to speak....Listen, if he knew about the hooters, he might forego telling Kristin about the Denny family in favor of a discussion of her constitutional right to exploit her title charms. That was a chance I didn't care to take.

We walked into Hooters about 1:00. The Hooters Hostess behind the counter just inside the door immediately shouted at us, "Hi-welcome-to-Hooters! Can-I-show-you-to-a-table-for-lunch?" She had to shout because the place was so noisy. A dozen television sets blared sporting events, the play-by-play fighting for dominance with the rock and roll that spewed from speakers on every wall. A Hooters girl could have been having a wrestling match with a bear in there and Ned and I wouldn't have known unless it caught our eye.

There were many Hooters Girls lingering ten yards away, not wrestling bears but just chatting. Weekend lunch is apparently slow time in the land of Hooters. I glanced at Ned while we stood at the counter. Watching the nearby staff, his eyes were as big as Frisbees. I said yes to the Happy Hooters Hostess's invitation to lunch. I said it twice because of the noise, and because her attention was elsewhere. She was looking at Ned like he was leading an alien invasion from Mars. I doubt if many people with disabilities seek out the Hooters experience. It's not the kind of place the Parks Department green vans head for after an afternoon of bowling. When our hostess finally looked back at me, I inquired if a girl named Kristin happened to be on duty at the time.

This was a mistake. I should have waited until we were seated and more accepted within the Hooters milieu. The Hostess's demeanor changed instantly from professional gaiety to cold-eyed suspicion. "Kristin?" she said brusquely. "I don't know anybody named Kristin. There's nobody who works here named Kristin."

I could see where she was coming from. An old guy she's never seen before walks in the door with a young guy with Down syndrome and starts asking about a specific girl. They must get a lot of real creepy people in Hooters. I wouldn't be surprised if the creepy people/normal people ratio at any given time is ten to one, and a hundred to three on weekend evenings. For reasons of security, the management wants its girls thought of generically. One size fits all. Asking for a particular girl at the front desk has a whiff of the Hooters Whores about it, not the ambience you seek in a place that is only selling booze, barbecued chicken wings, and reportedly awful burgers, and emphatically not the staff.

I tried to explain. "I do television programs on Channel Nine," I said, "and Kristin is going to be in one of them."

She still wasn't having any of it. "You do programs on Channel Nine?" barked the lass, staring at me. "You? I watch Channel Nine all the time." I resisted the temptation to answer that I thought she was lying. Somehow I don't see *The Newshour* and *Nova* getting that big an audience amongst the Hooters lovelies.

"Yes. Many programs. On Channel Nine. KCTS."

Perhaps she realized that presenting herself as a devotee of public television was a stretch, because she said, "Actually my son watches it a lot. In the mornings. The kid's shows." And then she stared even harder at me, trying to see if I was Mr. Rogers, even though he's dead. Eventually she checked the staff roster and told me she had a Crystal, but no Kristin. I explained how a mutual friend had told me Kristin only worked the weekend lunch. The Hostess went off to ask the nearest girl if she knew Kristin. She came back immediately and said that Kristin had left half an hour before. The Hostess was about three degrees warmer, but it was still mighty frosty around the Hooters front desk.

"Well," I said, grabbing Ned by the arm and pulling him toward the door, "maybe we'll come back earlier next Saturday."

"I can't give you her number," the Hostess yelled after me, as if I'd been dumb enough to ask for it. And we were gone. Walking back to the car I explained to Ned about Hooters, how it was a restaurant chain whose popularity was based almost entirely on the underclad women waitresses. And I told him what hooters really means.

"That's disgusting!" Ned, the lifelong Puritan, said. Pause. "But I liked the waitresses."

We shall never return.

Sunday, May 23, 2004

Today we attended the Young Life Open Door picnic barbecue, which is about as far from lunch at Hooters as you can get and still have objects to eat. The barbecue ends the Young Life season for the year, and as usual was held at Gasworks, Seattle's most interesting city park. It's located on a peninsula that sticks out into Lake Union directly across from Hooters. (This is the last time I'll be saying that word.) Until 1956 the site was an industrial plant where large ominous machines converted coal and oil into manufactured gas. Cleaned and made safe, some of the old equipment is still there for kids to climb on.

It was a sunny, hot day, and all the usual Young Lifers and their parents were present. Ned had a good time, although once again he tended to hang out with the adult staff and not his fellow students. I spent most of the time off in a corner so as not to inhibit him. I watched Ned for a while, but the days when I tried to keep an eye on him all the time at events like this one are over. So I watched Renee again, lurching through an emotional range from sobbing to hysterical laughter and back again that would exhaust anybody else. I feel very sorry for her. Given the right circumstances, it will be possible for Ned to be generally happy throughout his life. But I can't see any circumstances short of some kind of miraculous cure that will let Renee be happy. She is doomed to a lifetime of destructive emotional upheaval. She's smart, and I think she knows it. No wonder she seems frightened so much of the time.

The theme for the party was the '70s. Most of the Young Life male staff were dressed like the guys who didn't get chosen on the original version of *The Dating Game*. The YL female collegians were all Joni Mitchelly.

The high point of the event for Ned was a round of 1970s-era *Name That Tune* in which he triumphed, even though his era of expertise is more the '60s. The high point for me was on the ground. Young Lifers were invited to write '70s-style slogans on the blacktop with big sticks of chalk. Heidi drew a very nice tribute to Jimi Hendrix, and there were peace signs here and there. Ned's first contribution was a scrawled "Rock and

One of the ways we are very lucky is that Ned has always had a splendid sense of humor.

Roll is here to stay." But he went back later, unbeknownst to me, and wrote carefully in large letters "IMPEACH BUSH. VOTE FOR JOHN KERRY." Then, sensing that a lot of the born-again Young Lifers and their parents were Republicans, he sat on the blacktop next to his creation and guarded it.

That's my boy.

Sunday, May 30, 2004

Last night Ned and Cathy went to a concert in Everett, half an hour north of Seattle. The stars of the evening were The Diamonds, the rock and roll quartet from the '50s and '60s that has become an essential part of Ned's core identity. John Felten, my cousin and therefore Ned's cousin once removed, was the bass singer in the Diamonds from 1958 until his death in a plane crash in 1982, the year after Ned was born. John's late mother, Helen, was my father's older sister. Long ago this combination of facts—rock singer, famous, tragic death, family connection—made John a mythical figure in Ned's life. I think if Ned found the legendary magic lamp on the beach, rubbed it, and a genie popped out to grant him three wishes, Ned's first wish would be the opportunity to meet John. He would not be disappointed either, because John was a wonderful guy, especially for someone in the music industry, which from my limited experience includes about as many wonderful guys as there were wonderful guys in Stalin's inner circle.

John was ten years older than I am. His family didn't live anywhere near us when we were all growing up, so I had little contact with him as a kid, but I always enjoyed the few times each year when we were together. John and his brother Jere and their parents would come for holiday parties. In the summer they would occasionally show up to go swimming. But I couldn't have been more than eight when John went south to college in California. The next thing I can remember about him was that The Diamonds were coming to town, including Cousin John the bass singer. They were performing in a nightclub, their rock and roll stardom days being over and done with by then. John's mother was a devoutly religious woman who wouldn't have been caught dead in a nightclub under normal circumstances. But to see her son perform she put on her best go-to-church frock and hat, while John's quiet, equally religious father Earnest put on his best brown suit. The Feltens went clubbing. (My mother found this image so amusing, it gave her moments of joy for years afterwards.) I'll bet Helen and Earnest nursed one Shirley Temple between them for three sets. It was not their world.

The story of how The Diamonds became rock and roll legends may be apocryphal or the work of an enthusiastic 1957 press agent, but it is legend in our family nonetheless. They never planned to be a rock act. They were more Four Freshmen/Kirby Stone Four-esque. Until one fateful day, The Diamonds were moderately successful on the nightclub and Vegas lounge circuit doing standards, show tunes, Patti Page covers, and a wonderful album of cowboy songs Ned and I finally found on eBay and bought a few months ago.

The fateful day. At the end of a 1957 recording session, they decided to cover a recent R&B (read black) hit by a group called The Gladiolas. The song was written by Gladiola Maurice Williams when he was sixteen years old. The Diamonds did it more as a joke than anything else, as a parody of the do-wop style then in vogue that was definitely not part of their existing repertoire. They worked on it for a half hour or so, but that's all it took because they were all very good musicians and picked things up quickly. The recording took even less time, and then they forgot about it. But their manager didn't. He put that song out there.

The song was *Little Darlin'*. In 1957 it was the Number One record in America for two weeks, and the Number Two record for a very long time after that. 1957 was the same year as such classic rock hits as *All Shook Up*, *Peggy Sue*, and *Whole Lotta Shakin' Going On*, so *Little Darlin's* rising to the top and staying there for months was a singular achievement for a quartet that wasn't even trying. It changed their lives, their act, and their audience. Those like Ned Palmer with a particular interest in the group's bass singer were amply rewarded in The Diamonds' recording of *Little Darlin'* by its most famous feature, a talking bass break in the middle of the song:

> *My darlin', I need you, to call my own, and*
> *never do wrong. To hold in mine, your little*
> *hand. I'll know, too soon, that all is so grand.*
> *Please, hold my hand.*

Regardless of his mood or what's going on in his world, Ned always smiles happily when that bass narration comes on. And I have never had the heart to tell him that most of the time it probably isn't John.

Careful readers will note that *Little Darlin'* was recorded in 1957. John joined The Diamonds in 1958, replacing Bill Reed, who left the group to get married shortly after performing in the original recording of the song. John was a much better bass, which is one of those rare family biases that happens to be true. Because of his abilities, the group eventually re-recorded the song with him. The *Little Darlin'* often played on

Golden Oldies radio stations today, and included in numerous nostalgia CDs, is sometimes the original Bill Reed recording, and sometimes the John Felten re-recording. The two versions sound so similar that the only way you can tell them apart is by listening carefully to the talking bass part, and even then it is extremely difficult. But not for Ned. For Ned they are all John, even when they aren't.

One of the other reasons John is such a powerful presence for Ned is his brother Jere, who lives west of Seattle in Kitsap County. The area encompasses the very westernmost part of Puget Sound and is quite beautiful, with lovely little bays and headlands. In the early 1930s the Palmer family looked around for summer home property over there. Eventually they bought five lots on a cliff, near the mouth of Liberty Bay in a small town named Keyport. It was the Depression, so the lots were cheap enough that my postman grandfather, his heirs and in-laws could just afford them. The senior Palmers got one lot, Helen and Earnest Felten took the one next door, and so on down the cliff top. Little houses went up, and every summer thereafter the Palmers were in residence in Keyport. My parents, brother, and I used to go over there often in the summers when I was young, though I have to admit to finding the operation a bit dull as a wee child. There are only so many hours you can spend on a beach turning over rocks to make the tiny crabs run away before you start hanging around the car, hoping somebody will get in it and drive you to anywhere else in the universe.

I'm sorry now I was too young to enjoy the experience, and especially too young to get to know my grandparents. Because my father was the youngest of six kids, his parents were quite a bit older than most of the other grandparents I knew. Wallace and Caroline Palmer seemed ancient to me, and not particularly warm and fuzzy. If I had tried to climb up into Wallace B. Palmer's lap, he would have said, "What the hell do you think you're doing?" and stood up. Even as a little kid I didn't blame them for their obvious disinterest in me. They had undoubtedly seen enough children to last them for the rest of the millennium, and I was the final grandchild. Not that they were unfriendly. They just didn't have anything to say to me, and I never knew what to say to them.

After the senior Palmers began passing away, most of their Keyport homes were sold to other families. But that room in my grandparents' house where those awkward non-conversations took place is now the John Felten Memorial Recording Studio, created and presided over by John's younger brother Jere. He's in his mid-sixties, with a wide variety of interests and occupations, including being one of the best ham radio operators in the world. (On a NASA flight years ago, hams were given an hour window to try to contact the astronauts in flight. Only one of them succeeded—a guy in Keyport, Washington.)

I don't think Jere would mind my saying that he is also a bit eccentric, and proud of it. He and his wife, Sharon, a former marketing director, moved into his folks' old Keyport summer home a long time ago. They proceeded to create a world in and around that small house that they find immensely satisfying and entirely their own. Jere was never a hippie, but he and Sharon now live as all those old organic types I knew decades ago thought they'd be living today. She has a magnificent garden in the front yard that produces many useful vegetables as well as some lovely flowers. They have cars but spend a lot of time traveling around on their bikes. A man who is a giant in one area of communications technology has no telephone, a computer he constructed from the parts of many other computers, and a home heated by a spectacular fireplace his father built.

Ned and Jere share many interests, especially music of various kinds. Jere knew Elvis and Johnny Cash, and that alone would be enough to endear him to Ned forever. But I don't think they would be the close friends they are, were it not for Jere's and Sharon's obvious fondness for Ned. They are probably his favorite relatives, and deserve to be—always enthusiastic, friendly, and interested in his doings. Every year we have a Christmas Eve gathering for family in our house. Ned starts waiting in the doorway forty-five minutes before Jere and Sharon are due to arrive. When they show up, he attaches himself to his cousin until it's time for them to go. Jere not only doesn't mind, he seems to enjoy it.

Three or four times a year Ned and I drive over to Keyport for a visit. While Sharon and I sit and watch the view or wander around in the garden, Jere and Ned go into the John Felten Studio in the old Wallace B. Palmer summerhouse. They mess around with music in there—talking about it, playing it, listening to it, singing it together. Lined up along one wall are twenty guitars or more. Tape recorders and microphones sit on benches and racks, and hanging on the walls are pictures of John and other mutual Ned-and-Jere heroes. In other words, if you had to design the absolutely perfect place for Ned Palmer, the one environment on earth that embodies so many things he cares about, it would be the John Felten Studio. But it wouldn't be complete without Jere in it. Theirs is a true friendship between two people from entirely different generations and almost entirely different worlds. And at its center is a shared sadness and loss. Nobody in this world misses John as much as Ned and Jere do. Their admiration for each other is grounded in a heartfelt longing for a lost brother, and a lost cousin once removed.

The last time I saw John perform was in a downtown Seattle club in the late 1970s when he was leading yet another Diamonds revival group. He was the only one left who had almost been a member of the original act. John informed us from the stage that his bass guitarist wasn't even born when *Little Darlin'* was recorded. That night they did a few quartet standards from the '50s, plus all their hits. Besides *Little Darlin'*, they also made a few dollars with an even funnier and to my taste better number called *She Say*, plus covers of *Silhouettes* and *The Stroll*. They sounded exactly like they did on the records, even though, with the exception of John, they were an entirely different group. This is now standard in the music business, as promoters try to squeeze a few more dollars out of somebody else's reputation. At one time I think there were half a dozen different groups touring the world as The Inkspots, and the Chad Mitchell Trio continued for years without Chad Mitchell. (Some guy named John Denver replaced him.) I look forward to the day when a promoter has the honesty to advertise "Tonight only! The Diamonds! Doing Their Impression of The Diamonds!"

That last time the John-led neo-Diamonds came to Seattle, I was working for KING Television News as the arts reporter. I wanted to shoot a tongue-in-cheek piece with my famous cousin about background singers. The bit started:

Me: "In the beginning...was the Oooooo."

Diamonds: "Oooooo."

Me: "And they followed that with the Ahhhhh."

Diamonds: "Ahhhhh."

Me: "And then they put the Oooo and the Ahhhhh together, and classic background singing was born!"

Diamonds: "OoooAhhh OoooAhhhOooAhhOooAhh..."

And so on. I don't know if John thought it was all that hot a bit, but he dutifully rousted his fellow Diamonds at 9:00 one morning so we could shoot it. He organized all the music and suggested songs we could include that sound especially stupid if you just sing the background vocals and go silent during the leads. (Listen to the Beach Boys backgrounds some time. Ludicrous.) I thought it was a wonderful piece, although my memory of it will always be sad. Just a few years later, that was the film I used to do his obituary.

John was a consummate musician with an extraordinary singing and speaking voice. If you listen much to oldies music on the radio, you probably hear that voice daily. He's the unbilled background bass in hundreds and maybe thousands of records. I should have been envious of John, because he got the voice I should have gotten. For generations, almost all of the Palmer males (and some of the females) have had bass voices. When we sang carols together at family Christmas parties, there'd be fifteen people doing the bass part, including my brother and me two octaves up. The only people singing the melody line in the face of all that deep rumbling were my poor mother and the other married-in women. At the end of each song, Wallace B. would harrumph and say, "Well, that wasn't bad...for a *normal* family." It was from this annual and often repeated remark that I concluded around the age of five that we were not a normal family, although it was many years before I understood why.

All the Palmer males had respectable bass voices, but the truly great bass singing and speaking voice has landed on only a few of us in the past hundred years. My father has it, and even in high school was famous as a local singer in his school choir and the various churches where he worked. Sunday mornings he used to dash from congregation to congregation, selling his pipes for five bucks a service. Pop worked his way through college doing the same thing, singing in churches and on the radio, including doing the first singing radio commercial in Seattle. Later on as a lawyer my father used his resonant bass speaking voice to great advantage. It is the voice of authority and power.

Last year for my episode of *The Perilous Fight*, I asked my father to read a quotation from General Hap Arnold. The general had taken a lot of criticism about the area bombing of German cities. Regardless of what Franklin Roosevelt said about sparing civilian populations, the targets of these raids weren't military. Hundreds of thousands of German civilians died because of our area bombing. Arnold responded to the criticism, and my father said in the show, "We must not get soft. War must be destructive and to a certain extent inhuman and ruthless." I told Pop to sound as cold and mean as he could. When Executive Producer Martin Smith heard the track for the first time he said, "Oh my God, that's your father? You poor boy!" But Martin doesn't understand what a real bass can do with a real bass voice. I was proud as hell to be able to use my Pop in the show.

(A digression. I was once visiting a friend's house when the phone rang. My friend's mother, a devout Catholic, answered it. Her expression almost immediately changed to one of shock, even fear. "It's for you," she said, looking at me. She was acting so weird that I said, "Good Lord, who is it?" She said, "I don't know. It sounds like God." "Oh," I said, "that's my father." And it was.)

The Palmer Voice has skipped me, and my brother, and my sons, although I think one of the reasons Ned has the unusual ability for a person with Down syndrome to sing well is part of the family legacy. John and Jere had no children, so the last hope for The Voice's reemergence is Ira's offspring, should there be offspring. Ira's kids may very well be the last of the Palmers anyway, so it would only be fair if at least one of them gets the real Palmer pipes.

The Diamonds in Everett last night included one performer who's been with the act for thirty years. Ned tells me he chatted briefly with this guy during intermission, but the guy was interested in selling CDs, not meeting cousins once removed. All in all I think Ned had a good night. His devotion to the memory of John Felten will continue forever. John is the man he never met, never knew, and yet truly loves. As long as Ned is alive, John is immortal. It's significant, I think, that of all the singing Ned does of old rock hits, he never performs songs associated with John. For Ned that would be a kind of sacrilege.

On that Bravo television show *Inside the Actor's Studio* where James Lipton interviews movie and stage folk, the final question of each interview is always, "If heaven exists, what do you want God to say to you when you arrive?" I think Ned would answer, "I want God to say, 'Ah, Ned Palmer at last! John's been waiting for you, over there by that pile of cheeseburgers. He's with an old guy named Denny. And some of that crowd from the *Titanic.*'"

Monday, May 31, 2004

Memorial Day

For the past decade, Ned and I have annually attended the Memorial Day events at Washelli, the cemetery about ten miles north of our home that includes a large military section. Quite a few of our family members are in Washelli, or Evergreen Memorial Park right across the road, including the grandparent Palmers and my Uncle Herb. Ned's particular delight is that the cemetery's 1884 founder was David Denny, brother of Arthur and therefore a distant shirttail relative. David, his wife, Louisa, and a few other Dennys and their relatives are in Washelli. The rest of the pioneer Dennys—the group that might accurately be called the rich Dennys, like Arthur—are in the far fancier Denny enclosure at Lakeview Cemetery, which sits on top of Capitol Hill overlooking downtown Seattle.

As per our regular Memorial Day routine, the only family grave Ned and I visited today at Washelli is that of Luther

Crowder, Ned's great-great-grandfather on his father's side. Luther is the veteran we've come to memorialize, and as he usually does in cemeteries with those to whom he has a connection, Ned memorializes Luther by sitting by his grave and quietly talking to him. I don't know what he says on these occasions, because just as when he talks to Great Aunt Dorothy up in Oak Harbor, he doesn't want me too close. I suspect he tells Luther about his neighbor, David Denny, entombed a few hundred yards away. But that's a guess.

Luther was a sergeant in the Civil War with the 122nd Illinois Volunteers. After the war he followed some of his family west to Seattle and died here in 1916. Ned and I agree that there's something very cool about attending Memorial Day events to honor a Civil War ancestor. Somehow it makes the World War One/World War Two/Korea/Vietnam/Iraq crowd seem like Johnny-come-marching-home-latelys. We keep this feeling to ourselves.

Washelli's Memorial Day ceremonies are organized by an old friend of mine, Michael Eagan, who got out of the theater public relations business and into the veterans' ceremonies business some years ago. Other than what must be a major hassle dealing with all the veterans' groups, Michael doesn't have to do much for this event because the ceremony has been exactly the same for years. Today the Seattle Pacific College band played patriotic tunes for half an hour, finishing with that number where the veterans of each branch of the armed forces stand when their theme song floats by. Ned and I always like this bit, watching these usually ancient men and women spring to their feet as anchors go a weighing, caissons go rolling along, and a melodic moment is spent in the halls of Montezuma.

Today, as always, the music was followed by a prayer and then the presentation of the colors. Twisting through the folding chairs, it was a lengthy parade by various organizations brandishing their American and organizational flags. I don't know what happens during this parade in other cities, but here in very liberal Seattle, the traditional military organizations are intermixed with groups like "Veterans for Peace" and "Vietnam Veterans Against the War." To my city's credit they are all honored equally, even in a year and on a day like this, when the fact that

American men and women are dying in an increasingly controversial war in Iraq floated over the ceremonies like a dark cloud.

This year's address was delivered by a career bureaucrat general who should have spent the extra hundred bucks for a writer. Like every other speaker on today's program he talked a lot about "the supreme sacrifice." The minister at the end even asked us to thank God that men and women were "allowed" to make the supreme sacrifice. I'm not going to blame God for that, but I'm certainly not going to thank Her either.

After the laying of wreaths on a representative tomb by the various organizations, and twenty-one rings of a Liberty Bell knockoff, it was over. Ned and I walked to the car, proud that we had attended once again.

We made one stop on the way, a stop we make every year. In the middle of the military headstones are those of the 442nd Infantry Regimental Combat Team. There are about twenty graves, instantly identifiable because all of the names on the stones are Japanese. The 442nd was the famous and highly decorated Nisei Brigade, composed of Japanese-Americans who fought like tigers in Europe and sustained heavy casualties, while at home many of their countrymen were in "relocation" camps. Of the hundreds of military graves in Washelli, I find those of the 442nd the most moving. These men volunteered to fight for a country that was shamefully violating the rights of their parents, siblings, and friends. The ultimate sacrifice represented by the men buried in Washelli must have been doubly painful for the men of the 442nd who survived. They came home to find their families had been cheated out of their businesses. They saw "No Japs Allowed" signs on some of those same "Now 100% American" firms.

Ned's voting now. He hasn't missed an election since he reached his majority. We are very proud of that, while at the same time we contend to anyone who might wonder that it's no big deal that both of our sons are registered voters. Why shouldn't they be? On an episode of *L.A. Law* many years ago, the lawyers were involved in the struggle to register Benny, the firm's developmentally disabled office clerk. As I remember, they eventually had to go to court, but even back then I didn't understand the plotline. Benny was an adult, holding down a job, and living independently. He was obviously capable of reading a voter's manual and making decisions about the kind of representation and legislation he favored. Surely the State of California, or any state, wouldn't deny such a person the most basic of American rights?

But because of memories of that show, I never inquired as to whether there was any special procedure in our state to register Ned. We just did it. Sometimes he votes as his parents suggest, but not always. Every vote Ned makes is Ned's vote, but he goes to the polling place a lot more informed than far too many Americans are. With and without our help, he's read over the Voter's Pamphlet and actually given some thought to his choices.

As a voting citizen it's important to me that Ned knows and understands the second half of that famous quotation by Carl Schurz that begins "My country right or wrong." Schurz was a German immigrant, a general in the Civil War, an acclaimed reporter, a United States Senator from Missouri, and a Secretary of the Interior. He was an environmentalist and an advocate of racial tolerance before both causes even existed. He was a hell of a guy, apparently, although he was far too eager to steal the lands of Native American peoples.

The second half of his quotation is: "When right, to be kept right. When wrong, to be put right."

That's why Ned and I always visit the dead heroes of the 442nd.

Tuesday, June 1, 2004, 2:00 p.m.

Nathan Hale High School

I'm sitting in a hallway outside the Music Room of Nathan Hale, listening to the wind ensemble play John Phillip Sousa's *Liberty Bell* under the baton of Mr. Ned Palmer. I am not actually in the room for this one-and-only rehearsal because Maestro Palmer asked me to leave. I hadn't planned on leaping up and correcting him, snatching the baton from his hand and doing it myself, or otherwise embarrassing him in any way, but apparently he didn't want to take the chance. So here I sit, listening. I have spent many hours in past years sitting and listening in this hallway, waiting for Ned to get done with Choir class, waiting for Music Supporters meetings to begin, waiting to go next door to the cafeteria and cook more pancakes. I suppose there is something appropriately symbolic about my sitting here now, listening to Ned fulfill his final scholastic musical fantasy by leading the band. He has reached his high school musical peak, albeit two years after high school, and I have waited in this hallway for the last time. We have come to the end together, as it were.

They've just run through *The Bell*. The student musicians are applauding. I'm sure Ned is smiling happily. Away we go.

Wednesday, June 3, 2004, midnight

It's been a long and unpleasant day, with one notable exception. My father's caregiver, Belinda, called at work to tell me Pop was going to see his doctor at 11:15 about possible pneumonia. If he had it, he would be admitted to Swedish Hospital in Ballard. One doesn't mess around with pneumonia in eighty-nine-year-old people. I said I'd meet them there for the appointment, but on the drive from KCTS, a woman turning left into a Taco Time smashed into my car, bashing in my left rear tire and accompanying metal. It was a clear day on a clear road with hardly any traffic. She just turned into me as if I didn't exist. I guess when some people want to eat tacos they want to eat them *right now*. This led to three hours of tow trucks, damage estimates (three grand), and rental cars. I spent the rest of the day and will probably spend the next two weeks driving a Dodge Neon. It's the kind of vehicle you figure was made exclusively for the rental car industry. At least I can't imagine why any private citizen would actually buy one for personal use.

In the accident, my cell phone flew off and then under the seat so I thought I didn't have it with me. I was trying to call various people to tell them what had happened using the Taco Time phone and getting the stink eye from the assembled Taco-istas.

A number of those calls were to the hospital where my father was, in fact, admitted. I also called KCTS, where Ned was working away at his computer assuming I would return soon to take him to the back door where Cathy was going to pick him up at 1:00. And then I had to call...well, this litany of the day's events is almost as tedious as the events themselves, so I'm cutting to...

The evening. Ever since the rehearsal on Tuesday, Ned has been clutching the baton Rich Sumstad gave him and conducting things—traffic, rock and roll CDs, the dog's stomach growls, and, at least in the car, a recording of *The Liberty Bell*. And so the evening of his potential musical triumph finally arrived.

Getting him into his new black suit reminded me of the scene in *Cat Ballou* where Jane Fonda and her team get drunken Lee Marvin into his old gunfighter's suit of lights so he can go kill his brother. It was an intense, feverish effort in the movie and in the Palmer family room. Ned endured it in silence and was at least slightly helpful. The only real crisis that arose involved the pants. The principal hook to hold them closed at the waist was missing.

"Oh yeah," Ned said, "that fell off when I tried on the pants at the store."

"Why didn't you tell me then when we could have done something about it?" I inquired with perhaps more volume than was absolutely necessary. The question went unanswered. Fortunately, we didn't need the hook because he had suspenders and buttons and I was also fully prepared to slap them pants on with duct tape if I had to. Eventually we got it all on him so it wasn't about to fall off. He looked good in the black suit, like somebody in the background of a *Sopranos* party scene, and that's not a bad look to have these days.

Because Nathan Hale High has no auditorium of its own, the music department does its concerts in the auditorium at Ingraham High ten miles away. We got there as required at 7:00, went in, and found Rich Sumstad. He showed us the backstage area where Ned was to wait before his entrance. With Rich, we did one practice of Ned walking out, shaking the maestro's hand, and then becoming the maestro by taking the podium and striking the downbeat. After that we were on our own until intermission.

I was most definitely on my own. Ned made it very clear that he was going to hang out with his old music friends and I could do anything I wanted to do as long as it wasn't anywhere near him. He disappeared into the school cafeteria, which the musicians use as a staging area. I walked around looking like the guy who makes sure nobody throws cherry bombs into the toilets.

The concert started at 7:30 with Nathan Hale's two jazz ensembles and then Ned's old concert choir. The first half closed with Ladies First, a girls' only singing group. Ned was nowhere in sight for any of this, and once again I realized how far we have come. The first time he and I were ever in this building was in the fall of 1998. He was a freshman then and the occasion was his first appearance with the concert choir. A big school building, otherwise empty except for the hundred or so musicians and their parents in the cafeteria or auditorium. I never let him out of my sight, nor did he want me to. Six years later, I didn't see him for an hour and a half and it didn't worry me at all.

We told those of his family and friends who wanted to see him conduct that if they got there at 8:30 they could avoid sitting through the other groups but still arrive in plenty of time to see Ned rampant. Eventually amongst the conductor's posse were Cathy, her sister Maralyn, Ned's old teachers Marcy Wynhoff and Kathy Schaeffer, and our friend Jimi Lou Steambarge. Ira even attended. When Ned was in the Nathan Hale choir, he appeared in fifteen concerts over four years but Ira successfully avoided almost every one of them. We never tried to force him to attend, even though Ned would have been genuinely thrilled to have him there. I suppose it was a part of not inflicting your kids on others. You don't inflict them on each other, either. Ned was eager to attend Ira's football games but we rarely stayed for the whole contest, in part because Ira, the beginning footballer, was in so few plays and when he was, he looked like a larger version of everybody else on the field. Helmets and pads will do that. Ira came tonight ostensibly to videotape the proceedings. It will be nice to have the videotape and it was even nicer to have Ira there supporting his brother.

Those who couldn't come included Tim Hilton, Cousin Jere, and Marcie Finnila. I think Ned was truly disappointed about their absence, especially Tim's, because he misses Tim. He's also been talking for months about dedicating his conducting to his Grandpa Harvard in honor of his ninetieth birthday, even though his ninetieth isn't until September. But Grandpa Harvard is in the hospital, and there wasn't going to be any opportunity for dedications anyway. Walk out, shake hands, mount the podium, big downbeat, keep the time, watch the band, turn and bow at the end, walk off. I've repeated this litany to Ned a dozen times in the last four or five days. Mostly he's either ignored me or stared at his shoes, hoping I'd shut up.

The Wind Ensemble was first on the program after intermission. I went looking for Ned while Ladies First wrapped up. I wanted to get him backstage and settled before the lobby was full of cookie eaters. I finally found him sitting on the floor in the hall outside the cafeteria. With all the other musicians gone to the auditorium he was alone by then, with his baton in hand, conducting the imaginary music in his head. He looked very small and very tense. Together we waited in the back of the hall until the intermission started, and then with Ira we went down the side aisle, up onto the stage, and into the stage left wings. Ira was going to shoot the video from backstage. If he shot from the audience we would have found ourselves watching five minutes of the back of Ned's head instead of his face. After twenty-five years in television, you do develop some idea of where the shot is.

In the gloom backstage. Ned took the only chair and sat in it, staring at the floor. I've been around a lot of performers before a show and you never can tell how they wish to be treated. Some actors can sit in the green room drinking coffee, smoking, telling stories, ostensibly not listening to what's happening on stage. A few moments before their cue, they casually rise, walk through the wings and into the light, and give a splendid performance. I've known other actors who would probably strike you if you tried to speak to them right before they go on. A friend of mine once played Ophelia to a Gertrude who stripped naked before each performance and then applied her costume slowly, one garment at a time, while glaring into a full-length mirror. She timed the routine so her cue to enter on stage coincided with the final costume element, her crown. My friend understood that if she spoke to Gertrude any time during this ritual she would have been struck repeatedly. "And Ophelia's the one who's supposed to be nuts," my friend said at the time.

For the past week or so Ned has made it clear that he wanted me to butt out as far as anything to do with his conducting is concerned. I haven't been able to resist the temptation to give him a few suggestions, like not looking at the score, which he can't read anyway, and instead looking at the players. Otherwise I've tried as much as possible to leave him in peace. But back in the dark corner of the stage, as the band members took their places on the other side of the curtain and started playing their first number, he was as nervous as I've ever seen him. He wasn't afraid. Afraid was right before he had some teeth pulled. Just very nervous. Now he wanted me to sit with him, talk to him, and be his dad. I didn't go through all the things he had to remember. I just told him to have fun. "If you're obviously having fun doing this, Ned, there isn't a person in the audience who won't enjoy it too."

I moved back to the curtain, watching the crowd out front, hoping to see Tim or some of the others arrive at the last minute. I glanced back at Ned once. Ira had found a chair and was sitting next to him, supporting him by his presence alone. In the dim light backstage, they looked like brothers for the first time in a very long time. I felt terrible for what might have been, but never was, and probably never could be. I wondered if Ira missed having a brother he could talk to and share his life with, a brother who would keep in touch no matter where they went or what they did. Before Ned was born, when we knew he was on the way but didn't know anything about him, that was what we hoped would happen. We hoped that one of the things we were doing was providing a companion for Ira, somebody he could always trust to be there if needed, and somebody who could always trust him. I've been able to adjust pretty well to Ned's situation in the years we've had together, but never to that loss of real brotherhood. It will always hurt me.

On the other side of the curtain the Wind Ensemble was playing its first piece, *Scenes from 'The Louvre'* by Norman Dello Joio. When they finished, after what seemed like three hours to me and probably seemed like thirty seconds to Ned, Rich Sumstad faced the audience and introduced the guest conductor. At least I assume that's what he did. With his voice from the sound system bouncing off the rear wall of the theater and then coming to us backstage after a few seconds' delay, I could barely understand what he was saying. Ned was standing just behind the curtain by then, clutching his baton so tightly it looked like rigor had set in. Ira took up his position so he could see the podium but the audience couldn't see him. "Good luck, Ned," Ira whispered in the dark. "Thanks, Ira," Ned said. Then we finally heard the words "Ned Palmer," the audience applauded, I gave Ned a quick hug, and he walked around the corner into the light.

Of course he did fine. His downbeat was strong, and he kept the beat fairly accurately, not that there was a musician on the stage who was looking at him. They were all concentrating on the music in front of them. But he watched them anyway, and he was smiling. In a few minutes it was over. He turned, beaming, to the audience, took his bow, and then waved at the band for their bow. The applause was polite. Rich joined him at the podium, they shook hands, and then to my surprise Ned hugged him. The audience applauded again.

When Ned came back into the wings, he seemed relieved more than anything else. The band was playing *Three Ayres from Gloucester* by then. Ira and I told him he had done very well. "Thanks," he said. The three of us snuck out a back door of the auditorium, walked around the building, and returned to the lobby. Once again I was on my own. As Ira took off for another function, Ned went back to working the hall, starting with the Vocal Jazz Ensemble kids who were out there getting ready to go on. I sat in a chair on the other side of the lobby, watching him in his element, realizing that for him conducting the band was good, but talking to as many people as possible about conducting the band was even better.

The only other adult in the lobby was a woman I didn't know, sitting behind the table where the Music Supporters group sells cookies. First she smiled at me, and then she stared at me. A little tiny thought formed in her little tiny brain. Apparently she hadn't seen me come in with Ned because after a few minutes she leaned forward and said, almost as an accusation, "Do you have a child in the music program?"

"No, I don't, " I told her. "Not for about fifteen minutes now." She obviously thought I was a creepy old man come to ogle the teens. My answer didn't preclude this possibility, so I explained who I was and what I was doing there. She seemed satisfied, although she continued to watch me with a slightly disapproving expression until the concert was over and the lobby filled with people.

That was four hours ago, and now it's very late. I just checked on the Maestro. He's sleeping soundly, with his baton on the floor by his bed for easy access, and the evening's program ("Special guest conductor Mr. Ned Palmer") beside his pillow.

Rich Sumstad is departing for teaching and playing trumpet in Canada next fall, when presumably Ned will have a job that puts him in a different and adult world. I have to believe that we are now, finally and forever, out of high school business, and certainly out of high school *music* business. No more concerts, pancake breakfasts, auctions, or standing around in the lobby talking to the people. No more applause. I wouldn't have said this six months ago, but I think Ned is ready to move on. He will miss opportunities to perform, but maybe we can find some others. It would be a shame if this was it for the rest of his life.

Friday, July 2, 2004

Peter Simonson called from the UW the other day to discuss how things are going in the search for a job for Ned. He said he has a few other cases that have taken up most of his time. We haven't been pressing him, but that's coming. He suggested to Cathy that he and Ned have a private meeting to discuss some possibilities. The meeting took place this morning at Irwin's, a small coffee/latte/espresso place just a few blocks from our house. Peter wanted Ned to walk there by himself and do the whole meeting solo, which Ned did. This evening when I came home, Ned was kind enough to provide me with a report.

My Meeting with Peter Simonson
Friday, July 2
By Ned Palmer

Friday morning my mother took me all the way up to the corner of Bagley Street, and after that she took me down to where Irwin's is. Then we walked home together. A few hours later was when I had my meeting with Peter Simonson. After I left the house I went back to Bagley and then I took a left turn and walked down toward Irwin's. The hardest part was crossing 40th street, which can be very busy. When I got there Peter Simonson was late, so I waited outside on the bench for him. My mother eventually came by and waited with me. [Ned walked it alone, but he had a surreptitious shadow who declared herself when Peter was late.]

Peter finally showed up and Peter and I went inside Irwin's. Mostly for a while we talked about how we were doing. I told him about the few jobs that I did for you and also for Jennie Cunningham at KCTS. Then after that I told him about the family reunion coming up pretty soon.

After that Peter got into the main thing I was there for. First he showed me a huge list of jobs and had me look through them. The list was really long, and some of the jobs were kind of strange, like office work, working in factories, and pretty weird business ideas like real estate. And a lot of washers—people who wash dishes— and also stuff involving money and math. Luckily I did find two jobs that went well with me. The first one was being a courtesy clerk, probably at the QFC in the University District. A courtesy clerk basically is the person who bags the groceries and helps the customer outside to that person's car. That job sounded good to me because it's the only job that didn't require using a cash register. The reason I'm not fond of the money and math stuff is knowing of my poor math skills. I think my skills are more directly to other things, like how to hold stuff, and to help other people. I like to work directly with people.

The other job on the list that looked good to me was assistant teacher to little kids. It's like little kids, like changing diapers for babies, and also preparing their meals, and also teaching them their ABCs and 1,2,3s. There is one school which I have found on the side of Thornton Creek on the grounds of Nathan Hale that does this kind of thing with little kids. I told Peter about that, and he went for that idea.

Peter suggested the idea of me being an usher in a movie theater. When I heard of that idea for a while I did like the idea. Unfortunately, Peter told me that the only loophole to that job is that the work is both on the weekends and at night. I don't want to do that because I have the nagging problem of sleeping on the job. Peter did mention the idea of working in a music store, one with books, and doing things like knowing the books and helping people find them.

When our meeting was over Peter and I walked out of Irwin's. That was when I mentioned to him about my love affair with animals. I told him how I'd like to work with dogs and cats. He considered that as a kind of a nice idea, and that he'd work on that. Peter said goodbye to me, and I walked home. When I got home my mom gave me an ice cream treat for doing a good job at the meeting.

Sunday, July 18, 2004

Ned and Cathy left yesterday morning for her friend Nathan's wedding, being held outdoors at a retreat center on the Kitsap peninsula. I don't know the bridegroom well, but he and Cathy have been friends ever since they traveled together in India in July 2000, looking for a Chhau dance company to present at the Children's Festival. Several artist-in-residence projects (with Nathan as artist and Cathy as fundraiser) have followed: on the most recent, a project for Día de los Muertos (Day of the Dead) at Hamilton International Middle School which culminated in a parade of both giant puppets and regulation-size students, Ned was tangentially involved. Nathan had brought along a mask for Ned, and Ned was not at all put off that the mask said "Barbara" across the forehead—especially once Nathan explained that Mexicans often parade in masks adorned with the name of someone they want to honor.

Ned chugged along without urging for the entire parade, and was rewarded for this unusual display of physical exertion by being able to pick himself out among the paraders, right at the front with the puppeteers and the musicians, in the picture that appeared in the *Seattle P.I.* the next day. This experience alone would have been sufficient for Ned to consider himself Nathan's "close friend," certainly worthy of a wedding invitation. Luckily, Nathan and his fiancée, Kathryn, included Ned in the invite.

Because I am approaching a video game production deadline, and the drive was going to be at least two hours each way, I passed on going. Cathy was probably relieved, knowing that I am not an outdoor-wedding-at-a-retreat-center kind of guy. I believe weddings should be indoors and fifteen minutes long, with ham sandwiches to follow, although in truth the best wedding I ever attended—other than my own, of course—was outdoors and very long. But then the bride's father spent almost a million dollars on the event, which made up for no ham sandwiches.

When they got back about 11:00 last night, she told me what happened and how it affected her view of Ned and the ways he's changed. She was kind enough to write an account of the day.

"First stroke of luck: there *was* a McDonald's on the road into Belfair, the last town in the Kitsap hinterlands before the scenic but narrow, twisting road out to Sahale, the retreat center. I'd been hoping there would be enough time to fuel Ned with a burger before the wedding, as it was unlikely that dinner would be to his taste and I didn't want to rely solely on his emergency roll of Chips Ahoys and carton of raisins. We arrived in good time for the 4:00 wedding, only to hear that the ceremony would be delayed, to await the arrival of a large number of guests whose ferry from Seattle was late. I quickly fell into an extended conversation with Nathan's boss, Jane. (Nathan now works part-time as the North American representative for two schools in India, where he grew up; his job is to convince American high-schoolers to spend a year, semester, or summer program there.) Ned listened quietly for a while, but found no way to enter this conversation. So he wandered around the field, introducing himself to other wedding guests, and, when Nathan and Kathryn arrived for pictures, making sure that he was front and center for conversation and hugs. I intervened only when I thought he had taken his share of their time and attention.

For the ceremony itself we walked through the field to a dense grove of trees, where chairs were set up around a central clearing. The ceremony was deeply moving: written by Nathan and Kathryn, with their passion and appreciation for each other apparent throughout, it was a perfect instrument for the collective love of family and friends, for each of them as individuals, to be reinforced by witnessing the love they were pledging to each other. The readings reflected many religions and cultures—Judaic, Hindu, Muslim, Christian.

At one point guests were invited to contribute their own comments about, and to, the bride and groom, and many in the group of a hundred fifty did so. I censor myself in such situations, convinced that I will not be eloquent or pithy enough to warrant standing and speaking. But it was immediately clear that Ned intended to speak, and despite some urgent whispering, I could not dissuade him. If I could have physically held him down I would have; I was worried that he would interrupt, and perhaps really spoil, this carefully planned ceremony by rambling on about the

Dennys, or something else completely beside the point. But after a moment of silence when he rose, to calm his nerves, he spoke clearly—and loudly enough to be heard—saying that he wanted to thank Nathan for helping his mom when they went to India together, that he really liked Nathan, and that he brought to this wedding a tribute from Seattle's first family. With a military-style salute, he took his seat. Most of the guests may have been a bit puzzled by the last bit, but Nathan understands Ned's pride in his ancestry, and there was certainly nothing disruptive or inappropriate about what he said.

As I sighed with relief, I found myself realizing, more immediately than I have in a long time, what a very different temperament Ned has than I do. He is much more gregarious: he loves to be out, chatting up new folks, part of any event, while I would usually prefer to be in a corner, talking to a close friend or at home, with my nose in a book. I can no longer shelter Ned from the world, or the world from Ned. He has the urge, and the right, to express himself. If he is, on occasion, rebuffed or embarrassed or hurt, he'll learn from those experiences. Nonetheless, today I am grateful that there was no need for any lessons to be learned.

For dinner Nathan and Kathryn provided pizza for the kids. We were seated with Nathan's honorary aunt, whom I had met two years ago when she came to Seattle from the Bay area to see a performance that Nathan was part of at the Children's Festival, and with Alex, and his wife Emma, a school friend of Nathan's, whom he and I had visited for a few hours in Singapore on the way to India. As we filled each other in on what we'd been up to for the past few years, the subject of conversation, at one point, turned to Washington State history. (Alex was interested in why the Pacific Northwest seemed so much more progressive than other parts of the West coast.) Astonishing: an uncontrived opportunity for Ned to contribute his extensive knowledge of the region's history to the conversation. A lengthy exchange, kept lively and alive by Ned's "And I bet you didn't know this" ploy, resulted. As we were leaving an hour or so later, Alex said quietly to me that he enjoyed meeting Ned, that he has a nephew with Down syndrome but that Ned is "in a different universe."

I had two hours, once we hit the freeway, to think about this comment, and the day, as Ned had fallen asleep. I had to pull him away from a conversation with the director of the retreat center, about why the grove where the wedding took place was established, and the American Indian it honors. (Ned had spied the plaque pinned inconspicuously to a tree.) He had then discovered an "amazing" connection between this honoree and an Indian singer whose work he knows, which he had wanted to explain at length. All in a day's work for Ned. He's intensely interested in his "universe," and, as I've seen clearly today, has the expressive power, given some luck and good will, to interest others in it as well. He doesn't need, or want, me to run conversational interference for him."

But on one topic we will interfere. Since mid-June, Cathy has been "no longer with" the Children's Festival, which is all that her severance agreement allows us to say publicly. She has been surprisingly calm about this turn of events: her attitude seems to be that when there's no recourse, "Don't even ignore 'em," as the great Sam Goldwyn once said. Ned, however, is outraged. Ever since Cathy began working for the Festival eighteen years ago, he has designated himself a "programming consultant" to advise on singers for little kids. He is determined to send Cathy's boss a note that the Festival will lose these services unless his mother is rehired. No amount of careful explaining that, in such a situation, his note will have no effect, has calmed him. We have simply refused to mail various versions of this communiqué.

And we will all move on. Perhaps at this moment, when we're really gearing up for Ned's job search, it will prove useful to be reminded that a job is just a job, that most people will probably have many jobs, that no matter how much energy and dedication you bring to the workplace, you should leave your heart at home, with family and friends, to make the inevitable transitions less painful.

Tuesday, August 10, 2004, 7:45 p.m.

Trinity United Methodist Church, Ballard

A few weeks ago, Cathy saw a flyer announcing the formation of the Arts Ballard Festival Choir. "Choral singers of all ages and ranges are encouraged to join in for what will undoubtedly be an exciting, inspirational, and fun event," the flyer promised. Someone named Chris Vincent was putting a group together to perform one night only in an arts center in Ballard, the northwest Seattle neighborhood once famous for its predominantly Scandinavian population. Ballard still promotes itself as being "all lutefisk all the time," but over the years it's become a far more diverse middle-class community.

It sounded to us like an ideal opportunity for Ned to be part of a choir again. If he didn't like it or they didn't like him, he could always walk away without much time or energy invested. But before we asked Ned about his interest we e-mailed Chris Vincent about Ned.

> Dear Chris Vincent, or organizer,
>   I recently picked up a flyer...and want to inquire about the feasibility of our son's participating. Ned is 22 and a graduate of Nathan Hale, where he sang in the choir (tenor or baritone, depending on needs) for four years...He also has Down syndrome. Although he does not read music, he required no special adaptations or instructions to participate in all choir performances and competitions. Thanks for your consideration...

Chris responded that the purpose of the choir was to have fun, and if we thought Ned would have fun it was fine with him.

I took Ned to the first rehearsal a week ago, held in this Ballard church. I planned to stay for the whole two hours. I didn't want to dump Ned at the first rehearsal of his first out-of-school adult choir and just hope he did all right in a room full of singing strangers. I thought I could sit in a back pew while Ned rehearsed. But when we arrived Chris asked me to stay and sing with the group, even if I wasn't going to join up. I didn't think I could refuse. This guy was being most generous to allow Ned in his choir, and at the moment he asked me to sing with them, he wasn't sure how many men were going to walk in the door. I was going to be there anyway, so I stayed to sing with Ned.

This was a huge mistake. About thirty people eventually showed up, mostly experienced church choir singers, some from the congregation where Chris is their director. The majority of them were women, so we few men were up front. Ned and I sat side-by-side between the basses and the baritones in the first row directly in front of Chris. He started the evening with vocal warm-up exercises. For four years Ned began every choir class at Nathan Hale with vocal warming up, but this time he declined to participate. Not making a single sound, he stared at the floor while the rest of us were all la-la-la-ing like crazy. Ned continued to stare at the floor for the entire rehearsal. One would have thought he was nonverbal, non-vocal, and non-alive, except that he was breathing and occasionally shooting me dire glances.

I was having my own troubles. Like Ned, I don't read music. With only six rehearsals before the performance, Chris understandably doesn't have the time or inclination to work with the sheet-music-challenged. We—and that would be Ned and me alone—have to pick up our parts by listening to those around us. I was trying to do that and at the same time trying to get Ned into the game.

He absolutely refused. His behavior suggested that when we told Chris by e-mail how experienced and functional our son is, we were blatantly lying. Either that or we are the kind of parents who are in denial about their kid's real abilities. Needless to say I was both embarrassed and angry.

Driving home that night, Ned told me what the problem was. The problem was me. Ned wants to do his singing alone, not with Dad standing next to him singing too. If I would butt out, he would be eager to participate in the Arts Ballard Festival Choir. I told him he may have blown that chance by his behavior. I couldn't think of a single reason why Chris would want him to come back. And that's how we left it.

Yesterday we sent an e-mail to Chris Vincent:

> Dear Chris, I understand that, unfortunately, Ned
> was largely a non-participant at last week's
> rehearsal...According to Ned, he hadn't expected
> Greg to stay, and was shy about singing in front of
> him. *[Bit of a stretcher, that. Shyness had nothing to do
> with it.]* Although we've discussed with Ned that he
> might feel more at ease with another kind of choir,
> he says that he would like to try another rehearsal,
> by himself...We'd appreciate your guidance here. If
> you're willing to bear with Ned for another re-
> hearsal, to see if he will start participating, Greg
> will bring him tomorrow, and then depart. If not,
> we do understand, and will look for a different
> setting...Thanks, Cathy Palmer

Return e-mail from Chris Vincent:

> I really appreciate your considerate and thoughtful
> approach. I did notice that Ned was working hard
> to keep up, but at the same time he seemed to be
> having a fairly good time. *[Real stretcher here from
> my memory of the evening, but perhaps Chris, who was
> looking directly at Ned, saw something I didn't.]* This
> particular project was meant to be fun. My feeling
> is that if he can enjoy himself, I am really not
> opposed in this least to his continuing...I think it
> might indeed be constructive to let him try again
> tomorrow evening and decide after that. Does that
> work for you and Ned? Chris Vincent

It did work for us, which is why at the moment I'm hiding in
the foyer of the church as they rehearse in the sanctuary. All his
life Ned has looked for situations he can control. Performing is
definitely one of them, and one of the ways he controls it is by
insisting on doing it alone, without parental involvement. If he's
playing his guitar in the family room, he always has the door closed

and will immediately stop when Cathy or I come in. If he is singing along with the radio while we're driving somewhere, he stops instantly if I try to join in. It's not that he's the least bit embarrassed, shy, or uncertain about his talents, regardless of what we told Chris. Ned thinks he's great, and in formal performance situations he doesn't mind sharing that opinion with everybody. He was not only happy to have us there when he sang with the Nathan Hale choir, he very much wanted us there. But he wanted us in the audience, not beside him on the stage. I knew this general feeling of his. Staying for the last rehearsal was my mistake. Although it would have been rude, I should have insisted on leaving, or hiding in the back of the church like a Scandinavian Quasimodo (Quasimoddersköld?), which is just what I'm doing now.

The second rehearsal has been going on for about an hour. As far as I can tell, Ned is participating. I can't hear him, and other than forty-five minutes ago when I snuck around behind some pillars to get a better view, I can't see him either. During a brief break, however, Chris told me he's doing fine. I worry that he will have a hard time picking up his part, but some of the other male choir members seem to be helping him. He is depending on the kindness of strangers.

Tuesday, August 24, 2004

Peter called today to tell us he's spoken with Roger Jones, manager of the huge Safeway store that's only five miles from our house and directly across the street from the bowling alley where Ned does his kegling. They discussed Ned, and Peter must have sold the kid well because he says Jones would be interested in hiring Ned as a part-time clerk. It's not a formal job offer yet. Before that happens, Ned will have to do an interview with the Safeway personnel department and pass a drug test, that mandatory ritual of the new millennium that makes everyone feel for one whiz like an Olympic athlete. If those events go well, he gets the offer and gets the job.

Given the thousands of adults with developmental disabilities who don't have jobs, I guess I should be overjoyed by the news that Ned will soon be working and making a salary. Because I know the alternative. Years ago I did a news story about a young woman with developmental disabilities who had completed high school and a work training program. She was pleasant, verbal, and a rudimentary reader. There were a lot of useful things she could have done as a worker. But there was no work for her, so the young woman's name went on some waiting list. At the age of twenty-one, having exhausted all the available state programs, she went home to live with her single mom and wait for a job. I met them seven years later. She was still waiting, but she had changed.

"I have to go to work every day to support us," her mother told me. "She's able to stay home alone by herself, but she doesn't have anything to do. So she just sits. I try to do things with her on the weekend, but that's not enough, and I'm exhausted all the time. I can't afford to have anyone here with her. We're pretty much alone in this."

After seven years of vegetating, the young woman was no longer verbal, nor could she read. Without the stimulation of other people and places, and without anything to do, her hard-won skills had evaporated. The tragic irony was that while she was waiting for a job, she lost the ability to do almost any job outside a sheltered workshop.

People with developmental disabilities need stimulation as much or more than everyone else. Without some kind of social interaction, a decrease in functional ability is not uncommon. Even so, the young woman's mother blamed herself. She thought she had failed her only child. She was wracked with guilt about the present and fear for the future. We both knew that her daughter was eventually destined for some state institution for the rest of her life. And there she'd just be sitting too, not waiting for a job, but waiting to die.

I thought about the two of them today. Ned obviously has far better prospects, and so I should be happy that those prospects have just improved. But after all these years of work, and knowing what he's capable of, it's hard to be giddy about his being a grocery store clerk. It's a dull, tiring, dead-end job historically filled by high school kids trying to make a few dollars and seniors trying to find something to do. In fact, it's exactly the kind of employment "lucky" adults with disabilities most often get. I've seen many of them working in grocery stores, including the store where Ned might be going. One of the last times I was there, I pulled into the large parking lot on a rainy Saturday afternoon. I had a few things to pick up while Ned was across the street bowling with the Parks Department.

A tall man wearing a white shirt and a green apron was standing in the middle of the lot. I parked nearby just as he started following a woman pushing a cart to her car. While she emptied the cart he stood ten feet away, silently watching her. When she was done, he stepped forward, took the cart, and wheeled it toward the entrance to the store. When I came back fifteen minutes later, he was still out there and still pushing carts around in the rain. He took mine and I thanked him. He smiled very quickly but didn't say anything. He was concentrating on the job and had no time to chat. He was soaking wet.

I thought about that man today, too. There is certainly one aspect of the box boy job Ned will enjoy. He'll like meeting new and different people every day and having the opportunity to chat with them, even if that chat is limited to the time it takes him to get their groceries from the check-stand to their car. But standing up for four hours a day, carrying heavy bags and boxes around, pushing carts around in the rain in a grocery store parking lot? I'd predict that two hours into his first day of work they'll find him sitting in a dark corner of the store staring at his shoes. There's no question he can do the work, but he'll be miserable doing it.

I realize there's some of my own ego at play here. What father can honestly say he raised his son to be a box boy, no matter what that son's situation might be? My hope for Ned's life is very simple. I want him to be happy regardless of what he's doing or where he is. I accept the fact that happiness might be possible for him if he's working as a part-time grocery store clerk. Ned describes himself as a singer/songwriter. If he is going to pursue that, he is going to need time to do so. Working at the store, he may develop a life like his Auntie Maralyn's.

Cathy's sister is a printmaker and watercolorist who does wonderful work. But like far too many artists, Maralyn can't support herself just doing her art. So for more than twenty years she has risen long before dawn and gone to work in the mailroom at the *Seattle Times*. She delivers mail and packages and is usually done by 11:00. The mailroom job puts three squares on her table, gives her medical benefits, usually takes only a little of her physical, emotional, and intellectual energy, and frees her to do what she really wants to do in the afternoons—be an artist. In a better world she could be an artist all the time, but the Medicis are dead and aren't coming back. So the *Times* serves unwittingly as her patron. The difference is that instead of being required to paint occasional portraits of Lorenzo di *Seattle Times* and his family, she delivers his mail five mornings a week.

Maybe that's Ned's life to be—dull work in the morning, art in the afternoon. But it still seems so impossible to me that I just can't imagine it for him. I appreciate Peter's efforts, and I certainly appreciate the Safeway manager who has agreed to hire my son. I know from personal experience that he has hired other people with developmental disabilities for his store and that's always to be commended. Nevertheless, it's going to be very hard to see Ned slip on a green apron and head for that parking lot in a few weeks.

Friday, August 27, 2004

A remarkable day. Ned and Peter went to the huge Safeway store in south Seattle that serves as the company's Northwest District office. Ned had an appointment to be interviewed by somebody in the Human Resources department about the pending box boy job in Ballard. While he's there, he'll take the mandatory drug test. Last night he was far more intrigued about the test than the interview. We assured him that they wouldn't be taking any blood, that no needles of any kind would be involved. Originally we thought he'd have to pee in a jar. I would have given a lot to be present when somebody tried to explain that process to him and the need for it. But Peter says that all they have to do is take a swab from his cheek. Ned still pronounced this "disgusting," and spent some time yesterday incensed that anyone could even suggest that he ever took drugs. Ned is, as they say, high on life. Exclusively life.

At exactly the same moment Ned was being swabbed, I heard an interesting bit of news at KCTS. For the past few years the mailroom at the station has been run by a fellow in his fifties named Jim Hoy. Jim was gone for some time last year to have major surgery. He returned to work but he has never been what you'd call robust. The surgery took a lot out of him, and, ever since returning, Jim has often seemed to me to be suffering. I heard today that his doctor has told him to stop working immediately. He's leaving KCTS, and he and his partner are moving to Arizona as soon as they can.

Jim is a full-time employee whose job involves sorting and delivering the incoming mail every morning and then putting postage on all the letters and packages going out in the afternoon. The first half of the job is exactly what Ned did that summer seven years ago when he worked with Merritt Klarsch. The afternoon task of stamping I don't think Ned could do, at least not yet. There's just too much math involved, plus the operation of a large, complicated postage meter apparatus.

In late morning I went to see Jay Parikh, Ned's boss-of-record in the marketing department, even though Ned hasn't done anything directly for Jay in months. But they are friends, and Jay has always been very big on Ned. I told him I didn't know what the company had in mind for Jim's mailroom replacement but that there was an experienced mailroom person in the building just now who was looking for part-time work. Jay was intrigued by the possibility of Ned's taking over the mailroom. He didn't know what the company's plans are either, but said he'd chat with Michal.

Michal (pronounced Michelle) Anderson Jacob is the new Director of Finance for KCTS. Why the Director of Finance oversees the mailroom I don't know, but stranger things happen in the glittering world of broadcasting. Born and raised in the Seattle area, she is most recently from Hawaii, where her husband is a Marine Corps helicopter pilot. When she was introduced at the monthly all-staff meeting a few weeks ago, Michal said she had made a deal with her hubby a long time ago. She'd follow him around during his active duty but they had to come back to the Northwest to live when that was over. And now they have. Or she has. He's still over there wrapping up his career in the Corps. He gets out early in November and comes to Seattle to teach.

Michal is the money person in a company that's currently operating on a seven million dollar loan and trying to keep its nonprofit head above water. It's a company that endured charges of near-fatal financial mismanagement not that long ago. Her predecessor in the job "resigned" on a day's notice and was gone. Michal wears a lot of black and dark blue to her brand new job. Combine all these things, and you might expect her to be intense, serious, and well aware of her important role in the survival of KCTS. If she acted like the toughest cowboy in the bunkhouse you wouldn't blame her. In fact, she seems just the opposite: light-hearted, a big laugher, and not given to taking herself or much else all that seriously. I might wish that I was hustling the "Mailroom Ned" deal with someone who had been here longer and knew him better, but Michal should be okay. Along with everything else, she's a mom with three daughters, I suspect a very good mom, and good moms are almost always compassionate, understanding people who are willing to take a chance on somebody else's kid.

Jay pitched her about Ned this morning, I followed up with an e-mail, and we met this afternoon. We haven't really talked since she was hired, being in different ends of the building doing entirely different things. She told me today that we had met once before, sort of. Many years ago when I was the film critic for KING I sat behind Michal and some of her pals at a movie, an event I have completely and understandably forgotten. She was then a senior at Chief Sealth High School in south Seattle and I was a minor local celebrity in the greater Seattle area. The teens thought that having the teevee movie guy in the theater sitting behind them was exciting. I don't know about her friends, but I suspect Michal rapidly overcame finding me all that big a thrill.

We talked about Ned and his abilities and the fact that he has a job coach who would stay with him in the mailroom until he clearly understands the job and can do it. She told me that the management had indeed thought of trying to make the mailroom clerk a part-time position. They would hire a half-timer in the morning to handle the incoming mail, and in the afternoon the still-to-be-hired building manager assistant would take care of the outgoing mail. This was the perfect deal for Ned if they were willing to give him a shot. Michal was indeed willing, but she had to check it out with the HR department. And though she didn't say it, I suspect she wanted to run hiring Ned by the company's president and CEO, Bill Mohler. She said she'd be back in touch.

I called Cathy and told her about the job possibility at KCTS. We both thought it was a strange situation. After all this time with no job, Ned might very soon have to pick between two companies that have agreed to hire him. I assume he will eagerly pick the KCTS mailroom if given the chance, but Cathy thinks there's at least the possibility he'll be so attracted by the social possibilities of grocery store clerking that he'll choose that. "Even after he finds out he'll be standing up for four hours a day?" I asked. "He could surprise us," she said, and she's right.

Right now it's a question of timing. We certainly wouldn't want to turn down one job if the other doesn't come through, and we have no idea when either work will be offered officially. There is every indication Safeway will step up almost immediately. There's also the chance that Ned could do both jobs, working at KCTS in the morning and at the grocery store in the afternoons for at least a few days a week. Given his stamina I don't see that happening, but it is at least a possibility.

Michal came by just before I left KCTS this afternoon to tell me that the company would consider hiring Ned for the position but that the process could take two weeks. "We may have to post the job," she said, "but Ned would be encouraged to apply for it."

That's where we left it. Michal has made it obvious to me that she really wants Ned to have this job. I suspect her boss Bill Mohler feels the same way. But there is red tape to negotiate which may make the timing of Ned's choice difficult. Can we, in good conscience, turn down the box boy job without having in hand a firm offer from KCTS? Can we even mention the KCTS job to Ned yet?

When Ned got back from his interview/swab this afternoon, Peter told us that Safeway has officially made a job offer if Ned isn't a drug addict. We didn't tell Ned or Peter about the KCTS possibility. No reason to get the chickens all a-dither before they are hatched.

Tuesday, August 31, 2004

Michal came by my desk this morning to offer Ned the job officially: "a two-month, twenty-hours-a-week, 'lets-see-how-this-goes' contract." It's been decided that the part-time mailroom position doesn't have to be posted. Again, I sense the hand of Michal and Bill Mohler in this. He came to KCTS last May after a decade as President of Bates Technical College in Tacoma. With 22,000 students, Bates is the biggest vocational college in the state as well as the licensee of KBTC, the only other public television station in the market. Before that, Bill was the assistant superintendent for vocational education for the Tacoma public schools. He's had a lot of experience in the areas of job training and job acquisition, and I'm sure some of that experience involved people with disabilities. If Bill were a crusty forty-year veteran of nothing but television station management, he would probably be far less likely to care about whether Ned worked in his mailroom. But we've been lucky again. He's a nice, friendly guy who knows firsthand and from many years' experience what it means to take a chance on a worker with disabilities: what it means to the worker, to his family, and what it means to the company where he is employed. And he is a dad.

The question now is whether that potential worker wants to take a chance on KCTS. This evening Cathy and I told him about the mailroom offer. You have an important decision to make, we said, although you don't have to make it right at this moment.

We sincerely want this to be Ned's choice, so it was with consider-able effort that I refrained from mentioning that in my opinion he would be out of his mind not to take the KCTS job.

Ned's reaction to news, both good and bad, is rarely what I anticipate, or at least rarely at the intensity I expect. Tell him bad news and he usually goes silent, looks intently at the ground, and then walks away to ponder. (The exception is if the news involves the death of someone he knows. Then he is always shocked—and a little thrilled—and looks it.) Tell him some good news and he smiles but doesn't do much else, at least not immediately. When I told him about the KCTS job, I wanted him to start whooping and hollering and jumping around the room in gay abandon.

"Really?" was the total of his response, as if I'd just men-tioned that Mick Jagger has a spare set of lips on the back of his neck. (This is probably untrue.) Ned didn't say there's no question in his mind that the KCTS deal is the way to go. He didn't say anything. It occurs to me that he doesn't see a dif-ference between what he's doing now at KCTS, and the mailroom offer. Ned has been sitting at a Channel Nine desk since last October. I know he hasn't been doing any real work for a long time, but he describes what he does here as work to everyone who asks him what he's been up to. Ned thinks he works at KCTS, so presenting him with the wonderful possi-bility of working at KCTS is naturally confusing. For him it's like comparing apples and apples.

Wednesday, September 1, 2004

This morning Ned hadn't made any decision yet between the mail and "plastic or paper?" and we didn't press him for one. According to his drug test, he is apparently not addicted to controlled substances, so the Safeway deal is in place. We can't find the food handler's permit he got in high school, but grocery store clerks need a different kind of permit anyway, because they don't actually lay hands upon food. At least as a regular grocery store patron I hope they don't.

Box boys are adjacent to food, however, spending all day in a big room that has a lot of food in it, and they handle packages and cans that contain food. So according to Peter, Ned needs some kind of Washington State Not-Quite-Food-Handler's Permit. To get such a thing you don't have to take a test, as you do to handle food. That's fortunate, because you never know how you're going to do on a test. Though part of me wishes there were a test I could see, because I can't imagine what kinds of questions it might contain to determine an applicant's suitability to not handle food. Perhaps:

3. If given the opportunity to handle food, you should:
   A. Handle food.
   B. Not handle food.
   C. Handle food but don't let anybody see you handling it or don't handle food and make sure someone sees that you aren't handling it.
   D. None of the above.

4. Which of the following can be handled because it is not food:
   A. Cheese
   B. A plastic bag
   C. A different kind of cheese
   D. A Twinkie (This one's tricky!)

To get an official Washington State Not-Quite-Food-Handler's Card all you have to do is watch a movie about the proper non-handling of food, so Ned and Peter went off today to watch it. When Ned returned he was up to speed on all that's required for someone who won't be handling food. Thank God.

He won't have any immediate opportunity to put his newfound non-food knowledge into practice, however, because this evening he decided to take the KCTS mailroom job. It seemed so obvious a choice to me that his actual decision wasn't a big deal. Ned knows KCTS and they know him. He's done the job before, and it isn't nearly as demanding physically as being a box boy. It also pays a third again more than box-boying. Ned still gave it a lot of thought. KCTS is well-known to him, so the grocery store had the attraction of being a brand new adventure with brand new people around, none of them his father. Ned may take a very long time adjusting to new circumstances and situations, but he still wants the opportunity to make that adjustment. I hope he won't regret the decision he's made. I hope none of us will regret it.

Thursday, September 2, 2004

Cathy called Peter Simonson today and told him about the KCTS job and that Ned had decided to take it. Peter has worked hard for Ned and succeeded in finding him a job that we are now rejecting at practically the last moment. Monday, September 13, was supposed to be the day Ned started at Safeway. Now it's the day Ned starts at KCTS—a job that's come out of the blue for Peter. He has every right to be miffed, and probably is. I certainly hope we haven't embarrassed him with his Safeway contacts. They thought they were doing Peter, and us, and especially Ned, a favor, and they were. Now they find that their admirable efforts to hire the handicapped have been rejected by the handicapped person himself. To them, Ned must seem like a baseball player who hit .184 last season but still threatens to go free agent if he doesn't get a no-cut contract.

I hope Peter sees the reality here. Ned has the opportunity to do a real job he already knows for a lot better money in a familiar place where his father can keep an eye on him. He would have been nuts not to pick that option.

Wednesday, September 3, 2004

Ned's twenty-third birthday followed the now familiar pattern of a hamburger lunch with adults in the back yard of the Two Bells Tavern, and then a hamburger dinner with his pals at a place called the Red Robin. The lunch was different only because I invited Michal Jacob to join us. She's about to be his boss, but she also hadn't met Cathy and all agreed that she should. They had a nice chat about various things.

This is Ned's third birthday party with adults in an adult place. No decorative paper plates, noisemakers, presents, or singing, just friends, relatives, and coworkers—or coworkers to be— gathered over burgers to celebrate one of their colleagues. The only way an observer would have known that it was a birthday party was the cupcake-with-candle the Two Bells staff brought out just before we were leaving.

The young man who for the past two decades has planned extremely elaborate festivities on his birthday seemed happy and satisfied with what happened. We still did the burger dinner tonight with Santosh, Lily, and Tanyss, and may for a few years to come. But Ned realizes that even the minimally lavish events of years past are over forever, and low-key adult observances are the future. He doesn't seem to have any problem with that. He's grown up, he knows it, and he likes it.

Monday, September 6, 2004

Labor Day

Cathy's father, John, and stepmother, Marcia, have lived on the east side of Lake Washington as part of the Hilltop Community for decades. Hilltop was one of Washington's first cooperative communities, with jointly-owned land, jointly-agreed-upon restrictions on individual property use, and a fine old sense of working together. It may sound corny, but Hilltop is one of those places that is so very "America working" that it makes you proud to be an American.

Every year on Labor Day, the Hilltop clans gather in the playfield/campfire area for a salmon barbecue. It's a nice event, the eats are good and plentiful, and nowadays a lot of the original families have third generation grandkids running around, so there's an enjoyable mix of the wise elders who have been at Hilltop for fifty years and the young people who will eventually have the responsibility for maintaining the community.

The Palmers attended this year as we have for a long time. We usually gather at one place on the lawn and stay there with Cathy's siblings, step-siblings, and parents, making occasional forays into the rest of the crowd. In the past, Ned has stayed with us, but this year he settled fifty yards away by the fire and stayed there for the entire evening. Instead of his contacts at the barbecue being entirely driven by his relatives as they have in the past, he had his own conversations with other Hilltop folks. This was a conscious decision on his part, and not driven by that desire to leave dad in the dust I've seen so often when he's with his peers, musical and otherwise. Ned wanted to be his own man in his own way, and was. Part of coming of age is not being solely identified in the context of your family. It's taken Ned a bit longer than a lot of young people to reach that phase of growing up, but now he has. He's inching away from us.

Tuesday, September 7, 2004

In preparation for Ned's starting work next week, Peter Simonson toured KCTS today for the second time and got the short course in the mailroom clerk's job. The tour was easy; the instruction not so easy. Jim, the previous mailroom operator, has already left town, and Ned's two immediate supervisors, Michal and Facilities Manager Michael Cooper, are relatively new to the company and probably not up to speed in the specifics of KCTS mail room operation. That leaves fill-in mailroom guy Eric, who has a lot of other things to do around the building. Shortly after Peter arrived today we discussed this problem. He asked me who in the place really knew the mailroom and could help him. And that's when it hit me.

"Peter, there's only one person at KCTS right now who's ever worked in the mailroom for any length of time. Ned."

When I got home, Cathy told me that after his visit today Peter called to chat about the job. He doesn't think there's anything involved that Ned can't handle with training and a little experience. His only concern is that there won't be enough for Ned to do. That doesn't worry me, because of Ned's renowned ability to amuse himself. But Peter's concern is that the company will discover they are paying Ned for four hours when he only works two, and either cut back his hours when the contract expires in two months or find a different way to do the mail that won't involve him.

Neither Peter nor Cathy knows KCTS and its management as well as I do. My guess is that nobody's going to mess with Ned if he can do the basic job. The general feeling amongst the management folk involved, including Bill Mohler and Michal, is that they are pleased, intrigued, and proud that they've given this job to an adult with developmental disabilities. At the same time they are comforted by the fact that they know him, he's got a job coach to assist in the first few weeks, and a father who isn't far away for the weeks and months after that. Hiring Ned is a gamble for the company, but not much of a gamble. It would take a lot to get them to take their job back. And having turned down the job offer at Safeway, it would be a shame if they did.

They should still be proud to have given it to him. Ned is taking over work that has been performed for half a century at KCTS by fully abled people, except for that summer Ned himself did it, and then he had a supervisor who was always in the room. It's an important job, too. A lot of necessary material comes through the mailroom, including all those checks from people who keep the place on the air with their contributions. In just a few days, the first KCTS employee who lays hands on those checks is going to be Ned.

Twenty years ago when I was working for KING, I hustled the station to do some public service announcements that would encourage businesses to hire workers with developmental disabilities. Ned was three at the time. I'd started to have some contact with King County ARC, which then stood for Association for Retarded Citizens but at the insistence of the "retarded" citizens themselves was changed a few years later to Advocates, Resources, and Counseling, and is now just ARC. As I remember, it was some people there who asked me to see if I could get KING to run PSAs promoting the hiring of folks with disabilities.

The KING public affairs office agreed, and I wrote and produced three thirty-second spots. For video we shot workers on the production line at Microsoft, a young woman with Down syndrome who helped at a daycare, and a genial, nonverbal man who was a janitor at a huge government office building. The message in the spots was simple: these people are providing a useful service to their employers, and there are thousands more like them who could do the same thing for your business. If you have more than twenty employees, chances are you have jobs that properly trained adults with developmental disabilities could do. All you have to do is give them a chance.

I couldn't help noticing that we had to go outside the broadcast industry to find examples to photograph. As far as I could tell, there wasn't a single adult with mental retardation working for any of Seattle's broadcasters, including KING, the other five television stations in town, and the dozens of radio stations licensed to Seattle and environs. KING's CEO at the time was Ancil Payne, a man whose integrity, intelligence, compassion, and humor set the tone for the entire operation. KING was a legendary station in America then, and the two people most responsible for that were two of the finest people I have ever known. Dorothy Bullitt, founder and owner of the KING Broadcasting Company, believed that if you were allowed to make tons of money using the public airwaves, then you had a responsibility to serve the public, not just claim you were. Ancil Payne took Mrs. Bullitt's ideas, added his own beliefs about good public affairs programming and an independent news operation, and made it all work.

The day we finished the spots, I sent Ancil a memo that included the scripts of the PSAs and the results of my research about the paucity of people with disabilities at KING or anywhere else in Northwest broadcasting. "If we put these spots on the air," I wrote him, "then we are being shamelessly hypocritical."

Ancil wrote back almost immediately. He included a copy of a letter he was sending that day to every human resources director in the company. In the letter he quoted from the spots and told all of his HR directors that he strongly supported employing workers with developmental disabilities whenever and wherever possible. He didn't exactly order them to do so. Telling people how to do their jobs once they were hired was not the way Ancil operated. But he came very close.

I don't know what happened at the other stations as a result of this letter from the boss. At KING I had a conversation a few months later with the HR director, a fatuous bureaucrat who specialized in lunch. I asked her whether she was doing anything about hiring developmentally disabled people as a result of Ancil's letter. She looked at me like I was crazy and said, "Oh, there's nothing here those people could do." And then she walked away. When I left KING six years later (shortly after Ancil retired), the station still had not hired anyone with developmental disabilities, nor to my knowledge had any other Seattle broadcaster. (Peter Simonson recently told me that a few years ago he placed a client at KOMO, the ABC affiliate, where she worked for a few years. That's one.)

I was relatively new to issues regarding the developmentally disabled way back then. But certainly a hope for Ned's future was part of my motivation to push KING to do the spots in the first place, and follow up with a note to Ancil afterwards. Before Ned could read or do much of anything else, before we had any idea of how capable he would be as an adult, I dreamed of his working at KING. Maybe in the mailroom.

A different television station, a different mailroom, but on Monday that dream comes true. On Monday, Ned Palmer becomes one of the first adults with a developmental disability to work for a Northwest broadcast station. Damned right Bill Mohler should be proud.

(A necessary digression about KING. By the time I started there, Dorothy Bullitt was in her mid-nineties. She was still a considerable force around the station, but her daughter, Patsy Bullitt Collins, was directly responsible for overseeing KING's operation. Patsy was then in her sixties, shy but friendly, with as powerful a commitment as her mother's to doing good works with her company, her wealth, and her power. On that very long day shortly after Ned was born, when our pediatrician, Steve Dassel, called to say the tests were positive and his suspicions about Ned were confirmed, I took his call in the KING news room. Sitting nearby was a wonderful colleague named Mary Rothschild, who knew Dr. Dassel, heard me say his name, and watched my half of the call. Mary realized something was wrong, so I told her what was going on when I got off the line. I told a few other people as well, and I guess the word went through the building very quickly. A few minutes after I got back to my office, there was a knock on the door. It was Patsy Collins.

"It's not the end of the world," Patsy said immediately. She stayed for almost an hour. She told me about her own developmentally disabled son and how he was working happily on a loading dock at a downtown department store. Patsy's boy was in his late twenties, living independently, and writing poetry. She gave me a book of his poems that he had also illustrated and she had published. Then she told me to go home and be with Cathy and Ned and not come back until I was ready. I have never forgotten her encouragement, her friendship, and her generosity of spirit. Her death last year was a great loss for all of us who knew her.)

I suspect Ned's biggest problem working in the KCTS mailroom is one anybody would have starting and doing that job. The company has downsized a lot in the last few years, and the workforce for a public television station is already quite fluid compared to that of many other businesses. It seems like half the mail that arrives now is addressed to people who are no longer with the station, and in some cases haven't been around for a decade or more. Many other letters and packages come addressed solely to job titles and not to individuals. In broadcasting such titles can be confusing. Are the Unit Production Manager, the Production Manager, the Production Business Manager, the Unit Manager, and the Executive in Charge of Production different people, or are they all the same person? In fact, they can be five different people in one television station and the same poor overworked wretch in another. Then there are the missives for jobs that don't apply to a public television station, or at least not this one. KCTS gets dozens of letters and faxes daily that are meant for the News Director, even though the station has never done a regular newscast and has no such person. Nor does KCTS have a Farm Director, Consumer Affairs Editor, Movie Critic, Traffic Manager, Food Editor, Station Ombudsman, Environmental Reporter, Ad

Manager, Sales Director, or Truck Parts Purchasing Manager. But mail comes in for all of them.

Here's how Ned's problem could manifest itself. If the press release is addressed to the Consumer Affairs department and concerns a new design in bedroom slippers, including an offer to interview Miss Bedroom Slipper of 2005 during her nation-wide tour, it can and should be thrown away. There's certainly nobody who wants to waste time dealing with it. But if it's a notification sent to the Farm Editor that the city's comptroller has decided to marry this year's county fair prize-winning goat, then chances are the people who do the weekly public affairs program will want to know about that.

Ned can't be responsible for making decisions about what's important and what's not. That shouldn't be the responsibility of anyone who sorts and distributes mail and faxes at KCTS. There are far too many different kinds of things going on in various departments that the mailroom clerk understandably knows nothing about. For now, we plan to have a box in the mailroom that will be labeled the equivalent of "Stuff We Can't Figure Out." KCTS employees will be encouraged to paw through the box to see if there's anything of interest to them. As time goes on and Ned gets a better sense of who's who and what they do, I think the volume of material in that box will diminish. He'll connect names with faces and faces with jobs, and that will make a big difference.

As far as the confusion over who still works for the company and who has replaced them, one of the things Peter will work on after he sets Ned up on Monday is a chart that will help get letters to the right people. ("If a letter is for ex-Production Manager Bill Smith, it should go to Production Supervisor Bob Jones..."—that kind of thing.) But again, time, experience, and familiarity will help Ned get the right letters and packages to the right people. The longer he's in the job the more it will be-come a function of his memory, not his ability to analyze. And you can never go wrong betting on Ned's memory.

He's lucky to be at KCTS and public television. The kind of egomaniac one occasionally (ha!) finds in commercial broadcast operations rarely descends to the low-paying, underappreciated, non-glitzy world of public teevee—at least you don't find them at the local level. (Not so sure about Bill Moyers. It's the soft-spoken, gentle-on-screen ones you have to watch out for.)

There is certainly an absence of prima donnas here. (I can faintly hear some of my KCTS colleagues saying "Look who's talkin'!") If some day Bill Mohler finds a press release addressed to the Farm Editor in his president's mailbox, his reaction is not going to be, "What's the matter with that kid in the mail room? Doesn't he know how important I am?" His reaction is going to be to laugh, deposit the farm news in the nearest paper-recycling can, and tell Ned to deliver all future letters for the Farm Editor to (probably) me.

Evidence of KCTS's general good feeling about hiring Ned appeared shortly before I left for the day. The station distributes a weekly, on-line company newsletter called *FYI*, edited by a young woman named Daphne Adair, the station's Internal Communications Coordinator. (I should think no letter has ever arrived addressed to the Internal Communications Coordinator, even though a lot of letters are meant for Daphne. That's the problem.) This morning she had a chat with Ned about his pending new job, and this afternoon *FYI* arrived on all our computers, with one story of particular interest:

Personnel News
Facilities Welcomes Ned Palmer...

As the woman in charge of KCTS facilities, Michal Anderson Jacob is pleased to announce that Ned Palmer has accepted an offer to become our Mail Clerk, a new, temporary part-time position charged with sorting mail, processing out-going mail, and other duties assigned from 9:00 a.m. to 1:00 p.m. Monday through Friday. Ned is the son of veteran producer Greg Palmer and has previous mailroom experience, thanks to a summer stint a few years back in our very own mailroom. He is also a Seattle long-timer, as great-great-grandnephew of Arthur

Armstrong Denny, one of the City of Seattle's founders and our first postmaster. Congratulations, Ned!

Daphne has been trying to make *FYI* more visually and editorially interesting than your average company newsletter. For the Ned story she outdid herself, first by discovering that Arthur Denny was Seattle's original postmaster (Ned was unaware of this fact, believe it or not) and then by running the story about Ned beside photographs of Arthur Denny, looking properly dour, and a shot she took today of Ned Palmer, looking properly gleeful. The photos had the perfect caption as far as the new hire is concerned.

Left: Arthur Armstrong Denny. Right: Ned Palmer. *Leaders in Seattle mail service since 1853.*

(KCTS company newsletter, September 7, 2004.)

Putting a little extra effort into the "new mail clerk" story was a very nice thing for her to do, and an encouraging indication of how the company will take to Ned.

Wednesday, September 8, 2004

11:15 p.m.

Because the video game documentary ran tonight on PBS, I started the day at 4 a.m., doing talk show interviews on the phone with east coast radio stations. Many of the interviewers assumed I am some kind of game crazy, but I was able to sidestep most of the inevitable questions about my favorite video game. (*Solitaire* would be the accurate answer, but disappointing to many gamey radio listeners.) More than anything else, today I felt relief that the videogame show is finally done, over, and out.

The family gathered to watch the show tonight at 9:00. At 10:10 I glanced over at Cathy and Ned. They were both sound asleep, thus confirming a long-held belief of mine. When they hired me to do this show I said on the first day of production that a two-hour show about video games is one hour too long for any sane person, and by that I meant any person who isn't a devout gamer. We weren't doing the program for devout gamers anyway, because they would be playing video games, not watching a PBS special about playing video games. My wife and child proved my point by fading out shortly after the start of hour two. They went up to bed, with Ned even passing on the chance to see his name in the credits. I stayed and watched the whole program to the bitter end. I didn't particularly want to see it all—I have already seen it a few thousand times—but I thought it was important that at least one person in America stayed the course. I was willing to make the sacrifice to be that person. But now it's bye bye forever, video games.

Thursday, September 9, 2004, 10 a.m.

KCTS

This is Ned's last day as a marketing intern at KCTS after almost a year. He returns Monday to sit at a desk on the next floor down and a hundred feet from where he is sitting at this moment. So his departure from the marketing internship means exactly nothing to anyone in the building except Ned. He's beginning to realize that what he does here will change a lot come Monday, change in ways that he won't necessarily enjoy. I know this because we had the following conversation a few minutes ago:

Ned: "What happens to the computer I'm using now?"

Dad: "I think it stays on your old desk up here for a while. But I think Gordon *(Hayes, the computer guy)* will transfer you to the computer in the mailroom. Your password and like that, so you can use the computer that's already in there."

Ned: "He doesn't have to do that because I'm going to be coming up here and using this computer when I'm not working in the mailroom. When I don't have anything to do there."

Dad: "But you'll still be in the mailroom even if there's nothing to do. You're supposed to be in the mailroom. That's where you'll be, starting Monday, from 9:00 when you get here, until 1:00 when your shift is over."

Ned: "You mean I have to stay in the mailroom?"

Dad: "Yes. That's where you work. Unless you're delivering packages and things to people's desks around the building. And I don't think there's going to be that much time when you don't have anything to do. There'll be a lot to do, especially right after you start, and especially because we're doing Pledge right now, so there's a lot of money coming in. All those white envelopes you saw. After your shift is over you could come work at your old desk, you know, go on the net, but..."

Ned: "Okay, I'll do that."

Dad: "...I think you'll probably be tired and want to go home and have something to eat. And as I say, your old computer won't be here after a while, or somebody else will be using it. You'll have a computer in the mailroom. But you won't have time to do the things you have been doing. You'll be doing the mail."

Ned: (walking away, shaking his head) "Yeah, right."

I refuse to let this conversation make me nervous.

Same day, 11:30 p.m.

This evening Ned and I went to the opening of the musical *Hairspray* at the Fifth Avenue Theatre. *Hairspray* originated at the Fifth a few years ago before going on to great Broadway success, so it's only logical that the first bus-and-truck national touring company also gets the kinks out in Seattle.

The kinks were out in force tonight, actually, with many persons in the audience not as God originally intended them to be. *Hairspray's* fan base is affected by the fact that the show has a famous cross-dressed performance: that is, a man playing a woman, which is different from a drag performance, which is a man playing a man dressed as a woman. In the 1988 John Waters movie on which it is based, *Hairspray's* lead character was a largish teenage girl named Tracy Turnblad, played by Ricki ("Icky") Lake. The most famous role and performance in the film, however, was that of her mother, Edna, played by the late great Divine, a.k.a. Harris Glenn Milstead. The stage adaptation originally at the Fifth and in New York had Harvey Fierstein in the mother role. On Broadway, Fierstein has since been replaced by Bruce Vilanch, comedy writer and former *Hollywood Squares* middle row/box one/left side. (And a very nice guy, incidentally. I interviewed him for the *Death* series.)

Given the musical's continuing success, for decades to come the role of Edna should be a godsend for overweight aging gay male actors, rather like the Elwood P. Dowd role in *Harvey* was a make-your-last-big paycheck retirement role for aging straight male heavy drinkers. (And I do not mean Jimmy Stewart, who played the part on film.) If the Edna I saw tonight, a standup comedian named John Pinette, is not overweight, aging, gay, and/or male, my apologies for the assumptions.

Hairspray concerns Tracy Turnblad's efforts to integrate an *American Bandstand*-style television show in the 1960s. She's successful after a lot of singing and dancing takes place. Ned enjoyed it and would have enjoyed it more if there were at least one song in the piece he recognized. But it was *Grease*-like enough (he adores *Grease*) to keep him in there. That's good, because I would have walked out halfway through the first act if I hadn't thought Ned were having a good time.

In the Baltimore high school Turnblad attends, the black students are so shunned and ignored that they are all dumped into Special Education classes. They realize, and Ms. Turnblad agrees, that any future they might have is impossible because once you're a Special Ed student your life is over. In and around a lot of re-tard jokes, much of the first act of the musical concerns our heroine's trying to convince the rest of the student body, the school administration, and the black students themselves that they are so much better than all those hopeless Special Ed students, none of whom is seen, of course. *Hairspray the Musical*, in other words, champions the cause of fat kids, African-Americans and their contributions to our culture, and aging overweight men in ugly frocks, but sees absolutely nothing wrong in the insulting denigration of people with disabilities. I'm just grateful that Ned, like every other person in the audience as far as I could tell, didn't pick up on any of this crap. That's why we stayed to the end.

Yeah, I know, I am overly sensitive to this issue. But I also know that the first people Hitler rounded up after he came to power weren't the Jews, the Gypsies, or the Seventh Day Adventists. The first people he killed were the mentally retarded. And almost nobody cared.

Friday, September 10, 2004

As part of station efforts to boost morale, this afternoon the KCTS staff gathered out in the back driveway for a company barbecue. Until he starts in the mailroom next week, Ned usually isn't at the station on Fridays, but Cathy brought him in for this event. I was happy to see he was definitely part of the group, accepted as just another employee. He chatted with a lot of people about this and that, had a burger or two, and watched the skits. He didn't even take offense when the mailroom was lampooned, although he clearly now sees it as his domain even before he's started working there.

Saturday, September 11, 2004

Tonight the Ballard Arts Festival Choir performed at last in a new center where a lot of visual artists have their studios. It might be a great place for print makers and painters, but as a venue for the performing arts it is terrible. Ned and his cochoristers were jammed into a space between an electric piano and a large letter press. There was hardly enough room for the choir, much less those of us who were there to hear them. Throughout their set, a noisy opening night party was going on a dozen yards away in another room. Nevertheless, the choir sounded very good and Ned did fine. He was relaxed and calm throughout, and looked like a guy who knew his way around a choir performance.

Afterwards the choir members gathered for dinner at a restaurant down on the ship canal. I drove Cathy home and came back with Ned. He dropped me like a bad habit at the door of the restaurant and took a seat at the big round table where his colleagues were about to have dinner. I headed for the bar and eventually a whole lot of coffee, because we were still there two hours later. I finally dragged him away to home and bed, because we arise early tomorrow to go to the church where the choir used to practice. To thank the congregation for the use of their hall, the Ballard Arts Festival Choir will make its second and last appearance during the morning service. It will be nice to hear them perform in a decent space.

There may be further opportunities to hear them, too. On the drive home from the restaurant tonight Ned told me that because the performance went so well, much of the dinner conversation concerned establishing a permanent choir. Director Chris Vincent likes the idea and so do many of the others, including Ned. They'll have to think up a new name for the group. That's an assignment I know Ned will eagerly assume. He loves to name things. So far he has already come up with one for the choir: The Ballardeers.

Me: "It's wonderful, Ned, but there's a problem. Your choir doesn't really do ballads. You do things like the Fauré *Requiem*. 'Ballardeers' makes you sound like folk singers."

Ned: "We can work around that."

Monday, September 13, 2004

Midnight

In the years to come, we will probably look back on this day as hugely important to the family, and especially to Ned. It was the real beginning of his adult life. For the first time ever he is going to be providing for himself by working at a paid job, something thousands of adults with developmental disabilities never get a chance to do, regardless of their skills. Ned is very lucky, but he also worked hard to reach this day, and so did his parents.

Though it is ultimately his achievement, he has never been alone in the process. Being a playwright now and then, all morning long I kept thinking we needed a big second act curtain, some excuse to bring all the characters back. Walking into KCTS with the new mailroom clerk was when it should have happened. I envisioned all those people who have been a part of his life lined up along the driveway as Ned went by. In that crowd would be the school teachers who saw his potential rather than his disability and went above and beyond the requirements of their jobs to help him: Debbie Bush, Kathi Titus, Sharon Mason, Marcy Wynhoff, Kathy Schaeffer, Tim Hilton, Darol Reynolds, Glenda Feyes, Rich Sumstad, and many others. His grandparents should have been there too, and cousin Jere, and wonderfully nutsy Aunt Dorothy, who gave him a mandolin and her songbooks and allowed him to be one of the last pleasures of her long life.

Cathy's sister, Maralyn Crosetto, and her partner, Tommy Smith, most certainly should have joined us, wonderful, gentle people who know something about the challenges life can present and keeping your spirit alive no matter what comes along. It would have been nice to see the whole supportive Crosetto clan, going back to great-great-grandparents Domenico and Abrosina, whose journey to America a hundred and six years ago to seek better, freer lives enthralls Ned second only to the migration of the Dennys. And as long as the dead are allowed to attend, John Felten, Eric *"Rawhide"* Fleming, Luther Crowder, and hell yes, Arthur and David Denny all deserved a spot on the curb. It would have been wonderful to see Charlotte Garretson one more time. I think she truly loved Ned, and taught him to sing, and died quietly before we ever really had a chance to thank her.

There should have been a place in the driveway for Anders, the barman from the *Endeavour*, who never treated Ned as anything other than an interesting guest. Ditto Tom Ritchie, Tom Heffernan, Gail Wagner, and many of the other people on the expedition around Britain that seems so long ago. Ned's friends should have been there, too, those from Room 104 and those from the rest of his world: Heidi, Santosh, Tanyss, both Lilys, Vicki Noon, Marcie Finnila, Debbie Hadley, Bob Newman, and all those others through the years who have enjoyed his company as much as he has enjoyed theirs.

One of the ways Ned has been lucky is that few people have ever been anything less than cordial to him, and those who weren't have been easily ignored or avoided. The great majority of people with whom he's had regular contact have been generous with their time, their friendship, and their encouragement. It is the nature of life that we rarely get the chance to gather those folks together and thank them, but if there were ever a time that should have happened, it was this morning at 8:45 at the corner of Republican and Fifth Avenue in Seattle, when Mr. Ned Palmer walked into work for the first time.

But instead of a gathering of souls, a "Welcome Ned!" banner over the door, and a brass band over by the dumpster symbolically playing *The Liberty Bell*, there was just the two of us, on just another Monday. This unusually hot Seattle summer is finally over, and fall has arrived. The daytime sky is the gun metal gray we Seattleites know so well. With few exceptions it will be like that for months, causing a profound depression in the lingering tourists. We locals, far from depressed, know it's time to get out our parkas, lose another pair of sunglasses, buy an umbrella to replace the one we lost last June, and move on.

I dropped Ned off in the mailroom a few minutes before 9:00. Peter Simonson showed up shortly thereafter. I walked away, because it's not my business any more. It's Ned's. Which is not to say that all morning long I didn't sneak up to the mailroom door every fifteen minutes or so and peek around the corner. I wanted to make sure he wasn't lying on the floor asleep, or writing down lists of the dead while the mail lay ignored. Sitting at his table sorting envelopes, he caught me checking up on him a few times. Mostly he enjoyed ignoring me, and I enjoyed being ignored. He's on his own, as it should be.

An hour after he started, Michal stopped by my desk to tell me he was doing fine. She showed me a note he had given her after I dropped him off.

"He told me it was written anonymously for him by someone else," she said. The note, in Ned's unmistakable handwriting, said:

> *Dear Michal Jacob and Mary Cudding* [the KCTS Human Resources Director, whose name is actually Cutting], *Ned would like to inform you that after this contract expires at the end of October Ned would like to return to his old job as an Intern. Sincerely*

It was signed with a question mark. Michal was clearly enjoying this announcement from the anonymous friend of her new mail clerk. "I think this is the first time I've ever gotten a letter of resignation from a new employee on his first day," she said. Indeed.

Ned must have written the letter last night and hidden it from me in his satchel this morning. He knew I wouldn't allow him to present it, because he then waited until I was gone and Peter was apparently not around before he gave it to Michal. Fortunately, she didn't take offense or make any connection between the letter and Ned's interest in the job or his ability to do it. Instead she found it both funny and cute. We both agreed it was a very Ned-like presentation.

I could have developed quite a lot of heat about what he did. He was being sneaky, and I think sneakiness is one of his worst traits. At the same time, I feel some responsibility for what the letter really means. Ned's under-appreciation of the power and necessity of money is almost entirely due to his parents' negligence and inability to educate him in the areas of finance. As a result, Ned makes little distinction between a job that pays and a job that doesn't. Earning ten dollars an hour loses its thrill if ten dollars isn't important to you. We have tried to describe his salary as the equivalent of one and a half action figures an hour, and each four-hour workday as eleven bags of Chips Ahoy cookies, but this hasn't worked at all.

I can see where Ned is coming from. If you eliminate the money attraction, his occupational choices are either sitting at his office computer listening to music on his headphones and doing whatever he wants, or doing something completely new and different: sorting mail, delivering packages, and carrying heavy boxes around. Given a person with a legendary reluctance to try new experiences, new objects, new food, and new anything, it's no wonder he wants to go back to interning.

But this was just the first day. If Ned follows his usual pattern, in a month's time he should be settled into the job and the routine and even enjoying himself. When the contract expires two months from today, I hope he agrees to re-up for a while. Thirty years sounds about right to me.

The new mailroom clerk went home at 1:00 with his mom. Before he left I asked him how it had gone. He told me the job was okay, that he liked it "a little," and that he was hungry and his feet hurt and he was going to go home to relax, watch the History Channel, and have a few hot dogs. He didn't say he hated the job and never wanted to come back, which was a good sign. If that's the case, though, he now has a letter of resignation on file. He didn't say anything about that, either.

He and I have had the exchange of, "How did you like it, Ned?" "A little..." at least a thousand times during the past decade or so. It's the highest praise he gives almost any experience immediately after the experience is over. The trip to Britain, date night at *Wizard of Oz* with Vicki, conducting the school orchestra, and now becoming a mailroom clerk are all things Ned first said he liked "a little." So I'm encouraged.

It is over. Ned has a job I know he can do, and more to the point, a job he knows he can do. He's working in a safe, benign, and I hope nurturing environment, under the supervision of good and compassionate people who are eager to help him, eager to see him succeed. As an extra bonus, I have a legitimate excuse to hang around and be handy if needed, not that I think I will be.

The parents of kids with developmental disabilities can never put their full weight down, never completely relax and enjoy the ride where their offspring are concerned. That's still the case for us with Ned, and it always will be. No job is forever, and nowadays no employer is forever either. Public television stations across the country are endangered. They survive through the largesse of the community—a community that seems to have become increasingly largesse-impaired. At the same time, cable broadcasters have appropriated a lot of public television's core programming and thus its core audience as well. It's no secret KCTS came very close to shutting down a few years ago under the previous management. Given the vagaries of the economy, changing broadcast technology, and the evolving market, there's no real assurance that the station won't be in trouble again some time before Ned's retirement party. If that crisis looms, the board of directors will undoubtedly bring in new managers to "rescue" the station. They might decide that one of the ways to do that is to ditch the guy in the mailroom for some other postal configuration, thereby saving one and a half action figures an hour. I hope it won't happen, but it would be naïve to assume it can't.

For now Ned has a job for two months, and if he wants it maybe for a year, or a decade, or the rest of his working life. Some kind of independent living still seems unlikely, but once upon a time so was the idea that he would go off to a job in the morning. We'll work on the living arrangements together, because eventually we know he's not going to have us around. He'll have to be somewhere.

It's late now, the end of a long day that seemed oddly both climactic and anticlimactic. I'm happy that he has a job working with people I know and respect. At the same time I feel I've lost something forever. He will always be the son I love, and the friend I respect. But it won't ever be the same. The day will come when I forget and say, "Hey, Ned, let's go do something," and he'll answer, "I'd like to, Dad, but I have to work." And whatever it is, I'll go do it alone. He's been a very good man to ride with, but today he started riding off in a slightly different direction, without me.

Once before I mentioned the Bravo Channel show *Inside the Actor's Studio*, where James Lipton interviews actors and directors about their work. He always concludes with the same question. Lipton's big finish is, "If heaven exists, what do you want God to say to you when you arrive?" Of the dozens of these shows I've watched, none of the performers who are also parents has ever given the answer that seems so obvious to me.

So let it be my big finish now. I want God to say to me, "You can stop worrying. I'm going to watch out for Ned. He'll have a great life, and be happy, and every day he'll be glad he's alive."

So long, partner.

About the Author

Greg Palmer has been writing professionally since 1968 for a variety of media. His PBS television work as writer, producer, and sometime host includes *The Video Game Revolution* (2004), *The Perilous Fight: America's World War Two in Color* (2004), and *Inside Passage: A Sea and Its Peoples* (expected Summer 2005). He is the co-editor of *The GI's Rabbi: World War II Letters of David Max Eichhorn* (2004, University Press of Kansas). His essay *He Canters When He Can* appears in *UNCOMMON FATHERS* (Woodbine House, 1995). Palmer and his family live in Seattle.